THE
WORKS OF ARISTOTLE

TRANSLATED INTO ENGLISH
UNDER THE EDITORSHIP

OF

W. D. ROSS, M.A.
FELLOW AND TUTOR OF ORIEL COLLEGE

VOLUME X

POLITICA
By BENJAMIN JOWETT

OECONOMICA
By E. S. FORSTER

ATHENIENSIUM RESPUBLICA
By SIR FREDERIC G. KENYON

OXFORD
AT THE CLARENDON PRESS

Oxford University Press, Amen House, London E.C.4

GLASGOW NEW YORK TORONTO MELBOURNE WELLINGTON
BOMBAY CALCUTTA MADRAS KARACHI KUALA LUMPUR
CAPE TOWN IBADAN NAIROBI ACCRA

FIRST EDITION 1921
SET IN GREAT BRITAIN
AT THE UNIVERSITY PRESS, OXFORD
AND REPRINTED LITHOGRAPHICALLY
FROM SHEETS OF THE FIRST EDITION
1946, 1952
REPRINTED LITHOGRAPHICALLY
BY D. R. HILLMAN & SONS LTD., FROME
1961

CONTENTS

POLITICA

BY

BENJAMIN JOWETT

REVISED EDITION

OXFORD
AT THE CLARENDON PRESS

PREFACE

PIETY towards Dr. Jowett, whose munificence has made possible the production of this translation of Aristotle, suggested that no new rendering of the *Politics* should be attempted, but that his translation should be re-issued. Much valuable work has been done, however, on the *Politics* since his translation was published in 1885, and of this I have endeavoured, in revising his translation, to take account, while preserving as far as possible the ease and grace of the original rendering. The revised translation is based on Immisch's edition in the Teubner series (1909), but I have not hesitated to depart from his text where he deserts the MSS. unnecessarily, or where a better emendation seemed possible ; all such departures have been indicated in the notes. In particular, I have added one more to the many attempts that have been made to emend the corrupt passage iv. 1300^a 23–^{b} 5.

By the kindness of Mr. H. W. C. Davis, Fellow of Balliol, I am permitted to use the table of contents prefixed to his edition of Dr. Jowett's translation.

W. D. ROSS.

ANALYSIS

BOOK I.

CH.

9. But we do not need that form of finance which accumulates wealth for its own sake. This is unnatural finance. It has been made possible by the invention of coined money. It accumulates money by means of exchange. Natural and unnatural finance are often treated as though they were the same, but differ in their aims ;

10. Also in their subject-matter; for natural finance is only concerned with the fruits of the earth and animals.

11. Natural finance is necessary to the householder; he must therefore know about live stock, agriculture, possibly about the exchange of the products of the earth, such as wood and minerals, for money. Special treatises on finance exist, and the subject should be specially studied by statesmen.

12. Lastly, we must discuss and distinguish the relations of husband to wife, of father to child.

13. In household management persons call for more attention than things ; free persons for more than slaves. Slaves are only capable of an inferior kind of virtue. Socrates was wrong in denying that there are several kinds of virtue. Still the slave must be trained in virtue. The education of the free man will be subsequently discussed.

BOOK II.

cc. 1-8. *Ideal Commonwealths—Plato, Phaleas, Hippodamus.*

1. To ascertain the nature of the ideal state we should start by examining both the best states of history and the best that theorists have imagined. Otherwise we might waste our . time over problems which others have already solved.

Among theorists, Plato in the *Republic* raises the most fundamental questions. He desires to abolish private property and the family.

2. But the end which he has in view is wrong. He wishes to make all his citizens absolutely alike ; but the differentiation of functions is a law of nature. There can be too much unity in a state.

3. And the means by which he would promote unity are wrong. The abolition of property will produce, not remove, dissension. Communism of wives and children will destroy natural affection.

4. Other objections can be raised ; but this is the fatal one.

5. To descend to details. The advantages to be expected from communism of property would be better secured if private property were used in a liberal spirit to relieve the wants of others. Private property makes men happier, and enables them to cultivate such virtues as generosity. The *Republic*

makes unity the result of uniformity among the citizens, which is not the case. The good sense of mankind has always been against Plato, and experiment would show that his idea is impracticable.

6. Plato sketched another ideal state in the *Laws*; it was meant to be more practicable than the other. In the *Laws* he abandoned communism, but otherwise upheld the leading ideas of the earlier treatise, except that he made the new state larger and too large. He forgot to discuss foreign relations, and to fix a limit of private property, and to restrict the increase of population, and to distinguish between ruler and subject. The form of government which he proposed was bad.

7. Phaleas of Chalcedon made equal distribution of property the main feature of his scheme. This would be difficult to effect, and would not meet the evils which Phaleas had in mind. Dissensions arise from deeper causes than inequality of wealth. His state would be weak against foreign foes. His reforms would anger the rich and not satisfy the poor.

8. Hippodamus, who was not a practical politician, aimed at symmetry. In his state there were to be three classes, three kinds of landed property, three sorts of laws. He also proposed to (1) create a Court of Appeal, (2) let juries qualify their verdicts, (3) reward those who made discoveries of public utility. His classes and his property system were badly devised. Qualified verdicts are impossible since jurymen may not confer together. The law about discoveries would encourage men to tamper with the Constitution. Now laws when obsolete and absurd should be changed; but needless changes diminish the respect for law.

cc. 9–12. *The best existent states—Sparta, Crete, and Carthage—Greek lawgivers.*

9. The Spartans cannot manage their serf population. Their women are too influential and too luxurious. Their property system has concentrated all wealth in a few hands. Hence the citizen body has decreased. There are points to criticize in the Ephorate, the Senate, the Kingship, the common meals, the Admiralty. The Spartan and his state are only fit for war. Yet even in war Sparta is hampered by the want of a financial system.

10. The Cretan cities resemble Sparta in their constitutions, but are more primitive. Their common meals are better managed. But the Cosmi are worse than the Ephors. The

CH.

Cretan constitution is a narrow and factious oligarchy ; the cities are saved from destruction only by their inaccessibility.

11. The Carthaginian polity is highly praised, and not without reason. It may be compared with the Spartan ; it is an oligarchy with some democratic features. It lays stress upon wealth ; in Carthage all offices are bought and sold. Also, one man may hold several offices together. These are bad features. But the discontent of the people is soothed by schemes of emigration.

12. Of lawgivers, Solon was the best ; conservative when possible, and a moderate democrat. About Philolaus, Charondas, Phaleas, Draco, Pittacus, and Androdamas there is little to be said.

BOOK III.

cc. 1–5. *The Citizen, civic virtue, and the civic body.*

1. How are we to define a citizen ? He is more than a mere denizen ; private rights do not make a citizen. He is ordinarily one who possesses political power ; who sits on juries and in the assembly. But it is hard to find a definition which applies to all so-called citizens. To define him as the son of citizen parents is futile.

2. Some say that his civic rights must have been justly acquired. But he is a citizen who has political power, however acquired.

3. Similarly the state is defined by reference to the distribution of political power ; when the mode of distribution is changed a new state comes into existence.

4. The good citizen may not be a good man ; the good citizen is one who does good service to his state, and this state may be bad in principle. In a constitutional state the good citizen knows both how to rule and how to obey. The good man is one who is fitted to rule. But the citizen in a constitutional state learns to rule by obeying orders. Therefore citizenship in such a state is a moral training.

5. Mechanics will not be citizens in the best state. Extreme democracies, and some oligarchies, neglect this rule. But circumstances oblige them to do this. They have no choice.

cc. 6–13. *The Classification of Constitutions ; Democracy and Oligarchy ; Kingship.*

6. The aims of the state are two : to satisfy man's social instinct, and to fit him for the good life. Political rule differs from

that over slaves in aiming primarily at the good of those who are ruled.

7. Constitutions are bad or good according as the common welfare is, or is not, their aim. Of good Constitutions there are three : Monarchy, Aristocracy, and Polity. Of bad there are also three : Tyranny, Oligarchy, Extreme Democracy. The bad are perversions of the good.

8. Democracies and Oligarchies are not made by the numerical proportion of the rulers to the ruled. Democracy is the rule of the poor ; oligarchy is that of the rich.

9. Democrats take Equality for their motto ; oligarchs believe that political rights should be unequal and proportionate to wealth. But both sides miss the true object of the state, which is virtue. Those who do most to promote virtue deserve the greatest share of power.

10. On the same principle, Justice is not the will of the majority or of the wealthier, but that course of action which the moral aim of the state requires.

11. But are the Many or the Few likely to be the better rulers ? It would be unreasonable to give the highest offices to the Many. But they have a faculty of criticism which fits them for deliberative and judicial power. The good critic need not be an expert ; experts are sometimes bad judges. Moreover, the Many have a greater stake in the city than the Few. But the governing body, whether Few or Many, must be held in check by the laws.

12. On what principle should political power be distributed? Granted that equals deserve equal shares ; who are these equals? Obviously those who are equally able to be of service to the state.

13. Hence there is something in the claims advanced by the wealthy, the free born, the noble, the highly gifted. But no one of these classes should be allowed to rule the rest. A state should consist of men who are equal, or nearly so, in wealth, in birth, in moral and intellectual excellence. The principle which underlies Ostracism is plausible. But in the ideal state, if a pre-eminent individual be found, he should be made a king.

cc. 14–18. *The Forms of Monarchy.*

14. Of Monarchy there are five kinds, (1) the Spartan, (2) the Barbarian, (3) the elective dictatorship, (4) the Heroic, (5) Absolute Kingship.

15. The last of these forms might appear the best polity to some ; that is, if the king acts as the embodiment of law. For he

will dispense from the law in the spirit of the law. But this power would be less abused if reserved for the Many. Monarchy arose to meet the needs of primitive society; it is now obsolete and on various grounds objectionable.

16. It tends to become hereditary; it subjects equals to the rule of an equal. The individual monarch may be misled by his passions, and no single man can attend to all the duties of government.

17. One case alone can be imagined in which Absolute Kingship would be just.

18. Let us consider the origin and nature of the best polity, now that we have agreed not to call Absolute Kingship the best.

BOOK IV (VI).

cc. 1–10.   *Variations of the main types of Constitutions.*

1. Political science should study (1) the ideal state, (2) those states which may be the best obtainable under special circumstances, and even (3) those which are essentially bad. For the statesman must sometimes make the best of a bad Constitution.

2. Of our six main types of state, Kingship and Aristocracy have been discussed (cf. Bk. III, c. 14 fol.). Let us begin by dealing with the other four and their divisions, inquiring also when and why they may be desirable.

3. First as to Democracy and Oligarchy. The common view that Democracy and Oligarchy should be taken as the main types of Constitution is at variance with our own view and wrong. So is the view that the numerical proportion of rulers to ruled makes the difference between these two types; in a Democracy the Many are also the poor, in an Oligarchy the Few are also the wealthy. In every state the distinction between rich and poor is the most fundamental of class-divisions. Still Oligarchy and Democracy are important types; and their variations arise from differences in the character of the rich and the poor by whom they are ruled.

4. Of Democracies there are four kinds. The worst, extreme Democracy, is that in which all offices are open to all, and the will of the people overrides all law.

5. Of Oligarchies too there are four kinds; the worst is that in which offices are hereditary and the magistrates uncontrolled by law.

6. These variations arise under circumstances which may be briefly described.

CH.

7. Of Aristocracy in the strict sense there is but one form, that in which the best men alone are citizens.

8. Polity is a compromise between Democracy and Oligarchy, but inclines to the Democratic side. Many so-called Aristocracies are really Polities.

9. There are different ways of effecting the compromise which makes a Polity. The Laconian Constitution is an example of a successful compromise.

10. Tyranny is of three kinds: (1) the barbarian despotism, and (2) the elective dictatorship have already been discussed; in both there is rule according to law over willing subjects. But in (3) the strict form of tyranny, there is the lawless rule of one man over unwilling subjects.

cc. 11–13.   *Of the Best State both in general and under special circumstances.*

11. For the average city-state the best constitution will be a mean between the rule of rich and poor; the middle-class will be supreme. No state will be well administered unless the middle-class holds sway. The middle-class is stronger in large than in small states. Hence in Greece it has rarely attained to power; especially as democracy and oligarchy were aided by the influence of the leading states.

12. No constitution can dispense with the support of the strongest class in the state. Hence Democracy and Oligarchy are the only constitutions possible in some states. But in these cases the legislator should conciliate the middle-class.

13. Whatever form of constitution be adopted there are expedients to be noted which may help in preserving it.

cc. 14–16.   *How to proceed in framing a Constitution.*

14. The legislator must pay attention to three subjects in particular: (a) The Deliberative Assembly which is different in each form of constitution.

15. (b) The Executive. Here he must know what offices are indispensable and which of them may be conveniently combined in the person of one magistrate; also whether the same offices should be supreme in every state; also which of the twelve or more methods of making appointments should be adopted in each case.

16. (c) The Courts of Law. Here he must consider the kinds of law-courts, their spheres of action, their methods of procedure.

BOOK V (VIII).

CH.

1. Ordinary states are founded on erroneous ideas of justice, which lead to discontent and revolution. Of revolutions some are made to introduce a new Constitution, others to modify the old, others to put the working of the Constitution in new hands. Both Democracy and Oligarchy contain inherent flaws which lead to revolution, but Democracy is the more stable of the two types.

2. We may distinguish between the frame of mind which fosters revolution, the objects for which it is started, and the provocative causes.

3. The latter deserve a more detailed account.

4. Trifles may be the occasion but are never the true cause of a sedition. One common cause is the aggrandizement of a particular class; another is a feud between rich and poor when they are evenly balanced and there is no middle-class to mediate. As to the manner of effecting a revolution: it may be carried through by force or fraud.

5. (a) In Democracies revolutions may arise from a persecution of the rich; or when a demagogue becomes a general, or when politicians compete for the favour of the mob.

6. (b) In Oligarchies the people may rebel against oppression; ambitious oligarchs may conspire, or appeal to the people, or set up a tyrant. Oligarchies are seldom destroyed except by the feuds of their own members; unless they employ a mercenary captain, who may become a tyrant.

7. (c) In Aristocracies and Polities the injustice of the ruling class may lead to revolution, but less often in Polities. Aristocracies may also be ruined by an unprivileged class, or an ambitious man of talent. Aristocracies tend to become oligarchies. Also they are liable to gradual dissolution; which is true of Polities as well.

8. The best precautions against sedition are these: to avoid illegality and frauds upon the unprivileged; to maintain good feeling between rulers and ruled; to watch destructive agencies; to alter property qualifications from time to time; to let no individual or class become too powerful; not to let magistracies be a source of gain; to beware of class-oppression.

CH.

9. In all magistrates we should require loyalty, ability, and justice ; we should not carry the principle of the constitution to extremes ; we should educate the citizens in the spirit of a constitution.

10. (*d*) The causes which destroy and the means which preserve a Monarchy must be considered separately. Let us first distinguish between Tyranny and Kingship. Tyranny combines the vices of Democracy and Oligarchy. Kingship is exposed to the same defects as Aristocracy. But both these kinds of Monarchy are especially endangered by the insolence of their representatives and by the fear or contempt which they inspire in others. Tyranny is weak against both external and domestic foes ; Kingship is strong against invasion, weak against sedition.

11. Moderation is the best preservative of Kingship. Tyranny may rely on the traditional expedients of demoralizing and dividing its subjects, or it may imitate Kingship by showing moderation in expenditure, and courtesy and temperance in social relations, by the wise use of ministers, by holding the balance evenly between the rich and poor.

12. But the Tyrannies of the past have been short-lived.

Plato's discussion of revolutions in the *Republic* is inadequate ; e.g. he does not explain the results of a revolution against a tyranny, and could not do so on his theory ; nor is he correct about the cause of revolution in an Oligarchy ; nor does he distinguish between the different varieties of Oligarchy and Democracy.

BOOK VI (VII).

cc. 1–8. *Concerning the proper organization of Democracies and Oligarchies.*

1. (A) Democracies differ *inter se* (1) according to the character of the citizen body, (2) according to the mode in which the characteristic features of democracy are combined.

2. Liberty is the first principle of democracy. The results of liberty are that the numerical majority is supreme, and that each man lives as he likes. From these characteristics we may easily infer the other features of democracy.

3. In oligarchies it is not the numerical majority, but the wealthier men, who are supreme. Both these principles are unjust if the supreme authority is to be absolute and above the law. Both numbers and wealth should have their share of influence. But it is hard to find the true principles of political justice, and harder still to make men act upon them.

CH.

4. Democracy has four species (cf. Bk. IV, c. 4). The best is (1) an Agricultural Democracy, in which the magistrates are elected by, and responsible to, the citizen body, while each office has a property qualification proportionate to its importance. These democracies should encourage agriculture by legislation. The next best is (2) the Pastoral Democracy. Next comes (3) the Commercial Democracy. Worst of all is (4) the Extreme Democracy with manhood suffrage.

5. It is harder to preserve than to found a Democracy. To preserve it we must prevent the poor from plundering the rich; we must not exhaust the public revenues by giving pay for the performance of public duties; we must prevent the growth of a pauper class.

6. (B) The modes of founding Oligarchies call for little explanation. Careful organization is the best way of preserving these governments.

7. Much depends on the military arrangements; oligarchs must not make their subjects too powerful an element in the army. Admission to the governing body should be granted on easy conditions. Office should be made a burden, not a source of profit.

8. Both in oligarchies and democracies the right arrangement of offices is important. Some kinds of office are necessary in every state; others are peculiar to special types of state.

BOOK VII (IV).

cc. 1–3. *The Summum Bonum for individuals and states.*

1. Before constructing the ideal state we must know what is the most desirable life for states and individuals. True happiness flows from the possession of wisdom and virtue, and not from the possession of external goods. But a virtuous life must be equipped with external goods as instruments. These laws hold good of both states and individuals.

2. But does the highest virtue consist in contemplation or in action? The states of the past have lived for action in the shape of war and conquest. But war cannot be regarded as a reasonable object for a state.

3. A virtuous life implies activity, but activity may be speculative as well as practical. Those are wrong who regard the life of a practical politician as degrading. But again they are wrong who treat political power as the highest good.

CC. 4–12. *A picture of the Ideal State.*

CH.

4. We must begin by considering the population and the territory. The former should be as small as we can make it without sacrificing independence and the capacity for a moral life. The smaller the population the more manageable it will be.

5. The territory must be large enough to supply the citizens with the means of living liberally and temperately, with an abundance of leisure. The city should be in a central position.

6. Communication with the sea is desirable for economic and military reasons; but the moral effects of sea-trade are bad. If the state has a marine, the port town should be at some distance from the city.

7. The character of the citizens should be a mean between that of Asiatics and that of the northern races; intelligence and high spirit should be harmoniously blended as they are in some Greek races.

8. We must distinguish the members of the state from those who are necessary as its servants, but no part of it. There must be men who are able to provide food, to practise the arts, to bear arms, to carry on the work of exchange, to supervise the state religion, to exercise political and judicial functions.

9. But of these classes we should exclude from the citizen body (1) the mechanics, (2) the traders, (3) the husbandmen. Warriors, rulers, priests remain as eligible for citizenship. The same persons should exercise these three professions, but at different periods of life. Ownership of land should be confined to them.

10. Such a distinction between a ruling and a subject class, based on a difference of occupation, is nothing new. It still exists in Egypt, and the custom of common meals in Crete and Italy proves that it formerly existed there. Most of the valuable rules of politics have been discovered over and over again in the course of history.

   In dealing with the land of the state we must distinguish between public demesnes and private estates. Both kinds of land should be tilled by slaves or barbarians of a servile disposition.

11. The site of the city should be chosen with regard (1) to public health, (2) to political convenience, (3) to strategic requirements. The ground-plan of the city should be regular enough for beauty, not so regular as to make defensive warfare difficult. Walls are a practical necessity.

12. It is well that the arrangement of the buildings in the city should be carefully thought out.

CH.

13. The nature and character of the citizens must be determined with reference to the kind of happiness which we desire them to pursue. Happiness was defined in the *Ethics* as the perfect exercise of virtue, the latter term being understood not in the conditional, but in the absolute sense. Now a man acquires virtue of this kind by the help of nature, habit, and reason.

Habit and reason are the fruits of education, which must therefore be discussed.

14. The citizens should be educated to obey when young and to rule when they are older. Rule is their ultimate and highest function. Since the good ruler is the same as the good man, our education must be so framed as to produce the good man. It should develop all man's powers and fit him for all the activities of life; but the highest powers and the highest activities must be the supreme care of education. An education which is purely military, like the Laconian, neglects this principle.

15. The virtues of peace (intellectual culture, temperance, justice) are the most necessary for states and individuals; war is nothing but a means towards securing peace. But education must follow the natural order of human development, beginning with the body, dealing next with the appetites, and training the intellect last of all.

16. To produce a healthy physique the legislator must fix the age of marriage, regulate the physical condition of the parents, provide for the exposure of infants, and settle the duration of marriage.

17. He must also prescribe a physical training for infants and young children. For their moral education the very young should be committed to overseers; these should select the tales which they are told, their associates, the pictures, plays, and statues which they see. From five to seven years of age should be the period of preparation for intellectual training.

BOOK VIII (V).

CH.

1. Education should be under state-control and the same for all the citizens.

2. It should comprise those useful studies which every one must master, but none which degrade the mind or body.

3. Reading, writing, and drawing have always been taught on the score of their utility; gymnastic as producing valour. Music is taught as a recreation, but it serves a higher purpose. The noble employment of leisure is the highest aim which a man can pursue; and music is valuable for this purpose. The same may be said of drawing, and other subjects of education have the same kind of value.

4. Gymnastic is the first stage of education; but we must not develop the valour and physique of our children at the expense of the mind, as they do in Sparta. Until puberty, and for three years after, bodily exercise should be light.

5. Music, if it were a mere amusement, should not be taught to children; they would do better by listening to professionals. But music is a moral discipline and a rational enjoyment.

6. By learning music children become better critics and are given a suitable occupation. When of riper age they should abandon music; professional skill is not for them; nor should they be taught difficult instruments.

7. The various musical harmonies should be used for different purposes. Some inspire virtue, others valour, others enthusiasm. The ethical harmonies are those which children should learn. The others may be left to professionals. The Dorian harmony is the best for education. The Phrygian is bad; but the Lydian may be beneficial to children.

Cetera desunt.

BOOK I

1 EVERY state is a community of some kind, and every **1252**ᵃ community is established with a view to some good; for mankind always act in order to obtain that which they think good. But, if all communities aim at some good, the state or political community, which is the highest of all, and which embraces all the rest, aims at good in a 5 greater degree than any other, and at the highest good.

Some people think [1] that the qualifications of a statesman, king, householder, and master are the same, and that they differ, not in kind, but only in the number of their subjects. For example, the ruler over a few is called 10 a master; over more, the manager of a household; over a still larger number, a statesman or king. as if there were no difference between a great household and a small state. The distinction which is made between the king and the statesman is as follows: When the government is personal, the ruler is a king; when, according to the 15 rules of the political science, the citizens rule and are ruled in turn, then he is called a statesman.

But all this is a mistake; for governments differ in kind, as will be evident to any one who considers the matter according to the method [2] which has hitherto guided us. As in other departments of science, so in 20 politics, the compound should always be resolved into the simple elements or least parts of the whole. We must therefore look at the elements of which the state is composed, in order that we may see in what the different kinds of rule differ from one another, and whether any scientific result can be attained about each one of them.

2 He who thus considers things in their first growth

---

[1] Cp. Plato, *Politicus*, 258 E-259 D.　　[2] Cp. 1256ᵃ2.

₂₅ and origin, whether a state or anything else, will obtain
the clearest view of them. In the first place there must
be a union of those who cannot exist without each other ;
namely, of male and female, that the race may continue
(and this is a union which is formed, not of deliberate
purpose, but because, in common with other animals and
with plants, mankind have a natural desire to leave
₃₀ behind them an image of themselves), and of natural ruler
and subject, that both may be preserved. For that which
can foresee by the exercise of mind is by nature intended to be lord and master, and that which can with its
body give effect to such foresight is a subject, and by
nature a slave ; hence master and slave have the same
1252ᵇ interest. Now nature has distinguished between the
female and the slave. For she is not niggardly, like the
smith who fashions the Delphian knife for many uses ;
she makes each thing for a single use, and every instrument is best made when intended for one and not for
₅ many uses. But among barbarians no distinction is made
between women and slaves, because there is no natural
ruler among them : they are a community of slaves, male
and female. Wherefore the poets say,—

' It is meet that Hellenes should rule over barbarians '[1] ;

as if they thought that the barbarian and the slave were
by nature one.

Out of these two relationships between man and woman,
₁₀ master and slave, the first thing to arise is the family,
and Hesiod is right when he says,—

' First house and wife and an ox for the plough '[2]

for the ox is the poor man's slave. The family is the
association established by nature for the supply of men's
everyday wants, and the members of it are called
by Charondas ' companions of the cupboard ', and by
Epimenides the Cretan, ' companions of the manger '.[3]
₁₅ But when several families are united, and the association

---

[1] Eurip. *Iphig. in Aul.* 1400.   [2] *Op. et Di.* 405.
[3] Or, reading in l. 15 with some MSS. and the old translator
(William of Moerbeke) ὁμοκάπνους, 'companions of the hearth'.

aims at something more than the supply of daily needs, the first society to be formed is the village. And the most natural form of the village appears to be that of a colony from the family, composed of the children and grandchildren, who are said to be 'suckled with the same milk'. And this is the reason why Hellenic states were originally governed by kings ; because the Hellenes [20] were under royal rule before they came together, as the barbarians still are. Every family is ruled by the eldest, and therefore in the colonies of the family the kingly form of government prevailed because they were of the same blood. As Homer says : [1]

'Each one gives law to his children and to his wives.'
For they lived dispersedly, as was the manner in ancient times. Wherefore men say that the Gods have a king, because they themselves either are or were in ancient [25] times under the rule of a king. For they imagine, not only the forms of the Gods, but their ways of life to be like their own.

When several villages are united in a single complete community, large enough to be nearly or quite self-sufficing, the state comes into existence, originating in the bare needs of life, and continuing in existence for the sake of a good life. And therefore, if the earlier forms [30] of society are natural, so is the state, for it is the end of them, and the nature of a thing is its end. For what each thing is when fully developed, we call its nature, whether we are speaking of a man, a horse, or a family. Besides, the final cause and end of a thing is the best, and to be self-sufficing is the end and the best.   1253[a]

Hence it is evident that the state is a creation of nature, and that man is by nature a political animal. And he who by nature and not by mere accident is without a state, is either a bad man or above humanity ; he is like the

'Tribeless, lawless, hearthless one,'   [5]
whom Homer[2] denounces—the natural outcast is forthwith

---

[1] *Od.* ix. 114, quoted by Plato, *Laws*, iii. 680 B, and in *N. Eth.* x. 1180[a] 28.
[2] *Il.* ix. 63.

a lover of war; he may be compared to an isolated piece at draughts.

Now, that man is more of a political animal than bees or any other gregarious animals is evident. Nature, as we often say, makes nothing in vain,[1] and man is the only animal whom she has endowed with the gift of 10 speech.[2] And whereas mere voice is but an indication of pleasure or pain, and is therefore found in other animals (for their nature attains to the perception of pleasure and pain and the intimation of them to one another, and no further), the power of speech is intended to set forth the expedient and inexpedient, and therefore likewise the 15 just and the unjust. And it is a characteristic of man that he alone has any sense of good and evil, of just and unjust, and the like, and the association of living beings who have this sense makes a family and a state.

Further, the state is by nature clearly prior to the family and to the individual, since the whole is of 20 necessity prior to the part; for example, if the whole body be destroyed, there will be no foot or hand, except in an equivocal sense, as we might speak of a stone hand; for when destroyed the hand will be no better than that. But things are defined by their working and power; and we ought not to say that they are the same when they no longer have-their proper quality, but only that they 25 have the same name. The proof that the state is a creation of nature and prior to the individual is that the individual, when isolated, is not self-sufficing; and therefore he is like a part in relation to the whole. But he who is unable to live in society, or who has no need because he is sufficient for himself, must be either a beast or a god : he is no part of a state. A social instinct is 30 implanted in all men by nature, and yet he who first founded the state was the greatest of benefactors. For man, when perfected, is the best of animals, but, when separated from law and justice, he is the worst of all; since armed injustice is the more dangerous, and he is

---

[1] Cp. 1256[b] 20.   [2] Cp. vii. 1332[b] 5.

equipped at birth with arms, meant to be used by intelligence and virtue, which he may use for the worst ends. Wherefore, if he have not virtue, he is the most 35 unholy and the most savage of animals, and the most full of lust and gluttony. But justice is the bond of men in states, for the administration of justice, which is the determination of what is just,[1] is the principle of order in political society.

3   Seeing then that the state is made up of households, before speaking of the state we must speak of the management of the household. The parts of household management correspond to the persons who compose the **1253ᵇ** household, and a complete household consists of slaves and freemen. Now we should begin by examining everything in its fewest possible elements; and the first and 5 fewest possible parts of a family are master and slave, husband and wife, father and children. We have therefore to consider what each of these three relations is and ought to be:—I mean the relation of master and servant, 10 the marriage relation (the conjunction of man and wife has no name of its own), and thirdly, the procreative relation[2] (this also has no proper name). And there is another element of a household, the so-called art of getting wealth, which, according to some, is identical with household management, according to others, a principal part of it; the nature of this art will also have to be considered by us.

Let us first speak of master and slave, looking to the 15 needs of practical life and also seeking to attain some better theory of their relation than exists at present. For some are of opinion that the rule of a master is a science, and that the management of a household, and the mastership of slaves, and the political and royal rule, as I was saying at the outset,[3] are all the same. Others 20 affirm that the rule of a master over slaves is contrary to nature, and that the distinction between slave and free-

---

[1] Cp. *N. Eth.* v. 1134ᵃ 31.
[2] Reading τεκνοποιητική in l. 10 with the MSS.
[3] Plato in *Pol.* 258 E–259 D, referred to already in 1252ᵃ 7–16.

man exists by law only, and not by nature; and being
an interference with nature is therefore unjust.

Property is a part of the household, and the art 4
of acquiring property is a part of the art of managing
the household; for no man can live well, or indeed live
25 at all, unless he be provided with necessaries. And as
in the arts which have a definite sphere the workers
must have their own proper instruments for the accom-
plishment of their work, so it is in the management of
a household.[1] Now instruments are of various sorts;
some are living, others lifeless; in the rudder, the pilot
of a ship has a lifeless, in the look-out man, a living
instrument; for in the arts the servant is a kind of in-
30 strument. Thus, too, a possession is an instrument for
maintaining life. And so, in the arrangement of the
family, a slave is a living possession, and property a
number of such instruments; and the servant is himself an instrument which takes precedence of all other
instruments. For if every instrument could accomplish its own work, obeying or anticipating the will of
35 others, like the statues of Daedalus, or the tripods
of Hephaestus, which, says the poet,[2]

' of their own accord entered the assembly of the Gods';

if, in like manner, the shuttle would weave and the plec-
trum touch the lyre without a hand to guide them, chief
workmen would not want servants, nor masters slaves.
1254ᵃ Here, however, another distinction must be drawn: the instruments commonly so called are instruments of production, whilst a possession is an instrument of action. The
shuttle, for example, is not only of use; but something
else is made by it, whereas of a garment or of a bed
5 there is only the use. Further, as production and action
are different in kind, and both require instruments, the
instruments which they employ must likewise differ in
kind. But life is action and not production, and therefore

---

[1] Retaining οὕτω καὶ τῷ οἰκονομικῷ in l. 27, and omitting τῷ
οἰκονομικῷ in l. 31.
[2] Hom. *Il.* xviii. 376.

the slave is the minister of action. Again, a possession is spoken of as a part is spoken of; for the part is not only a part of something else, but wholly belongs to it; 10 and this is also true of a possession. The master is only the master of the slave; he does not belong to him, whereas the slave is not only the slave of his master, but wholly belongs to him. Hence we see what is the nature and office of a slave; he who is by nature not his own but another's man, is by nature a slave; and he 15 may be said to be another's man who, being a human being, is also a possession. And a possession may be defined as an instrument of action, separable from the possessor.

5   But is there any one thus intended by nature to be a slave, and for whom such a condition is expedient and right, or rather is not all slavery a violation of nature?

There is no difficulty in answering this question, on 20 grounds both of reason and of fact. For that some should rule and others be ruled is a thing not only necessary, but expedient; from the hour of their birth, some are marked out for subjection, others for rule.

And there are many kinds both of rulers and subjects (and that rule is the better which is exercised over 25 better subjects—for example, to rule over men is better than to rule over wild beasts; for the work is better which is executed by better workmen, and where one man rules and another is ruled, they may be said to have a work); for in all things which form a composite whole and which are made up of parts, whether continuous or discrete, 30 a distinction between the ruling and the subject element comes to light. Such a duality exists in living creatures, but not in them only; it originates in the constitution of the universe; even in things which have no life there is a ruling principle, as in a musical mode. But we are wandering from the subject. We will therefore restrict ourselves to the living creature, which, in the first place, consists of soul and body: and of these two, the one is 35 by nature the ruler, and the other the subject. But then we must look for the intentions of nature in things which retain their nature, and not in things which are corrupted. And therefore we must study the man who is in the most perfect state both of body and soul, for in him we shall see the true relation of the two; although in bad

1254^b or corrupted natures the body will often appear to rule' over the soul, because they are in an evil and unnatural condition. At all events we may firstly observe in living creatures both a despotical and a constitutional rule ; for the soul rules the body with a despotical rule, whereas the intellect rules the appetites with a constitutional and royal rule. And it is clear that the rule of the soul over the

5 body, and of the mind and the rational element over the passionate, is natural and expedient ; whereas the equality of the two or the rule of the inferior is always hurtful. The same holds good of animals in relation to

10 men ; for tame animals have a better nature than wild, and all tame animals are better off when they are ruled by man ; for then they are preserved. Again, the male is by nature superior, and the female inferior ; and the

15 one rules, and the other is ruled ; this principle, of necessity, extends to all mankind. Where then there is such a difference as that between soul and body, or between men and animals (as [1] in the case of those whose business is to use their body, and who can do nothing better), the lower sort are by nature slaves, and it is better for them as for all inferiors that they should be under the

20 rule of a master. For he who can be, and therefore is, another's, and he who participates in rational principle enough to apprehend, but not to have, such a principle, is a slave by nature. Whereas the lower animals cannot even apprehend a principle ; [2] they obey their instincts. And indeed the use made of slaves and of tame animals

25 is not very different ; for both with their bodies minister to the needs of life. Nature would like to distinguish between the bodies of freemen and slaves, making the

---

[1] Reading διάκεινται δὲ τοῦτον in l. 17, with the 'old translation' and some MSS.

[2] Reading λόγου in l. 23 with some MSS.

one strong for servile labour, the other upright, and
although useless for such services, useful for political life 30
in the arts both of war and peace. But the opposite often
happens—that some have the souls and others have the
bodies of freemen. And doubtless if men differed from
one another in the mere forms of their bodies as much as
the statues of the Gods do from men, all would acknow- 35
ledge that the inferior class should be slaves of the
superior. And if this is true of the body, how much
more just that a similar distinction should exist in the
soul? but the beauty of the body is seen, whereas the 1255^a
beauty of the soul is not seen. It is clear, then, that
some men are by nature free, and others slaves, and
that for these latter slavery is both expedient and right.

6   But that those who take the opposite view have in
a certain way right on their side, may be easily seen.
For the words slavery and slave are used in two senses.
There is a slave or slavery by law as well as by nature. 5
The law of which I speak is a sort of convention—the
law by which whatever is taken in war is supposed to
belong to the victors. But this right many jurists impeach, as they would an orator who brought forward an
unconstitutional measure : they detest the notion that,
because one man has the power of doing violence and is
superior in brute strength, another shall be his slave and 10
subject. Even among philosophers there is a difference of
opinion. The origin of the dispute, and what makes the
views invade each other's territory, is as follows : in some
sense virtue, when furnished with means, has actually the
greatest power of exercising force : and as superior power
is only found where there is superior excellence of some
kind, power seems to imply virtue, and the dispute to be 15
simply one about justice (for it is due to one party iden-
tifying [1] justice with goodwill,[2] while the other identifies

---

[1] No thoroughly satisfactory explanation has been given for
διὰ τοῦτο, l. 17, and it appears better to read διὰ γὰρ τὸ . . . εὔνοιαν
(or ἐν εὐνοίᾳ) δοκεῖν.

[2] i.e. mutual goodwill, which is held to be incompatible with the
relation of master and slave.

it with the mere rule of the stronger). If these views are
thus set out separately, the other views [1] have no force
20 or plausibility against the view that the superior in virtue
ought to rule, or be master. Others, clinging, as they
think, simply to a principle of justice (for law and custom
are a sort of justice), assume that slavery in accordance
with the custom of war is justified by law, but at the same
moment they deny this. For what if the cause of the war
25 be unjust ? And again, no one would ever say that he is a
slave who is unworthy to be a slave. Were this the case,
men of the highest rank would be slaves and the children
of slaves if they or their parents chance to have been taken
captive and sold. Wherefore Hellenes do not like to call
Hellenes slaves, but confine the term to barbarians. Yet,
30 in using this language, they really mean the natural slave
of whom we spoke at first ; [2] for it must be admitted that
some are slaves everywhere, others nowhere. The same
principle applies to nobility. Hellenes regard themselves
as noble everywhere, and not only in their own country,
35 but they deem the barbarians noble only when at home,
thereby implying that there are two sorts of nobility
and freedom, the one absolute, the other relative. The
Helen of Theodectes says : [3]

'Who would presume to call me servant who am on
both sides sprung from the stem of the Gods ? '

What does this mean but that they distinguish freedom
40 and slavery, noble and humble birth, by the two
1255ᵇ principles of good and evil ? They think that as men
and animals beget men and animals, so from good men a
good man springs. But this is what nature, though she
may intend it, cannot always accomplish.

We see then that there is some foundation for this
5 difference of opinion, and that all are not either slaves
by nature or freemen by nature, and also that there is
in some cases a marked distinction between the two

---

[1] i. e. those stated in ll. 5–12, that the stronger always has, and that
he never has, a right to enslave the weaker. Aristotle finds that these
views cannot maintain themselves against his intermediate view,
that the superior in *virtue* should rule.
[2] Chap. 5.   [3] *Helena*, fr. 3, Nauck².

classes, rendering it expedient and right for the one to
be slaves and the others to be masters : the one practising obedience, the others exercising the authority and
lordship which nature intended them to have.   The abuse
of this authority is injurious to both ; for the interests of
part and whole,[1] of body and soul, are the same, and the 10
slave is a part of the master, a living but separated part
of his bodily frame.   Hence, where the relation of master
and slave between them is natural they are friends
and have a common interest, but where it rests merely
on law and force the reverse is true.   15

7   The previous remarks are quite enough to show that
the rule of a master is not a constitutional rule, and
that all the different kinds of rule are not, as some
affirm, the same with each other.[2]   For there is one rule
exercised over subjects who are by nature free, another
over subjects who are by nature slaves.   The rule
of a household is a monarchy, for every house is under
one head : whereas constitutional rule is a government
of freemen and equals.   The master is not called a 20
master because he has science,[3] but because he is of
a certain character, and the same remark applies to the
slave and the freeman.   Still there may be a science for
the master and a science for the slave.   The science of
the slave would be such as the man of Syracuse taught,
who made money by instructing slaves in their ordinary
duties.   And such a knowledge may be carried further, 25
so as to include cookery and similar menial arts.   For
some duties are of the more necessary, others of the
more honourable sort ; as the proverb says, ' slave before
slave, master before master '.[4]   But all such branches of 30
knowledge are servile.   There is likewise a science of
the master, which teaches the use of slaves ; for the
master as such is concerned, not with the acquisition,
but with the use of them.   Yet this so-called science is

---

[1] Cp. 1254^a 8.
[2] Plato, *Polit.* 258 E–259 D, referred to already in 1252^a 7–16,
1253^b 18–20.
[3] *Polit.* 259 C, 293 C.
[4] Philemon, *Pancratiastes*, fr. 2, Meineke.

not anything great or wonderful ; for the master need only know how to order that which the slave must know
35 how to execute. Hence those who are in a position which places them above toil have stewards who attend to their households while they occupy themselves with philosophy or with politics. But the art of acquiring slaves, I mean of justly acquiring them, differs both from the art of the master and the art of the slave, being a species of hunting or war.[1] Enough of the distinction
40 between master and slave.

1256ᵃ Let us now inquire into property generally, and into **8** the art of getting wealth, in accordance with our usual method,[2] for a slave has been shown[3] to be a part of property. The first question is whether the art of getting wealth is the same with the art of managing a household or a part of it, or instrumental to it ; and if the last, whether in the way that the art of making shuttles is
5 instrumental to the art of weaving, or in the way that the casting of bronze is instrumental to the art of the statuary, for they are not instrumental in the same way, but the one provides tools and the other material ; and by material I mean the substratum out of which any work is made ; thus wool is the material of the weaver,
10 bronze of the statuary. Now it is easy to see that the art of household management is not identical with the art of getting wealth, for the one uses the material which the other provides. For the art which uses household stores can be no other than the art of household management. There is, however, a doubt whether the art of getting wealth is a part of household management or a distinct
15 art. If the getter of wealth has to consider whence wealth and property can be procured, but there are many sorts of property and riches,[4] then are husbandry, and the care and provision of food in general, parts of the wealth-getting art[5] or distinct arts ? Again, there are many

---

[1] Cp. vii. 1333ᵇ 38.
[2] Of understanding the whole by the part, cp. 1252ᵃ 17.
[3] Chap. 4.   [4] Reading a comma after ἔσται in l. 16.
[5] Reading τῆς χρηματιστικῆς in l. 17 with the MSS.

sorts of food, and therefore there are many kinds of lives
both of animals and men ; they must all have food, and ₂₀
the differences in their food have made differences in
their ways of life. For of beasts, some are gregarious,
others are solitary ; they live in the way which is best
adapted to sustain them, accordingly as they are carnivorous or herbivorous or omnivorous : and their habits are ₂₅
determined for them by nature in such a manner that
they may obtain with greater facility the food of their
choice. But, as different species have different tastes, the
same things are not naturally pleasant to all of them ;
and therefore the lives of carnivorous or herbivorous
animals further differ among themselves. In the lives ₃₀
of men too there is a great difference. The laziest are
shepherds, who lead an idle life, and get their subsistence without trouble from tame animals ; their flocks
having to wander from place to place in search of pas-
ture, they are compelled to follow them, cultivating a
sort of living farm. Others support themselves by hunt- ₃₅
ing, which is of different kinds. Some, for example, are
brigands, others, who dwell near lakes or marshes or rivers
or a sea in which there are fish, are fishermen, and
others live by the pursuit of birds or wild beasts. The
greater number obtain a living from the cultivated fruits
of the soil. Such are the modes of subsistence which ₄₀
prevail among those whose industry springs up of itself,
and whose food is not acquired by exchange and retail **1256ᵇ**
trade—there is the shepherd, the husbandman, the
brigand, the fisherman, the hunter. Some gain a comfort-
able maintenance out of two employments, eking out the
deficiencies of one of them by another : thus the life of
a shepherd may be combined with that of a brigand, the ₅
life of a farmer with that of a hunter. Other modes of
life are similarly combined in any way which the needs
of men may require. Property, in the sense of a bare
livelihood, seems to be given by nature herself to all, both
when they are first born, and when they are grown up. ₁₀
For some animals bring forth, together with their offspring,
so much food as will last until they are able to supply

themselves; of this the vermiparous or oviparous animals
are an instance; and the viviparous animals have up to
a certain time a supply of food for their young in them-
15 selves, which is called milk. In like manner we may
infer that, after the birth of animals, plants exist for
their sake, and that the other animals exist for the sake
of man, the tame for use and food, the wild, if not all,
at least the greater part of them, for food, and for the
20 provision of clothing and various instruments. Now if
nature makes nothing incomplete, and nothing in vain,
the inference must be that she has made all animals for
the sake of man. And so, in one point of view, the art
of war is a natural art of acquisition, for the art of
acquisition includes hunting, an art which we ought to
practise against wild beasts, and against men who, though
25 intended by nature to be governed, will not submit; for
war of such a kind is naturally just.[1]

Of the art of acquisition then there is one kind which
by nature is a part of the management of a household, in
so far as the art of household management must either
find ready to hand, or itself provide, such things necessary
30 to life, and useful for the community of the family or
state, as can be stored. They are the elements of true
riches; for the amount of property which is needed for
a good life is not unlimited, although Solon in one of his
poems says that

'No bound to riches has been fixed for man'.[2]

But there is a boundary fixed, just as there is in the other
35 arts; for the instruments of any art are never unlimited,
either in number or size, and riches may be defined as
a number of instruments to be used in a household or
in a state. And so we see that there is a natural art
of acquisition which is practised by managers of households and by statesmen, and what is the reason of this.

40   There is another variety of the art of acquisition which 9
is commonly and rightly called an art of wealth-getting,

---

[1] Cp. 1255^b 38, 1333^b 38.   The brackets round ἡ γὰρ θηρευτικὴ
μέρος αὐτῆς in l. 23 should be removed.
[2] Bergk, *Poet. Lyr.*⁴, Solon, 13. 71.

and has in fact suggested the notion that riches and 1257ᵃ
property have no limit. Being nearly connected with
the preceding, it is often identified with it. But though
they are not very different, neither are they the same.
The kind already described is given by nature, the other
is gained by experience and art.

Let us begin our discussion of the question with the 5
following considerations :

Of everything which we possess there are two uses :
both belong to the thing as such, but not in the same
manner, for one is the proper, and the other the improper or secondary use of it. For example, a shoe is
used for wear, and is used for exchange ; both are uses of
the shoe. He who gives a shoe in exchange for money 10
or food to him who wants one, does indeed use the shoe
as a shoe, but this is not its proper or primary purpose,
for a shoe is not made to be an object of barter. The
same may be said of all possessions, for the art of exchange extends to all of them, and it arises at first from 15
what is natural, from the circumstance that some have
too little, others too much. Hence we may infer that
retail trade is not a natural part of the art of getting
wealth ; had it been so, men would have ceased to exchange when they had enough. In the first community,
indeed, which is the family, this art is obviously of no 20
use, but it begins to be useful when the society increases.
For the members of the family originally had all things
in common ; later, when the family divided into parts,
the parts shared in many things, and different parts in
different things, which they had to give in exchange for
what they wanted, a kind of barter which is still practised
among barbarous nations who exchange with one another 25
the necessaries of life and nothing more ; giving and receiving wine, for example, in exchange for corn, and the
like. This sort of barter is not part of the wealth-
getting art and is not contrary to nature, but is needed
for the satisfaction of men's natural wants. The other 30
or more complex form of exchange grew, as might have
been inferred, out of the simpler. ' When the inhabitants

of one country became more dependent on those of another, and they imported what they needed, and exported what they had too much of, money necessarily
35 came into use. For the various necessaries of life are not easily carried about, and hence men agreed to employ in their dealings with each other something which was intrinsically useful and easily applicable to the purposes of life, for example, iron, silver, and the like. Of this the value was at first measured simply by size and
40 weight, but in process of time they put a stamp upon it, to save the trouble of weighing and to mark the value.

1257ᵇ When the use of coin had once been discovered, out of the barter of necessary articles arose the other art of wealth-getting, namely, retail trade ; which was at first probably a simple matter, but became more complicated as soon as men learned by experience whence and by what exchanges the greatest profit might be made.
5 Originating in the use of coin, the art of getting wealth is generally thought to be chiefly concerned with it, and to be the art which produces riches and wealth ; having to consider how they may be accumulated. Indeed, riches is assumed by many to be only a quantity of coin, because the arts of getting wealth and retail
10 trade are concerned with coin. Others maintain that coined money is a mere sham, a thing not natural, but conventional only, because, if the users substitute another commodity for it, it is worthless, and because it is not useful as a means to any of the necessities of life, and, indeed, he who is rich in coin may often be in want of necessary food. But how can that be wealth of which
15 a man may have a great abundance and yet perish with hunger, like Midas in the fable, whose insatiable prayer turned everything that was set before him into gold ?

Hence men seek after a better notion of riches and of the art of getting wealth than the mere acquisition of coin, and they are right. For natural riches and the natural art of wealth-getting are a different thing ; in their true
20 form they are part of the management of a household ; whereas retail trade is the art of producing wealth, not

in every way, but by exchange. And it is thought
to be concerned with coin; for coin is the unit of exchange and the measure or limit of it. And there is
no bound to the riches which spring from this art of
wealth-getting.[1] As in the art of medicine there is no 25
limit to the pursuit of health, and as in the other arts
there is no limit to the pursuit of their several ends, for
they aim at accomplishing their ends to the uttermost
(but of the means there is a limit, for the end is always
the limit), so, too, in this art of wealth-getting there is no
limit of the end, which is riches of the spurious kind,
and the acquisition of wealth. But the art of wealth- 30
getting which consists in household management, on the
other hand, has a limit[2]; the unlimited acquisition of
wealth is not its business. And, therefore, in one point
of view, all riches must have a limit; nevertheless, as a
matter of fact, we find the opposite to be the case; for all
getters of wealth increase their hoard of coin without limit.
The source of the confusion is the near connexion between
the two kinds of wealth-getting; in either, the instrument 35
is the same, although the use is different, and so they pass
into one another; for each is a use of the same property,
but with a difference: accumulation is the end in the one
case, but there is a further end in the other. Hence some
persons are led to believe that getting wealth is the
object of household management, and the whole idea of
their lives is that they ought either to increase their
money without limit, or at any rate not to lose it. The 40
origin of this disposition in men is that they are intent
upon living only, and not upon living well; and, as their 1258^{a}
desires are unlimited, they also desire that the means of
gratifying them should be without limit. Those who do
aim at a good life seek the means of obtaining bodily
pleasures; and, since the enjoyment of these appears to 5
depend on property, they are absorbed in getting wealth :
and so there arises the second species of wealth-getting.
For, as their enjoyment is in excess, they seek an art

[1] Cp. 1256^{b} 32.
[2] Reading αὖ for οὐ in l. 30, with Bernays.

which produces the excess of enjoyment ; and, if they
are not able to supply their pleasures by the art of getting
wealth, they try other arts, using in turn every faculty
10 in a manner contrary to nature. The quality of courage,
for example, is not intended to make wealth, but to
inspire confidence ; neither is this the aim of the general's
or of the physician's art ; but the one aims at victory and
the other at health. Nevertheless, some men turn every
quality or art into a means of getting wealth ; this they
conceive to be the end, and to the promotion of the end
they think all things must contribute.

Thus, then, we have considered the art of wealth-
15 getting which is unnecessary, and why men want it ; and
also the necessary art of wealth-getting, which we have
seen to be different from the other, and to be a natural
part of the art of managing a household, concerned with
the provision of food, not, however, like the former kind,
unlimited, but having a limit.

And we have found the answer to our original ques- 10
tion,[1] Whether the art of getting wealth is the business
of the manager of a household and of the statesman or
20 not their business ?—viz. that wealth is presupposed by
them. For as political science does not make men, but
takes them from nature and uses them, so too nature
provides them with earth or sea or the like as a source of
food. At this stage begins the duty of the manager
of a household, who has to order the things which nature
25 supplies ;—he may be compared to the weaver who has
not to make but to use wool, and to know, too, what sort
of wool is good and serviceable or bad and unserviceable.
Were this otherwise, it would be difficult to see why the
art of getting wealth is a part of the management of
a household and the art of medicine not ; for surely the
members of a household must have health just as they
30 must have life or any other necessary. The answer is
that as from one point of view the master of the house
and the ruler of the state have to consider about health,

----

[1] 1256ᵃ 3.

from another point of view not they but the physician; so in one way the art of household management, in another way the subordinate art, has to consider about wealth. But, strictly speaking, as I have already said, the means of life must be provided beforehand by nature; for the business of nature is to furnish food to 35 that which is born, and the food of the offspring is always what remains over of that from which it is produced.[1] Wherefore the art of getting wealth out of fruits and animals is always natural.

There are two sorts of wealth-getting, as I have said [2]; one is a part of household management, the other is retail trade : the former necessary and honourable, while that 40 which consists in exchange is justly censured ; for it **1258ᵇ** is unnatural, and a mode by which men gain from one another. The most hated sort, and with the greatest reason, is usury, which makes a gain out of money itself, and not from the natural object of it. For money was intended to be used in exchange, but not to increase at interest. And this term interest,[3] which means the 5 birth of money from money, is applied to the breeding of money because the offspring resembles the parent. Wherefore of all modes of getting wealth this is the most unnatural.

11   Enough has been said about the theory of wealth-getting ; we will now proceed to the practical part. The discussion of such matters is not unworthy of philo- 10 sophy, but to be engaged in them practically is illiberal and irksome.[4] The useful parts of wealth-getting are, first, the knowledge of live-stock,—which are most profit-able, and where, and how,—as, for example, what sort of horses or sheep or oxen or any other animals are most likely to give a return. A man ought to know which of 15 these pay better than others, and which pay best in par-ticular places, for some do better in one place and some in another. Secondly, husbandry, which may be either

---

[1] Cp. 1256ᵇ 10.   [2] 1256ª 15–1258ª 18.   [3] τόκος, lit. 'offspring'.
[4] Or, 'We are free to speculate about them, but in practice we are limited by circumstances.' (Bernays.)

tillage or planting, and the keeping of bees and of fish,
or fowl, or of any animals which may be useful to man.
20 These are the divisions of the true or proper art of
wealth-getting and come first.   Of the other, which consists in exchange, the first and most important division
is commerce (of which there are three kinds—the
provision of a ship, the conveyance of goods, exposure
for sale—these again differing as they are safer or more
25 profitable), the second is usury, the third, service for hire
—of this, one kind is employed in the mechanical arts,
the other in unskilled and bodily labour.   There is still
a third sort of wealth-getting intermediate between this
and the first or natural mode which is partly natural, but
is also concerned with exchange, viz. the industries that
make their profit from the earth, and from things growing
30 from the earth which, although they bear no fruit, are
nevertheless profitable ; for example, the cutting of timber
and all mining.   The art of mining, by which minerals
are obtained, itself has many branches, for there are
various kinds of things dug out of the earth.   Of the
several divisions of wealth-getting I now speak generally ;
a minute consideration of them might be useful in practice,
but it would be tiresome to dwell upon them at greater
length now.

35   Those occupations are most truly arts in which there
is the least element of chance ; they are the meanest
in which the body is most deteriorated, the most
servile in which there is the greatest use of the body,
and the most illiberal in which there is the least need
of excellence.

Works have been written upon these subjects by
40 various persons ; for example, by Chares the Parian, and
Apollodorus the Lemnian, who have treated of Tillage
1259^a and Planting, while others have treated of other branches ;
any one who cares for such matters may refer to their
writings.   It would be well also to collect the scattered
stories of the ways in which individuals have succeeded in
5 amassing a fortune ; for all this is useful to persons who
value the art of getting wealth.   There is the anecdote

of Thales the Milesian and his financial device, which
involves a principle of universal application, but is attributed to him on account of his reputation for wisdom.
He was reproached for his poverty, which was supposed
to show that philosophy was of no use. According to 10
the story, he knew by his skill in the stars while it was
yet winter that there would be a great harvest of olives
in the coming year; so, having a little money, he gave
deposits for the use of all the olive-presses in Chios and
Miletus, which he hired at a low price because no one
bid against him. When the harvest-time came, and many
were wanted all at once and of a sudden, he let them 15
out at any rate which he pleased, and made a quantity
of money. Thus he showed the world that philosophers
can easily be rich if they like, but that their ambition
is of another sort. He is supposed to have given a
striking proof of his wisdom, but, as I was saying, his
device for getting wealth is of universal application, and 20
is nothing but the creation of a monopoly. It is an art
often practised by cities when they are in want of money;
they make a monopoly of provisions.

  There was a man of Sicily, who, having money deposited with him, bought up all the iron from the iron
mines; afterwards, when the merchants from their various 25
markets came to buy, he was the only seller, and without much increasing the price he gained 200 per cent.
Which when Dionysius heard, he told him that he might
take away his money, but that he must not remain at
Syracuse, for he thought that the man had discovered 30
a way of making money which was injurious to his own
interests. He made the same discovery as Thales; they
both contrived to create a monopoly for themselves. And
statesmen as well ought to know these things; for a state
is often as much in want of money and of such devices for
obtaining it as a household, or even more so; hence 35
some public men devote themselves entirely to finance.

12   Of household management we have seen[1] that there
are three parts—one is the rule of a master over slaves,
                    [1] 1253ᵇ 3–11.

which has been discussed already,[1] another of a father,
and the third of a husband. A husband and father, we
40 saw, rules over wife and children, both free, but the rule
differs, the rule over his children being a royal, over his
1259^b wife a constitutional rule. For although there may be
exceptions to the order of nature, the male is by nature
fitter for command than the female, just as the elder
and full-grown is superior to the younger and more
immature. But in most constitutional states the citizens
5 rule and are ruled by turns, for the idea of a constitutional state implies that the natures of the citizens are equal, and do not differ at all.[2] Nevertheless,
when one rules and the other is ruled we endeavour to
create a difference of outward forms and names and titles
of respect, which may be illustrated by the saying of
Amasis about his foot-pan.[3] The relation of the male
to the female is of this kind, but there the inequality
10 is permanent. The rule of a father over his children
is royal, for he rules by virtue both of love and of the
respect due to age, exercising a kind of royal power.
And therefore Homer has appropriately called Zeus
' father of Gods and men ', because he is the king of them
all. For a king is the natural superior of his subjects,
15 but he should be of the same kin or kind with them,
and such is the relation of elder and younger, of father
and son.

Thus it is clear that household management attends 13
more to men than to the acquisition of inanimate things,
and to human excellence more than to the excellence
20 of property which we call wealth, and to the virtue of
freemen more than to the virtue of slaves. A question
may indeed be raised, whether there is any excellence at
all in a slave beyond and higher than merely instrumental
and ministerial qualities—whether he can have the virtues
of temperance, courage, justice, and the like ; or whether
25 slaves possess only bodily and ministerial qualities. And,

---

[1] 1253^b 14–1255^b 39.   [2] Cp. ii. 1261^a 39, iii. 1288^a 12.
[3] Herod. ii. 172.

whichever way we answer the question, a difficulty arises ; for, if they have virtue, in what will they differ from freemen ? On the other hand, since they are men and share in rational principle, it seems absurd to say that they have no virtue. A similar question may be raised about women and children, whether they too have virtues : ₃₀ ought a woman to be temperate and brave and just, and is a child to be called temperate, and intemperate, or not ? So in general we may ask about the natural ruler, and the natural subject, whether they have the same or different virtues. For if a noble nature is equally required in both, why should one of them always rule, and the other always ₃₅ be ruled ? Nor can we say that this is a question of degree, for the difference between ruler and subject is a difference of kind, which the difference of more and less never is. Yet how strange is the supposition that the one ought, and that the other ought not, to have virtue ! For if the ruler is intemperate and unjust, how can he ₄₀ rule well ? if the subject, how can he obey well ? If he **1260^a** be licentious and cowardly, he will certainly not do his duty. It is evident, therefore, that both of them must have a share of virtue, but varying as natural subjects also vary among themselves. Here the very constitution of the soul¹ has shown us the way ; in it one part naturally rules, ₅ and the other is subject, and the virtue of the ruler we maintain to be different from that of the subject ;—the one being the virtue of the rational, and the other of the irrational part. Now, it is obvious that the same principle applies generally, and therefore almost all things rule and are ruled according to nature. But the kind of rule differs ;—the freeman rules over the slave after another manner from that in which the male rules over the female, or the man over the child ; although the parts of the soul ₁₀ are present in all of them, they are present in different degrees. For the slave has no deliberative faculty at all ; the woman has, but it is without authority,² and the child has, but it is immature. So it must necessarily be

¹ Reading ⟨τὰ⟩ περὶ τὴν ψυχήν in l. 4 with Schütz.
² Or, with Bernays, 'inconclusive'.

15 supposed to be with the moral virtues also ; all should partake of them, but only in such manner and degree as is required by each for the fulfilment of his duty. Hence the ruler ought to have moral virtue in perfection, for his function, taken absolutely, demands a master artificer, and rational principle is such an artificer ; the subjects, on the other hand, require only that measure of 20 virtue which is proper to each of them. Clearly, then, moral virtue belongs to all of them ; but the temperance of a man and of a woman, or the courage and justice of a man and of a woman, are not, as Socrates maintained,[1] the same ; the courage of a man is shown in commanding, of a woman in obeying. And this holds of all other virtues, as will be more clearly seen if we look at them in 25 detail, for those who say generally that virtue consists in a good disposition of the soul, or in doing rightly, or the like, only deceive themselves. Far better than such definitions is their mode of speaking, who, like Gorgias,[2] enumerate the virtues. All classes must be deemed to have their special attributes ; as the poet says of women,

30   ' Silence is a woman's glory ',[3]

but this is not equally the glory of man. The child is imperfect, and therefore obviously his virtue is not relative to himself alone, but to the perfect man and to his teacher, and in like manner the virtue of the slave is relative to a master. Now we determined[4] that a slave is useful for the wants of life, and therefore he will obvi-
35 ously require only so much virtue as will prevent him from failing in his duty through cowardice or lack of self-control. Some one will ask whether, if what we are saying is true, virtue will not be required also in the artisans, for they often fail in their work through the lack of self-control ? But is there not a great difference in the 40 two cases ? For the slave shares in his master's life ; the artisan is less closely connected with him, and only attains excellence in proportion as he becomes a slave.

---

[1] Plato, *Meno*, 72 A–73 C.   [2] *Meno*, 71 E, 72 A.
[3] Soph. *Aj*. 293.   [4] 1254ᵇ 16–39, cf. 1259ᵇ 25 sq.

The meaner sort of mechanic has a special and separate 1260^b slavery; and whereas the slave exists by nature, not so the shoemaker or other artisan. It is manifest, then, that the master ought to be the source of such excellence in the slave, and not a mere possessor of the art of mastership which trains the slave in his duties.[1] Wherefore 5 they are mistaken who forbid us to converse with slaves and say that we should employ command only,[2] for slaves stand even more in need of admonition than children.

So much for this subject; the relations of husband and wife, parent and child, their several virtues, what in their intercourse with one another is good, and what is evil, 10 and how we may pursue the good and escape the evil, will have to be discussed when we speak of the different forms of government.[3] For, inasmuch as every family is a part of a state, and these relationships are the parts of a family, and the virtue of the part must have regard to the virtue of the whole, women and children must be 15 trained by education with an eye to the constitution,[4] if the virtues of either of them are supposed to make any difference in the virtues of the state. And they must make a difference: for the children grow up to be citizens, and half the free persons in a state are women.[5]

Of these matters, enough has been said; of what 20 remains, let us speak at another time. Regarding, then, our present inquiry as complete, we will make a new beginning. And, first, let us examine the various theories of a perfect state.

[1] Cp. 1255^b 23, 31–35.   [2] Plato, *Laws*, vi. 777 E.
[3] The question is not actually discussed in the *Politics*.
[4] Cp. v. 1310^a 12–36, viii. 1337^a 11–18.
[5] Plato, *Laws*, vi. 781 A.

BOOK II

OUR purpose is to consider what form of political **1**
community is best of all for those who are most able to
realize their ideal of life. We must therefore examine
30 not only this but other constitutions, both such as
actually exist in well-governed states, and any theoretical
forms which are held in esteem ; that what is good and
useful may be brought to light. And let no one suppose
that in seeking for something beyond them we are anxious
to make a sophistical display at any cost ; we only under-
35 take this inquiry because all the constitutions with which
we are acquainted are faulty.

We will begin with the natural beginning of the subject.
Three alternatives are conceivable : The members of a
state must either have (1) all things or (2) nothing in
common, or (3) some things in common and some not.
That they should have nothing in common is clearly
40 impossible, for the constitution is a community, and
1261ᵃ must at any rate have a common place—one city will be
in one place, and the citizens are those who share in that
one city. But should a well-ordered state have all things,
as far as may be, in common, or some only and not
others ? For the citizens might conceivably have wives
5 and children and property in common, as Socrates proposes in the *Republic* of Plato.[1] Which is better, our
present condition, or the proposed new order of society ?

10 There are many difficulties in the community of women. **2**
And the principle on which Socrates rests the necessity of such an institution evidently is not established
by his arguments. Further, as a means to the end
which he ascribes to the state, the scheme, taken literally,
is impracticable, and how we are to interpret it[2] is

---

[1] *Rep.* iv. 423 E, v. 457 C, 462 B.
[2] Reading in l. 14 διελεῖν, with good MS. authority.

nowhere precisely stated. I am speaking of the premiss 15
from which the argument of Socrates proceeds, 'that the
greater the unity of the state the better'. Is it not
obvious that a state may at length attain such a degree
of unity as to be no longer a state?—since the nature of
a state is to be a plurality, and in tending to greater unity,
from being a state, it becomes a family, and from being
a family, an individual ; for the family may be said to be 20
more one than the state, and the individual than the
family. So that we ought not to attain this greatest unity
even if we could, for it would be the destruction of the
state. Again, a state is not made up only of so many
men, but of different kinds of men ; for similars do not
constitute a state. It is not like a military alliance. The 25
usefulness of the latter depends upon its quantity even
where there is no difference in quality (for mutual
protection is the end aimed at), just as a greater weight
of anything is more useful than a less (in like manner,
a state differs from a nation, when the nation has not
its population organized in villages, but lives an Arcadian
sort of life) ; but the elements out of which a unity is to
be formed differ in kind. Wherefore the principle of 30
compensation,[1] as I have already remarked in the
Ethics,[2] is the salvation of states. Even among freemen
and equals this is a principle which must be maintained,
for they cannot all rule together, but must change at the
end of a year or some other period of time or in some
order of succession. The result is that upon this plan
they all govern ; just as if shoemakers and carpenters were 35
to exchange their occupations, and the same persons did
not always continue shoemakers and carpenters. And
since it is better[3] that this should be so in politics as
well, it is clear that while there should be continuance of the
same persons in power where this is possible, yet where
this is not possible by reason of the natural equality 1261ᵇ
of the citizens, and[4] at the same time it is just that

[1] Or, 'reciprocal proportion'.   [2] *N. Eth.* v. 1132ᵇ 32.
[3] Omitting the brackets in ª 37, ᵇ 4, and the marks of a lacuna
in ª 37.
[4] Reading in l. 1 ἅμα δέ with the MSS.

all should share in the government (whether to govern be
a good thing or a bad [1]), an approximation to this is that
equals should in turn retire from office and should, apart
from official position, be treated alike.[2] Thus the one
party rule and the others are ruled in turn, as if they were
5 no longer the same persons. In like manner when they hold
office there is a variety in the offices held. Hence it is
evident that a city is not by nature one in that sense which
some persons affirm ; and that what is said to be the greatest
good of cities is in reality their destruction ; but surely
the good of things must be that which preserves them.[3]
10 Again, in another point of view, this extreme unification
of the state is clearly not good ; for a family is more self-
sufficing than an individual, and a city than a family, and
a city only comes into being when the community is
large enough to be self-sufficing. If then self-sufficiency
is to be desired, the lesser degree of unity is more
15 desirable than the greater.

But, even supposing that it were best for the com- **3**
munity to have the greatest degree of unity, this unity
is by no means proved to follow from the fact 'of all
men saying " mine " and " not mine " at the same instant
of time', which, according to Socrates,[4] is the sign of
20 perfect unity in a state. For the word ' all ' is ambiguous.
If the meaning be that every individual says 'mine' and
'not mine' at the same time, then perhaps the result at
which Socrates aims may be in some degree accomplished ;
each man will call the same person his own son and the
same person his own wife, and so of his property and of all
that falls to his lot. This, however, is not the way in which
people would speak who had their wives and children in
25 common ; they would say ' all ' but not ' each '. In like
manner their property would be described as belonging
to them, not severally but collectively. There is an
obvious fallacy in the term ' all ': like some other words,
' both ', ' odd ', ' even ', it is ambiguous, and even in abstract

[1] Cp. Pl. *Rep.* i. 345–6.   [2] Cp. i. 1259ᵇ4, iii. 1288ª 12.
[3] Cp. Pl. *Rep.* i. 353.   [4] Pl. *Rep.* v. 462 C.

argument becomes a source of logical puzzles. That all 30
persons call the same thing mine in the sense in which
each does so may be a fine thing, but it is impracticable ;
or if the words are taken in the other sense, such a unity
in no way conduces to harmony. And there is another
objection to the proposal. For that which is common to
the greatest number has the least care bestowed upon it.
Every one thinks chiefly of his own, hardly at all of the
common interest ; and only when he is himself concerned
as an individual. For besides other considerations, every- 35
body is more inclined to neglect the duty which he expects
another to fulfil ; as in families many attendants are often
less useful than a few. Each citizen will have a thousand
sons who will not be his sons individually, but anybody
will be equally the son of anybody, and will therefore be **1262^a**
neglected by all alike. Further, upon this principle,
every one will use the word ' mine ' of one who is prosper-
ing or the reverse,[1] however small a fraction he may
himself be of the whole number ; the same boy will be
' my son ', ' so and so's son ', the son of each of the
thousand, or whatever be the number of the citizens ;
and even about this he will not be positive ; for it is 5
impossible to know who chanced to have a child, or
whether, if one came into existence, it has survived. But
which is better—for each to say ' mine ' in this way,
making a man the same relation to two thousand or ten
thousand citizens, or to use the word ' mine ' in the
ordinary and more restricted sense ? For usually the
same person is called by one man his own son whom 10
another calls his own brother or cousin or kinsman—blood
relation or connexion by marriage either of himself or of
some relation of his, and yet another his clansman or
tribesman ; and how much better is it to be the real
cousin of somebody than to be a son after Plato's
fashion ! Nor is there any way of preventing brothers
and children and fathers and mothers from sometimes 15
recognizing one another ; for children are born like their
parents, and they will necessarily be finding indications of

[1] Cp. *Rep.* v. 463 E.

their relationship to one another. Geographers declare
such to be the fact ; they say that in part of Upper Libya,
20 where the women are common, nevertheless the children
who are born are assigned to their respective fathers on
the ground of their likeness.[1] And some women, like
the females of other animals—for example, mares and
cows—have a strong tendency to produce offspring
resembling their parents, as was the case with the
Pharsalian mare called Honest.[2]

25   Other evils, against which it is not easy for the authors **4**
of such a community to guard, will be assaults and
homicides, voluntary as well as involuntary, quarrels and
slanders, all which are most unholy acts when committed
against fathers and mothers and near relations, but not
30 equally unholy when there is no relationship. Moreover,
they are much more likely to occur if the relationship is
unknown, and, when they have occurred, the customary
expiations of them cannot be made. Again, how
strange it is that Socrates,[3] after having made the
children common, should hinder lovers from carnal
intercourse only, but should permit love and familiarities
35 between father and son or between brother and brother,
than which nothing can be more unseemly, since even
without them love of this sort is improper. How
strange, too, to forbid intercourse for no other reason than
the violence of the pleasure, as though the relationship of
father and son or of brothers with one another made no
difference.

40   This community of wives and children seems better
suited to the husbandmen than to the guardians, for if
1262ᵇ they have wives and children in common, they will be
bound to one another by weaker ties, as a subject class
should be, and they will remain obedient and not rebel.[4]
In a word, the result of such a law would be just the
5 opposite of that which good laws ought to have, and the
intention of Socrates in making these regulations about

[1] Cp. Herod. iv. 180.   [2] Cp. *Hist. Anim.* vii. 586ª 13.
[3] *Rep*. iii. 403 A–C.   [4] Cp. vii. 1330ª 28.

women and children would defeat itself. For friendship we believe to be the greatest good of states [1] and the preservative of them against revolutions; neither is there anything which Socrates so greatly lauds as the unity of the state which he and all the world declare to 10 be created by friendship. But the unity which he commends [2] would be like that of the lovers in the *Symposium*,[3] who, as Aristophanes says, desire to grow together in the excess of their affection, and from being two to become one, in which case one or both would certainly perish. Whereas in a state having women and children 15 common, love will be watery; and the father will certainly not say 'my son', or the son 'my father'.[4] As a little sweet wine mingled with a great deal of water is imperceptible in the mixture, so, in this sort of community, the idea of relationship which is based upon these names will be lost; there is no reason why the so- 20 called father should care about the son, or the son about the father, or brothers about one another. Of the two qualities which chiefly inspire regard and affection— that a thing is your own and that it is your only one— neither can exist in such a state as this.

Again, the transfer of children as soon as they are born from the rank of husbandmen or of artisans to that of 25 guardians, and from the rank of guardians into a lower rank,[5] will be very difficult to arrange; the givers or transferrers cannot but know whom they are giving and transferring, and to whom. And the previously mentioned [6] evils, such as assaults, unlawful loves, homicides, 30 will happen more often amongst those who are transferred to the lower classes, or who have a place assigned to them among the guardians; for they will no longer call the members of the class they have left brothers, and children, and fathers, and mothers, and will not, therefore, be afraid of committing any crimes by reason of consanguinity. Touching the community of wives 35 and children, let this be our conclusion.

[1] Cp. *N. Eth.* viii. 1155^{a} 22.   [2] Cp. c. 2.
[3] *Symp.* 191 A, 192 C.   [4] Cp. c. 3.   [5] *Rep.* iii. 415 B.   [6] ^{a} 25–40.

Next let us consider what should be our arrangements 5
about property: should the citizens of the perfect state
40 have their possessions in common or not? This question
may be discussed separately from the enactments about
1263ᵃ women and children. Even supposing that the women
and children belong to individuals, according to the
custom which is at present universal, may there not be
an advantage in having and using possessions in
common? Three cases are possible: (1) the soil may
be appropriated, but the produce may be thrown for
consumption into the common stock; and this is the
5 practice of some nations. Or (2), the soil may be
common, and may be cultivated in common, but the
produce divided among individuals for their private use;
this is a form of common property which is said to exist
among certain barbarians. Or (3), the soil and the
produce may be alike common.

When the husbandmen are not the owners, the case
10 will be different and easier to deal with; but when they
till the ground for themselves the question of ownership
will give a world of trouble. If they do not share
equally in enjoyments and toils, those who labour much
and get little will necessarily complain of those who
15 labour little and receive or consume much. But indeed there
is always a difficulty in men living together and having all
human relations in common, but especially in their having
common property. The partnerships of fellow-travellers
are an example to the point; for they generally fall
out over everyday matters and quarrel about any
20 trifle which turns up. So with servants: we are most
liable to take offence at those with whom we most
frequently come into contact in daily life.

These are only some of the disadvantages which
attend the community of property; the present arrangement, if improved as it might be by good customs¹ and
laws, would be far better, and would have the advantages
25 of both systems. Property should be in a certain sense

¹ Reading in l. 23 ἔχει ἐπικοσμηθὲν ἔθεσι, with some good MSS.

common, but, as a general rule, private ; for, when every
one has a distinct interest,[1] men will not complain of one
another, and they will make more progress, because
every one will be attending to his own business. And yet
by reason of goodness, and in respect of use, ' Friends ',
as the proverb says, ' will have all things common.'[2] Even 30
now there are traces of such a principle, showing that it
is not impracticable, but, in well-ordered states, exists
already to a certain extent and may be carried further.
For, although every man has his own property, some
things he will place at the disposal of his friends, while
of others he shares the use with them. The Lace- 35
daemonians, for example, use one another's slaves, and
horses, and dogs, as if they were their own ; and when
they lack provisions on a journey, they appropriate what
they find[3] in the fields throughout the country. It is
clearly better that property should be private, but the
use of it common ; and the special business of the
legislator is to create in men this benevolent disposition.
Again, how immeasurably greater is the pleasure, when a 40
man feels a thing to be his own ; for surely the love of self[4]
is a feeling implanted by nature and not given in vain, 1263ᵇ
although selfishness is rightly censured ; this, however,
is not the mere love of self, but the love of self in excess,
like the miser's love of money ; for all, or almost all,
men love money and other such objects in a measure.
And further, there is the greatest pleasure in doing 5
a kindness or service to friends or guests or companions,
which can only be rendered when a man has private
property. These advantages are lost by excessive unification of the state. The exhibition of two virtues, besides, is
visibly annihilated in such a state : first, temperance towards
women (for it is an honourable action to abstain from 10
another's wife for temperance sake) ; secondly, liberality
in the matter of property. No one, when men have all
things in common, will any longer set an example of

---

[1] Cp. *Rep.* ii. 374.   [2] Cp. *Rep.* iv. 424 A.
[3] Reading ⟨τοῖς⟩ ἐν τοῖς ἀγροῖς, with Vahlen.
[4] Cp. *N. Eth.* ix. 8.

liberality or do any liberal action ; for liberality consists in the use which is made of property.[1]

15 Such legislation may have a specious appearance of benevolence ; men readily listen to it, and are easily induced to believe that in some wonderful manner everybody will become everybody's friend,-especially when some one[2] is heard denouncing the evils now existing in 20 states, suits about contracts, convictions for perjury, flatteries of rich men and the like, which are said to arise out of the possession of private property. These evils, however, are due to a very different cause—the wickedness of human nature. Indeed, we see that there is much more quarrelling among those who have all 25 things in common, though there are not many of them when compared with the vast numbers who have private property.

Again, we ought to reckon, not only the evils from which the citizens will be saved, but also the advantages which they will lose. The life which they are to lead 30 appears to be quite impracticable. The error of Socrates must be attributed to the false notion of unity from which he starts.[3] Unity there should be, both of the family and of the state, but in some respects only. For there is a point at which a state may attain such a degree of unity as to be no longer a state, or at which, without actually ceasing to exist, it will become an inferior state, 35 like harmony passing into unison, or rhythm which has been reduced to a single foot. The state, as I was saying, is a plurality,[4] which should be united and made into a community by education ; and it is strange that the author of a system of education which he thinks will make the state virtuous, should expect to improve his citizens by regulations of this sort, and not by philosophy 40 or by customs and laws, like those which prevail at Sparta and Crete respecting common meals, whereby 1264[a] the legislator has made property common. Let us remember that we should not disregard the experience

---

[1] Cp. *N. Eth.* iv. 1119^b 22. [2] *Rep.* v. 464, 465.
[3] Cp. c. 2. [4] Cp. 1261^a 18.

of ages; in the multitude of years these things, if they were good, would certainly not have been unknown; for almost everything has been found out, although sometimes they are not put together ; in other cases men do not use the knowledge which they have. Great light 5 would be thrown on this subject if we could see such a form of government in the actual process of construction ; for the legislator could not form a state at all without distributing and dividing its constituents into associations for common meals, and into phratries and tribes. But all this legislation ends only in forbidding agriculture to 10 the guardians, a prohibition which the Lacedaemonians try to enforce already.

But, indeed, Socrates has not said, nor is it easy to decide, what in such a community will be the general form of the state. The citizens who are not guardians are the majority, and about them nothing has been determined: are the husbandmen, too, to have their property in common? Or is each individual to have his 15 own? and are their wives and children to be individual or common? If, like the guardians, they are to have all things in common, in what do they differ from them, or what will they gain by submitting to their government? Or, upon what principle would they submit, unless indeed 20 the governing class adopt the ingenious policy of the Cretans, who give their slaves the same institutions as their own, but forbid them gymnastic exercises and the possession of arms. If, on the other hand, the inferior classes are to be like other cities in respect of marriage and property, what will be the form of the community? Must it not contain two states in one,[1] each hostile to 25 the other? He makes the guardians into a mere occupying garrison, while the husbandmen and artisans and the rest are the real citizens. But if so the suits and quarrels, and all the evils which Socrates affirms [2] to exist in other states, will exist equally among them. He says indeed that, having so good an education, the 30 citizens will not need many laws, for example laws about

[1] Cp. *Rep.* iv. 422 E.   [2] *Rep.* v. 464, 465.

the city or about the markets;[1] but then he confines his education to the guardians. Again, he makes the husbandmen owners of the property upon condition of their paying a tribute.[2] But in that case they are likely to be much more unmanageable and conceited than the 35 Helots, or Penestae, or slaves in general.[3] And whether community of wives and property be necessary for the lower equally with the higher class or not, and the questions akin to this, what will be the education, form of government, laws of the lower class, Socrates has nowhere determined: neither is it easy to discover this, nor is their character [4] of small importance if the common 40 life of the guardians is to be maintained.

1264ᵇ Again, if Socrates makes the women common, and retains private property, the men will see to the fields, but who will see to the house? And who will do so if the agricultural class have both their property and their wives in common? Once more: it is absurd to argue, 5 from the analogy of the animals, that men and women should follow the same pursuits,[5] for animals have not to manage a household. The government, too, as constituted by Socrates, contains elements of danger; for he makes the same persons always rule. And if this is often a cause of disturbance among the meaner sort, how much 10 more among high-spirited warriors? But that the persons whom he makes rulers must be the same is evident; for the gold which the God mingles in the souls of men is not at one time given to one, at another time to another, but always to the same: as he says, 'God mingles gold in some, and silver in others, from their very birth; but brass and iron in those who are meant 15 to be artisans and husbandmen.'[6] Again, he deprives the guardians even of happiness, and says that the legislator ought to make the whole state happy.[7] But the whole cannot be happy unless most, or all, or some of its parts enjoy happiness.[8] In this respect happiness

[1] *Rep.* iv. 425 D.   [2] *Rep.* v. 464 C.
[3] Cp. 1269ᵃ 36.   [4] Reading ποιούς τινας in l. 39 with some MSS.
[5] Cp. *Rep.* v. 451 D.   [6] Cp. *Rep.* iii. 415 A.
[7] *Rep.* iv. 419, 420.   [8] Cp. vii. 1329ᵃ 23.

is not like the even principle in numbers, which may ²⁰
exist only in the whole, but in neither of the parts ; not
so happiness.   And if the guardians are not happy, who
are?   Surely not the artisans, or the common people.
The Republic of which Socrates discourses has all these
difficulties, and others quite as great.   ²⁵

6   The same, or nearly the same, objections apply to
Plato's later work, the *Laws*, and therefore we had better
examine briefly the constitution which is therein described.
In the *Republic*, Socrates has definitely settled in all
a few questions only ; such as the community of women ³⁰
and children, the community of property, and the
constitution of the state.   The population is divided into
two classes—one of husbandmen, and the other of
warriors ;[1] from this latter is taken a third class of
counsellors and rulers of the state.[2]   But Socrates has
not determined whether the husbandmen and artisans
are to have a share in the government, and whether they, ³⁵
too, are to carry arms and share in military service, or
not.   He certainly thinks[3] that the women ought to
share in the education of the guardians, and to fight by
their side.   The remainder of the work is filled up with
digressions foreign to the main subject, and with ⁴⁰
discussions about the education of the guardians.   In the 1265ᵃ
Laws there is hardly anything but laws ; not much is
said about the constitution.   This, which he had intended
to make more of the ordinary type, he gradually brings
round to the other or ideal form.   For with the
exception of the community of women and property, he ⁵
supposes everything to be the same in both states ; there
is to be the same education ; the citizens of both are to
live free from servile occupations, and there are to be
common meals in both.   The only difference is that in
the *Laws*, the common meals are extended to women,[4]
and the warriors number 5000,[5] but in the *Republic*
only 1000.[6]

[1] *Rep.* ii. 373 E.   [2] *Rep.* iii. 412 B.   [3] *Rep.* v. 451 E.
[4] *Laws*, vi. 780 E.   [5] *Laws*, v. 737 E.   [6] *Rep.* iv. 423 A

10   The discourses of Socrates are never commonplace ;
they always exhibit grace and originality and thought ;
but perfection in everything can hardly be expected.
We must not overlook the fact that the number of 5000
citizens, just now mentioned, will require a territory as
15 large as Babylon, or some other huge site, if so many
persons are to be supported in idleness, together with
their women and attendants, who will be a multitude
many times as great. In framing an ideal we may
assume what we wish, but should avoid impossibilities.[1]

It is said that the legislator ought to have his eye
directed to two points,—the people and the country.[2]
20 But neighbouring countries also must not be forgotten
by him,[3] firstly because the state for which he legislates
is to have a political and not an isolated life.[4] For
a state must have such a military force as will be
serviceable against her neighbours, and not merely
25 useful at home. Even if the life of action is not admitted
to be the best, either for individuals or states,[5] still a city
should be formidable to enemies, whether invading or
retreating.

There is another point : Should not the amount of
property be defined in some way which differs from this by
being clearer ? For Socrates says that a man should have
30 so much property as will enable him to live temperately,[6]
which is only a way of saying 'to live well' ; this is too
general a conception. Further, a man may live temperately and yet miserably. A better definition would
be that a man must have so much property as will
enable him to live not only temperately but liberally ;[7] if
the two are parted, liberality will combine with luxury ;
temperance will be associated with toil. For liberality
and temperance are the only eligible qualities[8] which
35 have to do with the use of property. A man cannot use
property with mildness or courage, but temperately and

---

[1] Cp. vii. 1325ᵇ 38.
[2] Perhaps *Laws*, iv. 704–709, and v. 747 D.   [3] Cp. 1267ª 19.
[4] Cp. vii. 1327ª 41.   [5] Cp. vii. C. 2. and 3.   [6] *Laws*, v. 737 D.
[7] Cp. vii. 1326ᵇ 30.
[8] Reading ἕξεις αἱρεταί in l. 35 with Vettori.

liberally he may; and therefore the practice of these virtues is inseparable from property. There is an inconsistency, too, in equalizing the property and not regulating the number of the citizens;[1] the population is to remain unlimited, and he thinks that it will be suffi- 40 ciently equalized[2] by a certain number of marriages being unfruitful, however many are born to others, because he 1265ᵇ finds this to be the case in existing states. But greater care will be required than now; for among ourselves, whatever may be the number of citizens, the property is always distributed among them, and therefore no one is in want; but, if the property were incapable of division as in the *Laws*, the supernumeraries, whether few or 5 many, would get nothing. One would have thought that it was even more necessary to limit population than property; and that the limit should be fixed by calculating the chances of mortality in the children, and of sterility in married persons. The neglect of this subject, which 10 in existing states is so common, is a never-failing cause of poverty among the citizens; and poverty is the parent of revolution and crime. Pheidon the Corinthian, who was one of the most ancient legislators, thought that the families and the number of citizens ought to remain the same, although originally all the lots may have been of 15 different sizes: but in the *Laws* the opposite principle is maintained. What in our opinion is the right arrangement will have to be explained hereafter.[3]

There is another omission in the *Laws*: Socrates does not tell us how the rulers differ from their subjects; he only says that they should be related as the warp and 20 the woof, which are made out of different wools.[4] He allows that a man's whole property may be increased fivefold,[5] but why should not his land also increase to a certain extent? Again, will the good management of a household be promoted by his arrangement of home-

---

[1] But see *Laws*, v. 740 B–741 A.
[2] Reading ἀνομαλισθησομένην, in l. 40, with Madvig.
[3] Cp. vii. 1326ᵇ26–32, 1330ᵃ9–18, 1335ᵇ19–26; but the promise is hardly fulfilled.
[4] *Laws*, v. 734 E, 735 A.   [5] *Laws*, v. 744 E.

25 steads ? for he assigns to each individual two homesteads
in separate places,¹ and it is difficult to live in two houses.
The whole system of government tends to be neither
democracy nor oligarchy, but something in a mean
between them, which is usually called a polity, and is
composed of the heavy-armed soldiers. Now, if he
intended to frame a constitution which would suit the
30 greatest number of states, he was very likely right, but
not if he meant to say that this constitutional form came
nearest to his first or ideal state; for many would prefer
the Lacedaemonian, or, possibly, some other more aristocratic government. Some, indeed, say that the best
constitution is a combination of all existing forms, and
35 they praise the Lacedaemonian ² because it is made up of
oligarchy, monarchy, and democracy, the king forming
the monarchy, and the council of elders the oligarchy,
while the democratic element is represented by the
Ephors; for the Ephors are selected from the people.
40 Others, however, declare the Ephoralty to be a tyranny,
and find the element of democracy in the common meals
1266ª and in the habits of daily life. In the *Laws* ³ it is
maintained that the best constitution is made up of
democracy and tyranny, which are either not constitutions
at all, or are the worst of all. But they are nearer the
truth who combine many forms; for the constitution is
better which is made up of more numerous elements.
5 The constitution proposed in the *Laws* has no element
of monarchy at all; it is nothing but oligarchy and
democracy, leaning rather to oligarchy. This is seen in
the mode of appointing magistrates; ⁴ for although the
appointment of them by lot from among those who have
been already selected combines both elements, the way
10 in which the rich are compelled by law to attend the
assembly ⁵ and vote for magistrates or discharge other
political duties, while the rest may do as they like, and

¹ *Laws*, v. 745 C, but cp. infra, vii. 1330ª 9-18.
² Cp. iv. 1293ᵇ 16, 1294ᵇ 18-34.
³ iii. 693 D, 701 E, iv. 710, vi. 756 E.
⁴ *Laws*, vi. 756, 763 E, 765.
⁵ *Laws*, vi. 764 A ; and *Pol.* iv. 1294ª 37, 1298ᵇ 16.

the endeavour [1] to have the greater number of the magistrates appointed out of the richer classes and the highest officers selected from those who have the greatest incomes, both these are oligarchical features. The oligarchical principle prevails also in the choice of the council,[2] for all are compelled to choose, but the compulsion extends only to the choice out of the first class, and of an equal number out of the second class and out of the third class, but not in this latter case to all the voters but to those of the first three classes;[3] and the selection of candidates out of the fourth class is only compulsory on the first and second. Then, from the persons so chosen, he says that there ought to be an equal number of each class selected. Thus a preponderance will be given to the better sort of people, who have the larger incomes, because many of the lower classes, not being compelled, will not vote. These considerations, and others which will be adduced [4] when the time comes for examining similar polities, tend to show that states like Plato's should not be composed of democracy and monarchy. There is also a danger in electing the magistrates out of a body who are themselves elected;[5] for, if but a small number choose to combine, the elections will always go as they desire. Such is the constitution which is described in the *Laws*.

7   Other constitutions have been proposed; some by private persons, others by philosophers and statesmen, which all come nearer to established or existing ones than either of Plato's. No one else has introduced such novelties as the community of women and children, or public tables for women: other legislators begin with what is necessary. In the opinion of some, the regulation of property is the chief point of all, that being the question upon which all revolutions turn. This

---

[1] *Laws*, vi. 763 D E.   [2] *Laws*, vi. 756 B-E.
[3] Reading. τοῖς δ' ἐκ τῶν τριῶν [ἢ τετάρτων] in l. 17, cp. *Laws*, vi. 756 C 8.
[4] iv. 7-9, 12. 1296ᵇ 34-38, 1297ᵃ 7-13.
[5] *Laws*, vi. 753 D.

danger was recognized by Phaleas of Chalcedon, who
was the first to affirm that the citizens of a state
40 ought to have equal possessions. He thought that in
1266ᵇ a new colony the equalization might be accomplished
without difficulty, not so easily when a state was already
established ; and that then the shortest way of com-
passing the desired end would be for the rich to give
and not to receive marriage portions, and for the poor
not to give but to receive them.

5   Plato in the *Laws*[1] was of opinion that, to a certain
extent, accumulation should be allowed, forbidding, as
I have already observed,[2] any citizen to possess more
than five times the minimum qualification. But those
who make such laws should remember what they are
apt to forget,[3]—that the legislator who fixes the amount
10 of property should also fix the number of children ; for,
if the children are too many for the property, the law
must be broken. And, besides the violation of the law,
it is a bad thing that many from being rich should
become poor ; for men of ruined fortunes are sure to
stir up revolutions. That the equalization of property
15 exercises an influence on political society was clearly
understood even by some of the old legislators. Laws
were made by Solon and others prohibiting an individual from possessing as much land as he pleased ; and
there are other laws in states which forbid the sale of
property : among the Locrians, for example, there is a
20 law that a man is not to sell his property unless he can
prove unmistakably that some misfortune has befallen
him. Again, there have been laws which enjoin the preservation of the original lots. Such a law existed in the
island of Leucas, and the abrogation of it made the constitution too democratic, for the rulers no longer had the
prescribed qualification. Again, where there is equality
25 of property, the amount may be either too large or too
small, and the possessor may be living either in luxury
or penury. Clearly, then, the legislator ought not only

---

[1] v. 744 E.   [2] 1265ᵇ 21.   [3] Cp. 1265ª 38–ᵇ 16.

to aim at the equalization of properties, but at moderation in their amount. Further, if he prescribe this moderate amount equally to all, he will be no nearer the mark; for it is not the possessions but the desires of mankind which require to be equalized,[1] and this is impossible, 30 unless a sufficient education is provided by the laws. But Phaleas will probably reply that this is precisely what he means; and that, in his opinion, there ought to be in states, not only equal property, but equal education. Still he should tell us what will be the character of his education; there is no use in having one and the same for all, if it is of a sort that predisposes men to avarice, 35 or ambition, or both. Moreover, civil troubles arise, not only out of the inequality of property, but out of the inequality of honour, though in opposite ways. For the 40 common people quarrel about the inequality of property, 1267^a the higher class about the equality of honour; as the poet says,—

'The bad and good alike in honour share.'[2]

There are crimes of which the motive is want; and for these Phaleas expects to find a cure in the equalization of property, which will take away from a man the temptation to be a highwayman, because he is hungry or cold. But want is not the sole incentive to crime; men 5 also wish to enjoy themselves and not to be in a state of desire—they wish to cure some desire, going beyond the necessities of life, which preys upon them; nay, this is not the only reason—they may desire superfluities[3] in order to enjoy pleasures unaccompanied with pain, and therefore they commit crimes.

Now what is the cure of these three disorders? Of the first, moderate possessions and occupation; of the second, habits of temperance; as to the third, if any 10 desire pleasures which depend on themselves, they will find the satisfaction of their desires nowhere but in philosophy; for. all other pleasures we are dependent on others. The fact is that the greatest crimes are caused by excess and not by necessity. Men do not

---

[1] Cp. 1263^b22.   [2] *Il.* ix. 319.   [3] Keeping ἂν ἐπιθυμοῖεν.

become tyrants in order that they may not suffer cold;
and hence great is the honour bestowed, not on him who kills a thief, but on him who kills a tyrant. Thus we see that the institutions of Phaleas avail only against petty crimes.

There is another objection to them. They are chiefly designed to promote the internal welfare of the state. But the legislator should consider also its relation to neighbouring nations, and to all who are outside of it.[1] The government must be organized with a view to military strength; and of this he has said not a word. And so with respect to property: there should not only be enough to supply the internal wants of the state, but also to meet dangers coming from without. The property of the state should not be so large that more powerful neighbours may be tempted by it, while the owners are unable to repel the invaders; nor yet so small that the state is unable to maintain a war even against states of equal power, and of the same character. Phaleas has not laid down any rule; but we should bear in mind that abundance of wealth[2] is an advantage. The best limit will probably be, that a more powerful neighbour must have no inducement to go to war with you by reason of the excess of your wealth, but only such as he would have had if you had possessed less. There is a story that Eubulus, when Autophradates was going to besiege Atarneus, told him to consider how long the operation would take, and then reckon up the cost which would be incurred in the time. 'For', said he, 'I am willing for a smaller sum than that to leave Atarneus at once.' These words of Eubulus made an impression on Autophradates, and he desisted from the siege.

The equalization of property is one of the things that tend to prevent the citizens from quarrelling. Not that the gain in this direction is very great. For the nobles will be dissatisfied because they think themselves worthy of more than an equal share of honours; and this is often found

[1] Cp. 1265ᵃ 20.
[2] Or, reading ὅ τι in l. 28 with Stahr, 'what amount of wealth.

to be a cause of sedition and revolution.[1] And the avarice of mankind is insatiable; at one time two obols 1267ᵇ was pay enough; but now, when this sum has become customary, men always want more and more without end; for it is of the nature of desire not to be satisfied, and most men live only for the gratification of it. The 5 beginning of reform is not so much to equalize property as to train the nobler sort of natures not to desire more, and to prevent the lower from getting more; that is to say, they must be kept down, but not ill-treated. Besides, the equalization proposed by Phaleas is imperfect; 10 for he only equalizes land, whereas a man may be rich also in slaves, and cattle, and money, and in the abundance of what are called his movables. Now either all these things must be equalized, or some limit must be imposed on them, or they must all be let alone. It would appear that Phaleas is legislating for a small city 15 only, if, as he supposes, all the artisans are to be public slaves and not to form a supplementary part of the body of citizens. But if there is a law that artisans are to be public slaves, it should only apply to those engaged on public works, as at Epidamnus, or at Athens on the plan which Diophantus once introduced.

From these observations any one may judge how far 20 Phaleas was wrong or right in his ideas.

8   Hippodamus, the son of Euryphon, a native of Miletus, the same who invented the art of planning cities, and who also laid out the Piraeus,—a strange man, whose fondness for distinction led him into a general eccentricity of life, which made some think him affected (for 25 he would wear flowing hair and expensive ornaments; but these were worn on a cheap but warm garment [2] both in winter and summer); he, besides aspiring to be an adept in the knowledge of nature, was the first person not a statesman who made inquiries about the best form of government.

The city of Hippodamus was composed of 10,000 30

---

[1] Cp. l. 1.   [2] Reading ἐπί for ἔτι in l. 26.

citizens divided into three parts,—one of artisans, one of
husbandmen, and a third of armed defenders of the
state. He also divided the land into three parts, one
sacred, one public, the third private:—the first was set
apart to maintain the customary worship of the gods,
35 the second was to support the warriors, the third was the
property of the husbandmen. He also divided laws
into three classes, and no more, for he maintained that
there are three subjects of lawsuits,—insult, injury, and
homicide. He likewise instituted a single final court of
40 appeal, to which all causes seeming to have been impro-
perly decided might be referred ; this court he formed
1268^a of elders chosen for the purpose. He was further of
opinion that the decisions of the courts ought not to be
given by the use of a voting pebble, but that every one
should have a tablet on which he might not only write
a simple condemnation, or leave the tablet blank for a
simple acquittal ; but, if he partly acquitted and partly
5 condemned, he was to distinguish accordingly. To the
existing law he objected that it obliged the judges to be
guilty of perjury, whichever way they voted. He also
enacted that those who discovered anything for the good
of the state should be honoured ; and he provided that
the children of citizens who died in battle should be
maintained at the public expense, as if such an enactment
10 had never been heard of before, yet it actually exists
at Athens [1] and in other places. As to the magistrates,
he would have them all elected by the people, that is,
by the three classes already mentioned, and those who
were elected were to watch over the interests of the
public, of strangers, and of orphans. These are the
most striking points in the constitution of Hippodamus.
15 There is not much else.

    The first of these proposals to which objection may
be taken is the threefold division of the citizens. The
artisans, and the husbandmen, and the warriors, all
have a share in the government. But the husbandmen
have no arms, and the artisans neither arms nor land,

---

[1] Cp. Thuc. ii. 46.

and therefore they become all but slaves of the warrior
class. That they should share in all the offices is an im- 20
possibility; for generals and guardians of the citizens,
and nearly all the principal magistrates, must be taken
from the class of those who carry arms. Yet, if the two
other classes have no share in the government, how can
they be loyal citizens? It may be said that those who 25
have arms must necessarily be masters of both the
other classes, but this is not so easily accomplished unless
they are numerous; and if they are, why should the
other classes share in the government at all, or have
power to appoint magistrates? Further, what use are
farmers to the city? Artisans there must be, for these 30
are wanted in every city, and they can live by their
craft, as elsewhere; and the husbandmen, too, if they
really provided the warriors with food, might fairly
have a share in the government. But in the republic of
Hippodamus they are supposed to have land of their own,
which they cultivate for their private benefit. Again, as 35
to this common land out of which the soldiers are maintained, if they are themselves to be the cultivators of it,
the warrior class will be identical with the husbandmen, although the legislator intended to make a distinction between them. If, again, there are to be other
cultivators distinct both from the husbandmen, who have
land of their own, and from the warriors, they will make
a fourth class, which has no place in the state and no
share in anything. Or, if the same persons are to cul- 40
tivate their own lands, and those of the public as well,
they will have a difficulty in supplying the quantity of
produce which will maintain two households:[1] and why, 1268ᵇ
in this case, should there be any division, for they might
find food themselves and give to the warriors from the
same land[2] and the same lots? There is surely a great
confusion in all this.

Neither is the law to be commended which says that 5
the judges, when a simple issue is laid before them,

<hr>

[1] Reading δύο οἰκίαις in l. 1.
[2] Reading ἀπὸ τῆς ⟨αὐτῆς⟩ γῆς in l. 2 with Böcker.

should distinguish in their judgement; for the judge is
thus converted into an arbitrator. Now, in an arbitration, although the arbitrators are many, they confer with
one another about the decision, and therefore they can
distinguish; but in courts of law this is impossible, and,
10 indeed, most legislators take pains to prevent the judges
from holding any communication with one another.
Again, will there not be confusion if the judge thinks
that damages should be given, but not so much as the
suitor demands? He asks, say, for twenty minae, and the
judge allows him ten minae (or in general the suitor asks
for more and the judge allows less), while another judge
15 allows five, another four minae. In this way they will go on
splitting up the damages, and some will grant the whole
and others nothing: how is the final reckoning to be
taken? Again, no one contends that he who votes for
a simple acquittal or condemnation perjures himself, if
the indictment has been laid in an unqualified form; and
20 this is just, for the judge who acquits does not decide that
the defendant owes nothing, but that he does not owe the
twenty minae. He only is guilty of perjury who thinks
that the defendant ought not to pay twenty minae, and
yet condemns him.

To honour those who discover anything which is useful
to the state is a proposal which has a specious sound,
but cannot safely be enacted by law, for it may encourage
informers, and perhaps even lead to political commotions.
25 This question involves another. It has been doubted
whether it is or is not expedient to make any changes in
the laws of a country, even if another law be better. Now,
if all changes are inexpedient, we can hardly assent to the
30 proposal of Hippodamus; for, under pretence of doing
a public service, a man may introduce measures which
are really destructive to the laws or to the constitution.
But, since we have touched upon this subject, perhaps we
had better go a little into detail, for, as I was saying, there
is a difference of opinion, and it may sometimes seem de-
35 sirable to make changes. Such changes in the other arts
and sciences have certainly been beneficial; medicine, for

example, and gymnastic, and every other art and craft
have departed from traditional usage. And, if politics be
an art, change must be necessary in this as in any other art.
That improvement has occurred is shown by the fact
that old customs are exceedingly simple and barbarous.
For the ancient Hellenes went about armed [1] and bought 40
their brides of each other. The remains of ancient laws
which have come down to us are quite absurd; for 1269[a]
example, at Cumae there is a law about murder, to the
effect that if the accuser produce a certain number of
witnesses from among his own kinsmen, the accused shall
be held guilty. Again, men in general desire the good,
and not merely what their fathers had. But the primaeval
inhabitants, whether they were born of the earth or 5
were the survivors of some destruction, may be supposed
to have been no better than ordinary or even foolish people
among ourselves (such is certainly the tradition [2] concerning the earth-born men); and it would be ridiculous
to rest contented with their notions. Even when laws
have been written down, they ought not always to remain
unaltered. As in other sciences, so in politics, it is im- 10
possible that all things should be precisely set down in
writing; for enactments must be universal, but actions
are concerned with particulars.[3] Hence we infer that
sometimes and in certain cases laws may be changed;
but when we look at the matter from another point of
view, great caution would seem to be required. For
the habit of lightly changing the laws is an evil, and, 15
when the advantage is small, some errors both of lawgivers and rulers had better be left; the citizen will not
gain so much by making the change as he will lose by
the habit of disobedience. The analogy of the arts [4] is
false; a change in a law is a very different thing from
a change in an art. For the law has no power to com- 20
mand obedience except that of habit, which can only be
given by time, so that a readiness to change from old to

[1] Cp. Thucyd. i. 5 and 6.
[2] Cp. Plato, *Laws*, iii. 677 B; *Polit.* 274 C; *Tim.* 22 D.
[3] Cp. Plato, *Polit.* 295 A.   1268[b] 34 sqq.

new laws enfeebles the power of the law. Even if we
admit that the laws are to be changed, are they all to
25 be changed, and in every state? And are they to be
changed by anybody who likes, or only by certain
persons? These are very important questions; and
therefore we had better reserve the discussion of them to
a more suitable occasion.[1]

In the governments of Lacedaemon and Crete, and **9**
30 indeed in all governments, two points have to be considered: first, whether any particular law is good or bad,
when compared with the perfect state; secondly, whether
it is or is not consistent with the idea and character
which the lawgiver has set before his citizens. That in
a well-ordered state the citizens should have leisure and
35 not have to provide for their daily wants is generally
acknowledged, but there is a difficulty in seeing how this
leisure is to be attained. The Thessalian Penestae
have often risen against their masters, and the Helots
in like manner against the Lacedaemonians, for whose
misfortunes they are always lying in wait. Nothing,
however, of this kind has as yet happened to the Cretans;
40 the reason probably is that the neighbouring cities, even
1269ᵇ when at war with one another, never form an alliance
with rebellious serfs, rebellions not being for their interest,
since they themselves have a dependent population.[2]
Whereas all the neighbours of the Lacedaemonians,
whether Argives, Messenians, or Arcadians, were their
5 enemies. In Thessaly, again, the original revolt of the
slaves occurred because the Thessalians were still at
war with the neighbouring Achaeans, Perrhaebians and
Magnesians. Besides, if there were no other difficulty,
the treatment or management of slaves is a troublesome
affair; for, if not kept in hand, they are insolent, and think
10 that they are as good as their masters, and, if harshly
treated, they hate and conspire against them. Now it is
clear that when these are the results the citizens of a

---

[1] These questions are not actually discussed in the *Politics*.
[2] Cp. 1271ᵇ 41.

state have not found out the secret of managing their subject population. Again, the licence of the Lacedaemonian women defeats the intention of the Spartan constitution, and is adverse to the happiness of the state. For, a husband and a wife being each a part of every family, the state 15 may be considered as about equally divided into men and women ; and, therefore, in those states in which the condition of the women is bad, half the city[1] may be regarded as having no laws. And this is what has actually happened at Sparta ; the legislator wanted to make the whole state hardy and temperate, and he has 20 carried out his intention in the case of the men, but he has neglected the women, who live in every sort of intemperance and luxury. The consequence is that in such a state wealth is too highly valued, especially if the citizens fall under the dominion of their wives, after the 25 manner of most warlike races, except the Celts and a few others who openly approve of male loves. The old mythologer would seem to have been right in uniting Ares and Aphrodite, for all warlike races are prone to the love either of men or of women. This was exempli- 30 fied among the Spartans in the days of their greatness ; many things were managed by their women   But what difference does it make whether women rule, or the rulers are ruled by women ? The result is the same. Even in regard to courage, which is of no use in daily life, and is 35 needed only in war, the influence of the Lacedaemonian women has been most mischievous. The evil showed itself in the Theban invasion, when, unlike the women in other cities, they were utterly useless and caused more confusion than the enemy. This licence of the Lacedaemonian women existed from the earliest times, and was 40 only what might be expected. For, during the wars of 1270^a the Lacedaemonians, first against the Argives, and afterwards against the Arcadians and Messenians, the men were long away from home, and, on the return of peace, they gave themselves into the legislator's hand, already

[1] Cp. i. 1260^b 18.

E 2

5 prepared by the discipline of a soldier's life (in which
there are many elements of virtue), to receive his enactments. But, when Lycurgus, as tradition says, wanted to
bring the women under his laws, they resisted, and he gave
up the attempt. These then are the causes of what then
happened, and this defect in the constitution is clearly to
be attributed to them. We are not, however, considering
10 what is or is not to be excused, but what is right or wrong,
and the disorder of the women, as I have already said,[1] not
only gives an air of indecorum to the constitution considered in itself, but tends in a measure to foster avarice.
15 The mention of avarice naturally suggests a criticism
on the inequality of property. While some of the
Spartan citizens have quite small properties, others have
very large ones ; hence the land has passed into the
hands of a few. And this is due also to faulty laws ;
20 for, although the legislator rightly holds up to shame the
sale or purchase of an inheritance, he allows anybody
who likes to give or bequeath it. Yet both practices
lead to the same result. And nearly two-fifths of the
whole country are held by women; this is owing to
the number of heiresses and to the large dowries which
25 are customary. It would surely have been better to
have given no dowries at all, or, if any, but small or
moderate ones. As the law now stands, a man may
bestow his heiress on any one whom he pleases, and, if
he die intestate, the privilege of giving her away descends
to his heir.[2] Hence, although the country is able to
30 maintain 1500 cavalry and 30,000 hoplites, the whole
number of Spartan citizens[3] fell below 1000. The result
proves the faulty nature of their laws respecting property ;
for the city sank under a single defeat ; the want of men
was their ruin. There is a tradition that, in the days of
their ancient kings, they were in the habit of giving the
35 rights of citizenship to strangers, and therefore, in spite
of their long wars, no lack of population was experienced

[1] 1269ᵇ 12, 23.
[2] i. e. to the person who 'inherits' the heiress. Cf. Newman *ad loc.*
[3] At the time of the Theban invasion.

by them; indeed, at one time Sparta is said to have numbered not less than 10,000 citizens. Whether this statement is true or not, it would certainly have been better to have maintained their numbers by the equalization of property. Again, the law which relates to the procreation of children is adverse to the correction of this 40 inequality. For the legislator, wanting to have as many 1270ᵇ Spartans as he could, encouraged the citizens to have large families; and there is a law at Sparta that the father of three sons shall be exempt from military service, and he who has four from all the burdens of the state. Yet it is obvious that, if there were many children, the 5 land being distributed as it is, many of them must necessarily fall into poverty.

The Lacedaemonian constitution is defective in another point; I mean the Ephoralty. This magistracy has authority in the highest matters, but the Ephors are chosen from the whole people, and so the office is apt to fall into the hands of very poor men, who, being badly off, 10 are open to bribes. There have been many examples at Sparta of this evil in former times; and quite recently, in the matter of the Andrians, certain of the Ephors who were bribed did their best to ruin the state. And so great and tyrannical is their power, that even the kings have been compelled to court them, so that, in this way 15 as well, together with the royal office the whole constitution has deteriorated, and from being an aristocracy has turned into a democracy. The Ephoralty certainly does keep the state together; for the people are contented when they have a share in the highest office, and the result, whether due to the legislator or to chance, has been advantageous. For if a constitution is to be permanent, all 20 the parts of the state must wish that it should exist and the same arrangements be maintained.[1] This is the case at Sparta, where the kings desire its permanence because they have due honour in their own persons; the nobles because they are represented in the council of elders (for

---

[1] Reading διαμένειν ταὐτά in l. 22 with most MSS. Cp. iv. 1294ᵇ 38, v. 1309ᵇ 17.

25 the office of elder is a reward of virtue) ; and the people, because all are eligible to the Ephoralty. The election of Ephors out of the whole people is perfectly right, but ought not to be carried on in the present fashion, which is too childish. Again, they have the decision of great causes, although they are quite ordinary men, and therefore they should not determine them merely on their own 30 judgement, but according to written rules, and to the laws. Their way of life, too, is not in accordance with the spirit of the constitution—they have a deal too much licence ; whereas, in the case of the other citizens, the excess of strictness is so intolerable that they run away from the law into the secret indulgence of sensual pleasures.

35   Again, the council of elders is not free from defects. It may be said that the elders are good men and well trained in manly virtue ; and that, therefore, there is an advantage to the state in having them. But that judges of important causes should hold office for life is a disput-40 able thing, for the mind grows old as well as the body. **1271**^a And when men have been educated in such a manner that even the legislator himself cannot trust them, there is real danger. Many of the elders are well known to have taken bribes and to have been guilty of partiality 5 in public affairs. And therefore they ought not to be irresponsible ; yet at Sparta they are so. But (it may be replied), ' All magistracies are accountable to the Ephors.' Yes, but this prerogative is too great for them, and we maintain that the control should be exercised in some other manner. Further, the mode in which the 10 Spartans elect their elders is childish ; and it is improper that the person to be elected should canvass for the office ; the worthiest should be appointed, whether he chooses or not. And here the legislator clearly indicates the same intention which appears in other parts of his constitution ; he would have his citizens ambitious, and he has reckoned upon this quality in the election of 15 the elders ; for no one would ask to be elected if he were not. Yet ambition and avarice, almost more than any other passions, are the motives of crime.

Whether kings are or are not an advantage to states,
I will consider at another time[1]; they should at any rate 20
be chosen, not as they are now, but with regard to their
personal life and conduct. The legislator himself obviously did not suppose that he could make them really
good men ; at least he shows a great distrust of their
virtue. For this reason the Spartans used to join
enemies with them in the same embassy, and the quarrels 25
between the kings were held to be conservative of the
state.

Neither did the first introducer of the common meals,
called ' phiditia ', regulate them well. The entertainment
ought to have been provided at the public cost, as in
Crete[2]; but among the Lacedaemonians every one is
expected to contribute, and some of them are too poor to 30
afford the expense ; thus the intention of the legislator is
frustrated. The common meals were meant to be a
popular institution, but the existing manner of regulating
them is the reverse of popular. For the very poor can
scarcely take part in them ; and, according to ancient 35
custom, those who cannot contribute are not allowed to
retain their rights of citizenship.

The law about the Spartan admirals has often been
censured, and with justice; it is a source of dissension,
for the kings are perpetual generals, and this office of 40
admiral is but the setting up of another king.

The charge which Plato brings, in the *Laws*,[3] against 1271^b
the intention of the legislator, is likewise justified ; the
whole constitution has regard to one part of virtue only,
—the virtue of the soldier, which gives victory in war.
So long as they were at war, therefore, their power was
preserved, but when they had attained empire they fell,[4] 5
for of the arts of peace they knew nothing, and had never
engaged in any employment higher than war. There is
another error, equally great, into which they have fallen.
Although they truly think that the goods for which men
contend are to be acquired by virtue rather than by vice,

---

[1] iii. 14-17.   [2] Cp. 1272^a 13-21.
[3] *Laws*, i. 625 E, 630.   [4] Cp. vii. 1334^a 6.

they err in supposing that these goods are to be preferred to the virtue which gains them.

10   Once more: the revenues of the state are ill-managed;
there is no money in the treasury, although they are
obliged to carry on great wars, and they are unwilling to
pay taxes. The greater part of the land being in the
hands of the Spartans, they do not look closely into one
15 another's contributions. The result which the legislator
has produced is the reverse of beneficial; for he has
made his city poor, and his citizens greedy.

Enough respecting the Spartan constitution, of which
these are the principal defects.

20   The Cretan constitution nearly resembles the Spartan, 10
and in some few points is quite as good; but for the
most part less perfect in form. The older constitutions
are generally less elaborate than the later, and the Lacedaemonian is said to be, and probably is, in a very great
measure, a copy of the Cretan. According to tradition,
25 Lycurgus, when he ceased to be the guardian of King
Charillus, went abroad and spent most of his time in Crete.
For the two countries are nearly connected; the Lyctians
are a colony of the Lacedaemonians, and the colonists,
when they came to Crete, adopted the constitution which
30 they found existing among the inhabitants. Even to
this day the Perioeci, or subject population of Crete, are
governed by the original laws which Minos is supposed
to have enacted. The island seems to be intended by
nature for dominion in Hellas, and to be well situated;
it extends right across the sea, around which nearly all
35 the Hellenes are settled; and while one end is not far
from the Peloponnese, the other almost reaches to
the region of Asia about Triopium and Rhodes. Hence
Minos acquired the empire of the sea, subduing some of
the islands and colonizing others; at last he invaded
Sicily, where he died near Camicus.

The Cretan institutions resemble the Lacedaemonian.
40 The Helots are the husbandmen of the one, the Perioeci
1272^a of the other, and both Cretans and Lacedaemonians have

common meals, which were anciently called by the Lacedaemonians not 'phiditia' but 'andria'; and the Cretans
have the same word, the use of which proves that the
common meals originally came from Crete. Further, the
two constitutions are similar ; for the office of the Ephors 5
is the same as that of the Cretan Cosmi, the only difference being that whereas the Ephors are five, the Cosmi
are ten in number. The elders, too, answer to the elders
in Crete, who are termed by the Cretans the council.
And the kingly office once existed in Crete, but was
abolished, and the Cosmi have now the duty of leading
them in war. All classes share in the ecclesia, but it can 10
only ratify the decrees of the elders and the Cosmi.

The common meals of Crete are certainly better
managed than the Lacedaemonian ; for in Lacedaemon
every one pays so much per head, or, if he fails, the law, 15
as I have already explained,[1] forbids him to exercise the
rights of citizenship. But in Crete they are of a more
popular character. There, of all the fruits of the earth
and cattle raised on the public lands, and of the tribute
which is paid by the Perioeci, one portion is assigned to
the gods and to the service of the state, and another to the
common meals, so that men, women, and children are all 20
supported out of a common stock.[2] The legislator has
many ingenious ways of securing moderation in eating,
which he conceives to be a gain ; he likewise encourages
the separation of men from women, lest they should have
too many children, and the companionship of men with
one another—whether this is a good or bad thing I shall 25
have an opportunity of considering at another time.[3]
But [4] that the Cretan common meals are better ordered
than the Lacedaemonian there can be no doubt.

On the other hand, the Cosmi are even a worse institution than the Ephors, of which they have all the evils
without the good. Like the Ephors, they are any chance
persons, but in Crete this is not counterbalanced by a 30

---

[1] 1271^a 35.   [2] Cp. vii. 1330^a 5.
[3] The question is nowhere discussed by Aristotle.
[4] Reading ὅτι δέ in l. 26, with the MSS.

corresponding political advantage. At Sparta every one is eligible, and the body of the people, having a share in the highest office, want the constitution to be permanent.[1] But in Crete the Cosmi are elected out of certain families, and not out of the whole people, and the elders out of those who have been Cosmi.

35   The same criticism may be made about the Cretan, which has been already made about the Lacedaemonian elders.[2] Their irresponsibility and life tenure is too great a privilege, and their arbitrary power of acting upon their own judgement, and dispensing with written law, is dangerous. It is no proof of the goodness of the institution that the people are not discontented at being excluded 40 from it. For there is no profit to be made out of the 1272ᵇ office as out of the Ephoralty, since, unlike the Ephors, the Cosmi, being in an island, are removed from temptation.

The remedy by which they correct the evil of this institution is an extraordinary one, suited rather to a close oligarchy than to a constitutional state. For the Cosmi are often expelled by a conspiracy of their own colleagues, or of private individuals; and they are allowed also to resign before their term of office has expired· 5 Surely all matters of this kind are better regulated by law than by the will of man, which is a very unsafe rule. Worst of all is the suspension of the office of Cosmi, a device to which the nobles often have recourse when they will not submit to justice. This shows that the Cretan government, although possessing some of the characteristics of a constitutional state, is really a close 10 oligarchy.

The nobles have a habit, too, of setting up a chief;[3] they get together a party among the common people and their own friends and then quarrel and fight with one another. What is this but the temporary destruction 15 of the state and dissolution of society? A city is in a dangerous condition when those who are willing are also

---

[1] Cp. *supra*, 1270ᵇ 25.   [2] 1270ᵇ 35–1271ᵃ 18.
[3] Reading μοναρχίαν in l. 12, with the MSS.

able to attack her. But, as I have already said,[1] the island of Crete is saved by her situation ; distance has the same effect as the Lacedaemonian prohibition of strangers ; and the Cretans have no foreign dominions. This is the reason why the Perioeci are contented in Crete, whereas the Helots are perpetually revolting. But when lately foreign invaders found their way into 20 the island, the weakness of the Cretan constitution was revealed. Enough of the government of Crete.

11   The Carthaginians are also considered to have an excellent form of government, which differs from that of any other state in several respects, though it is in some very 25 like the Lacedaemonian. Indeed, all three states—the Lacedaemonian, the Cretan, and the Carthaginian—nearly resemble one another, and are very different from any others. Many of the Carthaginian institutions are excellent. The superiority of their constitution is proved by 30 the fact that the common people remains loyal to the constitution ; the Carthaginians have never had any rebellion worth speaking of, and have never been under the rule of a tyrant.

Among the points in which the Carthaginian constitution resembles the Lacedaemonian are the following :— The common tables of the clubs answer to the Spartan phiditia, and their magistracy of the 104 to the Ephors ; but, 35 whereas the Ephors are any chance persons, the magistrates of the Carthaginians are elected according to merit — this is an improvement. They have also their kings and their gerusia, or council of elders, who correspond to the kings and elders of Sparta. Their kings, unlike the Spartan, are not always of the same family, nor that an ordinary one, but if there is some distinguished 40 family they are selected out of it and not appointed by seniority — this is far better. Such officers have great power, and therefore, if they are persons of little worth, 1273^a do a great deal of harm, and they have already done harm at Lacedaemon.

----

[1] ^a41 sq.

Most of the defects or deviations from the perfect state, for which the Carthaginian constitution would be censured, apply equally to all the forms of government which we have mentioned. But of the deflections from
5 aristocracy and constitutional government, some incline more to democracy and some to oligarchy. The kings and elders, if unanimous, may determine whether they will or will not bring a matter before the people, but when they are not unanimous, the people decide on such matters as well. And whatever the kings and elders bring before the people is not only heard but also determined by them,
10 and any one who likes may oppose it ; now this is not permitted in Sparta and Crete. That the magistracies of five who have under them many important matters should be co-opted, that they should choose the supreme
15 council of 100, and should hold office longer than other magistrates (for they are virtually rulers both before and after they hold office)—these are oligarchical features ; their being without salary and not elected by lot, and any similar points, such as the practice of having all suits
20 tried by the magistrates,[1] and not some by one class of judges or jurors and some by another, as at Lacedaemon, are characteristic of aristocracy. The Carthaginian constitution deviates from aristocracy and inclines to oligarchy, chiefly on a point where popular opinion is on their side. For men in general think that magistrates should be chosen not only for their merit, but for their wealth : a man, they say, who is poor cannot rule well,—he has not
25 the leisure. If, then, election of magistrates for their wealth be characteristic of oligarchy, and election for merit of aristocracy, there will be a third form under which the constitution of Carthage is comprehended ; for the Carthaginians choose their magistrates, and particularly the
30 highest of them—their kings and generals—with an eye both to merit and to wealth.

But we must acknowledge that, in thus deviating from aristocracy, the legislator has committed an error. Nothing is more absolutely necessary than to provide that

---

[1] Cp. iii. 1275^b 8–12.

the highest class, not only when in office, but when out
of office, should have leisure and not disgrace themselves
in any way; and to this his attention should be first
directed. Even if you must have regard to wealth, in 35
order to secure leisure, yet it is surely a bad thing that
the greatest offices, such as those of kings and generals,
should be bought. The law which allows this abuse
makes wealth of more account than virtue, and the
whole state becomes avaricious. For, whenever the chiefs
of the state deem anything honourable, the other citizens 40
are sure to follow their example; and, where virtue has
not the first place, there aristocracy cannot be firmly 1273^b
established. Those who have been at the expense of
purchasing their places will be in the habit of repaying
themselves; and it is absurd to suppose that a poor and
honest man will be wanting to make gains, and that a
lower stamp of man who has incurred a great expense
will not. Wherefore they should rule who are able to 5
rule best. And even if the legislator does not care
to protect the good from poverty, he should at any rate
secure leisure for them when in office.[1]

   It would seem also to be a bad principle that the same
person should hold many offices, which is a favourite
practice among the Carthaginians, for one business is
better done by one man.[2] The legislator should see to 10
this and should not appoint the same person to be a
flute-player and a shoemaker. Hence, where the state
is large, it is more in accordance both with constitutional
and with democratic principles that the offices of state
should be distributed among many persons. For, as I
said,[3] this arrangement is fairer to all, and any action
familiarized by repetition is better and sooner performed.
We have a proof in military and naval matters; the 15
duties of command and of obedience in both these
services extend to all.

   The government of the Carthaginians is oligarchical,
but they successfully escape the evils of oligarchy by

[1] Cp. 1269^a 34.   [2] Cp. Plato, *Rep.* ii. 374 A.   [3] 1261^b 1.

enriching one portion of the people after another by sending them [1] to their colonies. This is their panacea 20 and the means by which they give stability to the state. Accident favours them, but the legislator should be able to provide against revolution without trusting to accidents. As things are, if any misfortune occurred, and the bulk of the subjects revolted, there would be no way of restoring peace by legal methods.

25 Such is the character of the Lacedaemonian, Cretan, and Carthaginian constitutions, which are justly celebrated.

Of those who have treated of governments, some 12 have never taken any part at all in public affairs, but have passed their lives in a private station; about most of them, what was worth telling has been already told.[2] 30 Others have been lawgivers, either in their own or in foreign cities, whose affairs they have administered; and of these some have only made laws, others have framed constitutions; for example, Lycurgus and Solon 35 did both. Of the Lacedaemonian constitution I have already spoken.[3] As to Solon, he is thought by some to have been a good legislator, who put an end to the exclusiveness of the oligarchy, emancipated the people, established the ancient Athenian democracy, and harmonized the different elements of the state. According to their view, the council of Areopagus was an oligarchical 40 element, the elected magistracy, aristocratical, and the **1274^a** courts of law, democratical. The truth seems to be that the council and the elected magistracy existed before the time of Solon, and were retained by him, but that he formed the courts of law out of all the citizens, thus creating the democracy, which is the very reason why he is sometimes blamed. For in giving the supreme power to the law courts, which are elected by lot, he is thought 5 to have destroyed the non-democratic element. When

---

[1] Reading τῷ πλουτίζειν αἰεί τι in l. 19, with Schneider; cp. iv. 1320^b 4.
[2] cc. 1-8.   [3] c. 9.

the law courts grew powerful, to please the people who were now playing the tyrant the old constitution was changed into the existing democracy. Ephialtes and Pericles curtailed the power of the Areopagus ; Pericles also instituted the payment of the juries, and thus every demagogue in turn increased the power of the demo- 10 cracy until it became what we now see. All this is true ; it seems, however, to be the result of circumstances, and not to have been intended by Solon. For the people, having been instrumental in gaining the empire of the sea in the Persian War,¹ began to get a notion of itself, and followed worthless demagogues, whom the better class opposed. Solon, himself, appears to have given 15 the Athenians only that power of electing to offices and calling to account the magistrates which was absolutely necessary ;² for without it they would have been in a state of slavery and enmity to the government. All the magistrates he appointed from the notables and the men of wealth, that is to say, from the pentacosio-medimni, or from the class called zeugitae,³ or from a third class 20 of so-called knights or cavalry. The fourth class were labourers who had no share in any magistracy.

Mere legislators were Zaleucus, who gave laws to the Epizephyrian Locrians, and Charondas, who legislated for his own city of Catana, and for the other Chalcidian cities in Italy and Sicily. Some people attempt to 25 make out that Onomacritus was the first people who had any special skill in legislation,⁴ and that he, although a Locrian by birth, was trained in Crete, where he, lived in the exercise of his prophetic art ; that Thales was his companion, and that Lycurgus and Zaleucus were dis- ciples of Thales, as Charondas was of Zaleucus. But their 30 account is quite inconsistent with chronology.

There was also Philolaus, the Corinthian, who gave laws to the Thebans. This Philolaus was one of the

---

¹ Cp. v. 1304ᵃ 20, viii. 1341ᵃ 29.   ² Cp. iii. 1281ᵇ 32.
³ Because they kept a yoke of oxen.
⁴ Or (with Bernays), 'to make out an unbroken series of great legislators, Onomacritus being considered the first.'

family of the Bacchiadae, and a lover of Diocles, the
Olympic victor, who left Corinth in horror of the inces-
tuous passion which his mother Halcyone had conceived
35 for him, and retired to Thebes, where the two friends
together ended their days. The inhabitants still point
out their tombs, which are in full view of one another, but
one is visible from the Corinthian territory, the other
not.[1] Tradition says the two friends arranged them thus,
40 Diocles out of horror at his misfortunes, so that the land
of Corinth might not be visible from his tomb; Philolaus
1274^b that it might. This is the reason why they settled at
Thebes, and so Philolaus legislated for the Thebans,
and, besides some other enactments, gave them laws
about the procreation of children, which they call the
'Laws of Adoption'. These laws were peculiar to him,
and were intended to preserve the number of the lots.
5   In the legislation of Charondas there is nothing remarkable, except the suits against false witnesses. He
is the first who instituted denunciation for perjury. His
laws are more exact and more precisely expressed than
even those of our modern legislators.

(Characteristic of Phaleas is the equalization of property; of Plato, the community of women, children, and
10 property, the common meals of women, and the law
about drinking, that the sober shall be masters of the
feast;[2] also the training of soldiers to acquire by practice
equal skill with both hands, so that one should be as
useful as the other.)[3]

15   Draco has left laws, but he adapted them to a constitution which already existed, and there is no peculiarity
in them which is worth mentioning, except the greatness
and severity of the punishments.

Pittacus, too, was only a lawgiver, and not the author
of a constitution; he has a law which is peculiar to him,
that, if a drunken man do something wrong, he shall be
20 more heavily punished than if he were sober;[4] he looked

---

[1] Reading τοῦ μὲν σύνοπτον τοῦ δ' οὐ σύνοπτον in l. 38.
[2] Cp. *Laws*, i. 640 D, ii. 671 D–672 A.   [3] Cp. *Laws*, vii. 794 D.
[4] Cp. *N. Eth.* 1113^b 31.

not to the excuse which might be offered for the
drunkard, but only to expediency, for drunken more
often than sober people commit acts of violence.

Androdamas of Rhegium gave laws to the Chalcidians of Thrace.   Some of them relate to homicide, and
to heiresses ; but there is nothing remarkable in them.   25

And here let us conclude our inquiry into the various
constitutions which either actually exist, or have been
devised by theorists.

BOOK III

HE who would inquire into the essence and attributes 1
of various kinds of government must first of all determine
' What is a state ? ' At present this is a disputed question.
Some say that the state has done a certain act ; others,
35 no, not the state,¹ but the oligarchy or the tyrant. And
the legislator or statesman is concerned entirely with the
state ; a constitution or government being an arrangement
of the inhabitants of a state. But a state is composite,
like any other whole made up of many parts ;—these
40 are the citizens, who compose it. It is evident, therefore,
1275ᵃ that we must begin by asking, Who is the citizen, and
what is the meaning of the term ? For here again there
may be a difference of opinion. He who is a citizen in a
democracy will often not be a citizen in an oligarchy.
5 Leaving out of consideration those who have been made
citizens, or who have obtained the name of citizen in any
other accidental manner, we may say, first, that a citizen
is not a citizen because he lives in a certain place,
for resident aliens and slaves share in the place ; nor is
he a citizen who has no legal right except that of suing
10 and being sued ; for this right may be enjoyed under
the provisions of a treaty. Nay, resident aliens in many
places do not possess even such rights completely, for
they are obliged to have a patron, so that they do but
imperfectly participate in citizenship, and we call them
citizens only in a qualified sense, as we might apply the
term to children who are too young to be on the register,
15 or to old men who have been relieved from state duties.
Of these we do not say quite simply that they are citizens,
but add in the one case that they are not of age, and in
the other, that they are past the age, or something
20 of that sort ; the precise expression is immaterial, for

¹ Cp. 1276ᵃ 8.

our meaning is clear. Similar difficulties to those which I have mentioned may be raised and answered about deprived citizens and about exiles. But the citizen whom we are seeking to define is a citizen in the strictest sense, against whom no such exception can be taken, and his special characteristic is that he shares in the administration of justice, and in offices. Now of offices some are discontinuous, and the same persons are not allowed to hold them twice, or can only hold 25 them after a fixed interval ; others have no limit of time, —for example, the office of dicast or ecclesiast.[1] It may, indeed, be argued that these are not magistrates at all, and that their functions give them no share in the government. But surely it is ridiculous to say that those who have the supreme power do not govern. Let us not dwell furt' er upon this, which is a purely verbal question ; what we want is a common term including both dicast 30 and ecclesiast. Let us, for the sake of distinction, call it 'indefinite office', and we will assume that those who share in such office are citizens. This is the most comprehensive definition of a citizen, and best suits all those who are generally so called.

But we must not forget that things of which the un- 35 derlying principles differ in kind, one of them being first, another second, another third, have, when regarded in this relation, nothing, or hardly anything, worth mentioning in common. Now we see that governments differ in kind, and that some of them are prior and that others are posterior ; those which are faulty or perverted 1275^b are necessarily posterior to those which are perfect. (What we mean by perversion will be hereafter explained.[2]) The citizen then of necessity differs under each form of government ; and our definition is best 5 adapted to the citizen of a democracy ; but not necessarily to other states. For in some states the people are not acknowledged, nor have they any regular assembly,

---

[1] ' Dicast '=juryman and judge in one : ' ecclesiast '=member of the ecclesia or assembly of the citizens.
[2] Cp. 1279^a 19.

but only extraordinary ones; and suits are distributed
by sections among the magistrates.   At Lacedaemon, for
instance, the Ephors determine suits about contracts,
10 which they distribute among themselves, while the elders
are judges of homicide, and other causes are decided
by other magistrates. A similar principle prevails at
Carthage ;[1] there certain magistrates decide all causes.
We may, indeed, modify our definition of the citizen so
as to include these states.   In them it is the holder
15 of a definite, not of an indefinite office, who legislates
and judges, and to some or all such holders of definite
offices is reserved the right of deliberating or judging
about some things or about all things. The conception
of the citizen now begins to clear up.

He who has the power to take part in the deliberative
or judicial administration of any state is said by us to be
20 a citizen of that state ; and, speaking generally, a state is
a body of citizens sufficing for the purposes of life.

But in practice a citizen is defined to be one of whom 2
both the parents are citizens ; others insist on going
further back ; say to two or three or more ancestors.
25 This is a short and practical definition ; but there are
some who raise the further question : How this third or
fourth ancestor came to be a citizen ? Gorgias of Leontini, partly because he was in a difficulty, partly in irony,
said—' Mortars are what is made by the mortar-makers,
and the citizens of Larissa are those who are made by the
magistrates ;[2] for it is their trade to make Larissaeans.'[3]
30 Yet the question is really simple, for, if according to the
definition just given they shared in the government,[4] they
were citizens. This is a better definition than the other.
For the words, ' born of a father or mother who is a
citizen ', cannot possibly apply to the first inhabitants or
founders of a state.

[1] Cp. ii. 1273ᵃ 19.
[2] An untranslatable play upon the word δημιουργός, which means
either ' a magistrate ' or ' an artisan '.
[3] Reading in l. 30 Λαρισαιοποιούς, which seems to have been read
by Aretinus.   [4] Cp. l. 18.

There is a greater difficulty in the case of those who have been made citizens after a revolution, as by 35 Cleisthenes at Athens after the expulsion of the tyrants, for he enrolled in tribes many metics, both strangers and slaves. The doubt in these cases is, not who is, but whether he who is ought to be a citizen; and there **1276^a** will still be a further doubt, whether he who ought not to be a citizen, is one in fact, for what ought not to be is what is false. Now, there are some who hold office, and yet ought not to hold office, whom we describe as ruling, but ruling unjustly. And the citizen was defined [1] by the fact of his holding some kind of rule or office,—he who holds a judicial or legislative office fulfils our definition of a citizen. It is evident, 5 therefore, that the citizens about whom the doubt has arisen must be called citizens.

3 Whether they ought to be so or not is a question which is bound up with the previous inquiry. [2] For a parallel question is raised respecting the state, whether a certain act is or is not an act of the state ; for example, in the transition from an oligarchy or a tyranny to a democracy. In such cases persons refuse 10 to fulfil their contracts or any other obligations, on the ground that the tyrant, and not the state, contracted them ; they argue that some constitutions are established by force, and not for the sake of the common good. But this would apply equally to democracies, for they too may be founded on violence, and then the acts of the democracy will be neither more nor less acts of the state in 15 question than those of an oligarchy or of a tyranny. This question runs up into another :—on what principle shall we ever say that the state is the same, or different ? It would be a very superficial view which considered only the place and the inhabitants (for the soil and the population may be separated, and some of the inhabitants may live in one 20 place and some in another). This, however, is not a very

---

[1] 1275^a 22 sqq.   [2] Cp. 1274^b 34

serious difficulty; we need only remark that the word
'state' is ambiguous.[1]

25 It is further asked: When are men, living in the same
place, to be regarded as a single city—what is the limit?
Certainly not the wall of the city, for you might surround
all Peloponnesus with a wall. Like this, we may say,
is Babylon,[2] and every city that has the compass of a
nation rather than a city; Babylon, they say, had been
taken for three days before some part of the inhabitants
30 became aware of the fact. This difficulty may, however, with
advantage be deferred[3] to another occasion ; the statesman has to consider the size of the state, and whether it
should consist of more than one nation or not.

Again, shall we say that while the race of inhabitants,
35 as well as their place of abode, remain the same, the city
is also the same, although the citizens are always dying
and being born, as we call rivers and fountains the same,
although the water is always flowing away and coming
again? Or shall we say that the generations of men, like
40 the rivers, are the same, but that the state changes? For,
1276ᵇ since the state is a partnership, and is a partnership of
citizens in a constitution, when the form of the government
changes, and becomes different, then it may be supposed
that the state is no longer the same, just as a tragic differs
5 from a comic chorus, although the members of both may
be identical. And in this manner we speak of every union
or composition of elements as different when the form of
their composition alters ; for example, a scale containing
the same sounds is said to be different, accordingly as
10 the Dorian or the Phrygian mode is employed. And if
this is true it is evident that the sameness of the state
consists chiefly in the sameness of the constitution, and
it may be called or not called by the same name, whether
the inhabitants are the same or entirely different. It is
quite another question, whether a state ought or ought

---

[1] i. e. πόλις means both 'state' and 'city'.
[2] Cp. ii. 1265ª 14.
[3] The size of the state is discussed in vii. 1326ª 8-1327ª 3; the
question whether it should consist of more than one nation is
barely touched upon, in v. 1303ª 25-ᵇ 3.

not to fulfil engagements when the form of government 15 changes.

4   There is a point nearly allied to the preceding : Whether the virtue of a good man and a good citizen is the same or not.[1] But, before entering on this discussion, we must certainly first obtain some general notion of the virtue of the citizen. Like the sailor, the citizen 20 is a member of a community. Now, sailors have different functions, for one of them is a rower, another a pilot, and a third a look-out man, a fourth is described by some similar term ; and while the precise definition of each individual's virtue applies exclusively to him, there is, at 25 the same time, a common definition applicable to them all. For they have all of them a common object, which is safety in navigation. Similarly, one citizen differs from another, but the salvation of the community is the common business of them all. This community is the constitution ; the virtue of the citizen must therefore be 30 relative to the constitution of which he is a member. If, then, there are many forms of government, it is evident that there is not one single virtue of the good citizen which is perfect virtue. But we say that the good man is he who has one single virtue which is perfect virtue. Hence it is evident that the good citizen need not of necessity possess the virtue which makes a good man.

The same question may also be approached by another 35 road, from a consideration of the best constitution. If the state cannot [2] be entirely composed of good men, and yet each citizen is expected to do his own business well, and must therefore have virtue, still, inasmuch as all the citizens 40 cannot be alike, the virtue of the citizen and of the good **1277**^a man cannot coincide. All must have the virtue of the good citizen—thus, and thus only, can the state be perfect ; but they will not have the virtue of a good man, unless we assume that in the good state all the citizens must be good.

---

[1] Cp. *N. Eth.* v. 1130^b 28.
[2] Reading ἀδύνατον in l. 38 with the MSS.

5   Again, the state, as composed of unlikes, may be compared to the living being : as the first elements into which
a living being is resolved are soul and body, as soul is
made up of rational principle and appetite, the family of
husband and wife, property of master and slave, so of all
these, as well as other dissimilar elements, the state is
10 composed ; and, therefore, the virtue of all the citizens
cannot possibly be the same, any more than the excellence of the leader of a chorus is the same as that of the
performer who stands by his side.   I have said enough
to show why the two kinds of virtue cannot be absolutely
and always the same.

But will there then be no case in which the virtue of
the good citizen and the virtue of the good man coin-
15 cide ?   To this we answer that the good *ruler* is a good
and wise man, and that he who would be a statesman
must be a wise man.   And some persons say that even
the education of the ruler should be of a special kind ;
for are not the children of kings instructed in riding and
military exercises ?   As Euripides says :

'No subtle arts for me, but what the state requires.'[1]

As though there were a special education needed by
20 a ruler.   If then[2] the virtue of a good ruler is the same
as that of a good man, and we assume further that the
subject is a citizen as well as the ruler, the virtue of the
good citizen and the virtue of the good man cannot be
absolutely the same, although in some cases they may ; for
the virtue of a ruler differs from that of a citizen.   It
was the sense of this difference which made Jason say
that ' he felt hungry when he was not a tyrant ', meaning
that he could not endure to live in a private station.
25 But, on the other hand, it may be argued that men are
praised for knowing both how to rule and how to obey,
and he is said to be a citizen of approved virtue who is
able to do both.   Now if we suppose the virtue of a
good man to be that which rules, and the virtue of the

---

[1] *Aeolus*, fr. 16, Nauck[2].
[2] Reading εἰ δή in l. 20, with some good MSS.

citizen to include ruling and obeying, it cannot be said that they are equally worthy of praise. Since, then, it is 30 sometimes thought that the ruler and the ruled must learn different things [1] and not the same, but that the citizen must know and share in them both, the inference is obvious. There is, indeed, the rule of a master, which is concerned with menial offices,[2]—the master need not know how to perform these, but may employ others in the execution of them : the other would 35 be degrading ; and by the other I mean the power actually to do menial duties, which vary much in character and are executed by various classes of slaves, such, for example, as handicraftsmen, who, as their name signifies, live by the labour of their hands :—under these the mechanic is 1277^b included. Hence in ancient times, and among some nations, the working classes had no share in the government—a privilege which they only acquired under the extreme democracy. Certainly the good man and the statesman and the good citizen ought not to learn the crafts of inferiors except for their own occasional use ;[3] 5 if they habitually practise them, there will cease to be a distinction between master and slave.[4]

This is not the rule of which we are speaking ; but there is a rule of another kind, which is exercised over freemen and equals by birth—a constitutional rule, which the ruler must learn by obeying, as he would learn 10 the duties of a general of cavalry by being under the orders of a general of cavalry, or the duties of a general of infantry by being under the orders of a general of infantry, and by having had the command of a regiment and of a company. It has been well said that ' he who has never learned to obey cannot be a good commander '. The two are not the same, but the good citizen ought to be capable of both ; he should know how to govern like a freeman, and how to obey like a freeman—these are the 15 virtues of a citizen. And, although the temperance and

---

[1] Reading ἄμφω ἕτερα for ἀμφότερα in l. 30, with Bernays.
[2] Cp. i. 1255^b 20-37.   [3] Cp. viii. 1337^b 15.
[4] Reading τὸν μέν . . . τὸν δέ in ll. 6, 7, with the MSS.

justice of a ruler are distinct from those of a subject, the virtue of a good man will include both ; for the virtue of the good man who is free and also a subject, e. g. his justice, will not be one but will comprise distinct kinds, the one qualifying him to rule, the other to obey, and dif-
20 fering as the temperance and courage of men and women differ.[1] For a man would be thought a coward if he had no more courage than a courageous woman, and a woman would be thought loquacious if she imposed no more restraint on her conversation than the good man ; and indeed their part in the management of the household is different, for the duty of the one is to acquire, and of the
25 other to preserve. Practical wisdom only is characteristic of the ruler :[2] it would seem that all other virtues must equally belong to ruler and subject. The virtue of the subject is certainly not wisdom, but only true opinion ; he may be compared to the maker of the flute, while his master is like the flute-player or user of the flute.[3]
30 From these considerations may be gathered the answer to the question, whether the virtue of the good man is the same as that of the good citizen, or different, and how far the same, and how far different.[4]

There still remains one more question about the 5 citizen : Is he only a true citizen who has a share of
35 office, or is the mechanic to be included ? If they who hold no office are to be deemed citizens, not every citizen can have this virtue of ruling and obeying ; for this man is a citizen. And if none of the lower class are citizens, in which part of the state are they to be placed ? For they are not resident aliens, and they are not foreigners.
1278ª May we not reply, that as far as this objection goes there is no more absurdity in excluding them than in excluding slaves and freedmen from any of the above-mentioned classes ? It must be admitted that we cannot consider all those to be citizens who are necessary to the existence of the state ; for example, children are not

---

[1] Cp. i. 1260ª 20.   [2] Cp. *Rep.* iv. 428.   [3] Cp. *Rep.* x. 601 D, E.
[4] Cp. 1278ª 40, 1288ª 39, iv. 1293ᵇ 5, vii. 1333ª 11.

citizens equally with grown-up men, who are citizens absolutely, but children, not being grown up, are only 5 citizens on a certain assumption.[1] Nay, in ancient times, and among some nations, the artisan class *were* slaves or foreigners, and therefore the majority of them are so now. The best form of state will not admit them to citizenship; but if they are admitted, then our definition of the virtue of a citizen will not apply to every citizen, nor to every free man as such, but only to those who are freed 10 from necessary services. The necessary people are either slaves who minister to the wants of individuals, or mechanics and labourers who are the servants of the community. These reflections carried a little further will explain their position; and indeed what has been said already[2] is of itself, when understood, explanation enough.

Since there are many forms of government there must 15 be many varieties of citizens, and especially of citizens who are subjects; so that under some governments the mechanic and the labourer will be citizens, but not in others, as, for example, in aristocracy or the so-called government of the best (if there be such an one), in which honours are given according to virtue and merit; for no man can practise virtue who is living the life of a 20 mechanic or labourer. In oligarchies the qualification for office is high, and therefore no labourer can ever be a citizen; but a mechanic may, for an actual majority of them are rich. At Thebes[3] there was a law that no man 25 could hold office who had not retired from business for ten years. But in many states the law goes to the length of admitting aliens; for in some democracies a man is a citizen though his mother only be a citizen; and a similar principle is applied to illegitimate children; the law is relaxed when there is a dearth of population. 30 But when the number of citizens increases, first the children of a male or a female slave are excluded; then those whose mothers only are citizens; and at last the

---

[1] Sc. that they grow up to be men.   [2] 1275ª 38 sqq.
[3] Cp. vi. 1321ª 28.

right of citizenship is confined to those whose fathers and mothers are both citizens.

35 Hence, as is evident, there are different kinds of citizens ; and he is a citizen in the highest sense who shares in the honours of the state. Compare Homer's words ' like some dishonoured stranger ' ; [1] he who is excluded from the honours of the state is no better than an alien. But when this exclusion is concealed, then the object is that the privileged class may deceive their fellow inhabitants.

40 As to the question whether the virtue of the good man
1278ᵇ is the same as that of the good citizen, the considerations already adduced prove that in some states the good man and the good citizen are the same, and in others different. When they are the same it is not every citizen who is a good man, but only the statesman and those who have or may have, alone or in conjunction with
5 others, the conduct of public affairs.

Having determined these questions, we have next to **6** consider whether there is only one form of government or many, and if many, what they are, and how many, and what are the differences between them.

A constitution is the arrangement of magistracies in a
10 state [2], especially of the highest of all. The government is everywhere sovereign in the state, and the constitution is in fact the government. For example, in democracies the people are supreme, but in oligarchies, the few ; and, therefore, we say that these two forms of government also are different : and so in other cases.

15 First, let us consider what is the purpose of a state, and how many forms of government there are by which human society is regulated. We have already said, in the first part of this treatise,[3] when discussing household management and the rule of a master, that man is
20 by nature a political animal. And therefore, men, even

---

[1] Achilles complains of Agamemnon's so treating him, *Il.* ix. 648, xvi. 59.
[2] Cp. 1274ᵇ 38, iv. 1289ª 15.   [3] Cp. i. 1253ª 2.

when they do not require one another's help, desire to live together ; not but that they are also brought together by their common interests in proportion as they severally attain to any measure of well-being. This is certainly the chief end, both of individuals and of states. And also for the sake of mere life (in which there is possibly 25 some noble element so long as the evils of existence do not greatly overbalance the good) mankind meet together and maintain the political community. And we all see that men cling to life even at the cost of enduring great misfortune, seeming to find in life a natural sweetness and happiness.

There is no difficulty in distinguishing the various 30 kinds of authority ; they have been often defined already in discussions outside the school. The rule of a master, although the slave by nature and the master by nature have in reality the same interests, is nevertheless exercised primarily with a view to the interest of the master, but 35 accidentally considers the slave, since, if the slave perish, the rule of the master perishes with him. On the other hand, the government of a wife and children and of a household, which we have called household management, is exercised in the first instance for the good of the governed or for the common good of both parties, but essentially for the good of the governed, as we see to 40 be the case in medicine, gymnastic, and the arts in 1279^a general, which are only accidentally concerned with the good of the artists themselves.[1] For there is no reason why the trainer may not sometimes practise gymnastics, and the helmsman is always one of the crew. The trainer or the helmsman considers the good of those committed to his care. But, when he is one of the persons 5 taken care of, he accidentally participates in the advantage, for the helmsman is also a sailor, and the trainer becomes one of those in training. And so in politics : when the state is framed upon the principle of equality and likeness, the citizens think that they ought to hold 10 office by turns. Formerly, as is natural, every one would

[2] Cp. Pl. *Rep.* i. 341 D.

take his turn of service; and then again, somebody else would look after his interest, just as he, while in office, had looked after theirs.¹ But nowadays, for the sake of the advantage which is to be gained from the public revenues and from office, men want to be always in office.

15 One might imagine that the rulers, being sickly, were only kept in health while they continued in office; in that case we may be sure that they would be hunting after places. The conclusion is evident: that governments which have a regard to the common interest are constituted in accordance with strict principles of justice, and are therefore true forms; but those which regard
20 only the interest of the rulers are all defective and perverted forms, for they are despotic, whereas a state is a community of freemen.

Having determined these points, we have next to con- **7** sider how many forms of government there are, and what they are; and in the first place what are the true forms, for when they are determined the perversions of
25 them will at once be apparent. The words constitution and government have the same meaning, and the government, which is the supreme authority in states, must be in the hands of one, or of a few, or of the many. The true forms of government, therefore, are those in which the one, or the few, or the many, govern with a view to the
30 common interest; but governments which rule with a view to the private interest, whether of the one, or of the few, or of the many, are perversions.² For the members of a state, if they are truly citizens, ought to participate in its advantages. Of forms of government in which one rules, we call that which regards the common interests, kingship or royalty; that in which more than one, but
35 not many, rule, aristocracy; and it is so called, either because the rulers are the best men, or because they have at heart the best interests of the state and of the citizens. But when the citizens at large administer the

---

¹ Cp. ii. 1261ᵃ 37–ᵇ 6.   ² Cp. *N. Eth.* viii. 10.

state for the common interest, the government is called by
the generic name,—a constitution. And there is a reason
for this use of language.   One man or a few may excel ₄₀
in virtue ; but as the number increases it becomes more
difficult for them to attain perfection in every kind of 1279ᵇ
virtue, though they may in military virtue, for this
is found in the masses.   Hence in a constitutional
government the fighting-men have the supreme power,
and those who possess arms are the citizens.

Of the above-mentioned forms, the perversions are as
follows :—of royalty, tyranny ; of aristocracy, oligarchy ; ₅
of constitutional government, democracy.   For tyranny
is a kind of monarchy which has in view the interest of
the monarch only ; oligarchy has in view the interest of
the wealthy ; democracy, of the needy : none of them the
common good of all.   10

8   But there are difficulties about these forms of government, and it will therefore be necessary to state a little
more at length the nature of each of them.   For he
who would make a philosophical study of the various
sciences, and does not regard practice only, ought not to
overlook or omit anything, but to set forth the truth in 15
every particular.   Tyranny, as I was saying, is monarchy
exercising the rule of a master over the political society ;
oligarchy is when men of property have the government
in their hands ; democracy, the opposite, when the in-
digent, and not the men of property, are the rulers.
And here arises the first of our difficulties, and it relates
to the distinction just drawn.   For democracy is said to ₂₀
be the government of the many.   But what if the many
are men of property and have the power in their hands ?
In like manner oligarchy is said to be the government
of the few ; but what if the poor are fewer than the rich,
and have the power in their hands because they are
stronger ?   In these cases the distinction which we have ₂₅
drawn between these different forms of government
would no longer hold good.

Suppose, once more, that we add wealth to the few

and poverty to the many, and name the governments accordingly—an oligarchy is said to be that in which the few and the wealthy, and a democracy that in which
30 the many and the poor are the rulers—there will still be a difficulty. For, if the only forms of government are the ones already mentioned, how shall we describe those other governments also just mentioned by us, in which the rich are the more numerous and the poor are the fewer, and both govern in their respective states?
35 The argument seems to show that, whether in oligarchies or in democracies, the number of the governing body, whether the greater number, as in a democracy, or the smaller number, as in an oligarchy, is an accident due to the fact that the rich everywhere are few, and the poor numerous. But if so, there is a misapprehension of the causes of the difference between them. For
40 the real difference between democracy and oligarchy is
1280^a poverty and wealth. Wherever men rule by reason of their wealth, whether they be few or many, that is an oligarchy, and where the poor rule, that is a democracy. But as a fact the rich are few and the poor many; for few are well-to-do, whereas freedom is enjoyed by all,
5 and wealth and freedom are the grounds on which the oligarchical and democratical parties respectively claim power in the state.

Let us begin by considering the common definitions **9** of oligarchy and democracy, and what is justice oligarchical and democratical. For all men cling to justice
10 of some kind, but their conceptions are imperfect and they do not express the whole idea. For example, justice is thought by them to be, and is, equality, not, however, for all, but only for equals. And inequality is thought to be, and is, justice; neither is this for all, but only for unequals. When the persons are omitted, then men judge erroneously. The reason is that they are
15 passing judgement on themselves, and most people are bad judges in their own case. And whereas justice implies a relation to persons as well as to things, and

a just distribution, as I have already said in the *Ethics*,[1] implies the same ratio between the persons and between the things, they agree about the equality of the things, but dispute about the equality of the persons, chiefly for the reason which I have just given,—because they are bad 20 judges in their own affairs; and secondly, because both the parties to the argument are speaking of a limited and partial justice, but imagine themselves to be speaking of absolute justice. For the one party, if they are unequal in one respect, for example wealth, consider themselves to be unequal in all; and the other party, if they are equal in one respect, for example free birth, consider themselves to be equal in all. But they leave out the 25 capital point. For if men met and associated out of regard to wealth only, their share in the state would be proportioned to their property, and the oligarchical doctrine would then seem to carry the day. It would not be just that he who paid one mina should have the same share of a hundred minae, whether of the principal 30 or of the profits, as he who paid the remaining ninety-nine. But [2] a state exists for the sake of a good life, and not for the sake of life only : if life only were the object, slaves and brute animals might form a state, but they cannot, for they have no share in happiness or in a life of free choice. Nor does a state exist for the sake of alliance and security from injustice, nor yet for the 35 sake of exchange and mutual intercourse; for then the Tyrrhenians and the Carthaginians, and all who have commercial treaties with one another,[3] would be the citizens of one state. True, they have agreements about imports, and engagements that they will do no wrong to one another, and written articles of alliance. But 40 there are no magistracies common to the contracting 1280^b parties who will enforce their engagements ; different states have each their own magistracies. Nor does one

---

[1] v. 1131ª 15.
[2] The sentence in the original becomes involved in so many parentheses that there is no true apodosis to the protasis beginning in l. 31. In *sense* the apodosis comes at 1281ª 4.
[3] Cp. 1275ª 10.

state take care that the citizens of the other are such
as they ought to be, nor see that those who come under
the terms of the treaty do no wrong or wickedness at
all, but only that they do no injustice to one another.
5 Whereas, those who care for good government take into
consideration virtue and vice in states. Whence it may
be further inferred that virtue must be the care of a state
which is truly so called, and not merely enjoys the name :
for without this end the community becomes a mere
alliance which differs only in place from alliances of which
the members live apart ; and law is only a convention,
10 'a surety to one another of justice,' as the sophist
Lycophron says, and has no real power to make the
citizens good and just.

This is obvious; for suppose distinct places, such as
Corinth and Megara, to be brought together so that their
walls touched, still they would not be one city, not even
15 if the citizens had the right to intermarry, which is one
of the rights peculiarly characteristic of states. Again,
if men dwelt at a distance from one another, but not so
far off as to have no intercourse, and there were laws
among them that they should not wrong each other in
20 their exchanges, neither would this be a state. Let us
suppose that one man is a carpenter, another a husbandman, another a shoemaker, and so on, and that their
number is ten thousand : nevertheless, if they have nothing
in common but exchange, alliance, and the like, that
would not constitute a state. Why is this ? Surely not
25 because they are at a distance from one another : for even
supposing that such a community were to meet in one
place, but that each man had a house of his own, which
was in a manner his state, and that they made alliance
with one another, but only against evil-doers ; still an
accurate thinker would not deem this to be a state, if their
intercourse with one another was of the same character
30 after as before their union. It is clear then that a state is not
a mere society, having a common place, established for the
prevention of mutual crime and for the sake of exchange.[1]

[1] Cp. *Protag.* 322 B.

These are conditions without which a state cannot exist; but all of them together do not constitute a state, which is a community of families and aggregations of families in well-being, for the sake of a perfect and self-sufficing life. Such a community can only be established among 35 those who live in the same place and intermarry. Hence arise in cities family connexions, brotherhoods, common sacrifices, amusements which draw men together. But these are created by friendship, for the will to live together is friendship. The end of the state is the good life, and these are the means towards it. And the state is the 40 union of families and villages in a perfect and self-sufficing 1281^a life,[1] by which we mean a happy and honourable life.[2]

Our conclusion, then, is that political society exists for the sake of noble actions, and not of mere companionship. Hence they who contribute most to such a society have a greater share in it than those who have 5 the same or a greater freedom or nobility of birth but are inferior to them in political virtue; or than those who exceed them in wealth but are surpassed by them in virtue.

From what has been said it will be clearly seen that all the partisans of different forms of government speak of a part of justice only.   10

10   There is also a doubt as to what is to be the supreme power in the state:—Is it the multitude? Or the wealthy? Or the good? Or the one best man? Or a tyrant? Any of these alternatives seems to involve disagreeable consequences. If the poor, for example, because they are more in number, divide among themselves the property of the rich,—is not this unjust? No, 15 by heaven (will be the reply), for the supreme authority justly willed it. But if this is not injustice, pray what is? Again, when in the first division all has been taken, and the majority divide anew the property of the minority, is it not evident, if this goes on, that they will ruin the state? Yet surely, virtue is not the ruin of those

---

[1] Omitting χάριν in l. 1.   [2] Cp. i. 1252^b 27; N. Eth. i. 1097^b 6.

G 2

who possess her, nor is justice destructive of a state;
20 and therefore this law of confiscation clearly cannot be
just. If it were, all the acts of a tyrant must of necessity be just ; for he only coerces other men by superior
power, just as the multitude coerce the rich. But is it
just then that the few and the wealthy should be the
25 rulers ? And what if they, in like manner, rob and
plunder the people,—is this just ? If so, the other case
will likewise be just. But there can be no doubt that all
these things are wrong and unjust.

Then ought the good to rule and have supreme
30 power ? But in that case everybody else, being excluded
from power, will be dishonoured. For the offices of a
state are posts of honour ; and if one set of men always
hold them, the rest must be deprived of them. Then
will it be well that the one best man should rule ? Nay,
that is still more oligarchical, for the number of those
who are dishonoured is thereby increased. Some one
may say that it is bad in any case for a man, subject as
35 he is to all the accidents of human passion, to have the
supreme power, rather than the law. But what if the law
itself be democratical or oligarchical, how will that help
us out of our difficulties ?[1] Not at all ; the same consequences [2] will follow.

Most of these questions may be reserved for another 11
40 occasion.[3] The principle that the multitude ought to be
supreme rather than the few best is one that is maintained, and, though not free from difficulty,[4] yet seems
to contain an element of truth. For the many, of
1281ᵇ whom each individual is but an ordinary person, when
they meet together may very likely be better than the
few good, if regarded not individually but collectively,
just as a feast to which many contribute is better
than a dinner provided out of a single purse. For
each individual among the many has a share of virtue

[1] Cp. 1282ᵇ6.   [2] Cp. ll. 11–34.   [3] cc. 12–17, iv., vi.
[4] Reading in l. 41 λέγεσθαι, as suggested by Richards, and
ἀπορίαν, with the MSS.

and prudence, and when they meet together, they be- 5
come in a manner one man, who has many feet, and
hands, and senses; that is a figure of their mind and
disposition. Hence the many are better judges than a
single man of music and poetry; for some understand
one part, and some another, and among them they understand the whole. There is a similar combination of 10
qualities in good men, who differ from any individual of
the many, as the beautiful are said to differ from those
who are not beautiful, and works of art from realities,
because in them the scattered elements are combined,
although, if taken separately, the eye of one person or
some other feature in another person would be fairer
than in the picture. Whether this principle can apply to 15
every democracy, and to all bodies of men, is not clear.
Or rather, by heaven, in some cases it is impossible of
application; for the argument would equally hold about
brutes; and wherein, it will be asked, do some men differ
from brutes? But there may be bodies of men about 20
whom our statement is nevertheless true. And if so, the
difficulty which has been already raised,[1] and also another
which is akin to it—viz. what power should be assigned
to the mass of freemen and citizens, who are not rich and
have no personal merit—are both solved. There is still 25
a danger in allowing them to share the great offices
of state, for their folly will lead them into error, and
their dishonesty into crime. But there is a danger also
in not letting them share, for a state in which many poor
men are excluded from office will necessarily be full of 30
enemies. The only way of escape is to assign to them
some deliberative and judicial functions. For this reason
Solon[2] and certain other legislators give them the power
of electing to offices, and of calling the magistrates to
account, but they do not allow them to hold office
singly. When they meet together their perceptions
are quite good enough, and combined with the better 35
class they are useful to the state (just as impure food
when mixed with what is pure sometimes makes the

<hr />

[1] c. 10.   [2] Cp. ii. 1274^a 15.

entire mass more wholesome than a small quantity of the pure would be), but each individual, left to himself, forms an imperfect judgement. On the other hand, the popular form of government involves certain difficulties.
40 In the first place, it might be objected that he who can judge of the healing of a sick man would be one who could himself heal his disease, and make him whole—
1282^a that is, in other words, the physician; and so in all professions and arts. As, then, the physician ought to be called to account by physicians, so ought men in general to be called to account by their peers. But physicians are of three kinds :—there is the ordinary practitioner, and there is the physician of the higher class, and thirdly the intelligent man who has studied the art : in all arts there
5 is such a class ; and we attribute the power of judging to them quite as much as to professors of the art. Secondly, does not the same principle apply to elections ? For a right election can only be made by those who have knowledge ; those who know geometry, for example, will choose a geometrician rightly, and those who know how
10 to steer, a pilot ; and, even if there be some occupations and arts in which private persons share in the ability to choose, they certainly cannot choose better than those who know. So that, according to this argument, neither the election of magistrates, nor the calling of them to account, should be entrusted to the many. Yet possibly these objections are to a great extent met by our old
15 answer,[1] that if the people are not utterly degraded, although individually they may be worse judges than those who have special knowledge—as a body they are as good or better. Moreover, there are some arts whose products are not judged of solely, or best, by the artists themselves, namely those arts whose products are recognized even by those who do not possess the art ;
20 for example, the knowledge of the house is not limited to the builder only ; the user, or, in other words, the master, of the house will even be a better judge than the

---

[1] 1281^a 40–^b 21.

builder, just as the pilot will judge better of a rudder than the carpenter, and the guest will judge better of a feast than the cook.

This difficulty seems now to be sufficiently answered, but there is another akin to it. That inferior persons 25 should have authority in greater matters than the good would appear to be a strange thing, yet the election and calling to account of the magistrates is the greatest of all. And these, as I was saying,[1] are functions which in some states are assigned to the people, for the assembly is supreme in all such matters. Yet persons of any age, and having but a small property qualification, sit in the 30 assembly and deliberate and judge, although for the great officers of state, such as treasurers and generals, a high qualification is required. This difficulty may be solved in the same manner as the preceding, and the present practice of democracies may be really defensible. For the power does not reside in the dicast, or senator, or ecclesiast, but in the court, and the senate, and the 35 assembly, of which individual senators, or ecclesiasts, or dicasts, are only parts or members. And for this reason the many may claim to have a higher authority than the few ; for the people, and the senate, and the courts consist of many persons, and their property collectively is greater than the property of one or of a few 40 individuals holding great offices. But enough of this.

The discussion of the first question [2] shows nothing so 1282ᵇ clearly as that laws, when good, should be supreme ; and that the magistrate or magistrates should regulate those matters only on which the laws are unable to speak with precision owing to the difficulty of any general principle 5 embracing all particulars.[3]   But what are good laws has not yet been clearly explained ; the old difficulty remains.[4]   The goodness or badness, justice or injustice, of laws varies of necessity with the constitutions of states. 10 This, however, is clear, that the laws must be adapted to the constitutions. But if so, true forms of government

[1] 1281ᵇ 32.   [2] c. 10.
[3] Cp. *N. Eth.* v. 1137ᵇ 19.   [4] Cp. 1281ᵃ 36.

will of necessity have just laws, and perverted forms of
government will have unjust laws.

15   In all sciences and arts the end is a good, and the 12
greatest good and in the highest degree a good in the most
authoritative of all [1]—this is the political science of which
the good is justice, in other words, the common interest.
All men think justice to be a sort of equality ; and to a
certain extent [2] they agree in the philosophical distinctions
20 which have been laid down by us about Ethics.[3]   For
they admit that justice is a thing and has a relation to
persons, and that equals ought to have equality.   But
there still remains a question : equality or inequality of
what ? here is a difficulty which calls for political
speculation.   For very likely some persons will say
that offices of state ought to be unequally distributed
25 according to superior excellence, in whatever respect, of
the citizen, although there is no other difference between
him and the rest of the community ; for that those who
differ in any one respect have different rights and claims.
But, surely, if this is true, the complexion or height of
a man, or any other advantage, will be a reason for his
30 obtaining a greater share of political rights.   The error
here lies upon the surface, and may be illustrated from
the other arts and sciences.   When a number of flute-
players are equal in their art, there is no reason why
those of them who are better born should have better
flutes given to them ; for they will not play any better
on the flute, and the superior instrument should be reserved for him who is the superior artist.   If what I am
saying is still obscure, it will be made clearer as we
35 proceed.   For if there were a superior flute-player who
was far inferior in birth and beauty, although either of
these may be a greater good than the art of flute-playing,
40 and may excel flute-playing in a greater ratio than he
excels the others in his art, still he ought to have the
1283ᵃ best flutes given to him, unless the advantages of wealth

---

[1] Cp. i. 1252ᵃ 2 ; *N. Eth.* i. 1094ᵃ 1.   [2] Cp. 1280ᵃ 9.
[3] Cp. *N. Eth.* v. 3.

and birth contribute to excellence in flute-playing, which they do not. Moreover, upon this principle any good may be compared with any other. For if a given height [1] may be measured against wealth and against freedom, 5 height in general may be so measured. Thus if A excels in height more than B in virtue, even if virtue in general excels height still more, all goods will be commensurable; for if a certain amount is better than some other, it is clear that some other will be equal. But since no such comparison can be made, it is evident 10 that there is good reason why in politics men do not ground their claim to office on every sort of inequality any more than in the arts. For if some be slow, and others swift, that is no reason why the one should have little and the others much; it is in gymnastic contests that such excellence is rewarded. Whereas the rival claims of candidates for office can only be based on the 15 possession of elements which enter into the composition of a state. And therefore the noble, or free-born, or rich, may with good reason claim office ; for holders of offices must be freemen and tax-payers : a state can be no more composed entirely of poor men than entirely of slaves. But if wealth and freedom are necessary elements, justice and valour are equally so ; [2] for without the former qualities a state cannot exist at all, without the latter not well.   20

13   If the existence of the state is alone to be considered, then it would seem that all, or some at least, of these claims are just ; but, if we take into account a good life, then, as I have already said,[3] education and virtue 25 have superior claims. As, however, those who are equal in one thing ought not to have an equal share in all, nor those who are unequal in one thing to have an unequal share in all, it is certain that all forms of goverpment which rest on either of these principles are perversions. All men have a claim in a certain sense, as I have

[1] Omitting μᾶλλον in l. 4 with Ridgeway.
[2] Cp. iv. 1291ᵃ 19-33.   [3] Cp. 1281ᵃ 4.

30 already admitted,[1] but all have not an absolute claim. The rich claim because they have a greater share in the land, and land is the common element of the state; also they are generally more trustworthy in contracts. The free claim under the same title as the noble; for they are nearly akin. For the noble are citizens in a truer sense than the ignoble, and good birth is always valued in a 35 man's own home and country.[2] Another reason is, that those who are sprung from better ancestors are likely to be better men, for nobility is excellence of race. Virtue, too, may be truly said to have a claim, for justice has been acknowledged by us to be a social[3] virtue, and it 40 implies all others.[4] Again, the many may urge their claim against the few; for, when taken collectively, and compared with the few, they are stronger and richer and **1283ᵇ** better. But, what if the good, the rich, the noble, and the other classes who make up a state, are all living together in the same city, will there, or will there not, be any doubt who shall rule?—No doubt at all in determining who ought to rule in each of the above-5 mentioned forms of government. For states are characterized by differences in their governing bodies—one of them has a government of the rich, another of the virtuous, and so on. But a difficulty arises when all these elements coexist. How are we to decide? Suppose the 10 virtuous to be very few in number: may we consider their numbers in relation to their duties, and ask whether they are enough to administer the state, or so many as will make up a state? Objections may be urged against all the aspirants to political power. For those 15 who found their claims on wealth or family might be thought to have no basis of justice; on this principle, if any one person were richer than all the rest, it is clear that he ought to be ruler of them. In like manner he who is very distinguished by his birth ought to have the superiority over all those who claim on the ground that 20 they are freeborn. In an aristocracy, or government of

---

[1] 1280ª 9 sqq. [2] Cp. i. 1255ª 32. [3] Cp. i. 1253ª 37.
[4] Cp. *N. Eth*. v. 1129ᵇ 25.

the best, a like difficulty occurs about virtue; for if one
citizen be better than the other members of the government, however good they may be, he too, upon the same
principle of justice, should rule over them. And if the
people are to be supreme because they are stronger than
the few, then if one man, or more than one, but not a ²⁵
majority, is stronger than the many, they ought to rule,
and not the many.

All these considerations appear to show that none of
the principles on which men claim to rule and to hold all
other men in subjection to them are strictly right. To ³⁰
those who claim to be masters of the government on the
ground of their virtue or their wealth, the many might
fairly answer that they themselves are often better and
richer than the few—I do not say individually, but
collectively. And another ingenious objection which is ³⁵
sometimes put forward may be met in a similar manner.
Some persons doubt whether the legislator who desires
to make the justest laws ought to legislate with a view
to the good of the higher classes or of the many, when
the case which we have mentioned occurs.¹ Now what ⁴⁰
is just or right is to be interpreted in the sense of 'what
is equal'; and that which is right in the sense of being
equal is to be considered with reference to the advantage
of the state, and the common good of the citizens. And
a citizen is one who shares in governing and being
governed. He differs under different forms of govern- **1284**^a
ment, but in the best state he is one who is able and
willing to be governed and to govern with a view to the
life of virtue.

If, however, there be some one person, or more than
one, although not enough to make up the full complement of a state, whose virtue is so pre-eminent
that the virtues or the political capacity of all the rest ₅
admit of no comparison with his or theirs, he or they
can be no longer regarded as part of a state; for justice
will not be done to the superior, if he is reckoned only

¹ i. e. when the many collectively are better than the few.
Cf. l. 33. The brackets in ll. 36, 39 should be removed.

as the equal of those who are so far inferior to him in
10 virtue and in political capacity. Such an one may truly
be deemed a God among men. Hence we see that
legislation is necessarily concerned only with those who
are equal in birth and in capacity; and that for men
of pre-eminent virtue there is no law—they are themselves a law. Any one would be ridiculous who
15 attempted to make laws for them : they would probably retort what, in the fable of Antisthenes, the lions
said to the hares,[1] when in the council of the beasts the
latter began haranguing and claiming equality for all.
And for this reason democratic states have instituted
20 ostracism ; equality is above all things their aim, and
therefore they ostracized and banished from the city for
a time those who seemed to predominate too much
through their wealth, or the number of their friends, or
through any other political influence. Mythology tells
us that the Argonauts left Heracles behind for a similar
25 reason ; the ship Argo would not take him because she
feared that he would have been too much for the rest of
the crew. Wherefore those who denounce tyranny and
blame the counsel which Periander gave to Thrasybulus
cannot be held altogether just in their censure. The
story is that Periander, when the herald was sent to ask
counsel of him, said nothing, but only cut off the tallest
30 ears of corn till he had brought the field to a level. The
herald did not know the meaning of the action, but came
and reported what he had seen to Thrasybulus, who
understood that he was to cut off the principal men in
the state ;[2] and this is a policy not only expedient for
35 tyrants or in practice confined to them, but equally
necessary in oligarchies and democracies. Ostracism[3] is
a measure of the same kind, which acts by disabling and
banishing the most prominent citizens. Great powers
do the same to whole cities and nations, as the Athenians
40 did to the Samians, Chians, and Lesbians ; no sooner had
they obtained a firm grasp of the empire, than they

[1] i. e. 'where are your claws and teeth?'   [2] Cp. v. 1311ᵃ 20.
[3] Cp. v. 1302ᵇ 18.

humbled their allies contrary to treaty ; and the Persian **1284^b** king has repeatedly crushed the Medes, Babylonians, and other nations, when their spirit has been stirred by the recollection of their former greatness.

The problem is a universal one, and equally concerns all forms of government, true as well as false; for, although perverted forms with a view to their own interests may adopt this policy, those which seek the 5 common interest do so likewise. The same thing may be observed in the arts and sciences ; [1] for the painter will not allow the figure to have a foot which, however beautiful, is not in proportion, nor will the ship-builder allow 10 the stern or any other part of the vessel to be unduly large, any more than the chorus-master will allow any one who sings louder or better than all the rest to sing in the choir. Monarchs, too, may practise compulsion and still live in harmony with their cities, if their own government is for the interest of the state. Hence where 15 there is an acknowledged superiority the argument in favour of ostracism is based upon a kind of political justice. It would certainly be better that the legislator should from the first so order his state as to have no need of such a remedy. But if the need arises, the next best thing is that he should endeavour to correct the evil by this or some similar measure. The principle, however, 20 has not been fairly applied in states ; for, instead of looking to the good of their own constitution, they have used ostracism for factious purposes. It is true that under perverted forms of government, and from their special point of view, such a measure is just and expedient, but it is also clear that it is not absolutely just. In the 25 perfect state there would be great doubts about the use of it, not when applied to excess in strength, wealth, popularity, or the like, but when used against some one who is pre-eminent in virtue,—what is to be done with him ? Mankind will not say that such an one is to be expelled and exiled ; on the other hand, he ought 30 not to be a subject—that would be as if mankind should

[1] Cp. v. 1302^b 34, 1309^b 21 ; vii. 1326^a 35 ; *Rep.* iv. 420.

claim to rule over Zeus, dividing his offices among them. The only alternative is that all should joyfully obey such a ruler, according to what seems to be the order of nature, and that men like him should be kings in their state for life.

35   The preceding discussion, by a natural transition, leads **14** to the consideration of royalty, which we admit to be one of the true forms of government. Let us see whether in order to be well governed a state or country should be under the rule of a king or under some other form of government; and whether monarchy, although 40 good for some, may not be bad for others. But first we must determine whether there is one species of royalty or **1285ᵃ** many. It is easy to see that there are many, and that the manner of government is not the same in all of them.

Of royalties according to law, (1) the Lacedaemonian is thought to answer best to the true pattern; but there the 5 royal power is not absolute, except when the kings go on an expedition, and then they take the command. Matters of religion are likewise committed to them. The kingly office is in truth a kind of generalship, irresponsible and perpetual. The king has not the power of life and death, except in a specified case,[1] as for instance, in ancient times, he had it when upon a 10 campaign, by right of force. This custom is described in Homer. For Agamemnon is patient when he is attacked in the assembly, but when the army goes out to battle he has the power even of life and death. Does he not say?—'When I find a man skulking apart from the battle, nothing shall save him from the dogs and vultures, for in my hands is death.'[2]

This, then, is one form of royalty—a generalship 15 for life: and of such royalties some are hereditary and others elective.

(2) There is another sort of monarchy not uncommon among the barbarians, which nearly resembles tyranny.

---

[1] Reading ἔν τινι without any noun, as proposed by Bernays.
[2] *Il.* ii. 391–393. The last clause is not found in our Homer.

But this is both legal and hereditary. For barbarians, being more servile in character than Hellenes, and 20 Asiatics than Europeans, do not rebel against a despotic government. Such royalties have the nature of tyrannies because the people are by nature slaves; [1] but there is no danger of their being overthrown, for they are hereditary and legal. Wherefore also their guards are such as a king and not such as a tyrant would employ, that is 25 to say, they are composed of citizens, whereas the guards of tyrants are mercenaries.[2] For kings rule according to law over voluntary subjects, but tyrants over involuntary; and the one are guarded by their fellow-citizens, the others are guarded against them.

These are two forms of monarchy, and there was a 30 third (3) which existed in ancient Hellas, called an Aesymnetia or dictatorship. This may be defined generally as an elective tyranny, which, like the barbarian monarchy, is legal, but differs from it in not being hereditary. Sometimes the office was held for life, sometimes for a term of years, or until certain duties had been performed. For example, the Mytilenaeans elected Pittacus 35 leader against the exiles, who were headed by Antimenides and Alcaeus the poet. And Alcaeus himself shows in one of his banquet odes[3] that they chose Pittacus tyrant, for he reproaches his fellow-citizens for 'having made the low-born Pittacus tyrant of the spiritless and ill-fated city, with one voice shouting his praises'.   1285ᵇ

These forms of government have always had the character of tyrannies, because they possess despotic power; but inasmuch as they are elective and acquiesced in by their subjects, they are kingly.

(4) There is a fourth species of kingly rule—that of the heroic times—which was hereditary and legal, and was exercised over willing subjects. For the first chiefs 5 were benefactors of the people[4] in arts or arms; they either gathered them into a community, or procured land for them; and thus they became kings of voluntary

---

[1] Cp. i. 1252ᵇ7.   [2] Cp. v. 1311ᵃ7.
[3] fr. 37 A, Bergk⁴   [4] Cp. v. 1310ᵇ10.

subjects, and their power was inherited by their descendants. They took the command in war and presided
10 over the sacrifices, except those which required a priest.
They also decided causes either with or without an
oath ; and when they swore, the form of the oath was
the stretching out of their sceptre. In ancient times
their power extended continuously to all things whatsoever,
in city and country, as well as in foreign parts ; but at a
15 later date they relinquished several of these privileges, and
others the people took from them, until in some states
nothing was left to them but the sacrifices; and where
they retained more of the reality they had only the right
of leadership in war beyond the border.
20 These, then, are the four kinds of royalty. First the
monarchy of the heroic ages ; this was exercised over
voluntary subjects, but limited to certain functions ; the
king was a general and a judge, and had the control of
religion. The second is that of the barbarians, which is
an hereditary despotic government in accordance with
25 law. A third is the power of the so-called Aesymnete
or Dictator ; this is an elective tyranny. The fourth
is the Lacedaemonian, which is in fact a generalship,
hereditary and perpetual. These four forms differ from
one another in the manner which I have described.

(5) There is a fifth form of kingly rule in which one
30 has the disposal of all, just as each nation or each state
has the disposal of public matters ; this form corresponds
to the control of a household. For as household management is the kingly rule of a house, so kingly rule [1] is the
household management of a city, or of a nation, or of
many nations.

Of these forms we need only consider two, the Lace- 15
35 daemonian and the absolute royalty ; for most of the
others lie in a region between them, having less power
than the last, and more than the first. Thus the inquiry is reduced to two points : first, is it advantageous
to the state that there should be a perpetual general,

¹ Reading βασιλεία in l. 32, with the MSS.

and if so, should the office be confined to one family, or
open to the citizens in turn?[1] Secondly, is it well that a 1286^a
single man should have the supreme power in all things?
The first question falls under the head of laws rather than of
constitutions; for perpetual generalship might equally exist
under any form of government, so that this matter may be
dismissed for the present.[2] The other kind of royalty 5
is a sort of constitution ; this we have now to consider, and
briefly to run over the difficulties involved in it. We
will begin by inquiring whether it is more advantageous
to be ruled by the best man or by the best laws.[3]

The advocates of royalty maintain that the laws speak 10
only in general terms, and cannot provide for circumstances ; and that for any science to abide by written
rules is absurd. In Egypt[4] the physician is allowed to
alter his treatment after the fourth day, but if sooner, he
takes the risk. Hence it is clear that a government 15
acting according to written laws is plainly not the best.
Yet surely the ruler cannot dispense with the general
principle which exists in law; and that is a better ruler
which is free from passion than that in which it is innate.
Whereas the law is passionless, passion must ever sway
the heart of man. Yes, it may be replied, but then on the 20
other hand an individual will be better able to deliberate
in particular cases.

The best man, then, must legislate, and laws must be
passed, but these laws will have no authority when they
miss the mark, though in all other cases retaining their
authority. But when the law cannot determine a point at 25
all, or not well, should the one best man or should all
decide? According to our present practice assemblies
meet, sit in judgement, deliberate, and decide, and their
judgements all relate to individual cases. Now any
member of the assembly, taken separately, is certainly
inferior to the wise man. But the state is made up of
many individuals. And as a feast to which all the guests

---

[1] Reading ἢ κατὰ μέρος in l. 39, with the best MSS.
[2] It is not discussed later.   [3] Cp. Plato, *Polit*. 294 A-295 C.
[4] Omitting πως in l. 12, with some MSS.

contribute is better than a banquet furnished by a single
30 man,[1] so a multitude is a better judge of many things
than any individual.

Again, the many are more incorruptible than the few ;
they are like the greater quantity of water which is less
easily corrupted than a little. The individual is liable to
be overcome by anger or by some other passion, and then
35 his judgement is necessarily perverted ; but it is hardly
to be supposed that a great number of persons would all
get into a passion and go wrong at the same moment.
Let us assume that they are the freemen, and that they
never act in violation of the law, but fill up the gaps
which the law is obliged to leave. Or, if such virtue is
scarcely attainable by the multitude, we need only
suppose that the majority are good men and good
citizens, and ask which will be the more incorruptible,
40 the one good ruler, or the many who are all good?
1286ᵇ Will not the many? But, you will say, there may be
parties among them, whereas the one man is not divided
against himself. To which we may answer that their
character is as good as his. If we call the rule of many
5 men, who are all of them good, aristocracy, and the rule
of one man royalty, then aristocracy will be better for
states than royalty, whether the government is supported
by force or not,[2] provided only that a number of men
equal in virtue can be found.

The first governments were kingships, probably for this
reason, because of old, when cities were small, men of
10 eminent virtue were few. Further, they were made kings
because they were benefactors,[3] and benefits can only
be bestowed by good men. But when many persons
equal in merit arose, no longer enduring the pre-eminence of one, they desired to have a commonwealth, and
set up a constitution. The ruling class soon deteriorated
and enriched themselves out of the public treasury ;
15 riches became the path to honour, and so oligarchies
naturally grew up. These passed into tyrannies and
tyrannies into democracies ; for love of gain in the ruling

---

[1] Cp. 1281ª 42.   [2] Cp. l. 27.   [3] Cp. 1285ᵇ 6.

classes was always tending to diminish their number, and so to strengthen the masses, who in the end set upon their masters and established democracies. Since cities 20 have increased in size, no other form of government appears to be any longer even easy to establish.[1]

Even supposing the principle to be maintained that kingly power is the best thing for states, how about the family of the king? Are his children to succeed him? If they are no better than anybody else, that will be mischievous. But, says the lover of royalty, the king, 25 though he might, will not hand on his power to his children. That, however, is hardly to be expected, and is too much to ask of human nature. There is also a diffi-culty about the force which he is to employ; should a king have guards about him by whose aid he may be able to coerce the refractory? if not, how will he 30 administer his kingdom? Even if he be the lawful sovereign who does nothing arbitrarily or contrary to law, still he must have some force wherewith to main-tain the law. In the case of a limited monarchy there is not much difficulty in answering this question; the 35 king must have such force as will be more than a match for one or more individuals, but not so great as that of the people. The ancients observed this principle when they gave guards to any one whom they appointed dictator or tyrant. Thus, when Dionysius asked the Syracusans to allow him guards, somebody advised that they should give him only such a number.   40

16   At this place in the discussion there impends the 1287^a inquiry respecting the king who acts solely according to his own will; he has now to be considered. The so-called limited monarchy, or kingship according to law, as I have already remarked,[2] is not a distinct form of government, for under all governments, as, for example, 5 in a democracy or aristocracy, there may be a general holding office for life, and one person is often made supreme over the administration of a state. A magistracy

---

[1] Cp. iv. 1293^a 1, 1297^b 22.   [2] 1286^a 2.

of this kind exists at Epidamnus,[1] and also at Opus, but
10 in the latter city has a more limited power. Now,
absolute monarchy, or the arbitrary rule of a sovereign
over all the citizens, in a city which consists of equals, is
thought by some to be quite contrary to nature; it is
argued that those who are by nature equals must have
the same natural right and worth, and that for unequals
to have an equal share, or for equals to have an unequal
15 share, in the offices of state, is as bad as for different
bodily constitutions to have the same food and clothing.
Wherefore it is thought to be just that among equals every
one be ruled as well as rule, and therefore that all should
have their turn. We thus arrive at law; for an order of
succession implies law. And the rule of the law, it is
20 argued, is preferable to that of any individual. On the
same principle, even if it be better for certain individuals
to govern, they should be made only guardians and
ministers of the law. For magistrates there must be,—
this is admitted; but then men say that to give authority
to any one man when all are equal is unjust. Nay, there
may indeed be cases which the law seems unable to
25 determine, but in such cases can a man? Nay, it will
be replied, the law trains officers for this express purpose,
and appoints them to determine matters which are left
undecided by it, to the best of their judgement. Further,
it permits them to make any amendment of the existing
laws which experience suggests. Therefore he who bids
the law rule may be deemed to bid God and Reason
alone rule, but he who bids man rule adds an element of
30 the beast; for desire is a wild beast, and passion perverts
the minds of rulers, even when they are the best of men.
The law is reason unaffected by desire. We are told [2] that
a patient should call in a physician; he will not get
better if he is doctored out of a book. But the parallel
35 of the arts is clearly not in point; for the physician does
nothing contrary to rule from motives of friendship; he
only cures a patient and takes a fee; whereas magistrates
do many things from spite and partiality. And, indeed,

[1] Cp. v. 1301ᵇ 21.   [2] Cp. 1286ᵃ 12–14, *Polit.* 296 B.

if a man suspected the physician of being in league with his 40
enemies to destroy him for a bribe, he would rather have
recourse to the book. But certainly physicians, when they
are sick, call in other physicians, and training-masters, 1287ᵇ
when they are in trainiñg, other training-masters, as if
they could not judge truly about their own case and
might be influenced by their feelings. Hence it is
evident that in seeking for justice men seek for the mean or
neutral,[1] for the law is the mean. Again, customary laws 5
have more weight, and relate to more important matters,
than written laws, and a man may be a safer ruler than
the written law, but not safer than the customary law.

Again, it is by no means easy for one man to superintend many things ; he will have to appoint a number
of subordinates, and what difference does it make whether 10
these subordinates always existed or were appointed by
him because he needed them ? If, as I said before,[2] the
good man has a right to rule because he is better, still
two good men are better than one : this is the old
saying,—

　　　'two going together,[3]

and the prayer of Agamemnon,—

　　　' would that I had ten such counsellors ! '[4]

And at this day there are magistrates, for example judges, 15
who have authority to decide some matters which the
law is unable to determine, since no one doubts that the
law would command and decide in the best manner whatever it could. But some things can, and other things
cannot, be comprehended under the law, and thi$ is the 20
origin of the vexed question whether the best law or the
best man should rule. For matters of detail about which
men deliberate cannot be included in legislation. Nor
does any one deny that the decision of such matters must
be left to man, but it is argued that there should be many
judges, and not one only. For every ruler [5] who has been 25
trained by the law judges well ; and it would surely seem

[1] Cp. N. Eth. v. 1132ᵃ22.   [2] 1283ᵇ21, 1284ᵇ32.
[3] Il. x. 224.   [4] Il. ii. 372.
[5] Cp. for similar arguments 1286ᵃ28-ᵇ7.

strange that a person should see better with two eyes, or
hear better with two ears, or act better with two hands
or feet, than many with many; indeed, it is already the
practice of kings to make to themselves many eyes and
30 ears and hands and feet. For they make colleagues of
those who are the friends of themselves [1] and their governments. They must be friends of the monarch and of his
government ; if not his friends, they will not do what he
wants ; but friendship implies likeness and equality ; and,
therefore, if he thinks that his friends ought to rule, he
must think that those who are equal to himself and like
35 himself ought to rule equally with himself. These are
the principal controversies relating to monarchy.

But may not all this be true in some cases and not in 17
others? for there is by nature both a justice and an
advantage appropriate to the rule of a master, another to
kingly rule,[2] another to constitutional rule ; but there is
none naturally appropriate to tyranny, or to any other
perverted form of government ; for these come into being
40 contrary to nature. Now, to judge at least from what
has been said, it is manifest that, where men are alike
1288^a and equal, it is neither expedient nor just that one man
should be lord of all, whether there are laws, or whether
there are no laws, but he himself is in the place of law.
Neither should a good man be lord over good men, nor
a bad man over bad ; nor, even if he excels in virtue,
should he have a right to rule, unless in a particular case,
at which I have already hinted, and to which I will
5 once more recur.[3] But first of all, I must determine
what natures are suited for government by a king, and
what for an aristocracy, and what for a constitutional
government.

A people who are by nature capable of producing a race
superior in the virtue needed for political rule are fitted for
kingly government ; and a people submitting to be ruled

---

[1] Reading αὐτοῖς in l. 31, with Schol. in Aristoph. *Acharn.* 92.
[2] Reading δεσποτικὸν καὶ ἄλλο βασιλευτικόν in l. 38.
[3] 1284^a 3, and 1288^a 15.

as freemen by men whose virtue renders them capable 10
of political command are adapted for an aristocracy:
while the people who are suited for constitutional freedom
are those among whom there naturally exists [1] a warlike
multitude [2] able to rule and to obey in turn by a law
which gives office to the well-to-do according to their
desert. But when a whole family, or some individual, 15
happens to be so pre-eminent in virtue as to surpass all
others, then it is just that they should be the royal family
and supreme over all, or that this one citizen should be
king of the whole nation. For, as I said before,[3] to give
them authority is not only agreeable to that ground of 20
right which the founders of all states, whether aristocratical, or oligarchical, or again democratical, are accustomed to put forward (for these all recognize the
claim of excellence, although not the same excellence),
but accords with the principle already laid down.[4] For 25
surely it would not be right to kill, or ostracize, or exile
such a person, or require that he should take his turn in
being governed. The whole is naturally superior to the
part, and he who has this pre-eminence is in the relation
of a whole to a part. But if so, the only alternative is
that he should have the supreme power, and that mankind
should obey him, not in turn, but always. These are the 30
conclusions at which we arrive respecting royalty and its
various forms, and this is the answer to the question,
whether it is or is not advantageous to states, and to
which, and how.

18   We maintain [5] that the true forms of government are
three, and that the best must be that which is ad- 35
ministered by the best, and in which there is one man, or
a whole family, or many persons, excelling all the others
together in virtue, and both rulers and subjects are fitted,
the one to rule, the others to be ruled, in such a manner
as to attain the most eligible life. We showed at the

[1] Retaining ἐν ᾧ . . . πλῆθος in l. 12.   [2] Cp. 1279ᵇ 2.
[3] 1283ᵇ 20, 1284ᵃ 3-17, ᵇ 25.
[4] Cp. 1284ᵇ 28. πάντῃ . . . τὴν αὐτήν in l. 23 is parenthetical.
[5] Cp. 1279ᵃ 22–ᵇ 4.

commencement of our inquiry[1] that the virtue of the good man is necessarily the same as the virtue of the citizen of the perfect state. Clearly then in the same manner, and by 40 the same means through which a man becomes truly good, 1288ᵇ he will frame a state that is to be ruled by an aristocracy or by a king, and the same education and the same habits will be found to make a good man and a man fit to be a statesman or king.

Having arrived at these conclusions, we must proceed 5 to speak of the perfect state, and describe how it comes into being and is established.

[1] cc. 4, 5.

BOOK IV

I   IN all arts and sciences which embrace the whole of 10
any subject, and do not come into being in a fragmentary
way, it is the province of a single art or science to consider all that appertains to a single subject. For example,
the art of gymnastic considers not only the suitableness
of different modes of training to different bodies (2), but
what sort is absolutely the best (1); (for the absolutely
best must suit that which is by nature best and best
furnished with the means of life), and also what common
form of training is adapted to the great majority of men 15
(4). And if a man does not desire the best habit of body,
or the greatest skill in gymnastics, which might be
attained by him, still [1] the trainer or the teacher of
gymnastic should be able to impart any lower degree of
either (3). The same principle equally holds in medicine
and ship-building, and the making of clothes, and in the 20
arts generally.[2]

Hence it is obvious that government too is the subject
of a single science, which has to consider what government is best and of what sort it must be, to be most in
accordance with our aspirations, if there were no external
impediment, and also what kind of government is adapted
to particular states. For the best is often unattainable, 25
and therefore the true legislator and statesman ought to
be acquainted, not only with (1) that which is best in the
abstract, but also with (2) that which is best relatively to
circumstances. We should be able further to say how a
state may be constituted under any given conditions (3);
both how it is originally formed and, when formed, how it
may be longest preserved ; the supposed state being so far 30

---

[1] Reading in l. 18, with Bekker's 2nd edition, ἀγωνίαν, οὐθὲν ἧττον
τοῦ παιδοτρίβου.
[2] The numbers in this paragraph are made to correspond with
the numbers in the next.

from having the best constitution that it is unprovided even with the conditions necessary for the best ; neither is it the best under the circumstances, but of an inferior type. He ought, moreover, to know (4) the form of govern-
35 ment which is best suited to states in general ; for political writers, although they have excellent ideas, are often unpractical. We should consider, not only what form of government is best, but also what is possible and what is easily attainable by all. There are some who would have none but the most perfect ; for this many
40 natural advantages are required. Others, again, speak of a more attainable form, and, although they reject the constitution under which they are living, they extol some one in particular, for example the Lacedaemonian.¹

1289ᵃ Any change of government which has to be introduced should be one which men, starting from their existing constitutions, will be both willing and able to adopt, since there is quite as much trouble in the reformation of an old constitution as in the establishment of a new one, just
5 as to unlearn is as hard as to learn. And therefore, in addition to the qualifications of the statesman already mentioned, he should be able to find remedies for the defects of existing constitutions, as has been said before.² This he cannot do unless he knows how many forms of government there are. It is often supposed that there is only one kind of democracy and one of oligarchy.
10 But this is a mistake ; and, in order to avoid such mistakes, we must ascertain what differences there are in the constitutions of states, and in how many ways they are combined. The same political insight will enable a man to know which laws are the best, and which are suited to different constitutions : for the laws are, and ought to be, relative to the constitution, and not the constitution
15 to the laws. A constitution is the organization of offices in a state, and determines what is to be the governing body, and what is the end of each community. But laws are not to be confounded with the principles of the constitution ; they are the rules according to which the

¹ Cp. ii. 1265ᵇ 35.   ² Cp. 1288ᵇ 29.

magistrates should administer the state, and proceed against offenders. So that we must know the varieties, and the number of varieties, of each form of government, if 20 only with a view to making laws. For the same laws cannot be equally suited to all oligarchies or to all democracies, since there is certainly more than one form both of democracy and of oligarchy.   25

2 In our original discussion [1] about governments we divided them into three true forms: kingly rule, aristocracy, and constitutional government, and three corresponding perversions—tyranny, oligarchy, and democracy. Of kingly rule and of aristocracy we have already spoken,[2] 30 for the inquiry into the perfect state is the same thing with the discussion of the two forms thus named, since both imply a principle of virtue provided with external means. We have already determined in what aristocracy and kingly rule differ from one another, and when the latter should be established.[3] In what follows we have 35 to describe the so-called constitutional government, which bears the common name of all constitutions, and the other forms, tyranny, oligarchy, and democracy.

It is obvious which of the three perversions is the worst, and which is the next in badness. That which is the perversion of the first and most divine is necessarily 40 the worst. And just as a royal rule, if not a mere name, 1289^b must exist by virtue of some great personal superiority in the king,[4] so tyranny, which is the worst of governments, is necessarily the farthest removed from a well-constituted form ; oligarchy is little better, for it is a long way from aristocracy, and democracy is the most tolerable of the three.

A writer [5] who preceded me has already made these 5 distinctions, but his point of view is not the same as mine. For he lays down the principle that when all the constitutions are good (the oligarchy and the rest being

[1] iii. 7 ; cp. *N. Eth.* viii. 10.   [2] iii. 14-18.
[3] iii. 1279^a 32-37, 1286^b 3-5, 1284^a 3-^b 34, ch. 17.
[4] Cp. iii. 1284^a 3-^b 34, chs. 17, 18, v. 1310^b 10 sq., vii. 1325^b 10-12.
[5] Plato, *Polit.* 302 E, 303 A.

virtuous), democracy is the worst, but the best when all
are bad. Whereas we maintain that they are in any
10 case defective, and that[1] one oligarchy is not to be
accounted better than another, but only less bad.
Not to pursue this question further at present, let us
begin by determining (1)[2] how many varieties of constitution there are (since of democracy and oligarchy there are
15 several) ; (2)[3] what constitution is the most generally ac-
ceptable, and what is eligible in the next degree after the
perfect state ; and besides this what other there is which
is aristocratical and well-constituted, and at the same
time adapted to states in general ; (3)[4] of the other forms
of government to whom each is suited. For democracy
may meet the needs of some better than oligarchy, and
20 conversely. In the next place (4)[5] we have to consider
in what manner a man ought to proceed who desires to
establish some one among these various forms, whether
of democracy or of oligarchy ; and lastly, (5)[6] having
briefly discussed these subjects to the best of our power,
we will endeavour to ascertain the modes of ruin and
preservation both of constitutions generally and of each
25 separately, and to what causes they are to be attributed.

The reason why there are many forms of government **3**
is that every state contains many elements. In the first
place we see that all states are made up of families,
30 and in the multitude of citizens there must be some
rich and some poor, and some in a middle condition ;
the rich are heavy-armed, and the poor not. Of the
common people, some are husbandmen, and some traders,
and some artisans. There are also among the notables
differences of wealth and property—for example, in the
35 number of horses which they keep, for they cannot
afford to keep them unless they are rich. And therefore
in old times the cities whose strength lay in their cavalry
were oligarchies, and they used cavalry in wars against
their neighbours ; as was the practice of the Eretrians

---

[1] Reading ἔχειν in l. 10, with Richards.   [2] C. 3-10.
[3] C. 11.   [4] C. 12.   [5] Book vi. 1-7.   [6] Book v.

and Chalcidians, and also of the Magnesians on the river Mæander, and of other peoples in Asia. Besides dif- 40 ferences of wealth there are differences of rank and merit, and there are some other elements which were 1290[a] mentioned by us when in treating of aristocracy we enumerated the essentials of a state.[1] Of these elements, sometimes all, sometimes the lesser and sometimes the greater number, have a share in the government. It is 5 evident then that there must be many forms of government, differing in kind, since the parts of which they are composed differ from each other in kind. For a constitution is an organization of offices, which all the citizens distribute among themselves, according to the power which different classes possess, for example the rich or the poor, or according to some principle of equality which 10 includes both. There must therefore be as many forms of government as there are modes of arranging the offices, according to the superiorities and the differences of the parts of the state.

There are generally thought to be two principal forms : as men say of the winds that there are but two—north and south, and that the rest of them are only variations of these, so of governments there are said to be only two 15 forms—democracy and oligarchy. For aristocracy is considered to be a kind of oligarchy, as being the rule of a few, and the so-called constitutional government to be really a democracy, just as among the winds we make the west a variation of the north, and the east of the south wind. Similarly of musical modes there are said 20 to be two kinds, the Dorian and the Phrygian ; the other arrangements of the scale are comprehended under one or other of these two. About forms of government this is a very favourite notion. But in either case the better and more exact way is to distinguish, as I have done,[2] the one or two which are true forms, and to regard the others 25 as perversions, whether of the most perfectly attempered mode or of the best form of government : we may

---

[1] iii. 1283[a] 14 sq., and cp. vii. 8, 9.
[2] 1289[a] 31–33, 40 sqq., cp. viii. 1340[a] 40–[b] 5, 1342[a] 28 sqq., [b] 29 sqq.

compare the severer and more overpowering modes to the oligarchical forms, and the more relaxed and gentler ones to the democratic.

30 It must not be assumed, as some are fond of saying, 4 that democracy is simply that form of government in which the greater number are sovereign,[1] for in oligarchies, and indeed in every government, the majority rules ; nor again is oligarchy that form of government in which a few are sovereign. Suppose the whole population of a 35 city to be 1300, and that of these 1000 are rich, and do not allow the remaining 300 who are poor, but free, and in all other respects their equals, a share of the government—no one will say that this is a democracy. In like manner, if the poor were few and the masters of the rich who outnumber them, no one would ever call such a government, in which the rich majority have no share of 40 office, an oligarchy. Therefore we should rather say **1290^b** that democracy is the form of government in which the free are rulers, and oligarchy in which the rich ; it is only an accident that the free are the many and the rich are the few. Otherwise a government in which the offices were given according to stature, as is said to be 5 the case in Ethiopia, or according to beauty, would be an oligarchy ; for the number of tall or good-looking men is small. And yet oligarchy and democracy are not sufficiently distinguished merely by these two characteristics of wealth and freedom. Both of them contain many other elements, and therefore we must carry our analysis further, and say that the government is not 10 a democracy[2] in which the freemen, being few in number, rule over the many who are not free, as at Apollonia, on the Ionian Gulf, and at Thera ; (for in each of these states the nobles, who were also the earliest settlers, were held in chief honour, although they were but a few out of many). Neither is it a democracy when the rich have the government because they exceed in number ; 15 as was the case formerly at Colophon, where the bulk of

---

[1] Cp. iii. 1279^b 21.   [2] Reading δῆμος in l. 11, with the MSS.

the inhabitants were possessed of large property before the Lydian War. But the form of government is a democracy when the free, who are also poor and the majority, govern, and an oligarchy when the rich and the noble govern, they being at the same time few in number. 20 I have said that there are many forms of government, and have explained to what causes the variety is due. Why there are more than those already mentioned,[1] and what they are, and whence they arise, I will now proceed to consider, starting from the principle already admitted,[2] which is that every state consists, not of one, but of many parts. If we were going to speak of the 25 different species of animals, we should first of all determine the organs which are indispensable to every animal, as for example some organs of sense and the instruments of receiving and digesting food, such as the mouth and the stomach, besides organs of locomotion. Assuming now that there are only so many kinds of organs, but that there may be differences in them—I 30 mean different kinds of mouths, and stomachs, and perceptive and locomotive organs—the possible combinations of these differences will necessarily furnish many varieties of animals. (For animals cannot be the same which have different kinds of mouths or of ears.) And when all the combinations are exhausted, there will be as many sorts 35 of animals as there are combinations of the necessary organs. The same, then,[3] is true of the forms of government which have been described; states, as I have repeatedly said,[4] are composed, not of one, but of many elements. One element is the food-producing class, who 40 are called husbandmen; a second, the class of mechanics 1291ᵃ who practise the arts without which a city cannot exist; —of these arts some are absolutely necessary, others contribute to luxury or to the grace of life. The third class is that of traders, and by traders I mean those who are engaged in buying and selling, whether in commerce or 5

[1] i.e. democracy and oligarchy, cp. 1290ᵃ 13.   [2] 1289ᵇ 27 sq.
[3] Reading τὸν αὐτὸν δὴ τρόπον in l. 37, with Coraes.
[4] ii. 1261ᵃ 22 sqq., iii. 1283ᵃ 14 sqq., iv. 1289ᵇ 27-1290ᵃ 5, 1290ᵇ 23 sq., cp. iii. 1277ᵃ 5 sqq.

in retail trade. A fourth class is that of the serfs or
labourers. The warriors make up the fifth class, and
they are as necessary as any of the others, if the country
is not to be the slave of every invader. For how can a
state which has any title to the name be of a slavish
nature? The state is independent and self-sufficing,
10 but a slave is the reverse of independent. Hence we
see that this subject, though ingeniously, has not been
satisfactorily treated in the *Republic*.[1] Socrates says
that a state is made up of four sorts of people who are
absolutely necessary ; these are a weaver, a husbandman,
a shoemaker, and a builder; afterwards, finding that
15 they are not enough, he adds a smith, and again a
herdsman, to look after the necessary animals; then
a merchant, and then a retail trader. All these together
form the complement of the first state, as if a state were
established merely to supply the necessaries of life, rather
than for the sake of the good, or stood equally in need
of shoemakers and of husbandmen. But he does not
20 admit into the state a military class until the country
has increased in size, and is beginning to encroach on its
neighbour's land, whereupon they go to war. Yet even
amongst his four original citizens, or whatever be the
number of those whom he associates in the state, there
must be some one who will dispense justice and determine what is just. And as the soul may be said to be
25 more truly part of an animal than the body, so the higher
parts of states, that is to say, the warrior class, the class
engaged in the administration of justice, and that engaged
in deliberation, which is the special business of political
common sense,—these are more essential to the state than
the parts which minister to the necessaries of life. Whether
their several functions are the functions of different citi-
30 zens, or of the same,—for it may often happen that the
same persons are both warriors and husbandmen,—is immaterial to the argument. The higher as well as the lower
elements are to be equally considered parts of the state,
and if so, the military element at any rate must be

[1] *Rep*. ii. 369.

included. There are also the wealthy who minister to
the state with their property; these form the seventh
class. The eighth class is that of magistrates and of
officers; for the state cannot exist without rulers. And 35
therefore some must be able to take office and to
serve the state, either always or in turn. There only
remains the class of those who deliberate and who judge
between disputants; we were just now distinguishing
them. If presence of all these elements, and their fair 40
and equitable organization, is necessary to states, then
there must also be persons who have the ability of 1291ᵇ
statesmen. Different functions appear to be often combined in the same individual; for example, the warrior
may also be a husbandman, or an artisan; or, again,
the counsellor a judge. And all claim to possess 5
political ability, and think that they are quite competent
to fill most offices. But the same persons cannot be rich
and poor at the same time. For this reason the rich and
the poor are regarded in an especial sense as parts of
a state. Again, because the rich are generally few in
number, while the poor are many, they appear to be 10
antagonistic, and as the one or the other prevails they
form the government. Hence arises the common opinion
that there are two kinds of government—democracy and
oligarchy.

I have already explained [1] that there are many forms
of constitution, and to what causes the variety is due.
Let me now show that there are different forms 15
both of democracy and oligarchy, as will indeed be
evident from what has preceded. For both in the common people and in the notables various classes are
included; of the common people, one class are husbandmen, another artisans; another traders, who are
employed in buying and selling; another are the sea- 20
faring class, whether engaged in war or in trade, as
ferrymen or as fishermen. (In many places any one of
these classes forms quite a large population; for example,
fishermen at Tarentum and Byzantium, crews of triremes

[1] Cp. iii. c. 6.

at Athens, merchant seamen at Aegina and Chios,
25 ferrymen at Tenedos.) To the classes already mentioned may be added day-labourers, and those who,
owing to their needy circumstances, have no leisure, or
those who are not of free birth on both sides; and there
may be other classes as well. The notables again may
be divided according to their wealth, birth, virtue, education, and similar differences.
30   Of forms of democracy first comes that which is said
to be based strictly on equality. In such a democracy
the law says that it is just for the poor to have no more
advantage than the rich;[1] and that neither should be
masters, but both equal. For if liberty and equality, as is
35 thought by some, are chiefly to be found in democracy,
they will be best attained when all persons alike share in
the government to the utmost. And since the people are
the majority, and the opinion of the majority is decisive,
such a government must necessarily be a democracy.
Here then is one sort of democracy. There is another,[2]
in which the magistrates are elected according to a cer-
40 tain property qualification, but a low one; he who has
the required amount of property has a share in the
government, but he who loses his property loses his
1292^a rights. Another kind is that in which all the citizens
who are under no disqualification share in the government, but still the law is supreme. In another, everybody,
if he be only a citizen, is admitted to the government,
but the law is supreme as before. A fifth form of de-
5 mocracy, in other respects the same, is that in which, not
the law, but the multitude, have the supreme power, and
supersede the law by their decrees. This is a state of
affairs brought about by the demagogues. For in democracies which are subject to the law the best citizens
10 hold the first place, and there are no demagogues; but

---

[1] Or, reading ἄρχειν in l. 32 with Vettori, 'that the poor should
no more govern than the rich'. The emendation is not absolutely
necessary, though supported by vi. 1318^a 6 ἴσον γὰρ τὸ μηθὲν μᾶλλον
ἄρχειν τοὺς ἀπόρους ἢ τοὺς εὐπόρους, μηδὲ κυρίους εἶναι μόνους ἀλλὰ πάντας
ἐξ ἴσου κατ᾽ ἀριθμόν.

[2] Retaining ἄλλο δέ in l. 39.

where the laws are not supreme, there demagogues spring up. For the people becomes a monarch, and is many in one ; and the many have the power in their hands, not as individuals, but collectively. Homer says that 'it is not good to have a rule of many ',[1] but whether he means this corporate rule, or the rule of many individuals, is uncertain. At all events this sort of democracy, which 15 is now a monarch, and no longer under the control of law, seeks to exercise monarchical sway, and grows into a despot ; the flatterer is held in honour ; this sort of democracy being relatively to other democracies what tyranny is to other forms of monarchy. The spirit of both is the same, and they alike exercise a despotic rule over the better citizens. The decrees of the demos correspond to the edicts of the tyrant ; and the dema- 20 gogue is to the one what the flatterer is to the other. Both have great power ;—the flatterer with the tyrant, the demagogue with democracies of the kind which we are describing. The demagogues make the decrees of the people override the laws, by referring all things to the popular assembly. And therefore they grow great, 25 because the people have all things in their hands, and they hold in their hands the votes of the people, who are too ready to listen to them. Further, those who have any complaint to bring against the magistrates say, 'let the people be judges'; the people are too happy to accept the invitation ; and so the authority of every office is undermined. Such a democracy is fairly open 30 to the objection that it is not a constitution at all ; for where the laws have no authority, there is no constitution. The law ought to be supreme over all, and the magistracies should judge of particulars, and only this should be considered a constitution. So that if democracy be a real form of government, the sort of system in which 35 all things are regulated by decrees is clearly not even a democracy in the true sense of the word, for decrees relate only to particulars.[2]

These then are the different kinds of democracy.

[1] *Il*. ii. 204.   [2] Cp. *N. Eth*. v. 1137^b 27.

Of oligarchies, too, there are different kinds:—one 5
40 where the property qualification for office is such that the
poor, although they form the majority, have no share in
the government, yet he who acquires a qualification may
1292ᵇ obtain a share. Another sort is when there is a qualification for office, but a high one, and the vacancies in
the governing body are filled by co-optation. If the
election is made out of all the qualified persons, a constitution of this kind inclines to an aristocracy, if out of
a privileged class, to an oligarchy. Another sort of
5 oligarchy is when the son succeeds the father. There
is a fourth form, likewise hereditary, in which the magistrates are supreme and not the law. Among oligarchies
this is what tyranny is among monarchies, and the last-
mentioned form of democracy among democracies ; and
10 in fact this sort of oligarchy receives the name of a
dynasty (or rule of powerful families).

These are the different sorts of oligarchies and democracies. It should however be remembered that in many
states[1] the constitution which is established by law,
although not democratic, owing to the education and
habits of the people may be administered democrati-
15 cally, and conversely in other states the established
constitution may incline to democracy, but may be administered in an oligarchical spirit. This most often
happens after a revolution : for governments do not
change at once ; at first the dominant party are content
20 with encroaching a little upon their opponents. The
laws which existed previously continue in force, but
the authors of the revolution have the power in their
hands.

From what has been already said we may safely infer 6
that there are so many different kinds of democracies and
of oligarchies. For it is evident that either all the classes
whom we mentioned[2] must share in the government, or
25 some only and not others. When the class of husbandmen and of those who possess moderate fortunes have

---

[1] Cp. v. 1301ᵇ 10.   [2] 1291ᵇ 17-30.

the supreme power, the government is administered according to law. For the citizens being compelled to live by their labour have no leisure ; and so they set up the authority of the law, and attend assemblies only when necessary. They all obtain a share in the government when they have acquired the qualification which is fixed by the law—the absolute exclusion of any class would be 30 a step towards oligarchy ; hence all who have acquired the property qualification are admitted to a share in the constitution. But leisure cannot be provided for them [1] unless there are revenues to support them. This is one sort of democracy, and these are the causes which give birth to it. Another kind is based on the distinction which naturally comes next in order ; in this, every one 35 to whose birth there is no objection is eligible, but actually shares in the government only if he can find leisure. Hence in such a democracy the supreme power is vested in the laws, because the state has no means of paying the citizens. A third kind is when all freemen have a right to share in the government, but do not actually share, for the reason which has been already given ; so that in 40 this form again the law must rule. A fourth kind of democracy is that which comes latest in the history of 1293^a states. In our own day, when cities have far outgrown their original size, and their revenues have increased, all the citizens have a place in the government, through the great preponderance of the multitude ; and they all, including the poor who receive pay, and therefore 5 have leisure to exercise their rights, share in the administration. Indeed, when they are paid, the common people have the most leisure, for they are not hindered by the care of their property, which often fetters the rich, who are thereby prevented from taking part in the assembly or in the courts, and so the state is governed by the poor, who are a majority, and not by the laws. So many kinds of democracies there are, and 10 they grow out of these necessary causes.

[1] Placing διὸ ... μετέχειν after ὀλιγαρχικόν in l. 32, and omitting the second ἐξεῖναι in l. 32 with Thurot.

Of oligarchies, one form is that in which the majority of the citizens have some property, but not very much ; and this is the first form, which allows to any one who obtains the required amount the right of sharing in 15 the government. The sharers in the government being a numerous body, it follows that the law must govern, and not individuals. For in proportion as they are further removed from a monarchical form of government, and in respect of property have neither so much as to be able to live without attending to business, nor so little 20 as to need state support, they must admit the rule of law and not claim to rule themselves. But if the men of property in the state are fewer than in the former case, and own more property, there arises a second form of oligarchy. For the stronger they are, the more power they claim, and having this object in view, they themselves select those of the other classes who are to be ad-25 mitted to the government ; but, not being as yet strong enough to rule without the law, they make the law represent their wishes.[1] When this power is intensified by a further diminution of their numbers and increase of their property, there arises a third and further stage of oligarchy, in which the governing class keep the offices in their own hands, and the law ordains that the 30 son shall succeed the father. When, again, the rulers have great wealth and numerous friends, this sort of family despotism approaches a monarchy ; individuals rule and not the law. This is the fourth sort of oligarchy, and is analogous to the last sort of democracy.

35   There are still two forms besides democracy and 7 oligarchy ; one of them is universally recognized and included among the four principal forms of government, which are said to be (1) monarchy, (2) oligarchy, (3) democracy, and (4) the so-called aristocracy or government of the best. But there is also a fifth, which retains the generic name of polity or constitutional

---

[1] i.e. they make a law that the governing class shall have the power of co-optation from other classes.

government ; this is not common, and therefore has not 40 been noticed by writers who attempt to enumerate the different kinds of government ; like Plato,[1] in their books 1293[b] about the state, they recognize four only. The term ' aristocracy ' is rightly applied to the form of government which is described in the first part of our treatise ;[2] for that only can be rightly called aristocracy which is a government formed of the best men absolutely, and not merely of men who are good when tried by any given standard. In the perfect state the good man is absolutely 5 the same as the good citizen ; whereas in other states the good citizen is only good relatively to his own form of government. But there are some states differing from oligarchies and also differing from the so-called polity or constitutional government; these are termed aristocracies, and in them magistrates are certainly chosen, both according to their wealth and according to their merit. 10 Such a form of government differs from each of the two just now mentioned, and is termed an aristocracy. For indeed in states which do not make virtue the aim of the community, men of merit and reputation for virtue may be found. And so where a government has regard to wealth, virtue, and numbers, as at Carthage,[3] that is 15 aristocracy ; and also where it has regard only to two out of the three, as at Lacedaemon, to virtue and numbers, and the two principles of democracy and virtue temper each other. There are these two forms of aristocracy in addition to the first and perfect state, and there is a third form, viz. the constitutions which incline 20 more than the so-called polity towards oligarchy.

8   I have yet to speak of the so-called polity and of tyranny. I put them in this order, not because a polity or constitutional government is to be regarded as a perversion any more than the above-mentioned aristocracies. The truth is, that they all fall short of the 25 most perfect form of government, and so they are reckoned among perversions, and the really perverted

---

[1] *Rep.* viii, ix.   [2] iii. 1279[a] 34, 1286[b] 3, cp. vii. 1328[b] 37.
[3] Cp. ii. 1273[a] 21–30.

forms are perversions of these, as I said in the original discussion.¹ Last of all I will speak of tyranny, which I place last in the series because I am inquiring into the constitutions of states, and this is the very reverse of a constitution.

30 Having explained why I have adopted this order, I will proceed to consider constitutional government; of which the nature will be clearer now that oligarchy and democracy have been defined. For polity or constitutional government may be described generally as a fusion of oligarchy and democracy; but the term is 35 usually applied to those forms of government which incline towards democracy, and the term aristocracy to those which incline towards oligarchy, because birth and education are commonly the accompaniments of wealth. Moreover, the rich already possess the external advantages the want of which is a temptation to crime, and hence they are called noblemen and gentlemen. 40 And inasmuch as aristocracy seeks to give predominance to the best of the citizens, people say also of oligarchies that they are composed of noblemen and gentlemen.

1294^a Now it appears to be an impossible thing that the state which is governed not by the best citizens but by the worst should be well-governed, and equally impossible that the state which is ill-governed should be governed by the best. But we must remember that good laws, if they are not obeyed, do not constitute good government. Hence there are two parts of good government; one is 5 the actual obedience of citizens to the laws, the other part is the goodness of the laws which they obey; they may obey bad laws as well as good. And there may be a further subdivision; they may obey either the best laws which are attainable to them, or the best absolutely.

The distribution of offices according to merit is a 10 special characteristic of aristocracy, for the principle of an aristocracy is virtue, as wealth is of an oligarchy, and freedom of a democracy. In all of them there of course exists the right of the majority, and whatever seems

¹ iii. 7.

good to the majority of those who share in the government has authority. Now in most states the form called 15 polity exists,[1] for the fusion goes no further than the attempt to unite the freedom of the poor and the wealth of the rich, who commonly take the place of the noble. But as there are three grounds on which men claim an equal share in the government, freedom, wealth, and virtue (for the fourth or good birth is the result of the two last, 20 being only ancient wealth and virtue), it is clear that the admixture of the two elements, that is to say, of the rich and poor, is to be called a polity or constitutional government ; and the union of the three is to be called aristocracy or the government of the best, and more than any other form of government, except the true and ideal, has a right to this name.

Thus far I have shown the existence of forms of states 25 other than monarchy, democracy, and oligarchy, and what they are, and in what aristocracies differ from one another, and polities from aristocracies—that the two latter are not very unlike is obvious.

9   Next we have to consider how by the side of oligarchy 30 and democracy the so-called polity or constitutional government springs up, and how it should be organized. The nature of it will be at once understood from a comparison of oligarchy and democracy ; we must ascertain their different characteristics, and taking a portion from each, put the two together, like the parts of an indenture. Now there are three modes in which fusions of govern- 35 ment may be effected.   In the first mode we must combine the laws[2] made by both governments, say concerning the administration of justice.   In oligarchies they impose a fine on the rich if they do not serve as judges, and to the poor they give no pay ; but in democracies they give pay to the poor and do not fine 40 the rich.   Now (1) the union of these two modes[3] is a common or middle term between them, and is

---

[1] Retaining καλεῖται in l. 15.
[2] Reading ἅ in l. 36 with some good MSS.   [3] Cp. 1297^a 38.

1294[b] therefore characteristic of a constitutional government, for it is a combination of both. This is one mode of uniting the two elements. Or (2) a mean may be taken between the enactments of the two: thus democracies require no property qualification, or only a small one, from members of the assembly, oligarchies a high
5 one; here neither of these is the common term, but a mean between them. (3) There is a third mode, in which something is borrowed from the oligarchical and something from the democratical principle. For example, the appointment of magistrates by lot is thought to be democratical, and the election of them oligarchical; democratical again when there is no property qualification,
10 oligarchical when there is. In the aristocratical or constitutional state, one element will be taken from each—from oligarchy the principle of electing to offices, from democracy the disregard of qualification. Such are the various modes of combination.

There is a true union of oligarchy and democracy
15 when the same state may be termed either a democracy or an oligarchy; those who use both names evidently feel that the fusion is complete. Such a fusion there is also in the mean; for both extremes appear in it. The Lacedaemonian constitution, for example, is often de-
20 scribed as a democracy, because it has many democratical features. In the first place the youth receive a democratical education. For the sons of the poor are brought up with the sons of the rich, who are educated in such a manner as to make it possible for the sons of the poor to be educated like them. A similar equality prevails in
25 the following period of life, and when the citizens are grown up to manhood the same rule is observed; there is no distinction between the rich and poor. In like manner they all have the same food at their public tables, and the rich wear only such clothing as any poor man can afford. Again, the people elect to one of the two greatest offices of state, and in the other they share;[1]
30 for they elect the Senators and share in the Ephoralty.

[1] Cp. ii. 1270[b] 17.

By others the Spartan constitution is said to be an oligarchy, because it has many oligarchical elements. That all offices are filled by election and none by lot, is one of these oligarchical characteristics ; that the power of inflicting death or banishment rests with a few persons is another; and there are others. In a well attempered polity there should appear to be both elements and 35 yet neither; also the government should rely on itself, and not on foreign aid, and on itself not through the good will of a majority [1]—they might be equally well-disposed when there is a vicious form of government— but through the general willingness of all classes in the state to maintain the constitution.

Enough of the manner in which a constitutional 40 government, and in which the so-called aristocracies ought to be framed.

10   Of the nature of tyranny I have still to speak, in order 1295^a that it may have its place in our inquiry (since even tyranny is reckoned by us to be a form of government), although there is not much to be said about it. I have already in the former part of this treatise [2] discussed royalty or kingship according to the most usual meaning 5 of the term, and considered whether it is or is not advantageous to states, and what kind of royalty should be established, and from what source, and how.

When speaking of royalty we also spoke [3] of two forms of tyranny, which are both according to law, and there- 10 fore easily pass into royalty. Among Barbarians there are elected monarchs who exercise a despotic power ; despotic rulers were also elected in ancient Hellas, called Aesymnetes or dictators. These monarchies, when compared with one another, exhibit certain differences. And 15 they are, as I said before,[4] royal, in so far as the monarch rules according to law over willing subjects ; but they are tyrannical in so far as he is despotic and rules according to his own fancy. There is also a third kind of tyranny,

---

[1] Omitting ἔξωθεν in l. 37, with Thurot.
[2] iii. 14–17.   [3] iii. 1285^a 16-^b 3.   [4] iii. 1285^b 2.

which is the most typical form, and is the counterpart of the perfect monarchy. This tyranny is just that arbitrary
20 power of an individual which is responsible to no one, and governs all alike, whether equals or betters, with a view to its own advantage, not to that of its subjects, and therefore against their will. No freeman, if he can escape from it, will endure such a government. The kinds of tyranny are such and so many, and for the reasons which I have given.

25 We have now to inquire what is the best constitution **11** for most states, and the best life for most men, neither assuming a standard of virtue which is above ordinary persons, nor an education which is exceptionally favoured by nature and circumstances, nor yet an ideal state which is an aspiration only, but having regard to the life
30 in which the majority are able to share, and to the form of government which states in general can attain. As to those aristocracies, as they are called, of which we were just now speaking,[1] they either lie beyond the possibilities of the greater number of states, or they approximate to the so-called constitutional government, and therefore need no separate discussion. And in fact the conclusion at which we arrive respecting all these forms
35 rests upon the same grounds. For if what was said in the *Ethics*[2] is true, that the happy life is the life according to virtue lived without impediment, and that virtue is a mean, then the life which is in a mean, and in a mean attainable by every one, must be the best. And the same principles of virtue and vice are characteristic
40 of cities and of constitutions; for the constitution is in
1295ᵇ a figure the life of the city.

Now in all states there are three elements: one class is very rich, another very poor, and a third in a mean. It is admitted that moderation and the mean are best, and therefore it will clearly be best to possess the gifts of
5 fortune in moderation; for in that condition of life men

---

[1] 1293ᵇ 7-21, cp. 1293ᵇ 36-1294ᵃ 25.
[2] *N. Eth.* i. 1098ᵃ 16. vii. 1153ᵇ 10, x. 1177ᵃ 12.

are most ready to follow rational principle. But he who greatly excels in beauty, strength, birth, or wealth, or on the other hand who is very poor, or very weak, or very much disgraced, finds it difficult to follow rational principle.[1] Of these two the one sort grow into violent and great criminals, the others into rogues and petty 10 rascals. And two sorts of offences correspond to them, the one committed from violence, the other from roguery. Again, the middle class is least likely to shrink from rule, or to be over-ambitious for it ; both of which are injuries to the state. Again, those who have too much of the goods of fortune, strength, wealth, friends, and the like, are neither 15 willing nor able to submit to authority. The evil begins at home ; for when they are boys, by reason of the luxury in which they are brought up,[2] they never learn, even at school, the habit of obedience. On the other hand, the very poor, who are in the opposite extreme, are too degraded. So that the one class cannot obey, and can only rule despotically ; the other knows not how to command and 20 must be ruled like slaves. Thus arises a city, not of freemen, but of masters and slaves, the one despising, the other envying ; and nothing can be more fatal to friendship and good fellowship in states than this : for good fellowship springs from friendship ; when men are at enmity with one another, they would rather not even share the same path. But a city ought to be composed, as far 25 as possible, of equals and similars ; and these are generally the middle classes. Wherefore the city which is composed of middle-class citizens is necessarily best constituted in respect of the elements of which we say the fabric of the state naturally consists.[3] And this is the class of citizens which is most secure in a state, for they do not, 30 like the poor, covet their neighbours' goods ; nor do others covet theirs, as the poor covet the goods of the rich ; and as they neither plot against others, nor are themselves plotted against, they pass through life safely. Wisely then did Phocylides pray,[4]—' Many things are best in

[1] Cp. Pl. *Rep.* iv. 421 D ff.   [2] Cp. v. 1310[a] 22.
[3] Cp. ll. 1-3.   [4] Fr. 12, Bergk[4].

the mean ; I desire to be of a middle condition in my city.'

35 Thus it is manifest that the best political community is formed by citizens of the middle class, and that those states are likely to be well-administered, in which the middle class is large, and stronger if possible than both the other classes, or at any rate than either singly ; for the addition of the middle class turns the scale, and prevents either of the extremes from being dominant. Great then
40 is the good fortune of a state in which the citizens have
1296^a a moderate and sufficient property ; for where some possess much, and the others nothing, there may arise an extreme democracy, or a pure oligarchy ; or a tyranny may grow out of either extreme,—either out of the most rampant democracy, or out of an oligarchy ; but it is not so likely to arise out of the middle constitutions and those
5 akin to them. I will explain the reason of this hereafter, when I speak of the revolutions of states.[1] The mean condition of states is clearly best, for no other is free from faction ; and where the middle class is large, there are least likely to be factions and dissensions. For a similar reason large states are less liable to faction than small
10 ones, because in them the middle class is large ; whereas in small states it is easy to divide all the citizens into two classes who are either rich or poor, and to leave nothing in the middle. And democracies are safer [2] and more permanent than oligarchies, because they have a middle
15 class which is more numerous and has a greater share in the government ; for when there is no middle class, and the poor greatly exceed in number, troubles arise, and the state soon comes to an end. A proof of the superiority of the middle class is that the best legislators have been of a middle condition ; for example, Solon, as
20 his own verses testify ; and Lycurgus, for he was not a king ; and Charondas, and almost all legislators.

These considerations will help us to understand why most governments are either democratical or oligarchical. The reason is that the middle class is seldom numerous in

---

[1] v. 1308^a 18-24.   [2] Cp. v. 1302^a 8, 1307^a 16.

them, and whichever party, whether the rich or the com- 25
mon people, transgresses the mean and predominates,
draws the constitution its own way, and thus arises either
oligarchy or democracy.   There is another reason—the
poor and the rich quarrel with one another, and whichever side gets the better, instead of establishing a just
or popular government, regards political supremacy as 30
the prize of victory, and the one party sets up a
democracy and the other an oligarchy.   Further, both the
parties which had the supremacy in Hellas looked only
to the interest of their own form of government, and
established in states, the one, democracies, and the other,
oligarchies ; they thought of their own advantage, of the 35
public not at all.   For these reasons the middle form of
government has rarely, if ever, existed, and among a very
few only.   One man alone of all who ever ruled in Hellas [1]
was induced to give this middle constitution to states.
But it has now become a habit among the citizens of 40
states, not even to care about equality; all men are 1296ᵇ
seeking for dominion, or, if conquered, are willing to
submit.

What then is the best form of government, and what
makes it the best, is evident ; and of other constitutions,
since we say [2] that there are many kinds of democracy and
many of oligarchy, it is not difficult to see which has the 5
first and which the second or any other place in the order
of excellence, now that we have determined which is the
best.   For that which is nearest [3] to the best must of
necessity be better, and that which is furthest from it
worse, if we are judging absolutely and not relatively to
given conditions :   I say ' relatively to given conditions ', 10
since a particular government may be preferable, but
another form may be better for some people.

12   We have now to consider what and what kind of
government is suitable to what and what kind of men.

---

[1] Retaining ἐφ' ἡγεμονίᾳ γενομένων in l. 39.   The reference is
probably to Theramenes.
[2] 1289ᵃ 8, ᵇ 13, 1291ᵇ 15–1292ᵇ 10, 1292ᵇ 22–1293ᵃ 10.
[3] Reading ἐγγύτατα in l. 8 with most MSS.

I may begin by assuming, as a general principle common
15 to all governments, that the portion of the state which
desires the permanence of the constitution ought to be
stronger than that which desires the reverse. Now every
city is composed of quality and quantity. By quality
I mean freedom, wealth, education, good birth, and by
20 quantity, superiority of numbers. Quality may exist in
one of the classes which make up the state, and quantity
in the other. For example, the meanly-born may be
more in number than the well-born, or the poor than the
rich, yet they may not so much exceed in quantity as
they fall short in quality; and therefore there must be
25 a comparison of quantity and quality. Where the
number of the poor is more than proportioned to the
wealth of the rich, there will naturally be a democracy,
varying in form with the sort of people who compose it
in each case. If, for example, the husbandmen exceed in
number, the first form of democracy will then arise; if
30 the artisans and labouring class, the last; and so with
the intermediate forms. But where the rich and the
notables exceed in quality more than they fall short in
quantity, there oligarchy arises, similarly assuming various
forms according to the kind of superiority possessed by
the oligarchs.

35 The legislator should always include the middle class
in his government; if he makes his laws oligarchical, to
the middle class let him look; if he makes them democratical, he should equally by his laws try to attach this
class to the state. There only can the government ever
be stable where the middle class exceeds one or both of
40 the others, and in that case there will be no fear that
1297^a the rich will unite with the poor against the rulers. For
neither of them will ever be willing to serve the other,
and if they look for some form of government more
suitable to both, they will find none better than this, for
the rich and the poor will never consent to rule in turn,
5 because they mistrust one another. The arbiter is always
the one trusted, and he who is in the middle is an
arbiter. The more perfect the admixture of the political

elements, the more lasting will be the constitution. Many even of those who desire to form aristocratical governments make a mistake, not only in giving too much power to the rich, but in attempting to overreach the people. There comes a time when out of a false good there 10 arises a true evil, since the encroachments of the rich are more destructive to the constitution than those of the people.

13   The devices by which oligarchies deceive the people are five in number ; they relate to (1) the assembly ; 15 (2) the magistracies ; (3) the courts of law ; (4) the use of arms ; (5) gymnastic exercises. (1) The assemblies are thrown open to all, but either the rich only are fined for non-attendance, or a much larger fine is inflicted upon them. (2) As to the magistracies, those who are qualified by property cannot decline office upon oath, but the poor may. (3) In the law-courts the rich, and 20 the rich only, are fined if they do not serve, the poor are let off with impunity, or, as in the laws of Charondas, a larger fine is inflicted on the rich, and a smaller one on the poor. In some states all citizens who have registered themselves are allowed to attend the assembly and to try causes ; but if after registration they do not attend 25 either in the assembly or at the courts, heavy fines are imposed upon them. The intention is that through fear of the fines they may avoid registering themselves, and then they cannot sit in the law-courts or in the assembly. Concerning (4) the possession of arms, and (5) gymnastic exercises, they legislate in a similar spirit. For the poor 30 are not obliged to have arms, but the rich are fined for not having them ; and in like manner no penalty is inflicted on the poor for non-attendance at the gymnasium, and consequently, having nothing to fear, they do not attend, whereas the rich are liable to a fine, and therefore they take care to attend.

These are the devices of oligarchical legislators, and in 35 democracies they have counter devices. They pay the poor for attending the assemblies and the law-courts,

and they inflict no penalty on the rich for non-attendance. It is obvious that he who would duly mix the
two principles should combine the practice of both, and
provide that the poor should be paid to attend, and the
40 rich fined if they do not attend, for then all will take
part; if there is no such combination, power will be in
1297ᵇ the hands of one party only. The government should
be confined to those who carry arms. As to the property
qualification, no absolute rule can be laid down, but we
must see what is the highest qualification sufficiently
5 comprehensive to secure that the number of those who
have the rights of citizens exceeds the number of those
excluded. Even if they have no share in office, the
poor, provided only that they are not outraged or deprived of their property, will be quiet enough.

But to secure gentle treatment for the poor is not an
easy thing, since a ruling class is not always humane.
10 And in time of war the poor are apt to hesitate unless
they are fed; when fed, they are willing enough to
fight. In some states the government is vested, not only
in those who are actually serving, but also in those
who have served; among the Malians, for example, the
15 governing body consisted of the latter, while the magistrates were chosen from those actually on service. And
the earliest government which existed among the Hellenes, after the overthrow of the kingly power, grew up
out of the warrior class, and was originally taken from the
knights (for strength and superiority in war at that time
depended on cavalry;[1] indeed, without discipline, in-
20 fantry are useless, and in ancient times there was no
military knowledge or tactics, and therefore the strength
of armies lay in their cavalry). But when cities increased
and the heavy-armed grew in strength, more had a
share in the government; and this is the reason why
the states which we call constitutional governments
25 have been hitherto called democracies. Ancient constitutions, as might be expected, were oligarchical and
royal; their population being small they had no con-

[1] Cp. 1289ᵇ 36, vi. 1321ᵃ 8.

siderable middle class ; the people were weak in numbers and organization, and were therefore more contented to be governed.

I have explained why there are various forms of government, and why there are more than is generally supposed ; for democracy, as well as other constitutions, 30 has more than one form: also what their differences are, and whence they arise, and what is the best form of government, speaking generally, and to whom the various forms of government are best suited ; all this has now been explained.

14 Having thus gained an appropriate basis of discussion 35 we will proceed to speak of the points which follow next in order. We will consider the subject not only in general but with reference to particular constitutions. All constitutions have three elements, concerning which the good lawgiver has to regard what is expedient for each constitution. When they are well-ordered, the con-stitution is well-ordered, and as they differ from one another, constitutions differ. There is (1) one element 40 which deliberates about public affairs ; secondly (2) that 1298ᵃ concerned with the magistracies—the questions being, what they should be, over what they should exercise authority, and what should be the mode of electing to them ; and thirdly (3) that which has judicial power.

The deliberative element has authority in matters of war and peace, in making and unmaking alliances ; it passes 5 laws, inflicts death, exile, confiscation, elects magistrates and audits their accounts. These powers must be assigned either all to all the citizens or all to some of them (for example, to one or more magistracies, or different causes to different magistracies),[1] or some of them to all, and others of them only to some. That all things should be decided by all is characteristic of democracy ; this is the 10 sort of equality which the people desire. But there are various ways in which all may share in the government ;

---

[1] Reading in l. 8 (οἷον . . . πλείοσιν, ἢ ἑτέραις ἑτέρας) with the best MSS.

they may deliberate, not all in one body, but by turns, as in the constitution of Telecles the Milesian. There are other constitutions in which the boards of magistrates meet 15 and deliberate, but come into office by turns, and are elected out of the tribes and the very smallest divisions of the state, until every one has obtained office in his turn. The citizens, on the other hand, are assembled only for the purposes of legislation, and to consult about the constitution, and to hear the edicts of the magistrates. In another 20 variety of democracy the citizens form one assembly, but meet only to elect magistrates, to pass laws, to advise about war and peace, and to make scrutinies. Other matters are referred severally to special magistrates, who are elected by vote or by lot out of all the citizens. Or 25 again, the citizens meet about election to offices and about scrutinies, and deliberate concerning war or alliances while other matters are administered by the magistrates, who, as far as is possible,[1] are elected by vote. I am speaking of those magistracies in which special knowledge is required. A fourth form of democracy is when all the 30 citizens meet to deliberate about everything, and the magistrates decide nothing, but only make the preliminary inquiries ; and that is the way in which the last and worst form of democracy, corresponding, as we maintain,[2] to the close family oligarchy and to tyranny, is at present administered. All these modes are democratical.

On the other hand, that some should deliberate about 35 all is oligarchical. This again is a mode which, like the democratical, has many forms. When the deliberative class being elected out of those who have a moderate qualification are numerous and they respect and obey the prohibitions of the law without altering it, and any one who has the required qualification shares in the government, then, just because of this moderation, the 40 oligarchy inclines towards polity. But when only selected individuals and not the whole people share in the **1298^b** deliberations of the state, then, although, as in the former

---

[1] Sc. in an advanced democracy. Cp. vi. 1317^b 21.
[2] 1292^a 17–21, ^b 7–10, 1293^a 32–34.

case, they observe the law, the government is a pure oligarchy. Or, again, when those who have the power of deliberation are self-elected, and son succeeds father, and they and not the laws are supreme—the government is of necessity oligarchical. Where, again, particular 5 persons[1] have authority in particular matters ;—for example, when the whole people decide about peace and war and hold scrutinies, but the magistrates regulate everything else, and they are elected by vote—there the government is an aristocracy. And if some questions are decided by magistrates elected by vote, and others by magistrates elected by lot, either absolutely or out of select candidates, or elected partly by vote, partly by lot—these practices are partly characteristic of an aristocratical government, 10 and partly of a pure constitutional government.

These are the various forms of the deliberative body ; they correspond to the various forms of government. And the government of each state is administered according to one or other of the principles which have been laid down. Now it is for the interest of democracy, according to the most prevalent notion of it (I am speaking of that extreme form of democracy in which the people are supreme even over the laws), with a view to 15 better deliberation to adopt the custom of oligarchies respecting courts of law. For in oligarchies the rich who are wanted to be judges are compelled to attend under pain of a fine, whereas in democracies the poor are paid to attend. And this practice of oligarchies should be adopted by democracies in their public assemblies, for they will advise better if they all deliberate together,— 20 the people with the notables and the notables with the people. It is also a good plan that those who deliberate should be elected by vote or by lot in equal numbers out of the different classes ; and that if the people greatly exceed in number those who have political training, pay should not be given to all, but only to as many as would 25 balance the number of the notables, or that the number

[1] Retaining τινές in l. 5 and omitting the comma before πάντες in l. 6.

in excess should be eliminated by lot. But in oligarchies either certain persons should be co-opted from the mass, or a class of officers should be appointed such as exist in some states, who are termed probuli and guardians of the law ; and the citizens should occupy themselves exclusively with matters on which these have previously 30 deliberated ; for so the people will have a share in the deliberations of the state, but will not be able to disturb the principles of the constitution. Again, in oligarchies either the people ought to accept the measures of the government, or not to pass anything contrary to them ; or, if all are allowed to share in counsel, the decision should rest with the magistrates. The opposite of what is done in constitutional governments should be the rule 35 in oligarchies ; the veto of the majority should be final, their assent not final, but the proposal should be referred back to the magistrates. Whereas in constitutional governments they take the contrary course ; the few have 40 the negative, not the affirmative power ; the affirmation 1299ᵃ of everything rests with the multitude.

These, then, are our conclusions respecting the deliberative, that is, the supreme element in states.

Next we will proceed to consider the distribution of 15 offices ; this, too, being a part of politics concerning 5 which many questions arise :—What shall their number be ? Over what shall they preside, and what shall be their duration ? Sometimes they last for six months, sometimes for less ; sometimes they are annual, whilst in other cases offices are held for still longer periods. Shall they be for life or for a long term of years ; or, if for a short term only, shall the same persons hold them over and 10 over again, or once only ? Also about the appointment to them,—from whom are they to be chosen, by whom, and how ? We should first be in a position to say what are the possible varieties of them, and then we may proceed to determine which are suited to different forms of government. But what are to be included under the term ' offices ' ? That is a question not quite so easily

answered. For a political community requires many 15
officers; and not every one who is chosen by vote or by
lot is to be regarded as a ruler. In the first place there
are the priests, who must be distinguished from political
officers; masters of choruses and heralds, even ambassadors, are elected by vote. Some duties of superinten- 20
dence again are political, extending either to all the
citizens in a single sphere of action, like the office of
the general who superintends them when they are in the
field, or to a section of them only, like the inspectorships
of women or of youth. Other offices are concerned
with household management, like that of the corn
measurers who exist in many states and are elected
officers. There are also menial offices which the rich
have executed by their slaves. Speaking generally, those 25
are to be called offices to which the duties are assigned
of deliberating about certain measures and of judging and
commanding, especially the last; for to command is the
especial duty of a magistrate. But the question is not of
any importance in practice; no one has ever brought
into court the meaning of the word, although such
problems have a speculative interest.   30
    What kinds of offices, and how many, are necessary to
the existence of a state, and which, if not necessary, yet
conduce to its well-being, are much more important considerations, affecting all constitutions, but more especially
small states. For in great states it is possible, and indeed 35
necessary, that every office should have a special function; where the citizens are numerous, many may hold
office. And so it happens that some offices a man holds
a second time only after a long interval, and others
he holds once only; and certainly every work is better
done which receives the sole, and not the divided 1299^b
attention of the worker. But in small states it is
necessary to combine many offices in a few hands, since
the small number of citizens does not admit of many
holding office:—for who will there be to succeed them?
And yet small states at times require the same offices 5
and laws as large ones; the difference is that the one

want them often, the others only after long intervals.
Hence there is no reason why the care of many offices
should not be imposed on the same person, for they will
not interfere with each other. When the population is
10 small, offices should be like the spits which also serve to
hold a lamp.¹ We must first ascertain how many
magistrates are necessary in every state, and also how
many are not exactly necessary, but are nevertheless
useful, and then there will be no difficulty in seeing ²
what offices can be combined in one. We should also
15 know over which matters several local tribunals are to
have jurisdiction, and in which authority should be
centralized: for example, should one person keep order
in the market and another in some other place, or should
the same person be responsible everywhere? Again,
should offices be divided according to the subjects with
which they deal, or according to the persons with whom
they deal : I mean to say, should one person see to good
order in general, or one look after the boys, another after
20 the women, and so on? Further, under different constitutions, should the magistrates be the same or different?
For example, in democracy, oligarchy, aristocracy, monarchy, should there be the same magistrates, although
they are elected, not out of equal or similar classes
of citizens, but differently under different constitutions
—in aristocracies, for example, they are chosen from the
25 educated, in oligarchies from the wealthy, and in democracies from the free,— or are there certain differences in
the offices answering to them as well,³ and may the same
be suitable to some, but different offices to others? For
in some states it may be convenient that the same office
should have a more extensive, in other states a narrower
30 sphere. Special offices are peculiar to certain forms of
government :—for example that of probuli, which is not
a democratic office, although a bule or council is. There
must be some body of men whose duty is to prepare

¹ Cp. 1252^b 2.　　² Reading συνίδοι in l. 12 with Bojesen.
³ Reading in l. 27 οὖσαι καὶ κατὰ ταύτας (with some good MSS.)
διαφοραί (with Vettori).

measures for the people in order that they may not be diverted from their business; when these are few in number, the state inclines to an oligarchy: or rather the probuli must always be few, and are therefore an 35 oligarchical element. But when both institutions exist in a state, the probuli are a check on the council; for the counsellor is a democratic element, but the probuli are oligarchical. Even the power of the council disappears when democracy has taken that extreme form in 1300^a which the people themselves are always meeting and deliberating about everything. This is the case when the members of the assembly receive abundant pay; for they have nothing to do and are always holding assemblies and deciding everything for themselves. A magistracy which controls the boys or the women, or any similar office, is suited to an aristocracy rather than to 5 a democracy; for how can the magistrates prevent the wives of the poor from going out of doors? Neither is it an oligarchical office; for the wives of the oligarchs are too fine to be controlled.

Enough of these matters. I will now inquire into appointments to offices. The varieties depend on three 10 terms, and the combinations of these give all possible modes: first, who appoints? secondly, from whom? and thirdly, how? Each of these three admits of three varieties: (A) All the citizens, or (B) only some, 15 appoint. Either (1) the magistrates are chosen out of all or (2) out of some who are distinguished either by a property qualification, or by birth, or merit, or for some special reason, as at Megara only those were eligible who had returned from exile and fought together against the democracy. They may be appointed either (a) by vote or (β) by lot. Again, these several varieties may be coupled, I mean that (C) some officers may be elected by 20 some, others by all, and (3) some again out of some, and others out of all, and (γ) some by vote and others by lot. Each variety of these terms admits of four modes.

For either (A 1 a) all may appoint from all by vote, or (A 1 β) all from all by lot, or (A 2 a) all from some by

vote, or (A 2 β) all from some by lot (and if from all,
25 either by sections, as, for example, by tribes, and wards,
and phratries, until all the citizens have been gone
through ; or the citizens may be in all cases eligible indis-
criminately) ; or again (A 1 γ, A 2 γ) to some offices in the
one way, to some in the other.   Again, if it is only some
that appoint, they may do so either (B 1 a) from all by
vote, or (B 1 β) from all by lot, or (B 2 a) from some by vote,
or (B 2 β) from same by lot, or to some offices in the
one way, to others in the other, i. e. (B 1 γ) from all, to some
offices by vote, to some by lot, and (B 2 γ) from some,
30 to some offices by vote, to some by lot.   Thus the modes
that arise, apart from two (C, 3) out of the three couplings,
number twelve.   Of these systems two are popular, that
all should appoint from all (A 1 a) by vote or (A 1 β) by
35 lot,—or (A 1 γ) by both.   That all should not appoint
at once, but should appoint from all or from some
either by lot or by vote or by both, or appoint to some
offices from all and to others from some ('by both' meaning to some offices by lot, to others by vote), is characteristic of a polity.   And (B 1 γ) that some should appoint
from all, to some offices by vote, to others by lot, is also
characteristic of a polity, but more oligarchical than the
40 former method.   And (A 3 a, β, γ, B 3 a, β, γ) to appoint
from both, to some offices from all, to others from some,
is characteristic of a polity with a leaning towards
1300ᵇ aristocracy.   That (B 2) some should appoint from some
is oligarchical,—even (B 2 β) that some should appoint
from some by lot (and if this does not actually occur, it is
none the less oligarchical in character), or (B 2 γ) that
some should appoint from some by both.   (B 1 a) that
some should appoint from all, and (A 2 a) that all
should appoint from some, by vote, is aristocratic.[1]

5   These are the different modes of constituting magistrates, and these correspond to different forms of govern-

---

[1] 1300ᵃ 10-ᵇ 5.   It is recognized by all the commentators that this
passage requires considerable emendation.   The text presupposed
by the translation in ᵃ 23-ᵇ 5 will be found at the end of this
note, and it will be observed that practically all the corruptions
presumed to have occurred are such as may well have resulted

ment :—which are proper to which, or how they ought to be established, will be evident when we determine the nature of their powers.[1] By powers I mean such powers from homoioteleuton or from dittography; most of the emendations have been anticipated by earlier scholars, though none has given quite the same interpretation of the passage as a whole.

The logic of the passage is as follows. The modes of appointment to office depend on three variants, each of which may have any one of three values. Twenty-seven modes are therefore possible. But one value of each variant is an intermediate between the other two, and it would seem that at first Aristotle means to ignore these intermediates. He therefore says, 1300^a22, that each variety has four, not nine, modes. In fact, however, in ll. 23-30 he introduces one of the intermediates (γ), and thus exhibits each of two varieties as having six, i. e. 2 × 3 modes. Thus, omitting two of the intermediates, he gets 12 (2 × 2 × 3) modes (l. 30).

It seems clear that the number 12 is arrived at solely by consideration of the original variants, and therefore that the further distinction drawn in ll. 24-26 is purely incidental. 1300^a 34-38 is likewise incidental.

On our interpretation of the passage, all the 27 possible combinations are in 1300^a 31-^b 5 assigned to their appropriate constitutions except:

1. The cases in which all appoint out of some by lot, or to some offices by vote, to others by lot (A 2 β, A 2 γ).

2. The case in which some appoint out of all by lot (B 1 β).

3. The cases in which *all* appoint to some offices, *some* to other offices (the nine combinations involving C).

(3) seems to be omitted as an unnecessary refinement. (1) could be introduced by adding καὶ τὸ πάντας ἐκ τινῶν ἢ κλήρῳ ἢ ἀμφοῖν after ἀμφοῖν in l. 33. As regards (2) the distinction between appointment by lot by all and by some is somewhat unmeaning. (2) could, however, be introduced by excising τὰς μὲν αἱρέσει in ^a 38, and by reading ἢ κλήρῳ (with some authority) and retaining ἢ ἀμφοῖν (τὰς μὲν κλήρῳ τὰς δ' αἱρέσει) in ^a 39.

1300^a 23-^b 5 ἢ γὰρ πάντες ἐκ πάντων αἱρέσει ἢ πάντες ἐκ πάντων κλήρῳ ⟨ἢ πάντες ἐκ τινῶν αἱρέσει ἢ πάντες ἐκ τινῶν κλήρῳ⟩ (καί, εἰ ἐξ ἁπάντων, ἢ ὡς ἀνὰ μέρος . . . ἢ ἀεὶ ἐξ ἁπάντων), ἢ καὶ τὰ μὲν οὕτως τὰ δὲ ἐκείνως· πάλιν εἰ τινὲς οἱ καθιστάντες, ἢ ἐκ πάντων αἱρέσει ἢ ἐκ πάντων κλήρῳ ἢ ἐκ τινῶν αἱρέσει ἢ ἐκ τινῶν κλήρῳ, ἢ τὰ μὲν οὕτως τὰ δὲ ἐκείνως, λέγω δὲ τὰ μὲν ἐκ πάντων αἱρέσει τὰ δὲ κλήρῳ ⟨καὶ τὰ μὲν ἐκ τινῶν αἱρέσει τὰ δὲ κλήρῳ⟩. ὥστε δώδεκα οἱ τρόποι γίνονται χωρὶς τῶν δύο συνδυασμῶν. τούτων δ' αἱ μὲν δύο καταστάσεις δημοτικαί, τὸ πάντας ἐκ πάντων αἱρέσει ἢ κλήρῳ [γίνεσθαι],—ἢ ἀμφοῖν, τὰς μὲν κλήρῳ τὰς δ' αἱρέσει τῶν ἀρχῶν· τὸ δὲ μὴ πάντας ἅμα μὲν καθιστάναι, ἐξ ἁπάντων δ' ἢ ἐκ τινῶν ἢ κλήρῳ ἢ αἱρέσει ἢ ἀμφοῖν, ἢ τὰς μὲν ἐκ πάντων τὰς δ' ἐκ τινῶν [ἀμφοῖν] (τὸ δὲ ἀμφοῖν λέγω τὰς μὲν κλήρῳ τὰς δ' αἱρέσει), πολιτικόν, καὶ τὸ τινὰς ἐκ πάντων τὰς αἱρέσει καθιστάναι τὰς δὲ κλήρῳ [ἢ ἀμφοῖν, τὰς μὲν κλήρῳ τὰς δ' αἱρέσει· ὀλιγαρχικόν] (ὀλιγαρχικώτερον δέ). καὶ τὸ ἐξ ἀμφοῖν, τὰς μὲν ἐκ πάντων τὰς δ' ἐκ τινῶν, πολιτικὸν ἀριστοκρατικῶς [ἢ τὰς μὲν αἱρέσει τὰς δὲ κλήρῳ]. τὸ δὲ τινὰς ἐκ τινῶν ὀλιγαρχικόν, καὶ τὸ τινὰς ἐκ τινῶν κλήρῳ (μὴ γινόμενον δ' ὁμοίως) καὶ τὸ τινὰς ἐκ τινῶν ἀμφοῖν. τὸ δὲ τινὰς ἐξ ἁπάντων τό τε ἐκ τινῶν πάντας αἱρέσει ἀριστοκρατικόν.

[1] The promise is not fulfilled in the *Politics*.

as a magistrate exercises over the revenue or in defence
10 of the country; for there are various kinds of power: the
power of the general, for example, is not the same with
that which regulates contracts in the market.

Of the three parts of government, the judicial remains 16
to be considered, and this we shall divide on the same
principle. There are three points on which the varieties
15 of law-courts depend: The persons from whom they
are appointed, the matters with which they are concerned,
and the manner of their appointment. I mean, (1) are
the judges taken from all, or from some only? (2) how
many kinds of law-courts are there? (3) are the judges
chosen by vote or by lot?

First, let me determine how many kinds of law-courts
there are. They are eight in number: One is the court
20 of audits or scrutinies; a second takes cognizance of
ordinary offences against the state; a third is concerned
with   treason   against   the   constitution;   the   fourth
determines disputes respecting penalties, whether[1] raised
by magistrates or by private persons; the fifth decides
the more important civil cases; the sixth tries cases of
25 homicide, which are of various kinds, (*a*) premeditated,
(*b*) involuntary, (*c*) cases in which the guilt is confessed
but the justice is disputed; and there may be a fourth
court (*d*) in which murderers who have fled from justice
are tried[2] after their return; such as the Court of Phreatto
is said to be at Athens. But cases of this sort rarely
30 happen at all even in large cities. The different kinds of
homicide may be tried either by the same or by
different courts. (7) There are courts for strangers:—of
these there are two subdivisions, (*a*) for the settlement
of their disputes with one another, (*b*) for the settlement
of disputes between them and the citizens. And besides
all these there must be (8) courts for small suits about
sums of a drachma up to five drachmas, or a little more,
which have to be determined, but they do not require
many judges.

---

[1] Retaining καί in l. 21.
[2] For a second murder. Cf. Dem. *c. Aristocr.* c. 77.

Nothing more need be said of these small suits, nor of 35 the courts for homicide and for strangers:—I would rather speak of political cases, which, when mismanaged, create division and disturbances in constitutions.

Now if all the citizens judge, in all the different cases which I have distinguished, they may be appointed by vote or by lot, or sometimes by lot and sometimes by 40 vote. Or when a single class of causes are tried, the judges who decide them may be appointed, some by vote, and some by lot. These then are the four modes 1301^a of appointing judges from the whole people, and there will be likewise four modes, if they are elected from a part only ; for they may be appointed from some by vote and judge in all causes; or they may be appointed from some by lot and judge in all causes ; or they may be elected in some cases by vote, and in some cases taken by lot, or some courts, even when judging the same causes, may be composed of members some appointed by vote and some by lot. These modes, then, as was said, answer[1] 5 to those previously mentioned.

Once more, the modes of appointment may be combined ; I mean, that some may be chosen out of the whole people, others out of some, some out of both ; for example, the same tribunal may be composed of some who were elected out of all, and of others who were elected out of some, either by vote or by lot or by both.

In how many forms law-courts can be established has 10 now been considered. The first form, viz. that in which the judges are taken from all the citizens, and in which all causes are tried, is democratical ; the second, which is composed of a few only who try all causes, oligarchical ; the third, in which some courts are taken from all classes, and some from certain classes only, aristocratical and 15 constitutional.

[1] Inserting ἀντίστροφοι after τρόποι in l. 6, with Newman.

BOOK V

THE design which we proposed to ourselves is now I
20 nearly completed.[1] Next in order follow the causes of
revolution in states, how many, and of what nature they
are; what modes of destruction apply to particular states,
and out of what, and into what they mostly change; also
what are the modes of preservation in states generally,
or in a particular state, and by what means each state
may be best preserved: these questions remain to be
considered.

25 In the first place we must assume as our starting-point
that in the many forms of government which have sprung
up there has always been an acknowledgement of justice
and proportionate equality, although mankind fail in
attaining them, as indeed I have already explained.[2]
Democracy, for example, arises out of the notion that
those who are equal in any respect are equal in all
30 respects; because men are equally free, they claim to
be absolutely equal. Oligarchy is based on the notion
that those who are unequal in one respect are in all
respects unequal; being unequal, that is, in property,
they suppose themselves to be unequal absolutely. The
democrats think that as they are equal they ought to be
equal in all things; while the oligarchs, under the idea
that they are unequal, claim too much, which is one form
35 of inequality. All these forms of government have a
kind of justice, but, tried by an absolute standard, they
are faulty; and, therefore, both parties, whenever their
share in the government does not accord with their pre-
conceived ideas, stir up revolution. Those who excel in
40 virtue have the best right of all to rebel (for they alone
1301^b can with reason be deemed absolutely unequal),[3] but then
they are of all men the least inclined to do so.[4]   There

---

[1] Cp. iv. c. 2.   [2] iii. 1282^b 18-30, cp. 1280^a 9 sqq.
[3] Cp. iii. 1284^b 28-34.   [4] Cp. 1304^b 4.

is also a superiority which is claimed by men of rank ;
for they are thought noble because they spring from
wealthy and virtuous ancestors.[1] Here then, so to speak,
are opened the very springs and fountains of revolution ; 5
and hence arise two sorts of changes in governments ; the
one affecting the constitution, when men seek to change
from an existing form into some other, for example, from
democracy into oligarchy, and from oligarchy into democracy, or from either of them into constitutional government or aristocracy, and conversely ; the other not 10
affecting the constitution, when, without disturbing the
form of government, whether oligarchy, or monarchy, or
any other, they try to get the administration into their
own hands.[2] Further, there is a question of degree ; an
oligarchy, for example, may become more or less oligarchical, and a democracy more or less democratical ; and 15
in like manner the characteristics of the other forms of
government may be more or less strictly maintained.
Or the revolution may be directed against a portion of
the constitution only, e.g. the establishment or overthrow
of a particular office : as at Sparta it is said that Lysander
attempted to overthrow the monarchy, and king Pausa- 20
nias,[3] the ephoralty. At Epidamnus, too, the change
was partial. For instead of phylarchs or heads of tribes,
a council was appointed ; but to this day the magistrates
are the only members of the ruling class who are compelled to go to the Heliaea when an election takes place,
and the office of the single archon[4] was another oligar- 25
chical feature. Everywhere inequality is a cause of revolution, but an inequality in which there is no proportion—
for instance, a perpetual monarchy among equals ; and
always it is the desire of equality which rises in rebellion.

Now equality is of two kinds, numerical and propor-
tional ; by the first I mean sameness or equality in 30
number or size ; by the second, equality of ratios. For
example, the excess of three over two is numerically equal
to the excess of two over one ; whereas four exceeds two

[1] Cp. iv. 1294^a21.   [2] Cp. iv. 1292^b 11.
[3] Cp. vii. 1333^b 34.   [4] Cp. iii. 1287^a 7.

in the same ratio in which two exceeds one, for two is the
35 same part of four that one is of two, namely, the half.
As I was saying before,[1] men agree that justice in the
abstract is proportion, but they differ in that some think
that if they are equal in any respect they are equal
absolutely, others that if they are unequal in any respect
they should be unequal in all. Hence there are two
40 principal forms of government, democracy and oligarchy;
1302ᵃ for good birth and virtue are rare, but wealth and numbers
are more common. In what city shall we find a hundred
persons of good birth and of virtue? whereas the rich
everywhere abound. That a state should be ordered,
simply and wholly, according to either kind of equality, is
not a good thing ; the proof is the fact that such forms of
5 government never last. They are originally based on
a mistake, and, as they begin badly, cannot fail to end
badly. The inference is that both kinds of equality should
be employed ; numerical in some cases, and proportionate
in others.

Still democracy appears to be safer and less liable to
revolution than oligarchy.[2] For in oligarchies[3] there is
10 the double danger of the oligarchs falling out among
themselves and also with the people ; but in democracies[4] there is only the danger of a quarrel with
the oligarchs. No dissension worth mentioning arises
among the people themselves. And we may further
remark that a government which is composed of the
middle class more nearly approximates to democracy
15 than to oligarchy, and is the safest of the imperfect forms
of government.

In considering how dissensions and political revolutions 2
arise, we must first of all ascertain the beginnings and
causes of them which affect constitutions generally. They
may be said to be three in number ; and we have now
20 to give an outline of each. We want to know (1) what
is the feeling? (2) what are the motives of those who
make them ? (3) whence arise political disturbances and

[1] ᵃ26.   [2] Cp. iv. 1296ᵃ 13.   [3] Cp. c. 6.   [4] Cp. c. 5.

quarrels? The universal and chief cause of this revolutionary feeling has been already mentioned ;[1] viz. the
desire of equality, when men think that they are equal to 25
others who have more than themselves; or, again, the
desire of inequality and superiority, when conceiving
themselves to be superior they think that they have not
more but the same or less than their inferiors; preten-
sions which may and may not be just. Inferiors revolt in
order that they may be equal, and equals that they may be 30
superior. Such is the state of mind which creates revolutions. The motives for making them are the desire of
gain and honour, or the fear of dishonour and loss; the
authors of them want to divert punishment or dishonour
from themselves or their friends. The causes and reasons
of revolutions, whereby men are themselves affected in 35
the way described, and about the things which I have
mentioned, viewed in one way may be regarded as seven,
and in another as more than seven. Two of them have
been already noticed ;[2] but they act in a different manner,
for men are excited against one another by the love of
gain and honour—not, as in the case which I have just 40
supposed, in order to obtain them for themselves, but at 1302^b
seeing others, justly or unjustly, engrossing them. Other
causes are insolence, fear, excessive predominance,
contempt, disproportionate increase in some part of the
state; causes of another sort are election intrigues,
carelessness, neglect about trifles, dissimilarity of elements.

3   What share insolence and avarice have in creating 5
revolutions, and how they work, is plain enough. When
the magistrates are insolent and grasping they conspire
against one another and also against the constitution
from which they derive their power, making their gains
either at the expense of individuals or of the public. It 10
is evident, again, what an influence honour exerts and
how it is a cause of revolution. Men who are themselves dishonoured and who see others obtaining honours

---

[1] 1301^a 33 sqq., [b] 35 sqq.   [2] l. 32.

rise in rebellion ; the honour or dishonour when un-
deserved is unjust ; and just when awarded according to
15 merit. Again, superiority is a cause of revolution when
one or more persons have a power which is too much for
the state and the power of the government ; this is a
condition of affairs out of which there arises a monarchy,
or a family oligarchy. And therefore, in some places,
as at Athens and Argos, they have recourse to ostracism.[1]
But how much better to provide from the first that there
20 should be no such pre-eminent individuals instead of letting
them come into existence and then finding a remedy.

Another cause of revolution is fear. Either men have
committed wrong, and are afraid of punishment, or they
are expecting to suffer wrong and are desirous of anticipating their enemy. Thus at Rhodes the notables
conspired against the people through fear of the suits
25 that were brought against them.[2]　Contempt is also a
cause of insurrection and revolution ; for example, in
oligarchies—when those who have no share in the state
are the majority, they revolt, because they think that they
are the stronger. Or, again, in democracies, the rich
despise the disorder and anarchy of the state ; at Thebes,
for example, where, after the battle of Oenophyta, the
30 bad administration of the democracy led to its ruin. At
Megara the fall of the democracy was due to a defeat
occasioned by disorder and anarchy. And at Syracuse
the democracy aroused contempt before the tyranny of
Gelo arose ; at Rhodes, before the insurrection.

Political revolutions also spring from a disproportionate
35 increase in any part of the state. For as a body is made
up of many members, and every member ought to grow
in proportion,[3] that symmetry may be preserved ; but
loses its nature if the foot be four cubits long and the
rest of the body two spans ; and, should the abnormal
increase be one of quality as well as of quantity, may even
40 take the form of another animal : even so a state has many
1303^a parts, of which some one may often grow imperceptibly ;
for example, the number of poor in democracies and in

---

[1] Cp. iii. 1284^a 17.　　[2] Cp. 1304^b 27.　　[3] Cp. iii. 1284^b 8.

constitutional states. And this disproportion may sometimes happen by an accident, as at Tarentum, from a defeat in which many of the notables were slain in a battle
with the Iapygians just after the Persian War, the consti- 5
tutional government in consequence becoming a democracy; or as was the case at Argos, where the Argives,
after their army had been cut to pieces on the seventh day
of the month by Cleomenes the Lacedaemonian, were
compelled to admit to citizenship some of their perioeci;
and at Athens, when, after frequent defeats of their
infantry at the time of the Peloponnesian War, the
notables were reduced in number, because the soldiers
had to be taken from the roll of citizens.   Revolutions 10
arise from this cause as well, in democracies as in other
forms of government, but not to so great an extent.
When the rich grow numerous or properties increase, the
form of government changes into an oligarchy or a government of families.   Forms of government also change—
sometimes even without revolution, owing to election contests, as at Heraea (where, instead of electing their magis- 15
trates, they took them by lot, because the electors were
in the habit of choosing their own partisans); or owing
to carelessness, when disloyal persons are allowed to find
their way into the highest offices, as at Oreum, where,
upon the accession of Heracleodorus to office, the oligarchy was overthrown, and changed by him into a
constitutional and democratical government.

Again, the revolution may be facilitated by the slight- 20
ness of the change; I mean that a great change may
sometimes slip into the constitution through neglect of
a small matter; at Ambracia, for instance, the qualification for office, small at first, was eventually reduced to
nothing.   For the Ambraciots thought that a small
qualification was much the same as none at all.

Another cause of revolution is difference of races 25
which do not at once acquire a common spirit; for a
state is not the growth of a day, any more than it grows
out of a multitude brought together by accident.   Hence
the reception of strangers in colonies, either at the time of

their foundation or afterwards, has generally produced revolution; for example, the Achaeans who joined the Troezenians in the foundation of Sybaris, becoming later
30 the more numerous, expelled them; hence the curse fell upon Sybaris. At Thurii the Sybarites quarrelled with their fellow-colonists; thinking that the land belonged to them, they wanted too much of it and were driven out. At Byzantium the new colonists were detected in a conspiracy, and were expelled by force of arms; the people of Antissa, who had received the Chian exiles, fought with
35 them, and drove them out; and the Zancleans, after having received the Samians, were driven by them out of their own city. The citizens of Apollonia on the Euxine, after the introduction of a fresh body of colonists, had a revolution; the Syracusans, after the expulsion of
1303ᵇ their tyrants, having admitted strangers and mercenaries to the rights of citizenship, quarrelled and came to blows; the people of Amphipolis, having received Chalcidian colonists, were nearly all expelled by them.

Now, in oligarchies the masses make revolution under
5 the idea that they are unjustly treated, because, as I said before,[1] they are equals, and have not an equal share, and in democracies the notables revolt, because they are not equals, and yet have only an equal share.

Again, the situation of cities is a cause of revolution when the country is not naturally adapted to preserve the unity of the state. For example, the Chytians at Clazomenae did not agree with the people of the island; and the people of Colophon quarrelled with the Notians;
10 at Athens, too, the inhabitants of the Piraeus are more democratic than those who live in the city. For just as in war the impediment of a ditch, though ever so small, may break a regiment, so every cause of difference, how-
15 ever slight, makes a breach in a city. The greatest opposition is confessedly that of virtue and vice; next comes that of wealth and poverty; and there are other antagonistic elements, greater or less, of which one is this difference of place.

[1] 1301ᵃ 33.

4   In revolutions the occasions may be trifling, but great
interests are at stake. Even trifles are most important
when they concern the rulers, as was the case of old at 20
Syracuse; for the Syracusan constitution was once
changed by a love-quarrel of two young men, who were in
the government. The story is that while one of them was
away from home his beloved was gained over by his
companion, and he to revenge himself seduced the other's
wife. They then drew the members of the ruling class 25
into their quarrel and so split all the people into portions.
We learn from this story that we should be on our guard
against the beginnings of such evils, and should put an
end to the quarrels of chiefs and mighty men. The mis- .
take lies in the beginning—as the proverb says—' Well
begun is half done'; so an error at the beginning, though 30
quite small, bears the same ratio to the errors in the other
parts. In general, when the notables quarrel, the whole
city is involved, as happened in Hestiaea after the Persian
War. The occasion was the division of an inheritance;
one of two brothers refused to give an account of 35
their father's property and the treasure which he had
found: so the poorer of the two quarrelled with him
and enlisted in his cause the popular party, the other,
who was very rich, the wealthy classes.

At Delphi, again, a quarrel about a marriage was the
beginning of all the troubles which followed. In this **1304ᵃ**
case the bridegroom, fancying some occurrence to be of
evil omen, came to the bride, and went away without
taking her. Whereupon her relations, thinking that they
were insulted by him, put some of the sacred treasure
among his offerings while he was sacrificing, and then
slew him, pretending that he had been robbing the
temple. At Mytilene, too, a dispute about heiresses
was the beginning of many misfortunes, and led to the 5
war with the Athenians in which Paches took their city.
A wealthy citizen, named Timophanes, left two daughters;
Dexander, another citizen, wanted to obtain them for his
sons; but he was rejected in his suit, whereupon he
stirred up a revolution, and instigated the Athenians (of

10 whom he was proxenus) to interfere. A similar quarrel about an heiress arose at Phocis between Mnaseas the father of Mnason, and Euthycrates the father of Onomarchus; this was the beginning of the Sacred War· A marriage-quarrel was also the cause of a change in the government of Epidamnus. A certain man betrothed his 15 daughter to a person whose father, having been made a magistrate, fined the father of the girl, and the latter, stung by the insult, conspired with the unenfranchised classes to overthrow the state.

Governments also change into oligarchy or into democracy or into a constitutional government because the magistrates, or some other section of the state, increase 20 in power or renown. Thus at Athens the reputation gained by the court of the Areopagus, in the Persian War, seemed to tighten the reins of government. On the other hand, the victory of Salamis,[1] which was gained by the common people who served in the fleet, and won for the Athenians the empire due to command of the sea, strength- 25 ened the democracy. At Argos, the notables, having distinguished themselves against the Lacedaemonians in the battle of Mantinea, attempted to put down the democracy. At Syracuse, the people, having been the chief authors of the victory in the war with the Athenians, changed the constitutional government into democracy. 30 At Chalcis, the people, uniting with the notables, killed Phoxus the tyrant, and then seized the government. At Ambracia,[2] the people, in like manner, having joined with the conspirators in expelling the tyrant Periander, transferred the government to themselves. And generally, it should be remembered that those who have 35 secured power to the state, whether private citizens, or magistrates, or tribes, or any other part or section of the state, are apt to cause revolutions. For either envy of their greatness draws others into rebellion, or they themselves, in their pride of superiority, are unwilling to remain on a level with others.

Revolutions also break out when opposite parties, e.g. the

---

[1] Cp. ii. 1274ᵃ 12 ; viii. 1341ᵃ 29.   [2] Cp. 1311ᵃ 39.

rich and the people, are equally balanced, and there is **1304^b**
little or no middle class ; for, if either party were manifestly superior, the other would not risk an attack upon
them. And, for this reason, those who are eminent in
virtue usually do not stir up insurrections, always a
minority. Such are the beginnings and causes of the 5
disturbances and revolutions to which every form of
government is liable.

Revolutions are effected in two ways, by force and by
fraud. Force may be applied either at the time of
making the revolution or afterwards. Fraud, again, is 10
of two kinds; for (1) sometimes the citizens are deceived
into acquiescing in a change of government, and afterwards
they are held in subjection against their will. This was
what happened in the case of the Four Hundred, who
deceived the people by telling them that the king would
provide money for the war against the Lacedaemonians,
and, having cheated the people, still endeavoured to retain the government. (2) In other cases the people are 15
persuaded at first, and afterwards, by a repetition of the
persuasion, their goodwill and allegiance are retained.
The revolutions which effect constitutions generally
spring from the above-mentioned causes.[1]

5 And now, taking each constitution separately, we must
see what follows from the principles already laid down.

Revolutions in democracies are generally caused by 20
the intemperance of demagogues, who either in their
private capacity lay information against rich men until
they compel them to combine (for a common danger
unites even the bitterest enemies), or coming forward
in public stir up the people against them. The truth
of this remark is proved by a variety of examples. At 25
Cos the democracy was overthrown because wicked
demagogues arose, and the notables combined. At
Rhodes the demagogues not only provided pay for the
multitude, but prevented them from making good to
the trierarchs the sums which had been expended by

[1] Cp. 1302^a 17.

them ; and they, in consequence of the suits which were
30 brought against them, were compelled to combine and
put down the democracy.¹ The democracy at Heraclea
was overthrown shortly after the foundation of the colony
by the injustice of the demagogues, which drove out the
notables, who came back in a body and put an end to
the democracy. Much in the same manner the demo-
35 cracy at Megara ² was overturned ; there the demagogues
drove out many of the notables in order that they might
be able to confiscate their property. At length the
exiles, becoming numerous, returned, and, engaging and
defeating the people, established the oligarchy. The
1305ᵃ same thing happened with the democracy of Cyme, which
was overthrown by Thrasymachus. And we may observe
that in most states the changes have been of this
character. For sometimes the demagogues, in order to
curry favour with the people, wrong the notables and so
force them to combine ;—either they make a division of
their property, or diminish their incomes by the impo-
5 sition of public services, and sometimes they bring
accusations against the rich that they may have their
wealth to confiscate.³

Of old, the demagogue was also a general, and then
democracies changed into tyrannies. Most of the ancient
10 tyrants were originally demagogues.⁴ They are not so
now, but they were then ; and the reason is that they
were generals and not orators, for oratory had not yet
come into fashion. Whereas in our day, when the art of
rhetoric has made such progress, the orators lead the
people, but their ignorance of military matters prevents
them from usurping power ; at any rate instances to the
15 contrary are few and slight. Tyrannies were more
common formerly than now, for this reason also, that great
power was placed in the hands of individuals ; thus a
tyranny arose at Miletus out of the office of the Prytanis,
who had supreme authority in many important matters.⁵

---

¹ Cp. 1302ᵇ 23.   ² Cp. 1302ᵇ 31, iv. 1300ᵃ 17.
³ Cp. 1309ᵃ 14.   ⁴ Cp. 1310ᵇ 14; Plato, *Rep.* viii. 565 D.
⁵ Cp. 1310ᵇ 20.

Moreover, in those days, when cities were not large, the people dwelt in the fields, busy at their work; and their 20 chiefs, if they possessed any military talent, seized the opportunity, and winning the confidence of the masses by professing their hatred of the wealthy, they succeeded in obtaining the tyranny. Thus at Athens Peisistratus led a faction against the men of the plain,[1] and Theagenes at Megara slaughtered the cattle of the wealthy, which he found by the river side, where they 25 had put them to graze in land not their own. Dionysius, again, was thought worthy of the tyranny because he denounced Daphnaeus and the rich; his enmity to the notables won for him the confidence of the people. Changes also take place from the ancient to the latest form of democracy; for where there is a popular election 30 of the magistrates and no property qualification, the aspirants for office get hold of the people, and contrive at last even to set them above the laws. A more or less complete cure for this state of things is for the separate tribes, and not the whole people, to elect the magistrates.

These are the principal causes of revolutions in demo- 35 cracies.

6   There are two patent causes of revolutions in oligarchies: (1) First, when the oligarchs oppress the people, for then anybody is good enough to be their champion, especially if he be himself a member of the oligarchy, as Lygdamis at Naxos, who afterwards came to be tyrant. 40 But revolutions which commence outside the governing 1305ᵇ class may be further subdivided. Sometimes, when the government is very exclusive, the revolution is brought about by persons of the wealthy class who are excluded, as happened at Massalia and Istros and Heraclea, and 5 other cities. Those who had no share in the government created a disturbance, until first the elder brothers, and then the younger, were admitted; for in some places father and son, in others elder and younger brothers, do not hold office together. At Massalia the oligarchy 10

[1] See Herod. i. 59.

became more like a constitutional government, but at
Istros ended in a democracy, and at Heraclea was en-
larged to 600. At Cnidos, again, the oligarchy under-
went a considerable change. For the notables fell out
among themselves, because only a few shared in the
government ; there existed among them the rule already
mentioned, that father and son could not hold office
15 together, and, if there were several brothers, only the
eldest was admitted. The people took advantage of the
quarrel, and choosing one of the notables to be their
leader, attacked and conquered the oligarchs, who were
divided, and division is always a source of weakness.
The city of Erythrae, too, in old times was ruled, and
20 ruled well, by the Basilidae, but the people took offence
at the narrowness of the oligarchy and changed the
constitution.

(2) Of internal causes of revolutions in oligarchies one is
the personal rivalry of the oligarchs, which leads them to
play the demagogue. Now, the oligarchical demagogue
is of two sorts : either (a) he practises upon the oligarchs
themselves (for, although the oligarchy are quite a small
25 number, there may be a demagogue among them, as at
Athens Charicles' party won power by courting the Thirty,
that of Phrynichus by courting the Four Hundred); or
(b) the oligarchs may play the demagogue with the
people. This was the case at Larissa, where the guardians
of the citizens endeavoured to gain over the people be-
30 cause they were elected by them ; and such is the fate of
all oligarchies in which the magistrates are elected, as at
Abydos, not by the class to which they belong, but by
the heavy-armed or by the people, although they may
be required to have a high qualification, or to be members of a political club ; or, again, where the law-courts
are composed of persons outside the government, the
35 oligarchs flatter the people in order to obtain a decision
in their own favour, and so they change the constitution ;
this happened at Heraclea in Pontus. Again, oligarchies
change whenever any attempt is made to narrow them ;
for then those who desire equal rights are compelled to

call in the people. Changes in the oligarchy also occur
when the oligarchs waste their private property by
extravagant living; for then they want to innovate, and 40
either try to make themselves tyrants, or install some 1306^a
one else in the tyranny, as Hipparinus did Dionysius at
Syracuse, and as at Amphipolis[1] a man named Cleotimus
introduced Chalcidian colonists, and when they arrived,
stirred them up against the rich. For a like reason in
Aegina the person who carried on the negotiation with
Chares endeavoured to revolutionize the state. Sometimes 5
a party among the oligarchs try directly to create a political change; sometimes they rob the treasury, and then
either the thieves or, as happened at Apollonia in Pontus,
those who resist them in their thieving quarrel with the
rulers. But an oligarchy which is at unity with itself is
not easily destroyed from within; of this we may see an 10
example at Pharsalus, for there, although the rulers are
few in number, they govern a large city, because they
have a good understanding among themselves.

Oligarchies, again, are overthrown when another oligarchy is created within the original one, that is to
say, when the whole governing body is small and yet
they do not all share in the highest offices. Thus at 15
Elis the governing body was a small senate; and very few
ever found their way into it, because the senators were
only ninety in number, and were elected for life and out
of certain families in a manner similar to the Lacedaemonian elders. Oligarchy is liable to revolutions alike 20
in war and in peace; in war because, not being able to
trust the people, the oligarchs are compelled to hire
mercenaries, and the general who is in command of them
often ends in becoming a tyrant, as Timophanes did at
Corinth; or if there are more generals than one they
make themselves into a company of tyrants. Sometimes 25
the oligarchs, fearing this danger, give the people a share
in the government because their services are necessary to
them. And in time of peace, from mutual distrust, the
two parties hand over the defence of the state to the

[1] Cp. 1303^b 2.

army and to an arbiter between the two factions, who often ends the master of both. This happened at Larissa when Simos the Aleuad had the government, and at Abydos in the days of Iphiades and the political clubs. Revolutions also arise out of marriages or lawsuits which lead to the overthrow of one party among the oligarchs by another. Of quarrels about marriages I have already
35 mentioned [1] some instances ; another occurred at Eretria, where Diagoras overturned the oligarchy of the knights because he had been wronged about a marriage. A revolution at Heraclea, and another at Thebes, both arose out of decisions of law-courts upon a charge of adultery ; in both cases the punishment was just, but executed in the
1306ᵇ spirit of party, at Heraclea upon Eurytion,[2] and at Thebes upon Archias ; for their enemies were jealous of them [3] and so had them pilloried in the agora. Many oligarchies have been destroyed by some members of the ruling
5 class taking offence at their excessive despotism ; for example, the oligarchy at Cnidus and at Chios.

Changes of constitutional governments, and also of oligarchies which limit the office of counsellor, judge, or other magistrate to persons having a certain money qualification, often occur by accident. The qualification may have been originally fixed according to the circumstances
10 of the time, in such a manner as to include in an oligarchy a few only, or in a constitutional government the middle class. But after a time of prosperity, whether arising from peace or some other good fortune, the same property becomes many times as valuable, and then everybody participates in every office ; this happens
15 sometimes gradually and insensibly, and sometimes quickly. These are the causes of changes and revolutions in oligarchies.

We must remark generally, both of democracies and oligarchies, that they sometimes change, not into the opposite forms of government, but only into another

---

[1] 1303ᵇ 37–1304ᵃ 17.
[2] Reading Εὐρυτίωνος in l. 39 with some MSS.
[3] Reading αὐτοῖς in l. 2, as suggested by Liddell and Scott.

variety of the same class ; I mean to say, from those forms of democracy and oligarchy which are regulated 20 by law into those which are arbitrary, and conversely.

7 In aristocracies revolutions are stirred up when a few only share in the honours of the state; a cause which has been already shown [1] to affect oligarchies ; [2] for an aristocracy is a sort of oligarchy, and, like an oligarchy, 25 is the government of a few, although few not for the same reason ; hence the two are often confounded. And revolutions will be most likely to happen, and must happen, when the mass [3] of the people are of the high-spirited kind, and have a notion that they are as good as their rulers. Thus at Lacedaemon the so-called Partheniae, who were the sons [4] of the Spartan peers, attempted 30 a revolution, and, being detected, were sent away to colonize Tarentum. Again, revolutions occur when great men who are at least of equal merit are dishonoured by those higher in office, as Lysander was by the kings of Sparta ; or, when a brave man is excluded from the honours of the state, like Cinadon, who conspired against 35 the Spartans in the reign of Agesilaus; or, again, when some are very poor and others very rich, a state of society which is most often the result of war, as at Lacedaemon in the days of the Messenian War ; this is proved from the poem of Tyrtaeus, entitled ' Good Order' ; for he 1307^a speaks of certain citizens who were ruined by the war and wanted to have a redistribution of the land. Again, revolutions arise when an individual who is great, and might be greater, wants to rule alone, as, at Lacedaemon, Pausanias, who was general in the Persian War, or like Hanno at Carthage.

Constitutional governments and aristocracies are com- 5 monly overthrown owing to some deviation from justice in the constitution itself; the cause of the downfall is, in the former, the ill-mingling of the two elements

---

[1] 1305^b 2 sqq.   [2] Reading a comma after ὀλιγαρχίας in l. 24.
[3] Reading τὸ πλῆθος in l. 28 with the MSS.
[4] i. e. the illegitimate sons.

democracy and oligarchy; in the latter, of the three ele-
10 ments, democracy, oligarchy, and virtue, but especially
democracy and oligarchy. For to combine these is the
endeavour of constitutional governments; and most of
the so-called aristocracies have a like aim,[1] but differ
from polities in the mode of combination; hence some
15 of them are more and some less permanent. Those
which incline more to oligarchy are called aristocracies,
and those which incline to democracy constitutional
governments. And therefore the latter are the safer of
the two; for the greater the number, the greater the
strength, and when men are equal they are contented.
But the rich, if the constitution gives them power, are
20 apt to be insolent and avaricious; and, in general, whichever way the constitution inclines, in that direction it
changes as either party gains strength, a constitutional
government becoming a democracy, an aristocracy an
oligarchy. But the process may be reversed, and aristocracy may change into democracy. This happens
when the poor, under the idea that they are being
wronged, force the constitution to take an opposite form.
25 In like manner constitutional governments change into
oligarchies. The only stable principle of government
is equality according to proportion, and for every man to
enjoy his own.

What I have just mentioned actually happened at
Thurii,[2] where the qualification for office, at first high,
was therefore reduced, and the magistrates increased in
number. The notables had previously acquired the
30 whole of the land contrary to law; for the government
tended to oligarchy, and they were able to encroach....
But the people, who had been trained by war, soon got
the better of the guards kept by the oligarchs, until
those who had too much gave up their land.

Again, since all aristocratical governments incline to
35 oligarchy, the notables are apt to be grasping; thus at
Lacedaemon, where property tends to pass into few hands,[3]
the notables can do too much as they like, and are

[1] Cp. iv. c. 7.   [2] Cp. 1303ᵃ 31.   [3] Cp. ii. 1270ᵃ 18.

allowed to marry whom they please. The city of Locri was ruined by a marriage connexion with Dionysius, but such a thing could never have happened in a democracy, or in a well-balanced aristocracy.

I have already remarked that in all states revolutions 40 are occasioned by trifles.[1] In aristocracies, above all, they **1307**ᵇ are of a gradual and imperceptible nature. The citizens begin by giving up some part of the constitution, and so with greater ease the government change something else which is a little more important, until they have under- 5 mined the whole fabric of the state. At Thurii there was a law that generals should only be re-elected after an interval of five years, and some young men who were popular with the soldiers of the guard for their military prowess, despising the magistrates and thinking that they would easily gain their purpose, wanted to abolish 10 this law and allow their generals to hold perpetual commands ; for they well knew that the people would be glad enough to elect them. Whereupon the magistrates who had charge of these matters, and who are called councillors, at first determined to resist, but they afterwards consented, thinking that, if only this one law was 15 changed, no further inroad would be made on the constitution. But other changes soon followed which they in vain attempted to oppose ; and the state passed into the hands of the revolutionists, who established a dynastic oligarchy.

All constitutions are overthrown either from within or from without ; the latter, when there is some govern- 20 ment close at hand having an opposite interest, or at a distance, but powerful. This was exemplified in the old times of the Athenians and the Lacedaemonians ; the Athenians everywhere put down the oligarchies, and the Lacedaemonians the democracies.[2]

I have now explained what are the chief causes of revolutions and dissensions in states.   25

8   We have next to consider what means there are of

---

[1] 1302ᵇ 4, 1303ᵃ 20-25, ᵇ 17.   [2] Cp. iv. 1296ᵃ 32.

preserving constitutions in general, and in particular cases. In the first place it is evident that if we know the causes which destroy constitutions, we also know the causes which preserve them ; for opposites produce opposites, and destruction is the opposite of preservation.[1]

30 In all well-attempered governments there is nothing which should be more jealously maintained than the spirit of obedience to law, more especially in small matters ; for transgression creeps in unperceived and at last ruins the state, just as the constant recurrence of small expenses in time eats up a fortune. The expense does not take place all at once, and therefore is not 35 observed ; the mind is deceived, as in the fallacy which says that 'if each part is little, then the whole is little'. And this is true in one way, but not in another, for the whole and the all are not little, although they are made up of littles.

In the first place, then, men should guard against the 40 beginning of change, and in the second place they should 1308^a not rely upon the political devices of which I have already spoken,[2] invented only to deceive the people, for they are proved by experience to be useless. Further, we note that oligarchies as well as aristocracies may last, not from any inherent stability in such forms of govern-5 ment, but because the rulers are on good terms both with the unenfranchised and with the governing classes, not maltreating any who are excluded from the government, but introducing into it the leading spirits among them.[3] They should never wrong the ambitious in a matter of honour, or the common people in a matter of 10 money ; and they should treat one another and their fellow-citizens in a spirit of equality. The equality which the friends of democracy seek to establish for the multitude is not only just but likewise expedient among equals. Hence, if the governing class are numerous, 15 many democratic institutions are useful ; for example, the restriction of the tenure of offices to six months, that

---

[1] Cp. *Nic. Eth.* v. 1129^a 13.   [2] Cp. iv. 1297^a 13–38.
[3] Cp. vi. 1321^a 26.

all those who are of equal rank may share in them. Indeed, equals or peers when they are numerous become a kind of democracy, and therefore demagogues are very likely to arise among them, as I have already remarked.[1] The short tenure of office prevents oligarchies and aristocracies from falling into the hands of families; it is not easy for a person to do any great harm when his tenure of office is short, whereas long pos- 20 session begets tyranny in oligarchies and democracies. For the aspirants to tyranny are either the principal men of the state, who in democracies are demagogues and in oligarchies members of ruling houses, or those who hold great offices, and have a long tenure of them.[2]

Constitutions are preserved when their destroyers are 25 at a distance, and sometimes also because they are near, for the fear of them makes the government keep in hand the constitution. Wherefore the ruler who has a care of the constitution should invent terrors, and bring distant dangers near, in order that the citizens may be on their guard, and, like sentinels in a night-watch, never relax their attention. He should endeavour too by help of 30 the laws to control the contentions and quarrels of the notables, and to prevent those who have not hitherto taken part in them from catching the spirit of contention. No ordinary man can discern the beginning of evil,[3] but only the true statesman.

As to the change produced in oligarchies and constitu- 35 tional governments[4] by the alteration of the qualification, when this arises, not out of any variation in the qualification but only out of the increase of money, it is well to compare the general[5] valuation of property with that of past years, annually in those cities in which the census 40 is taken annually, and in larger cities every third or fifth 1308[b] year. If the whole is many times greater or many times less than when the ratings recognized by the constitution were fixed, there should be power given by law to raise 5 or lower the qualification as the amount is greater or less.

---

[1] 1305[b] 23 sqq.   [2] Cp. 1305[a] 7.   [3] Cp. 1303[b] 17-31.
[4] Cp. 1306[b] 6-16.   [5] Reading κοινοῦ in l. 39 with the MSS.

Where this is not done[1] a constitutional government
passes into an oligarchy, and an oligarchy is narrowed to
a rule of families ; or in the opposite case constitutional
government becomes democracy, and oligarchy either
constitutional government or democracy.

10   It is a principle common to democracy, oligarchy, and
every other form of government not to allow the disproportionate increase of any citizen, but to give moderate
honour for a long time rather than great honour for a
short time. For men are easily spoilt ; not every one
15 can bear prosperity. But if this rule is not observed, at
any rate the honours which are given all at once should
be taken away by degrees and not all at once. Especially
should the laws provide against any one having too
much power, whether derived from friends or money ; if
20 he has, he should be sent clean out of the country.[2] And
since innovations creep in through the private life of
individuals also, there ought to be a magistracy which will
have an eye to those whose life is not in harmony with
the government, whether oligarchy or democracy or any
other. And for a like reason an increase of prosperity in
25 any part of the state should be carefully watched. The
proper remedy for this evil is always to give the management of affairs and offices of state to opposite elements ;
such opposites are the virtuous and the many, or the
rich and the poor. Another way is to combine the poor and
the rich in one body, or to increase the middle class : thus
30 an end will be put to the revolutions which arise from
inequality.

But above all every state should be so administered
and so regulated by law that its magistrates cannot
possibly make money.[3] In oligarchies special precautions
should be used against this evil. For the people do not
take any great offence at being kept out of the govern-
35 ment—indeed they are rather pleased than otherwise at
having leisure for their private business—but what irri-
tates them is to think that their rulers are stealing the

---

[1] Reading in l. 7 μὴ ποιούντων μὲν οὕτως, ἔνθα μέν, with the MSS.
[2] Cp. 1302^b 18 ; iii. 1284^a 17.   [3] Cp. 1316^a 39.

public money ; then they are doubly annoyed ; for they
lose both honour and profit.   If office brought no profit,
then and then only could democracy and aristocracy be
combined ; for both notables and people might have 40
their wishes gratified.   All would be able to hold office, 1309^{a}
which is the aim of democracy, and the notables would
be magistrates, which is the aim of aristocracy.   And
this result may be accomplished when there is no possibility of making money out of the offices ; for the poor
will not want to have them when there is nothing to be
gained from them—they would rather be attending to 5
their own concerns; and the rich, who do not want
money from the public treasury, will be able to take
them ; and so the poor will keep to their work and grow
rich, and the notables will not be governed by the lower
class.   In order to avoid peculation of the public money, 10
the transfer of the revenue should be made at a general
assembly of the citizens, and duplicates of the accounts
deposited with the different brotherhoods, companies,
and tribes.   And honours should be given by law to
magistrates who have the reputation of being incorruptible.   In democracies the rich should be spared ; not 15
only should their property not be divided, but their
incomes also, which in some states are taken from them
imperceptibly, should be protected.   It is a good thing
to prevent the wealthy citizens, even if they are willing,
from undertaking expensive and useless public services,
such as the giving of choruses, torch-races, and the like.
In an oligarchy, on the other hand, great care should be 20
taken of the poor, and lucrative offices should go to
them ; if any of the wealthy classes insult them, the
offender should be punished more severely than if he had
wronged one of his own class.   Provision should be
made that estates pass by inheritance and not by gift, and
no person should have more than one inheritance ; for in 25
this way properties will be equalized, and more of the
poor rise to competency.   It is also expedient both in a
democracy and in an oligarchy to assign to those who
have less share in the government (i. e. to the rich in a

M 2

democracy and to the poor in an oligarchy) an equality
30 or preference in all but the principal offices of state.
The latter should be entrusted chiefly or only to members
of the governing class.

There are three qualifications required in those who **9**
have to fill the highest offices,—(1) first of all, loyalty to
35 the established constitution; (2) the greatest administra-
tive capacity; (3) virtue and justice of the kind proper to
each form of government; for, if what is just is not the
same in all governments, the quality of justice must also
differ. There may be a doubt, however, when all these
40 qualities do not meet in the same person, how the selec-
1309ᵇ tion is to be made; suppose, for example, a good general
is a bad man and not a friend to the constitution, and
another man is loyal and just, which should we choose?
In making the election ought we not to consider two
points? what qualities are common, and what are rare.
Thus in the choice of a general, we should regard his
5 skill rather than his virtue; for few have military skill,
but many have virtue. In any office of trust or steward-
ship, on the other hand, the opposite rule should be
·observed; for more virtue than ordinary is required in
the holder of such an office, but the necessary knowledge
is of a sort which all men possess.

It may, however, be asked what a man wants with
10 virtue if he have political ability and is loyal, since these
two qualities alone will make him do what is for the
public interest. But may not men have both of them
and yet be deficient in self-control?- If, knowing and
loving their own interests, they do not always attend to
them, may they not be equally negligent of the interests
of the public?

Speaking generally, we may say that whatever legal
15 enactments are held to be for the interest of various
constitutions, all these preserve them. And the great
preserving principle is the one which has been repeatedly
mentioned,[1]—to have a care that the loyal citizens

¹ iv. 1296ᵇ 15, vi. 1320ª 14, cp. ii. 1270ᵇ 21 sq., iv. 1294ᵇ 37.

should be stronger than the disloyal. Neither should we
forget the mean, which at the present day is lost sight of
in perverted forms of government; for many practices
which appear to be democratical are the ruin of demo- 20
cracies, and many which appear to be oligarchical are the
ruin of oligarchies. Those who think that all virtue is
to be found in their own party principles push matters
to extremes; they do not consider that disproportion
destroys a state. A nose which varies from the ideal of
straightness to a hook or snub may still be of good shape
and agreeable to the eye; but if the excess be very 25
great, all symmetry is lost, and the nose at last ceases to
be a nose at all on account of some excess in one direction or defect in the other; and this is true of every
other part of the human body. The same law of propor- 30
tion equally holds in states. Oligarchy or democracy,
although a departure from the most perfect form, may
yet be a good enough government, but if any one attempts
to push the principles of either to an extreme, he will
begin by spoiling the government and end by having
none at all. Wherefore the legislator and the statesman 35
ought to know what democratical measures save and
what destroy a democracy, and what oligarchical measures
save or destroy an oligarchy. For neither the one nor
the other can exist or continue to exist unless both rich
and poor are included in it. If equality of property is
introduced, the state must of necessity take another form; 40
for when by laws carried to excess one or other element 1310ᵉ
in the state is ruined, the constitution is ruined.

There is an error common both to oligarchies and to
democracies:—in the latter the demagogues, when the
multitude are above the law, are always cutting the city
in two by quarrels with the rich, whereas they should 5
always profess to be maintaining their cause; just as in
oligarchies the oligarchs should profess to maintain the
cause of the people, and should take oaths the opposite
of those which they now take. For there are cities in
which they swear—'I will be an enemy to the people,
and will devise all the harm against them which I can';

10 but they ought to exhibit and to entertain the very opposite feeling; in the form of their oath there should be an express declaration—'I will do no wrong to the people.'

But of all the things which I have mentioned that which most contributes to the permanence of constitutions is the adaptation of education to the form of government,[1] and yet in our own day this principle is universally neglected.

15 The best laws, though sanctioned by every citizen of the state, will be of no avail unless the young are trained by habit and education in the spirit of the constitution, if the laws are democratical, democratically, or oligarchically, if the laws are oligarchical. For there may be a want of self-discipline in states as well as in individuals. Now, to have been educated in the spirit

20 of the constitution is not to perform the actions in which oligarchs or democrats delight, but those by which the existence of an oligarchy or of a democracy is made possible. Whereas among ourselves the sons of the ruling class in an oligarchy live in luxury,[2] but the sons of the poor are hardened by exercise and toil, and hence they are both more inclined and better able to make a

25 revolution.[3] And in democracies of the more extreme type there has arisen a false idea of freedom which is contradictory to the true interests of the state. For two principles are characteristic of democracy, the govern-

30 ment of the majority and freedom. Men think that what is just is equal; and that equality is the supremacy of the popular will; and that freedom means the doing what a man likes. In such democracies every one lives as he pleases, or in the words of Euripides,[4] 'according to his fancy.' But this is all wrong; men should not

35 think it slavery to live according to the rule of the constitution; for it is their salvation.

I have now discussed generally the causes of the revolution and destruction of states, and the means of their preservation and continuance.

[1] Cp. viii. 1337ᵃ 14. [2] Cp. iv. 1295ᵇ 17.
[3] Cp. Pl. *Rep.* viii. 556 D. [4] fr. 891, Nauck².

10   I have still to speak of monarchy, and the causes of its
destruction and preservation.   What I have said already 40
respecting forms of constitutional government applies 1310ᵇ
almost equally to royal and to tyrannical rule.   For royal
rule is of the nature of an aristocracy, and a tyranny is
a compound of oligarchy and democracy in their most
extreme forms ; it is therefore most injurious to its sub- 5
jects, being made up of two evil forms of government,
and having the perversions and errors of both.   These
two forms of monarchy are contrary in their very origin.
The appointment of a king is the resource of the better
classes against the people, and he is elected by them out 10
of their own number, because either he himself or his
family excel in virtue and virtuous actions ; whereas a
tyrant is chosen from the people to be their protector
against the notables, and in order to prevent them from
being injured.   History shows that almost all tyrants
have been demagogues who gained the favour of the 15
people by their accusation of the notables.[1]   At any rate
this was the manner in which the tyrannies arose in the
days when cities had increased in power.   Others which
were older originated in the ambition of kings wanting to
overstep the limits of their hereditary power and become
despots.   Others again grew out of the class which were 20
chosen to be chief magistrates ; for in ancient times
the people who elected them gave the magistrates,
whether civil or religious, a long tenure.   Others arose
out of the custom which oligarchies had of making some
individual supreme over the highest offices.   In any of
these ways an ambitious man had no difficulty, if he
desired, in creating a tyranny, since he had the power in 25
his hands already, either as king or as one of the officers
of state.[2]   Thus Pheidon at Argos and several others
were originally kings, and ended by becoming tyrants ;
Phalaris, on the other hand, and the Ionian tyrants,
acquired the tyranny by holding great offices.   Whereas
Panaetius at Leontini, Cypselus at Corinth, Peisistratus 30

---

[1] Cp. 1305ᵃ 8 ; Plato, *Rep.* viii. 565 D.
[2] Cp. 1305ᵃ 15.

at Athens, Dionysius at Syracuse, and several others who afterwards became tyrants, were at first demagogues.

And so, as I was saying,[1] royalty ranks with aristocracy, for it is based upon merit, whether of the individual or of his family, or on benefits conferred,[2] or on these claims with power added to them. For all who
35 have obtained this honour have benefited, or had in their power to benefit, states and nations; some, like Codrus, have prevented the state from being enslaved in war; others, like Cyrus, have given their country freedom, or have settled or gained a territory, like the Lace-
40 daemonian, Macedonian, and Molossian kings. The
1311ᵃ idea of a king is to be a protector of the rich against unjust treatment, of the people against insult and oppression. Whereas a tyrant, as has often been repeated,[3] has no regard to any public interest, except as conducive to his private ends; his aim is pleasure, the aim of a king,
5 honour. Wherefore also in their desires they differ; the tyrant is desirous of riches, the king, of what brings honour. And the guards of a king are citizens, but of a tyrant mercenaries.[4]

That tyranny has all the vices both of democracy and oligarchy is evident. As of oligarchy so of tyranny,
10 the end is wealth; (for by wealth only can the tyrant maintain either his guard or his luxury). Both mistrust the people, and therefore deprive them of their arms. Both agree too in injuring the people and driving them
15 out of the city and dispersing them. From democracy tyrants have borrowed the art of making war upon the notables and destroying them secretly or openly, or of exiling them because they are rivals and stand in the way of their power; and also because plots against them are contrived by men of this class, who either want to
20 rule or to escape subjection. Hence Periander advised Thrasybulus[5] by cutting off the tops of the tallest ears of corn, meaning that he must always put out of the way the

---

[1] l. 2 sq.   [2] Cp. iii. 1285ᵇ 6.
[3] iii. 1279ᵇ 6 sq., iv. 1295ᵃ 19.   [4] Cp. iii. 1285ᵃ 24.
[5] Cp. 1284ᵃ 26.

citizens who overtop the rest. And so, as I have already intimated,[1] the beginnings of change are the same in monarchies as in forms of constitutional government; 25 subjects attack their sovereigns out of fear or contempt, or because they have been unjustly treated by them. And of injustice, the most common form is insult, another is confiscation of property.

The ends sought by conspiracies against monarchies, whether tyrannies or royalties, are the same as the ends sought by conspiracies against other forms of government. Monarchs have great wealth and honour, which 30 are objects of desire to all mankind. The attacks are made sometimes against their lives, sometimes against the office ; where the sense of insult is the motive, against their lives. Any sort of insult (and there are many) may stir up anger, and when men are angry, they commonly act out of revenge, and not from ambition. For 35 example, the attempt made upon the Peisistratidae arose out of the public dishonour offered to the sister of Harmodius and the insult to himself. He attacked the tyrant for his sister's sake, and Aristogeiton joined in the attack for the sake of Harmodius. A conspiracy was also formed against Periander, the tyrant of Am- 40 bracia, because, when drinking with a favourite youth, he 1311ᵇ asked him whether by this time he was not with child by him. Philip, too, was attacked by Pausanias because he permitted him to be insulted by Attalus and his friends, and Amyntas the little, by Derdas, because he boasted of having enjoyed his youth. Evagoras of Cyprus, again, was slain by the eunuch to revenge an insult ; for 5 his wife had been carried off by Evagoras's son. Many conspiracies have originated in shameful attempts made by sovereigns on the persons of their subjects. Such was the attack of Crataeas upon Archelaus ; he had always hated the connexion with him, and so, when Archelaus, having promised him one of his two daughters 10 in marriage, did not give him either of them, but broke his word and married the elder to the king of Elymeia,

---

[1] 1310ᵃ 40 sqq.

when he was hard pressed in a war against Sirrhas and Arrhabaeus, and the younger to his own son Amyntas, under the idea that Amyntas would then be less likely to
15 quarrel with his son by Cleopatra—Crataeas made this slight a pretext for attacking Archelaus, though even a less reason would have sufficed, for the real cause of the estrangement was the disgust which he felt at his connexion with the king. And from a like motive Hellanocrates of Larissa conspired with him; for when Archelaus, who was his lover, did not fulfil his promise of restoring him to his country, he thought that the connexion between them had originated, not in affection, but in the
20 wantonness of power. Pytho, too, and Heracleides of Aenos, slew Cotys in order to avenge their father, and Adamas revolted from Cotys in revenge for the wanton outrage which he had committed in mutilating him when a child.

Many, too, irritated at blows inflicted on the person which they deemed an insult, have either killed or
25 attempted to kill officers of state and royal princes by whom they have been injured. Thus, at Mytilene, Megacles and his friends attacked and slew the Penthilidae, as they were going about [1] and striking people with clubs. At a later date Smerdis, who had been beaten and torn away from his wife by Penthilus, slew
30 him. In the conspiracy against Archelaus, Decamnichus stimulated the fury of the assassins and led the attack ; he was enraged because Archelaus had delivered him to Euripides to be scourged; for the poet had been irritated at some remark made by Decamnichus on the foulness of his breath. Many other examples might be
35 cited of murders and conspiracies which have arisen from similar causes.

Fear is another motive which, as we have said,[2] has caused conspiracies as well in monarchies as in more popular forms of government. Thus Artapanes conspired against Xerxes and slew him, fearing that he would

---

[1] Reading περιιόντας in l. 27 with some MSS.
[2] Cp. 1302^b 2, 21, 1311^a 25.

be accused of hanging Darius against his orders,—he having been under the impression that Xerxes would forget what he had said in the middle of a meal, and that the offence would be forgiven.

Another motive is contempt, as in the case of Sarda- 40 napalus, whom some one saw carding wool with his 1312^a women, if the story-tellers say truly; and the tale may be true, if not of him, of some one else.[1]   Dion attacked the younger Dionysius because he despised him, and saw 5 that he was equally despised by his own subjects, and that he was always drunk.   Even the friends of a tyrant will sometimes attack him out of contempt; for the confidence which he reposes in them breeds contempt, and they think that they will not be found out. The expectation of success is likewise a sort of contempt; the assailants are ready to strike, and think nothing of 10 the danger, because they seem to have the power in their hands.   Thus generals of armies attack monarchs; as, for example, Cyrus attacked Astyages, despising the effeminacy of his life, and believing that his power was worn out.   Thus again, Seuthes the Thracian conspired against Amadocus, whose general he was.

And sometimes men are actuated by more than one 15 motive, like Mithridates, who conspired against Ariobarzanes, partly out of contempt and partly from the love of gain.

Bold natures, placed by their sovereigns in a high military position, are most likely to make the attempt in the expectation of success; for courage is emboldened by power, and the union of the two inspires them with 20 the hope of an easy victory.

Attempts of which the motive is ambition arise in a different way as well as in those already mentioned. There are men who will not risk their lives in the hope of 25 gains and honours however great, but who nevertheless regard the killing of a tyrant simply as an extraordinary action which will make them famous and honourable in the world; they wish to acquire, not a kingdom, but 30 a name.   It is rare, however, to find such men; he who

[1] Cp. i. 1259^a 7.

would kill a tyrant must be prepared to lose his life if he
35 fail. He must have the resolution of Dion, who, when
he made war upon Dionysius, took with him very few
troops, saying 'that whatever measure of success he
might attain would be enough for him, even if he were
to die the moment he landed; such a death would be
welcome to him'. But this is a temper to which few can
attain.

40 Once more, tyrannies, like all other governments, are
1312ᵇ destroyed from without by some opposite and more
powerful form of government. That such a government
will have the will to attack them is clear; for the two are
opposed in principle; and all men, if they can, do what
they will. Democracy is antagonistic to tyranny, on
the principle of Hesiod,[1] 'Potter hates Potter', because
5 they are nearly akin, for the extreme form of democracy
is tyranny; and royalty and aristocracy are both alike
opposed to tyranny, because they are constitutions of a
different type. And therefore the Lacedaemonians put
down most of the tyrannies, and so did the Syracusans
during the time when they were well governed.

Again, tyrannies are destroyed from within, when the
10 reigning family are divided among themselves, as that
of Gelo was, and more recently that of Dionysius; in the
case of Gelo because Thrasybulus, the brother of Hiero,
flattered the son of Gelo and led him into excesses in
order that he might rule in his name. Whereupon the
family got together a party to get rid of Thrasybulus and
15 save the tyranny; but those of the people who conspired
with them seized the opportunity and drove them all out.
In the case of Dionysius, Dion, his own relative, attacked
and expelled him with the assistance of the people; he
afterwards perished himself.

There are two chief motives which induce men to
attack tyrannies — hatred and contempt. Hatred of
20 tyrants is inevitable, and contempt is also a frequent
cause of their destruction. Thus we see that most of
those who have acquired, have retained their power,

[1] *Op. et Dies* 25.

but those who have inherited,[1] have lost it, almost at
once; for, living in luxurious ease, they have become
contemptible, and offer many opportunities to their
assailants. Anger, too, must be included under hatred, 25
and produces the same effects. It is oftentimes even
more ready to strike—the angry are more impetuous in
making an attack, for they do not follow rational principle. And men are very apt to give way to their passions
when they are insulted. To this cause is to be attributed 30
the fall of the Peisistratidae and of many others. Hatred
is more reasonable, for anger is accompanied by pain,
which is an impediment to reason, whereas hatred is
painless.[2]

In a word, all the causes which I have mentioned [3] as
destroying the last and most unmixed form of oligarchy, 35
and the extreme form of democracy, may be assumed to
affect tyranny; indeed the extreme forms of both are
only tyrannies distributed among several persons. Kingly
rule is little affected by external causes, and is therefore
lasting; it is generally destroyed from within. And 40
there are two ways in which the destruction may come
about; (1) when the members of the royal family quarrel 1313[a]
among themselves, and (2) when the kings attempt to
administer the state too much after the fashion of a
tyranny, and to extend their authority contrary to the law.
Royalties do not now come into existence; where such
forms of government arise, they are rather monarchies or
tyrannies. For the rule of a king is over voluntary subjects, 5
and he is supreme in all important matters; but in our
own day men are more upon an equality, and no one is so immeasurably superior to others as to represent adequately
the greatness and dignity of the office. Hence mankind
will not, if they can help, endure it, and any one who obtains
power by force or fraud is at once thought to be a tyrant. 10
In hereditary monarchies a further cause of destruction is
the fact that kings often fall into contempt, and, although
possessing not tyrannical power, but only royal dignity,

---

[1] Cp. Plato, *Laws*, iii. 695.   [2] Cp. *Rhetoric*, ii. 1382[a] 12.
[3] 1302[b] 25–33, 1304[b] 20–1306[b] 21.

are apt to outrage others. Their overthrow is then
15 readily effected ; for there is an end to the king when his
subjects do not want to have him, but the tyrant lasts,
whether they like him or not.

The destruction of monarchies is to be attributed to
these and the like causes.

And they are preserved, to speak generally, by the **11**
opposite causes ; or, if we consider them separately,
(1) royalty is preserved by the limitation of its powers.
20 The more restricted the functions of kings, the longer
their power will last unimpaired ; for then they are more
moderate and not so despotic in their ways; and they
are less envied by their subjects. This is the reason why
the kingly office has lasted so long among the Molossians.
25 And for a similar reason it has continued among the
Lacedaemonians, because there it was always divided
between two, and afterwards further limited by Theopompus in various respects, more particularly by the
establishment of the Ephoralty. He diminished the
power of the kings, but established on a more lasting
basis the kingly office, which was thus made in a certain
30 sense not less, but greater. There is a story that when
his wife once asked him whether he was not ashamed to
leave to his sons a royal power which was less than he
had inherited from his father, ' No indeed,' he replied, ' for
the power which I leave to them will be more lasting.'

As to (2) tyrannies, they are preserved in two most
35 opposite ways. One of them is the old traditional
method in which most tyrants administer their government. Of such arts Periander of Corinth is said to have
been the great master, and many similar devices may be
gathered from the Persians in the administration of their
government. There are firstly the prescriptions mentioned some distance back,¹ for the preservation of a
tyranny, in so far as this is possible ; viz. that the tyrant
40 should lop off those who are too high ; he must put to

¹ 1311ᵃ 15-22.

death men of spirit ; he must not allow common meals, **1313^b**
clubs, education, and the like ; he must be upon his guard
against anything which is likely to inspire either courage
or confidence among his subjects ; he must prohibit
literary assemblies or other meetings for discussion, and
he must take every means to prevent people from
knowing one another (for acquaintance begets mutual 5
confidence).   Further, he must compel all persons staying
in the city to appear in public and live at his gates ; then he
will know what they are doing : if they are always kept
under, they will learn to be humble.   In short, he should
practise these and the like Persian and barbaric arts,
which all have the same object.   A tyrant should also 10
endeavour to know what each of his subjects says or does,
and should employ spies, like the 'female detectives' at
Syracuse, and the eavesdroppers whom Hiero was in the
habit of sending to any place of resort or meeting ; for 15
the fear of informers prevents people from speaking their
minds, and if they do, they are more easily found out.
Another art of the tyrant is to sow quarrels among the
citizens ; friends should be embroiled with friends, the
people with the notables, and the rich with one another.
Also he should impoverish his subjects ; he thus provides
against the maintenance of a guard by the citizens, and
the people, having to keep hard at work, are prevented 20
from conspiring.   The Pyramids of Egypt afford an example of this policy; also the offerings of the family of
Cypselus, and the building of the temple of Olympian
Zeus by the Peisistratidae, and the great Polycratean
monuments at Samos ; all these works were alike intended to occupy the people and keep them poor. 25
Another practice of tyrants is to multiply taxes, after the
manner of Dionysius at Syracuse, who contrived that
within five years his subjects should bring into the
treasury their whole property.   The tyrant is also fond
of making war in order that his subjects may have
something to do and be always in want of a leader.
And whereas the power of a king is preserved by his 30
friends, the characteristic of a tyrant is to distrust his

friends, because he knows that all men want to overthrow him, and they above all have the power.

Again, the evil practices of the last and worst form of democracy[1] are all found in tyrannies. Such are the power given to women in their families in the hope that they will inform against their husbands, and the licence which is allowed to slaves in order that they may betray
35 their masters; for slaves and women do not conspire against tyrants; and they are of course friendly to tyrannies and also to democracies, since under them they have a good time. For the people too would fain be a monarch, and therefore by them, as well as by the tyrant,
40 the flatterer is held in honour; in democracies he is the demagogue; and the tyrant also has those who associate
1314^a with him in a humble spirit, which is a work of flattery.

Hence tyrants are always fond of bad men,[2] because they love to be flattered, but no man who has the spirit of a freeman in him will lower himself by flattery; good men love others, or at any rate do not flatter them. Moreover, the bad are useful for bad purposes; 'nail
5 knocks out nail', as the proverb says. It is characteristic of a tyrant to dislike every one who has dignity or independence; he wants to be alone in his glory, but any one who claims a like dignity or asserts his independence encroaches upon his prerogative, and is hated by him as
10 an enemy to his power. Another mark of a tyrant is that he likes foreigners better than citizens, and lives with them and invites them to his table; for the one are enemies, but the others enter into no rivalry with him.

Such are the notes of the tyrant and the arts by which he preserves his power; there is no wickedness too great for him. All that we have said may be summed up
15 under three heads, which answer to the three aims of the tyrant. These are, (1) the humiliation of his subjects; he knows that a mean-spirited man will not conspire against anybody: (2) the creation of mistrust among them; for a tyrant is not overthrown until men begin to

---

[1] Cp. vi. 1319^b 27.
[2] Reading πονηρόφιλον in l. 1 with the MSS.

have confidence in one another; and this is the reason
why tyrants are at war with the good; they are under
the idea that their power is endangered by them, not 20
only because they will not be ruled despotically, but also
because they are loyal to one another, and to other men,
and do not inform against one another or against other
men: (3) the tyrant desires that his subjects shall be
incapable of action, for no one attempts what is impossible,
and they will not attempt to overthrow a tyranny, if they
are powerless.   Under these three heads the whole policy 25
of a tyrant may be summed up, and to one or other of
them all his ideas may be referred: (1) he sows distrust
among his subjects; (2) he takes away their power; (3)
he humbles them.

This then is one of the two methods by which tyrannies 30
are preserved; and there is another which proceeds upon
an almost opposite principle of action.   The nature of
this latter method may be gathered from a comparison
of the causes which destroy kingdoms, for as one mode
of destroying kingly power is to make the office of king
more tyrannical, so the salvation of a tyranny is to make
it more like the rule of a king.   But of one thing the 35
tyrant must be careful; he must keep power enough to
rule over his subjects, whether they like him or not, for
if he once gives this up he gives up his tyranny.   But
though power must be retained as the foundation, in all
else the tyrant should act or appear to act in the
character of a king.   In the first place he should pretend [1] 40
a care of the public revenues, and not waste money in 1314^b
making [2] presents of a sort at which the common people
get excited when they see their hard-won earnings
snatched from them and lavished on courtesans and
strangers and artists.   He should give an account of 5
what he receives and of what he spends (a practice which
has been adopted by some tyrants); for then he will seem
to be a steward of the public rather than a tyrant; nor
need he fear that, while he is the lord of the city, he will

----

[1] Reading καλῶς—πρῶτον μὲν δοκεῖν in l. 40.
[2] Omitting εἰς in i. 1.

ever be in want of money. Such a policy is at all events much more advantageous for the tyrant when he goes 10 from home, than to leave behind him a hoard, for then the garrison who remain in the city will be less likely to attack his power ; and a tyrant, when he is absent from home, has more reason to fear the guardians of his treasure than the citizens, for the one accompany him, but the others remain behind. In the second place, he should be seen to collect taxes and to require public services 15 only for state purposes, and that he may form a fund in case of war, and generally he ought to make himself the guardian and treasurer of them, as if they belonged, not to him, but to the public. He should appear, not harsh, but dignified, and when men meet him they should look 20 upon him with reverence, and not with fear. Yet it is hard for him to be respected if he inspires no respect, and therefore whatever virtues he may neglect, at least he should maintain the character of a great soldier, and produce the impression that he is one. Neither he nor any of his associates should ever be guilty of the least offence against modesty towards the young of either sex 25 who are his subjects, and the women of his family should observe a like self-control towards other women ; the insolence of women has ruined many tyrannies. In the indulgence of pleasures he should be the opposite of our modern tyrants, who not only begin at dawn and pass 30 whole days in sensuality, but want other men to see them, that they may admire their happy and blessed lot. In these things a tyrant should if possible be moderate, or at any rate should not parade his vices to the world ; for a drunken and drowsy tyrant is soon despised and 35 attacked ; not so he who is temperate and wide awake. His conduct should be the very reverse of nearly everything which has been said before[1] about tyrants. He ought to adorn and improve his city, as though he were not a tyrant, but the guardian of the state. Also he should appear to be particularly earnest in the service 40 of the Gods ; for if men think that a ruler is religious

---

[1] 1313ᵃ 35–1314ᵃ 29.

and has a reverence for the Gods, they are less afraid of **1315ᵃ**
suffering injustice at his hands, and they are less disposed
to conspire against him, because they believe him to have
the very Gods fighting on his side. At the same time
his religion must not be thought foolish. And he should
honour men of merit, and make them think that they 5
would not be held in more honour by the citizens if they
had a free government. The honour he should distribute
himself, but the punishment should be inflicted by
officers and courts of law. It is a precaution which is
taken by all monarchs not to make one person great ;
but if one, then two or more should be raised, that they
may look sharply after one another. If after all some one 10
has to be made great, he should not be a man of bold
spirit ; for such dispositions are ever most inclined to
strike. And if any one is to be deprived of his power,
let it be diminished gradually, not taken from him all at
once.¹ The tyrant should abstain from all outrage ; in 15
particular from personal violence and from wanton conduct towards the young. He should be especially
careful of his behaviour to men who are lovers of honour ;
for as the lovers of money are offended when their
property is touched, so are the lovers of honour and the
virtuous when their honour is affected. Therefore a 20
tyrant ought either not to commit such acts at all ; or
he should be thought only to employ fatherly correction,
and not to trample upon others,—and his acquaintance
with youth should be supposed 'to arise from affection,
and not from the insolence of power, and in general he
should compensate the appearance of dishonour by the
increase of honour.

Of those who attempt assassination they are the most 25
dangerous, and require to be most carefully watched, who
do not care to survive, if they effect their purpose
Therefore special precaution should be taken about any
who think that either they or those for whom they care
have been insulted ; for when men are led away by
passion to assault others they are regardless of themselve s

¹ Cp. 1308ᵇ 15.

₃₀ As Heracleitus says, ' It is difficult to fight against anger ; for a man will buy revenge with his soul.' [1]

And whereas states consist of two classes, of poor men and of rich, the tyrant should lead both to imagine that they are preserved and prevented from harming one ₃₅ another by his rule, and whichever of the two is stronger he should attach to his government ; for, having this advantage, he has no need either to emancipate slaves or to disarm the citizens ; either party added to the force which he already has, will make him stronger than his assailants.

₄₀ But enough of these details ;—what should be the general policy of the tyrant is obvious. He ought to show himself to his subjects in the light, not of a tyrant, but **1315ᵇ** of a steward and a king. He should not appropriate what is theirs, but should be their guardian ; he should be moderate, not extravagant in his way of life ; he should win the notables by companionship, and the multitude by flattery. For then his rule will of necessity be ₅ nobler and happier, because he will rule over better men [2] whose spirits are not crushed, over men to whom he himself is not an object of hatred, and of whom he is not afraid. His power too will be more lasting. His ₁₀ disposition will be virtuous, or at least half virtuous ; and he will not be wicked, but half wicked only.

Yet no forms of government are so short-lived as **12** oligarchy and tyranny. The tyranny which lasted longest was that of Orthagoras and his sons at Sicyon ; this continued for a hundred years. The reason was ₁₅ that they treated their subjects with moderation, and to a great extent observed the laws ; and in various ways gained the favour of the people by the care which they took of them. Cleisthenes, in particular, was respected for his military ability. If report may be believed, he crowned the judge who decided against him in the ₂₀ games ; and, as some say, the sitting statue in the Agora of Sicyon is the likeness of this person. (A similar story

---

[1] Fragm. 85 (ed. Diels).   [2] Cp. i. 1254ᵃ25.

is told of Peisistratus, who is said on one occasion to have allowed himself to be summoned and tried before the Areopagus.)

Next in duration to the tyranny of Orthagoras was that of the Cypselidae at Corinth, which lasted seventy-three years and six months: Cypselus reigned thirty years, Periander forty and a half, and Psammetichus the ₂₅ son of Gorgus three. Their continuance was due to similar causes: Cypselus was a popular man, who during the whole time of his rule never had a body-guard; and Periander, although he was a tyrant, was a great soldier. Third in duration was the rule of the Peisistratidae at Athens, but it was interrupted; for ₃₀ Peisistratus was twice driven out, so that during three and thirty years he reigned only seventeen; and his sons reigned eighteen—altogether thirty-five years. Of other tyrannies, that of Hiero[1] and Gelo at Syracuse was the most lasting. Even this, however, was short, not more ₃₅ than eighteen years in all; for Gelo continued tyrant for seven years, and died in the eighth; Hiero reigned for ten years, and Thrasybulus was driven out in the eleventh month. In fact, tyrannies generally have been of quite short duration.

I have now gone through almost all the causes by which ₄₀ constitutional governments and monarchies are either destroyed or preserved.   **1316^a**

In the *Republic* of Plato,[2] Socrates treats of revolutions, but not well, for he mentions no cause of change which peculiarly affects the first, or perfect state. He only says that the cause is that nothing is abiding, but all things change in a certain cycle; and that the origin of the ₅ change consists in those numbers ' of which 4 and 3, married with 5, furnish two harmonies ',[2]—(he means when

---

[1] Omitting τῶν in l. 34.

[2] This is an extract from the much fuller account in *Rep.* viii. 546 B.C. ἐπίτριτος πυθμήν is 'the ratio 4 : 3 in its lowest terms', i.e. the numbers 4, 3. These numbers when 'married' with 5 produce the right-angled triangle whose sides are as 3, 4, 5. When the 'number of this figure' is made solid, i.e. cubed, either by adding the cubes of the sides, or by cubing the area, the number 216 is produced, which gives in days the minimum period of

the number of this figure becomes solid) ; he conceives
that nature at certain times produces bad men who will
not submit to education; in which latter particular he may
very likely be not far wrong, for there may well be some
10 men who cannot be educated and made virtuous. But
why is such a cause of change peculiar to his ideal state,
and not rather common to all states, nay, to everything
which comes into being at all ? And is it by the agency
of time, which, as he declares, makes all things change,
15 that things which did not begin together, change together ? For example, if something has come into being
the day before the completion of the cycle, will it change
with things that came into being before ? Further, why
should the perfect state change into the Spartan ? [1]
For governments more often take an opposite form than
20 one akin to them. The same remark is applicable to the
other changes ; he says that the Spartan constitution
changes into an oligarchy, and this into a democracy, and
this again into a tyranny. And yet the contrary happens
quite as often ; for a democracy is even more likely to
25 change into an oligarchy than into a monarchy. Further,
he never says whether tyranny is, or is not, liable to
revolutions, and if it is, what is the cause of them, or into
what form it changes. And the reason is, that he could
not very well have told : for there is no rule ; according
to him it should revert to the first and best, and then
there would be a complete cycle. But in point of fact a
30 tyranny often changes into a tyranny, as that at Sicyon
changed from the tyranny of Myron into that of
Cleisthenes ; into oligarchy, as the tyranny of Antileon
did at Chalcis ; into democracy, as that of Gelo's family
did at Syracuse; into aristocracy, as at Carthage, and the
35 tyranny of Charilaus at Lacedaemon. Often an oligarchy

gestation in man, and therefore, according to Plato's fancy, is the
source of degeneration. The two harmonies are the square with
sides of 3,600, and the rectangle with sides of 4,800, 2,700, the
area of each of which, viz. 12,960,000, $= (3 \times 4 \times 5)^4$. For a full
discussion of the Nuptial Number in Plato cf. Adam's ed. of
the *Republic*, vol. ii, pp. 201–209, 264–312, and in particular see the
discussion of the Aristotelian passage on pp. 306–312.
  [1] *Rep.* viii. 544 C.

changes into a tyranny, like most of the ancient oligarchies in Sicily; for example, the oligarchy at Leontini
changed into the tyranny of Panaetius; that at Gela into
the tyranny of Cleander; that at Rhegium into the
tyranny of Anaxilaus; the same thing has happened in
many other states. And it is absurd to suppose that
the state changes into oligarchy merely because the ruling 40
class are lovers and makers of money,[1] and not because 1316ᵇ
the very rich think it unfair that the very poor should ,
have an equal share in the government with themselves.
Moreover, in many oligarchies there are laws against
making money in trade. But at Carthage, which is a 5
democracy, there is no such prohibition; and yet to this
day the Carthaginians have never had a revolution. It
is absurd too for him to say that an oligarchy is two
cities, one of the rich, and the other of the poor.[2]   Is
not this just as much the case in the Spartan constitution, or in any other in which either all do not
possess equal property, or all are not equally good men? 10
Nobody need be any poorer than he was before, and yet
the oligarchy may change all the same into a democracy,
if the poor form the majority; and a democracy may
change into an oligarchy, if the wealthy class are stronger
than the people, and the one are energetic, the other
indifferent.   Once more, although the causes of the 15
change[3] are very numerous, he mentions only one,[4]
which is, that the citizens become poor through dissipa-
tion and debt, as though he thought that all, or the
majority of them, were originally rich. This is not true :
though it is true that when any of the leaders lose their
property they are ripe for revolution ; but, when anybody else, it is no great matter, and an oligarchy does 20
not even then more often pass into a democracy than
into any other form of government. Again, if men are
deprived of the honours of state, and are wronged, and
insulted, they make revolutions, and change forms of

---

[1] *Rep.* viii. 550 E. χρηματισταί should be retained in l. 40.
[2] *Rep.* viii. 551 D.   [3] Sc. from oligarchy to democracy.
[4] *Rep.* viii. 555 D.

government, even although they have not wasted their substance because [1] they might do what they liked—of which extravagance he declares excessive freedom to be the cause.[2]

25   Finally, although there are many forms of oligarchies and democracies, Socrates speaks of their revolutions as though there were only one form of either of them.

[1] A lacuna need not be supposed to exist at l. 23.
[2] *Rep.* viii. 557 C, 564.

BOOK VI

1 WE have now considered the varieties of the deliberative or supreme power in states, and the various arrangements of law-courts and state offices, and which of
them are adapted to different forms of government.[1] We
have also spoken of the destruction and preservation of
constitutions, how and from what causes they arise.[2]

Of democracy and all other forms of government there
are many kinds; and it will be well to assign to them
severally the modes of organization which are proper
and advantageous to each, adding what remains to be said
about them.[3] Moreover, we ought to consider the various 40
combinations of these modes themselves; for such com- 1317ª
binations make constitutions overlap one another, so that
aristocracies have an oligarchical character, and constitutional governments incline to democracies.[4]

When I speak of the combinations which remain to be
considered, and thus far have not been considered by us,
I mean such as these:—when the deliberative part of 5
the government and the election of officers is constituted
oligarchically, and the law-courts aristocratically, or
when the courts and the deliberative part of the state are
oligarchical, and the election to offices aristocratical, or
when in any other way there is a want of harmony in
the composition of a state.[5]

I have shown already[6] what forms of democracy are 10
suited to particular cities, and what of oligarchy to
particular peoples, and to whom each of the other forms
of government is suited. Further, we must not only
show which of these governments is the best for each
state, but also briefly proceed to consider[7] how these 15
and other forms of government are to be established.

---

[1] Bk. iv. 14–16.   [2] Bk. v.
[3] 1318ᵇ 6–1319ª 6.   [4] Cp. iv. 1293ᵇ 34.
[5] These questions are not actually discussed by A.
[6] iv. 12.   [7] Cp. iv. 1289ᵇ 20.

First of all let us speak of democracy, which will also
bring to light the opposite form of government commonly
called oligarchy. For the purposes of this inquiry we
need to ascertain all the elements and characteristics of
20 democracy, since from the combinations of these the
varieties of democratic government arise. There are
several of these differing from each other, and the
difference is due to two causes. One (1) has been already
mentioned,[1]—differences of population ; for the popular
25 element may consist of husbandmen, or of mechanics, or
of labourers, and if the first of these be added to the
second, or the third to the two others, not only does the
democracy become better or worse, but its very nature
is changed. A second cause (2) remains to be mentioned :
30 the various properties and characteristics of democracy,
when variously combined, make a difference. For one
democracy will have less and another will have more, and
another will have all of these characteristics. There is
an advantage in knowing them all, whether a man wishes
to establish some new form of democracy, or only to re-
35 model an existing one.[2] Founders of states try to bring
together all the elements which accord with the ideas of
the several constitutions ; but this is a mistake of theirs,
as I have already remarked[3] when speaking of the
destruction and preservation of states. We will now set
forth the principles, characteristics, and aims of such
states.

40   The basis of a democratic state is liberty ; which, **2**
according to the common opinion of men, can only be
1317ᵇ enjoyed in such a state ;—this they affirm to be the
great end of every democracy.[4] One principle of liberty
is for all to rule and be ruled in turn, and indeed democratic justice is the application of numerical not propor-
5 tionate equality ; whence it follows that the majority
must be supreme, and that whatever the majority
approve must be the end and the just. Every citizen, it

---

[1] iv. 1291ᵇ 17-28, 1292ᵇ 25 sqq., 1296ᵇ 26-31.   [2] Cp. iv. 1289ᵃ 1.
[3] v. 1309ᵇ 18-1310ᵃ 36.   [4] Cp. Plato, *Rep.* viii. 557 sqq.

is said, must have equality, and therefore in a democracy the poor have more power than the rich, because there are more of them, and the will of the majority is supreme. This, then, is one note of liberty which all democrats affirm to be the principle of their state. Another is that a man should live as he likes.[1] This, they say, is the privilege of a freeman, since, on the other hand, not to live as a man likes is the mark of a slave. This is the second characteristic of democracy, whence has arisen the claim of men to be ruled by none, if possible, or, if this is impossible, to rule and be ruled in turns ; and so it contributes to the freedom based upon equality.

Such being our foundation and such the principle from which we start, the characteristics of democracy are as follows :—the election of officers by all out of all ; and that all should rule over each, and each in his turn over all ; that the appointment to all offices, or to all but those which require experience and skill,[2] should be made by lot ; that no property qualification should be required for offices, or only a very low one ; that a man should not hold the same office twice, or not often, or in the case of few except military offices : that the tenure of all offices, or of as many as possible, should be brief ; that all men should sit in judgement, or that judges selected out of all should judge, in all matters, or in most and in the greatest and most important,—such as the scrutiny of accounts, the constitution, and private contracts ; that the assembly should be supreme over all causes, or at any rate over the most important, and the magistrates over none or only over a very few.[3] Of all magistracies, a council is the most democratic [4] when there is not the means of paying all the citizens, but when they are paid even this is robbed of its power ; for the people then draw all cases to themselves, as I said in the previous discussion.[5] The next characteristic of democracy is payment for services ; assembly, law-courts, magistrates, everybody receives

[1] Cp. v. 1310^a 31.   [2] Cp. iv. 1298^a 27.
[3] Reading with the MSS. in ll. 29, 30 πάντων—ἀρχὴν ... ὀλιγίστων —ἢ τῶν μεγίστων κυρίαν.
[4] Cp. iv. 1299^b 32.   [5] Cp. iv. 1299^b 38.

pay, when it is to be had ; or when it is not to be had for all, then it is given to the law-courts and to the stated assemblies, to the council and to the magistrates, or at least to any of them who are compelled to have their meals together. And whereas oligarchy is characterized 40 by birth, wealth, and education, the notes of democracy appear to be the opposite of these,—low birth, poverty, mean employment. Another note is that no magistracy 1318ᵃ is perpetual, but if any such have survived some ancient change in the constitution it should be stripped of its power, and the holders should be elected by lot and no longer by vote. These are the points common to all democracies ; but democracy and demos in their truest 5 form are based upon the recognized principle of democratic justice, that all should count equally ; for equality implies that the poor should have no more share in the government than the rich, and should not be the only rulers, but that all should rule equally according to their numbers.[1] And in this way men think that they will 10 secure equality and freedom in their state.

Next comes the question, how is this equality to be 3 obtained ? Are we to assign to a thousand poor men the property qualifications of five hundred rich men ? and shall we give the thousand a power equal to that of the five hundred ? or, if this is not to be the mode, 15 ought we, still retaining the same ratio, to take equal numbers from each and give them the control of the elections and of the courts ?—Which, according to the democratical notion, is the juster form of the constitution,—this or one based on numbers only ? Democrats say that justice is that to which the majority agree, 20 oligarchs that to which the wealthier class ; in their opinion the decision should be given according to the amount of property. In both principles there is some inequality and injustice. For if justice is the will of the few, any one person who has more wealth than all the rest of the rich put together, ought, upon the oligarchical

[1] Cp. iv. 1291ᵇ 30.

principle, to have the sole power—but this would be
tyranny ; or if justice is the will of the majority, as I was 25
before saying,[1] they will unjustly confiscate the property
of the wealthy minority.   To find a principle of equality
in which they both agree we must inquire into their
respective ideas of justice.

Now they agree in saying that whatever is decided
by the majority of the citizens is to be deemed law.
Granted :—but not without some reserve ; since there are 30
two classes out of which a state is composed,—the poor
and the rich,—that is to be deemed law, on which both
or the greater part of both agree ; and if they disagree,
that which is approved by the greater number, and by
those who have the higher qualification.   For example,
suppose that there are ten rich and twenty poor, and
some measure is approved by six of the rich and is disapproved by fifteen of the poor, and the remaining four of 35
the rich join with the party of the poor, and the remaining five of the poor with that of the rich ; in such a case
the will of those whose qualifications, when both sides
are added up, are the greatest, should prevail.   If they turn
out to be equal, there is no greater difficulty than at
present, when, if the assembly or the courts are divided, 40
recourse is had to the lot, or to some similar expedient. 1318ᵇ
But, although it may be difficult in theory to know what
is just and equal, the practical difficulty of inducing those
to forbear who can, if they like, encroach, is far greater,
for the weaker are always asking for equality and justice,
but the stronger care for none of these things.   5

4   Of the four kinds of democracy, as was said in the
previous discussion,[2] the best is that which comes first in
order ; it is also the oldest of them all.   I am speaking
of them according to the natural classification of their
inhabitants.   For the best material of democracy is an
agricultural population ;[3] there is no difficulty in forming 10
a democracy where the mass of the people live by agriculture or tending of cattle.   Being poor, they have no

---

[1] Cp. iii. 1281ᵃ 14.   [2] iv. 1292ᵇ 22–1293ᵃ10.   [3] Cp. iv. 1292ᵇ 25–33.

leisure, and therefore do not often attend the assembly, and not[1] having the necessaries of life they are always at work, and do not covet the property of others. Indeed, they find their employment pleasanter than the cares of government or office where no great gains can be made out of them, for the many are more desirous of gain than of honour.[2] A proof is that even the ancient tyrannies were patiently endured by them, as they still endure oligarchies, if they are allowed to work and are not deprived of their property ; for some of them grow quickly rich and the others are well enough off. Moreover, they have the power of electing the magistrates and calling them to account ;[3] their ambition, if they have any, is thus satisfied ; and in some democracies, although they do not all share in the appointment of offices, except through representatives elected in turn out of the whole people, as at Mantinea ;—yet, if they have the power of deliberating, the many are contented. Even this form of government may be regarded as a democracy, and was such at Mantinea. Hence it is both expedient and customary in the afore-mentioned[4] type of democracy that all should elect to offices, and conduct scrutinies, and sit in the law-courts, but that the great offices should be filled up by election and from persons having a qualification ; the greater requiring a greater qualification, or, if there be no offices for which a qualification is required, then those who are marked out by special ability should be appointed. Under such a form of government the citizens are sure to be governed well (for the offices will always be held by the best persons ; the people are willing enough to elect them and are not jealous of the good). The good and the notables will then be satisfied, for they will not be governed by men who are their inferiors, and the persons elected will rule justly, because others will call them to account. Every man should be responsible to others, nor should any one be allowed to do just as he pleases ; for where absolute freedom is

---

[1] Retaining μή in l. 13.   [2] Cp. iv. 1297^b 6.
[3] Cp. ii. 1274^a 15.   [4] l. 6.

allowed there is nothing to restrain the evil which is inherent in every man. But the principle of responsibility 1319ᵃ secures that which is the greatest good in states; the right persons rule and are prevented from doing wrong, and the·people have their due. It is evident that this is the best kind of democracy, and why? because the people ⁵ are drawn from a certain class. Some of the ancient laws of most ¹ states were, all of them,² useful with a view to making the people husbandmen. They provided either that no one should possess more than a certain quantity of land, or that, if he did, the land should not be within a certain distance from the town or the acropolis. For- ₁₀ merly in many states there was a law forbidding any one to sell his original allotment of land.³ There is a similar law attributed to Oxylus, which is to the effect that there should be a certain portion of every man's land on which he could not borrow money. A useful corrective to the evil of which I am speaking would be the law of the ₁₅ Aphytaeans, who, although they are numerous, and do not possess much land, are all of them husbandmen. For their properties are reckoned in the census, not entire, but only in such small portions that even the poor may have more than the amount required.

Next best to an agricultural, and in many respects similar, are a pastoral people, who live by their flocks; ₂₀ they are the best trained of any for war, robust in body and able to camp out. The people of whom other democracies consist are far inferior to them, for their life ₂₅ is inferior; there is no room for moral excellence in any of their employments, whether they be mechanics or traders or labourers. Besides, people of this class can readily come to the assembly, because they are continually moving about in the city and in the agora; whereas husband- ₃₀ men are scattered over the country and do not meet, or equally feel the want of assembling together. Where the territory also happens to extend to a distance from the city,

---

¹ Retaining τοῖς in l. 7.
² Reading πάντες in l. 8 with the MSS. Cp. v. 1315ᵇ 38.
³ Cp. ii. 1266ᵇ 21.

there is no difficulty in making an excellent democracy or
35 constitutional government; for the people are compelled to
settle in the country, and even if there is a town population
the assembly ought not to meet, in democracies,[1] when
the country people cannot come. We have thus explained
how the first and best form of democracy should be
40 constituted ; it is clear that the other or inferior sorts
1319^b will deviate in a regular order, and the population which
is excluded will at each stage be of a lower kind.

The last form of democracy, that in which all share
alike, is one which cannot be borne by all states, and
will not last long unless well regulated by laws and
customs. The more general causes which tend to de-
5 stroy this or other kinds of government have been
pretty fully considered.[2] In order to constitute such a
democracy and strengthen the people, the leaders have
been in the habit of including as many as they can, and
making citizens not only of those who are legitimate, but
even of the illegitimate, and of those who have only one
10 parent a citizen, whether father or mother ;[3] for nothing
of this sort comes amiss to such a democracy. This is
the way in which demagogues proceed. Whereas the
right thing would be to make no more additions when
the number of the commonalty exceeds that of the
notables and of the middle class,—beyond this not to go.
When in excess of this point, the constitution becomes
15 disorderly, and the notables grow excited and impatient
of the democracy, as in the insurrection at Cyrene ; for
no notice is taken of a little evil, but when it increases it
strikes the eye. Measures like those which Cleisthenes[4]
20 passed when he wanted to increase the power of the
democracy at Athens, or such as were taken by the
founders of popular government at Cyrene, are useful in
the extreme form of democracy. Fresh tribes and
brotherhoods should be established ; the private rites of

---

[1] Reading in l. 37 μὴ ποιεῖν (MSS.) ἐν ταῖς δημοκρατίαις (Lambinus)
ἐκκλησίας (some MSS.).
[2] v. 2–7, 1311ᵃ 22–1313ᵃ 16.   [3] Cp. iii. 1278ᵃ 27.
[4] Cp. iii. 1275ᵇ 35.

families should be restricted and converted into public
ones; in short, every contrivance should be adopted 25
which will mingle the citizens with one another and get
rid of old connexions. Again, the measures which are
taken by tyrants appear all of them to be democratic ;
such, for instance, as the licence permitted to slaves
(which may be to a certain extent advantageous) and also
that of women and children, and the allowing everybody
to live as he likes.[1] Such a government will have many 30
supporters, for most persons would rather live in a disorderly than in a sober manner.

5 The mere establishment of a democracy is not the
only or principal business of the legislator, or of those
who wish to create such a state, for any state, however 35
badly constituted, may last one, two, or three days ; a far
greater difficulty is the preservation of it. The legislator
should therefore endeavour to have a firm foundation
according to the principles already laid down concerning
the preservation and destruction of states ;[2] he should
guard against the destructive elements, and should make 40
laws, whether written or unwritten, which will contain 1320[a]
all the preservatives of states. He must not think the
truly democratical or oligarchical measure to be that
which will give the greatest amount of democracy or
oligarchy, but that which will make them last longest.[3]
The demagogues of our own day often get property 5
confiscated [4] in the law-courts in order to please the
people. But those who have the welfare of the state
at heart should counteract them, and make a law that
the property of the condemned should not be public and
go into the treasury but be sacred. Thus offenders will
be as much afraid, for they will be punished all the same,
and the people, having nothing to gain, will not be so 10
ready to condemn the accused. Care should also be
taken that state trials are as few as possible, and heavy
penalties should be inflicted on those who bring ground-

---

[1] Cp. v. 1313[b] 32.   [2] Cp. Bk. v.
[3] Cp. v. 1313[a] 20-33.   [4] Cp. v. 1305[a] 3.

less accusations; for it is the practice to indict, not members of the popular party, but the notables, al-
15 though the citizens ought to be all attached to the constitution as well,[1] or at any rate should not regard their rulers as enemies.

Now, since in the last and worst form of democracy the citizens are very numerous, and can hardly be made to assemble unless they are paid, and to pay them when
20 there are no revenues presses hardly upon the notables (for the money must be obtained by a property-tax and confiscations and corrupt practices of the courts, things which have before now overthrown many democracies) ; where, I say, there are no revenues, the government should hold few assemblies, and the law-courts should consist of many persons, but sit for a few days only. This system has two advantages: first, the rich do not fear the expense,
25 even although they are unpaid themselves when the poor are paid; and secondly, causes are better tried, for wealthy persons, although they do not like to be long absent from their own affairs, do not mind going for a few days to the law-courts. Where there are revenues the demagogues should not be allowed after
30 their manner to distribute the surplus ; the poor are always receiving and always wanting more and more, for such help is like water poured into a leaky cask. Yet the true friend of the people should see that they be not too poor, for extreme poverty lowers the cha-
35 racter of the democracy ; measures therefore should be taken which will give them lasting prosperity ; and as this is equally the interest of all classes, the proceeds of the public revenues should be accumulated and distributed among its poor, if possible, in such quantities as may enable them to purchase a little farm, or, at any rate,
1320ᵇ make a beginning in trade or husbandry. And if this benevolence cannot be extended to all, money should be distributed in turn according to tribes or other divisions, and in the meantime the rich should pay the fee for the attendance of the poor at the necessary assemblies ; and

[1] Sc. 'as to οἱ κύριοι under it' (Newman). Omit ταύτῃ in l. 15.

should in return be excused from useless public services. By administering the state in this spirit the Carthaginians retain the affections of the people ; their policy is 5 from time to time to send some of them into their dependent towns, where they grow rich.[1] It is also worthy of a generous and sensible nobility to divide the poor amongst them, and give them the means of going to work. The example of the people of Tarentum is also well deserving of imitation, for, by sharing the use of 10 their own property with the poor, they gain their good will.[2] Moreover, they divide all their offices into two classes, some of them being elected by vote, the others by lot ; the latter, that the people may participate in them, and the former, that the state may be better administered. A like result may be gained by dividing the same offices, so as to have two classes of magistrates, one chosen by vote, the other by lot. 15

Enough has been said of the manner in which democracies ought to be constituted.

6 From these considerations there will be no difficulty in seeing what should be the constitution of oligarchies. We have only to reason from opposites and compare each form of oligarchy with the corresponding form of 20 democracy.

The first and best attempered of oligarchies is akin to a constitutional government. In this there ought to be two standards of qualification ; the one high, the other low—the lower qualifying for the humbler yet indispensable offices and the higher for the superior ones. He who 25 acquires the prescribed qualification should have the rights of citizenship. The number of those admitted should be such as will make the entire governing body stronger than those who are excluded, and the new citizen should be always taken out of the better class of the people. The principle, narrowed a little, gives another form of oligarchy ; until at length we reach the most cliquish 30 and tyrannical of them all, answering to the extreme

---

[1] Cp. ii. 1273^b 18.   [2] Cp. ii. 1263^a 37.

democracy, which, being the worst, requires vigilance in
proportion to its badness. For as healthy bodies and ships
35 well provided with sailors may undergo many mishaps
and survive them, whereas sickly constitutions and rotten
ill-manned ships are ruined by the very least mistake, so
do the worst forms of government require the greatest
1321^a care. The populousness of democracies generally preserves them (for number is to democracy in the place of
justice based on proportion); whereas the preservation of
an oligarchy clearly depends on an opposite principle,
viz. good order.

5   As there are four chief divisions of the common people, **7**
—husbandmen, mechanics, retail traders, labourers; so
also there are four kinds of military forces,—the cavalry,
the heavy infantry, the light-armed troops, the navy.[1]
When the country is adapted for cavalry, then a strong
10 oligarchy is likely to be established. For the security of
the inhabitants depends upon a force of this sort, and only
rich men can afford to keep horses. The second form
of oligarchy prevails when the country is adapted to
heavy infantry; for this service is better suited to the
rich than to the poor. But the light-armed and the
naval element are wholly democratic; and nowadays,
15 where they are numerous, if the two parties quarrel,
the oligarchy are often worsted by them in the struggle.
A remedy for this state of things may be found in the
practice of generals who combine a proper contingent of
light-armed troops with cavalry and heavy-armed. And
this is the way in which the poor get the better of the
20 rich in civil contests; being lightly armed, they fight
with advantage against cavalry and heavy infantry. An
oligarchy which raises such a force out of the lower classes
raises a power against itself. And therefore, since the
ages of the citizens vary and some are older and some
younger, the fathers should have their own sons, while
they are still young, taught the agile movements of light-
25 armed troops; and these, when they have been taken

[1] Cp. iv. 1289^b 32-40.

out of the ranks of the youth, should become light-armed
warriors in reality. The oligarchy should also yield
a share in the government to the people, either, as I said
before, to those who have a property qualification,[1] or,
as in the case of Thebes,[2] to those who have abstained
for a certain number of years from mean employments, 30
or, as at Massalia, to men of merit who are selected
for their worthiness, whether previously citizens or not.
The magistracies of the highest rank, which ought to be
in the hands of the governing body, should have expensive
duties attached to them, and then the people will not
desire them and will take no offence at the privileges
of their rulers when they see that they pay a heavy fine
for their dignity. It is fitting also that the magistrates 35
on entering office should offer magnificent sacrifices or
erect some public edifice, and then the people who
participate in the entertainments, and see the city
decorated with votive offerings and buildings, will not
desire an alteration in the government, and the notables
will have memorials of their munificence. This, however, 40
is anything but the fashion of our modern oligarchs, who
are as covetous of gain as they are of honour ; oligarchies
like theirs may be well described as petty democracies. **1321ᵇ**
Enough of the manner in which democracies and oligarchies should be organized.

8   Next in order follows the right distribution of offices,
their number, their nature, their duties, of which indeed 5
we have already spoken.[3] No state can exist not
having the necessary offices, and no state can be well
administered not having the offices which tend to preserve harmony and good order. In small states, as we
have already remarked,[4] there must not be many of
them, but in larger there must be a larger number, and 10
we should carefully consider which offices may properly
be united and which separated.

First among necessary offices is that which has the care

---

[1] 1320ᵇ 25.   [2] Cp. iii. 1278ᵃ 25.
[3] iv. 15.   [4] iv. 1299ᵃ 34–ᵇ 10.

of the market ; a magistrate should be appointed to inspect contracts and to maintain order.   For in every state
15 there must inevitably be buyers and sellers who will
supply one another's wants ; this is the readiest way to
make a state self-sufficing and so fulfil the purpose for
which men come together into one state.[1]   A second
office of a similar kind undertakes the supervision and
20 embellishment of public and private buildings, the maintaining and repairing of houses and roads, the prevention
of disputes about boundaries, and other concerns of a like
nature.   This is commonly called the office of City-
warden, and has various departments, which, in more
25 populous towns, are shared among different persons, one,
for example, taking charge of the walls, another of the
fountains, a third of harbours.   There is another equally
necessary office, and of a similar kind, having to do
with the same matters without the walls and in the
country :—the magistrates who hold this office are called
Wardens of the country, or Inspectors of the woods.
30 Besides these three there is a fourth office of receivers of
taxes, who have under their charge the revenue which is
distributed among the various departments ; these are
called Receivers or Treasurers.   Another officer registers
35 all private contracts, and decisions of the courts, all public
indictments, and also all preliminary proceedings.   This
office again is sometimes subdivided, in which case one
officer is appointed over all the rest.[2]   These officers are
called Recorders or Sacred Recorders, Presidents, and
the like.
40   Next to these comes an office of which the duties are
the most necessary and also the most difficult, viz. that
to which is committed the execution of punishments, or
the exaction of fines from those who are posted up accord-
1322[a] ing to the registers ; and also the custody of prisoners.
The difficulty of this office arises out of the odium which
is attached to it ; no one will undertake it unless great
profits are to be made, and any one who does is loath to

---

[1] Cp. i. 1252[b] 27 ; *Nic. Eth.* v. 1134[a] 26 ; Pl. *Rep.* ii. 369.
[2] Omitting οὐ in l. 38.

execute the law.   Still the office is necessary ; for judicial 5
decisions are useless if they take no 'effect ; and if society
cannot exist without them, neither can it exist without
the execution of them.   It is an office which, being so
unpopular, should not be entrusted to one person, but
divided among several taken from different courts.   In
like manner an effort should be made to distribute among
different persons the writing up of those who are on the
register of public debtors.   Some sentences should be 10
executed by the magistrates also, and in particular
penalties due to the outgoing magistrates should be
exacted by the incoming ones ; and as regards those due
to magistrates already in office, when one court has
given judgement, another should exact the penalty ; for
example, the wardens of the city should exact the fines
imposed by the wardens of the agora, and others again
should exact the fines imposed by *them.*   For penalties 15
are more likely to be exacted when less odium attaches
to the exaction of them ; but a double odium is incurred
when the judges who have passed also execute the
sentence, and if they are always the executioners, they will
be [1] the enemies of all.

In many places, while one magistracy executes the
sentence, another [2] has the custody of the prisoners, as, for
example, 'the Eleven' at Athens.   It is well to separate 20
off the jailorship also, and try by some device to render the
office less unpopular.   For it is quite as necessary as
that of the executioners ; but good men do all they can to
avoid it, and worthless persons cannot safely be trusted
with it ; for they themselves require a guard, and are not 25
fit to guard others.   There ought not therefore to be
a single or permanent officer set apart for this duty ; but
it should be entrusted to the young, wherever they are
organized into a band or guard, and different magistrates
acting in turn should take charge of it.

These are the indispensable officers, and should be
ranked first :—next in order follow others, equally neces- 30

---

[1] Inserting ποιεῖ after αὐτούς in l. 18, with Welldon.
[2] Reading δὲ διῄρηται in l. 19 with the MSS.

sary, but of higher rank, and requiring great experience
and fidelity. Such are the offices to which are committed
the guard of the city, and other military functions. Not
35 only in time of war but of peace their duty will be to
defend the walls and gates, and to muster and marshal
the citizens. In some states there are many such offices ;
in others there are a few only, while small states are content with one ; these officers are called generals or com-
1322ᵇ manders. Again, if a state has cavalry or light-armed
troops or archers or a naval force, it will sometimes
happen that each of these departments has separate
officers, who are called admirals, or generals of cavalry or
of light-armed troops. And there are subordinate officers
called naval captains, and captains of light-armed troops
5 and of horse ; having others under them :—all these are
included in the department of war. Thus much of
military command.

But since many, not to say all, of these offices handle
the public money, there must of necessity be another
office which examines and audits them, and has no other
10 functions. Such officers are called by various names,—
Scrutineers, Auditors, Accountants, Controllers. Besides
all these offices there is another which is supreme over
them, and to this is often entrusted both the introduction
and the ratification of measures, or at all events it presides, in a democracy, over the assembly. For there
15 must be a body which convenes the supreme authority
in the state. In some places they are called 'probuli',
because they hold previous deliberations, but in a
democracy more commonly 'councillors'.[1] These are
the chief political offices.

Another set of officers is concerned with the maintenance
20 of religion ; priests and guardians see to the preservation
and repair of the temples of the gods and to other matters
of religion. One office of this sort may be enough in small
places, but in larger ones there are a great many besides
the priesthood ; for example superintendents of public
25 worship, guardians of shrines, treasurers of the sacred

[1] Cp. iv. 1299ᵇ31.

revenues. Nearly connected with these there are also the officers appointed for the performance of the public sacrifices, except any which the law assigns to the priests ; such sacrifices derive their dignity from the public hearth of the city. They are sometimes called archons, sometimes kings,¹ and sometimes prytanes.

These, then, are the necessary offices, which may be ₃₀ summed up as follows : offices concerned with matters of religion, with war, with the revenue and expenditure, with the market, with the city, with the harbours, with the country ; also with the courts of law, with the records of contracts, with execution of sentences, with custody of ₃₅ prisoners, with audits and scrutinies and accounts of magistrates ; lastly, there are those which preside over the public deliberations of the state.² There are likewise magistracies characteristic of states which are peaceful and prosperous, and at the same time have a regard to good order : such as the offices of guardians of women, guardians of the laws, guardians of children, and directors of gymnastics ; also superintendents of gymnastic and 1323ᵃ Dionysiac contests, and of other similar spectacles. Some of these are clearly not democratic offices ; for example, the guardianships of women and children³—the poor, ₅ not having any slaves, must employ both their women and children as servants.

Once more : there are three offices according to whose directions the highest magistrates are chosen in certain states—guardians of the law, probuli, councillors,—of these, the guardians of the law are an aristocratical, the probuli an oligarchical, the council a democratical institution. Enough of the different kinds of offices.   ₁₀

¹ Cp. iii. 1285ᵇ 23.
² Reading εἰσι περὶ τῶν in l. 37, with Richards.
³ Cp. iv. 1300ᵃ 4.

BOOK VII

HE who would duly inquire about the best form of a 1
15 state ought first to determine which is the most eligible
life; while this remains uncertain the best form of the
state must also be uncertain; for, in the natural order of
things, those may be expected to lead the best life who
are governed in the best manner of which their circumstances admit. We ought therefore to ascertain, first of
20 all, which is the most generally eligible life, and then
whether the same life is or is not best for the state and
for individuals.

Assuming that enough has been already said in
discussions outside the school concerning the best life, we
will now only repeat what is contained in them. Certainly
no one will dispute the propriety of that partition of goods
25 which separates them into three classes,[1] viz. external
goods, goods of the body, and goods of the soul, or deny
that the happy man must have all three. For no one
would maintain that he is happy who has not in him a
particle of courage or temperance or justice or prudence,
who is afraid of every insect which flutters past him,
30 and will commit any crime, however great, in order to
gratify his lust of meat or drink, who will sacrifice his
dearest friend for the sake of half-a-farthing, and is as
feeble and false in mind as a child or a madman. These
propositions are almost universally acknowledged as soon
35 as they are uttered, but men differ about the degree or
relative superiority of this or that good. Some think
that a very moderate amount of virtue is enough, but
set no limit to their desires of wealth, property, power,
reputation, and the like. To whom we reply by an appeal
40 to facts, which easily prove that mankind do not acquire
or preserve virtue by the help of external goods, but

---

[1] Cp. *Laws*, iii. 697 B, v. 743 E ; *N. Eth.* i. 1098 ^{b}12.

external goods by the help of virtue, and that happiness, **1323**[b] whether consisting in pleasure or virtue, or both, is more often found with those who are most highly cultivated in their mind and in their character, and have only a moderate share of external goods, than among those who possess external goods to a useless extent but are 5 deficient in higher qualities; and this is not only matter of experience, but, if reflected upon, will easily appear to be in accordance with reason. For, whereas external goods have a limit, like any other instrument,[1] and all things useful are of such a nature that [2] where there is too much of them they must either do harm, or at any rate be of no use, to their possessors, every good of the soul, 10 the greater it is, is also of greater use, if the epithet useful as well as noble is appropriate to such subjects. No proof is required to show that the best state of one thing in relation to another corresponds in degree of excellence to the interval between the natures of which we say 15 that these very states are states : so that, if the soul is more noble than our possessions or our bodies, both absolutely and in relation to us, it must be admitted that the best state of either has a similar ratio to the other. Again, it is for the sake of the soul that goods external and goods of the body are eligible at all, and all wise men ought to choose them for the sake of the soul, and 20 not the soul for the sake of them.

Let us acknowledge then that each one has just so much of happiness as he has of virtue and wisdom, and of virtuous and wise action. God is a witness to us of this truth, for he is happy and blessed, not by reason of any external good, but in himself and by reason of his 25 own nature. And herein of necessity lies the difference between good fortune and happiness; for external goods come of themselves, and chance is the author of them, but no one is just or temperate by or through chance.[3] In like manner, and by a similar train of argument, 30

---

[1] Cp. i. 1256[b] 35.
[2] Reading (without brackets) πᾶν δὲ τὸ χρήσιμόν ἐστιν ὧν in l. 8, with the MSS.
[3] N. Eth. i. 1099[b] 20.

the happy state may be shown to be that which is best and which acts rightly; and rightly it cannot act without doing right actions, and neither individual nor state can do right actions without virtue and wisdom. Thus the courage, justice, and wisdom of a state have 35 the same form and nature as the qualities which give the individual who possesses them the name of just, wise, or temperate.

Thus much may suffice by way of preface: for I could not avoid touching upon these questions, neither could I go through all the arguments affecting them; these are the business of another science.

40 Let us assume then that the best life, both for individuals and states, is the life of virtue, when virtue has **1324**^a external goods enough for the performance of good actions. If there are any who controvert our assertion, we will in this treatise pass them over, and consider their objections hereafter.

5 There remains to be discussed the question, Whether **2** the happiness of the individual is the same as that of the state, or different? Here again there can be no doubt— no one denies that they are the same. For those who hold that the well-being of the individual consists in his wealth, also think that riches make the happiness of the 10 whole state, and those who value most highly the life of a tyrant deem that city the happiest which rules over the greatest number; while they who approve an individual for his virtue say that the more virtuous a city is, the happier it is. Two points here present themselves for con- 15 sideration: first (1), which is the more eligible life, that of a citizen who is a member of a state, or that of an alien who has no political ties; and again (2), which is the best form of constitution or the best condition of a state, either on the supposition that political privileges are desirable for all, or for a majority only? Since the 20 good of the state and not of the individual is the proper subject of political thought and speculation, and we are engaged in a political discussion, while the first of these

two points has a secondary interest for us, the latter will
be the main subject of our inquiry.

Now it is evident that the form of government is best
in which every man, whoever he is, can act best and live
happily. But even those who agree in thinking that the 25
life of virtue is the most eligible raise a question, whether
the life of business and politics is or is not more eligible
than one which is wholly independent of external goods,
I mean than a contemplative life, which by some is
maintained to be the only one worthy of a philosopher.
For these two lives—the life of the philosopher and the
life of the statesman—appear to have been preferred 30
by those who have been most keen in the pursuit of
virtue, both in our own and in other ages. Which is the
better is a question of no small moment ; for the wise
man, like the wise state, will necessarily regulate his life
according to the best end. There are some who think 35
that while a despotic rule over others is the greatest
injustice, to exercise a constitutional rule over them, even
though not unjust, is a great impediment to a man's
individual well-being. Others take an opposite view ;
they maintain that the true life of man is the practical
and political, and that every virtue admits of being 40
practised, quite as much by statesmen and rulers as by 1324ᵇ
private individuals. Others, again, are of opinion that
arbitrary and tyrannical rule alone consists with happiness ; indeed, in some states the entire aim both of
the laws and of the constitution[1] is to give men despotic
power over their neighbours. And, therefore, although 5
in most cities the laws may be said generally to be in
a chaotic state, still, if they aim at anything, they aim at
the maintenance of power : thus in Lacedaemon and Crete
the system of education and the greater part of the laws
are framed with a view to war.[2] And in all nations which 10
are able to gratify their ambition military power is held
in esteem, for example among the Scythians and Persians

---

[1] Reading in l. 4 δ' οὗτος καὶ τῶν νόμων καὶ τῆς πολιτείας ὅρος, with
the 'old translator' and one MS.

[2] Cp. Plato, Laws, i. 633 ff.

and Thracians and Celts. In some nations there are even laws tending to stimulate the warlike virtues, as at Carthage, where we are told that men obtain the honour of wear-
15 ing as many armlets as they have served campaigns. There was once a law in Macedonia that he who had not killed an enemy should wear a halter, and among the Scythians no one who had not slain his man was allowed to drink out of the cup which was handed round at a certain feast. Among the Iberians, a warlike nation, the number of enemies whom a man has slain is indicated by the
20 number of obelisks [1] which are fixed in the earth round his tomb ; and there are numerous practices among other nations of a like kind, some of them established by law and others by custom. Yet to a reflecting mind it must appear very strange that the statesman should be always
25 considering how he can dominate and tyrannize over others, whether they will or not. How can that which is not even lawful be the business of the statesman or the legislator? Unlawful it certainly is to rule without regard to justice, for there may be might where there is no right. The other arts and sciences offer no parallel ;
30 a physician is not expected to persuade or coerce his patients, nor a pilot the passengers in his ship. Yet most men appear to think that the art of despotic govern-ment is statesmanship, and what men affirm to be unjust and inexpedient in their own case they are not ashamed
35 of practising towards others ; they demand just rule for themselves, but where other men are concerned they care nothing about it. Such behaviour is irrational ; unless the one party is, and the other is not, born to serve, in which case men have a right to command, not indeed all their fellows, but only those who are intended to be subjects ; just as we ought not to hunt mankind, whether for food or sacrifice, but only the animals which
40 may be hunted for food or sacrifice,[2] that is to say, such wild animals as are eatable. And surely there may be
1325[a] a city happy in isolation, which we will assume to be well-governed (for it is quite possible that a city thus

---

[1] Or 'spits'.   [2] τά in l. 40 (Immisch) is a misprint for τό.

isolated might be well-administered and have good laws);
but such a city would not be constituted with any view
to war or the conquest of enemies,—all that sort of
thing must be excluded.   Hence we see very plainly 5
that warlike pursuits, although generally to be deemed
honourable, are not the supreme end of all things, but
only means.   And the good lawgiver should inquire
how states and races of men and communities may participate in a good life, and in the happiness which is
attainable by them.   His enactments will not be always 10
the same; and where there are neighbours[1] he will have
to see what sort of studies should be practised in relation
to their several characters, or how the measures appropriate in relation to each are to be adopted.   The end at
which the best form of government should aim may be
properly made a matter of future consideration.[2]   15

3   Let us now address those who, while they agree that
the life of virtue is the most eligible, differ about the
manner of practising it.   For some renounce political
power, and think that the life of the freeman is different 20
from the life of the statesman and the best of all; but
others think the life of the statesman best.   The argument
of the latter is that he who does nothing cannot do well,
and that virtuous activity is identical with happiness.
To both we say : 'you are partly right and partly wrong.'
The first class are right in affirming that the life of the
freeman is better than the life of the despot; for there 25
is nothing grand or noble in having the use of a slave, in
so far as he is a slave; or in issuing commands about
necessary things.   But it is an error to suppose that
every sort of rule is despotic like that of a master over
slaves, for there is as great a difference between the rule
over freemen and the rule over slaves as there is between
slavery by nature and freedom by nature, about which I 30
have said enough at the commencement of this treatise.[3]
And it is equally a mistake to place inactivity above

---

[1] Cp. ii. 1265[a] 20, 1267[a] 19.   [2] 1333[a] 11 sqq.   [3] i. 4-7.

action, for happiness is activity, and the actions of the just and wise are the realization of much that is noble.

But perhaps some one, accepting these premises, may still maintain that supreme power is the best of all things, 35 because the possessors of it are able to perform the greatest number of noble actions. If so, the man who is able to rule, instead of giving up anything to his neighbour, ought rather to take away his power; and the father should make no account[1] of his son, nor the son of his father, nor friend of friend; they should not bestow a thought on one another in comparison with this higher 40 object, for the best is the most eligible and 'doing well' is the best. There might be some truth in such a view **1325ᵇ** if we assume that robbers and plunderers attain the chief good. But this can never be; their hypothesis is false. For the actions of a ruler cannot really be honourable, unless he is as much superior to other men as a husband is to a wife, or a father to his children, 5 or a master to his slaves. And therefore he who violates the law can never recover by any success, however great, what he has already lost in departing from virtue. For equals the honourable and the just consist in sharing alike, as is just and equal. But that the unequal should be given to equals, and the unlike to those who are like, is contrary to nature, and nothing which is contrary to 10 nature is good. If, therefore, there is any one[2] superior in virtue and in the power of performing the best actions, him we ought to follow and obey, but he must have the capacity for action as well as virtue.

If we are right in our view, and happiness is assumed 15 to be virtuous activity, the active life will be the best, both for every city collectively, and for individuals. Not that a life of action must necessarily have relation to others, as some persons think, nor are those ideas only to be regarded as practical which are pursued for the sake of practical results, but much more the thoughts

---

[1] Reading ὑπόλογον ἔχειν in l. 39, as suggested by Dindorf and Madvig.
[2] Cp. iii. 1284ᵇ 32 and 1288ᵃ 28.

and contemplations which are independent and complete 20
in themselves ; since virtuous activity, and therefore
a certain kind of action, is an end, and even in the case
of external actions the directing mind is most truly said
to act.   Neither, again, is it necessary that states which
are cut off from others and choose to live alone should
be inactive ; for activity, as well as other things, may 25
take place by sections ; there are many ways in which
the sections of a state act upon one another.   The same
thing is equally true of every individual.   If this were
otherwise, God and the universe, who have no external
actions over and above their own energies, would be far
enough from perfection.   Hence it is evident that the 30
same life is best for each individual, and' for states and
for mankind collectively.

4   Thus far by way of introduction.   In what has preceded[1] I have discussed other forms of government ; in
what remains the first point to be considered is what 35
should be the conditions of the ideal or perfect state ;
for the perfect state cannot exist without a due supply
of the means of life.   And therefore we must pre-
suppose many purely imaginary conditions,[2] but nothing
impossible.   There will be a certain number of citizens,
a country in which to place them, and the like.   As the 40
weaver or shipbuilder or any other artisan must have
the material proper for his work (and in proportion as 1326^{a}
this is better prepared, so will the result of his art be
nobler), so the statesman or legislator must also have the
materials suited to him.

    First among the materials required by the statesman 5
is population : he will consider what should be the
number and character of the citizens, and then what should
be the size and character of the country.   Most persons
think that a state in order to be happy ought to be large;
but even if they are right, they have no idea what is a
large and what a small state.   For they judge of the 10

---

[1] Bk. ii.   [2] Cp. ii. 1265^{a}17.

size of the city by the number of the inhabitants; whereas they ought to regard, not their number, but their power. A city too, like an individual, has a work to do ; and that city which is best adapted to the fulfilment of its work is to be deemed greatest, in the same
15 sense of the word great in which Hippocrates might be called greater, not as a man, but as a physician, than some one else who was taller. And even if we reckon greatness by numbers, we ought not to include everybody, for there must always be in cities a multitude of
20 slaves and sojourners and foreigners; but we should include those only who are members of the state, and who form an essential part of it. The number of the latter is a proof of the greatness of a city; but a city which produces numerous artisans and comparatively few soldiers cannot be great, for a great city is not to be confounded
25 with a populous one. Moreover, experience shows that a very populous city can rarely, if ever, be well governed ; since all cities which have a reputation for good government have a limit of population. We may argue on grounds of reason, and the same result will follow. For
30 law is order, and good law is good order ; but a very great multitude cannot be orderly : to introduce order into the unlimited is the work of a divine power—of such a power as holds together the universe. Beauty is realized in number and magnitude,[1] and the state which combines magnitude with good order must necessarily
35 be the most beautiful. To the size of states there is a limit, as there is to other things, plants, animals, implements; for none of these retain their natural power when they are too large or too small, but they either
40 wholly lose their nature, or are spoiled. For example,[2] a ship which is only a span long will not be a ship at all, nor a ship a quarter of a mile long ; yet there may
1326ᵇ be a ship of a certain size, either too large or too small, which will still be a ship, but bad for sailing. In like manner a state when composed of too few is not, as a state ought to be, self-sufficing; when of too many,

---

[1] Cp. *Poet.* 1450ᵇ 36.   [2] Cp. v. 1309ᵇ 23.

though self-sufficing in all mere necessaries, as a nation may
be, it is ¹ not a state, being almost incapable of constitu- 5
tional government. For who can be the general of such a
vast multitude, or who the herald, unless he have the voice
of a Stentor ?
A state, then, only begins to exist when it has attained
a population sufficient for a good life in the political
community : it may indeed, if it somewhat exceed this 10
number, be a greater state. But, as I was saying, there
must be a limit. What should be the limit will be easily
ascertained by experience. For both governors and
governed have duties to perform ; the special functions
of a governor are to command and to judge. But if the 15
citizens of a state are to judge and to distribute offices
according to merit, then they must know each other's
characters ; where they do not possess this knowledge,
both the election to offices and the decision of lawsuits
will go wrong. When the population is very large they
are manifestly settled at haphazard, which clearly ought
not to be. Besides, in an over-populous state foreigners 20
and metics will readily acquire the rights of citizens, for
who will find them out ? Clearly then the best limit of
the population of a state is the largest number which
suffices for the purposes of life, and can be taken in at a
single view. Enough concerning the size of a state.   25

5   Much the same principle will apply to the territory of
the state : every one would agree in praising the territory
which is most entirely self-sufficing ; and that must be
the territory which is all-producing, for to have all things
and to want nothing is sufficiency. In size and extent it 30
should be such as may enable the inhabitants to live at
once temperately and liberally in the enjoyment of leisure.²
Whether we are right or wrong in laying down this limit
we will inquire more precisely hereafter,³ when we have
occasion to consider what is the right use of property 35
and wealth : a matter which is much disputed, because

¹ Reading ὥσπερ ἔθνος, ἀλλ' in l. 4, with the MSS.
² Cp. ii. 1265ª 32.   ³ This promise is not fulfilled.

men are inclined to rush into one of two extremes, some
into meanness, others into luxury.

It is not difficult to determine the general character of
the territory which is required (there are, however, some
40 points on which military authorities should be heard); it
should be difficult of access to the enemy, and easy of
1327ᵃ egress to the inhabitants. Further, we require that the
land as well as the inhabitants of whom we were just now
speaking[1] should be taken in at a single view, for a
country which is easily seen can be easily protected. As
to the position of the city, if we could have what we wish,
5 it should be well situated in regard both to sea and land.
This then is one principle, that it should be a convenient
centre for the protection of the whole country: the other
is, that it should be suitable for receiving the fruits of the
soil, and also for the bringing in of timber and any
10 other products that are easily transported.

Whether a communication with the sea is beneficial to **6**
a well-ordered state or not is a question which has often
been asked. It is argued that the introduction of strangers
brought up under other laws, and the increase of popula-
15 tion, will be adverse to good order; the increase arises
from their using the sea and having a crowd of merchants
coming and going, and is inimical to good government.[2]
Apart from these considerations, it would be undoubtedly
better, both with a view to safety and to the provision
20 of necessaries, that the city and territory should be
connected with the sea; the defenders of a country, if
they are to maintain themselves against an enemy,
should be easily relieved both by land and by sea; and
even if they are not able to attack by sea and land at once,
they will have less difficulty[3] in doing mischief to their
assailants on one element, if they themselves can use both.
25 Moreover, it is necessary that they should import from
abroad what is not found in their own country, and that
they should export what they have in excess; for a city

---

[1] 1326ᵇ 22–24.   [2] Cp. Plato, *Laws*, iv. 704 D–705 B.
[3] Omitting πρός in l. 23, with Argyriades.

ought to be a market, not indeed for others, but for
herself.

Those who make themselves a market for the world
only do so for the sake of revenue, and if a state ought 30
not to desire profit of this kind it ought not to have
such an emporium. Nowadays we often see in countries
and cities dockyards and harbours very conveniently
placed outside the city, but not too far off ; and they are
kept in dependence by walls and similar fortifications. 35
Cities thus situated manifestly reap the benefit of intercourse with their ports ; and any harm which is likely to
accrue may be easily guarded against by the laws, which
will pronounce and determine who may hold communication with one another, and who may not.

There can be no doubt that the possession of a 40
moderate naval force is advantageous to a city ; the
city should be formidable not only to its own citizens **1327ᵇ**
but to some of its neighbours,[1] or, if necessary, able to
assist them by sea as well as by land. The proper
number or magnitude of this naval force is relative to the
character of the state ; for if her function is to take a
leading part in politics, her naval power should be 5
commensurate with the scale of her enterprises. The
population of the state need not be much increased, since
there is no necessity that the sailors should be citizens :
the marines who have the control and command will be
freemen, and belong also to the infantry ; and wherever 10
there is a dense population of Perioeci and husbandmen,
there will always be sailors more than enough. Of this
we see instances at the present day. The city of Heraclea,
for example, although small in comparison with many 15
others, can man a considerable fleet. Such are our
conclusions respecting the territory of the state, its
harbours, its towns, its relations to the sea, and its
maritime power.

7   Having spoken of the number of the citizens,[2] we will
proceed to speak of what should be their character.

---

[1] Cp. ii. 1265ᵃ 20.   [2] 1326ᵃ 9–ᵇ 24.

20 This is a subject which can be easily understood by
any one who casts his eye on the more celebrated states
of Hellas, and generally on the distribution of races in
the habitable world. Those who live in a cold climate
and in Europe are full of spirit, but wanting in intelli-
25 gence and skill ; and therefore they retain comparative
freedom, but have no political organization, and are incapable of ruling over others. Whereas the natives of
Asia are intelligent and inventive, but they are wanting
in spirit, and therefore they are always in a state of subjection and slavery. But the Hellenic race, which is
situated between them, is likewise intermediate in cha-
30 racter, being high-spirited and also intelligent.[1] Hence
it continues free, and is the best-governed of any nation,
and, if it could be formed into one state, would be able
to rule the world. There are also similar differences in
the different tribes of Hellas ; for some of them are of a
one-sided nature, and are intelligent or courageous only,
35 while in others there is a happy combination of both
qualities. And clearly those whom the legislator will
most easily lead to virtue may be expected to be both
intelligent and courageous. Some [2] say that the
guardians should be friendly towards those whom
40 they know, fierce towards those whom they do not
know. Now, passion is the quality of the soul which
1328^a begets friendship and enables us to love ; notably the
spirit within us is more stirred against our friends and
acquaintances than against those who are unknown to
us, when we think that we are despised by them ; for
which reason Archilochus,[3] complaining of his friends,
very naturally addresses his soul in these words,

5 ' For surely thou art plagued on account of friends.'

The power of command and the love of freedom are
in all men based upon this quality, for passion is commanding and invincible. Nor is it right to say that the
guardians should be fierce towards those whom they do
not know, for we ought not to be out of temper with

---

[1] Cp. Plato, *Rep.* iv. 435 E, 436 A.   [2] *Rep.* ii. 375 C.
[3] Fr. 67, Bergk[4].

any one ; and a lofty spirit is not fierce by nature, but
only when excited against evil-doers. And this, as I 10
was saying before, is a feeling which men show most
strongly towards their friends if they think they have
received a wrong at their hands: as indeed is reasonable ; for, besides the actual injury, they seem[1] to be
deprived of a benefit by those who owe them one.
Hence the saying,   15

> ' Cruel is the strife of brethren ',[2]

and again,

> ' They who love in excess also hate in excess '.[3]

Thus we have nearly determined the number and
character of the citizens of our state, and also the size
and nature of their territory. I say ' nearly ', for we
ought not to require the same minuteness in theory as 20
in the facts given by perception.[4]

8   As in other natural compounds the conditions of a
composite whole are not necessarily organic parts of it,
so in a state or in any other combination forming a unity
not everything is a part, which is a necessary condition.[5]
The members of an association have necessarily some one 25
thing the same and common to all, in which they share
equally or unequally ; for example, food or land or any
other thing. But where there are two things of which
one is a means and the other an end, they have nothing
in common except that the one receives what the other
produces.   Such, for example, is the relation in which 30
workmen and tools stand to their work ; the house and
the builder have nothing in common, but the art of the
builder is for the sake of the house.   And so states
require property, but property, even though living beings 35
are included in it,[6] is no part of a state ; for a state
is not a community of living beings only, but a community of equals, aiming at the best life possible. Now,
whereas happiness is the highest good, being a realization

---

[1] μονίζουσιν in l. 15 (Immisch) is a misprint for νομίζουσιν.
[2] Eur. fr. 975, Nauck[4].   [3] Fr. adesp. 78, Nauck[4].   [4] Cp. 1331ᵇ 18.
[5] Cp. iii. 1278ᵃ 2.   [6] Cp. i. 1253ᵇ 32.

and perfect practice of virtue, which some can attain, while
others have little or none of it, the various qualities of
40 men are clearly the reason why there are various kinds
of states and many forms of government; for different
1328ᵇ men seek after happiness in different ways and by different
means, and so make for themselves different modes of
life and forms of government. We must see also how
many things are indispensable to the existence of a state,
for what we call the parts of a state will be found among
the indispensables.[1] Let us then enumerate the functions
of a state, and we shall easily elicit what we want:
5 First, there must be food; secondly, arts, for life requires many instruments; thirdly, there must be arms,
for the members of a community have need of them, and in
their own hànds, too, in order to maintain authority both
10 against disobedient subjects and against external assailants ; fourthly, there must be a certain amount of revenue,
both for internal needs, and for the purposes of war ;
fifthly, or rather first, there must be a care of religion,
which is commonly called worship; sixthly, and most
necessary of all, there must be a power of deciding what
is for the public interest, and what is just in men's
dealings with one another.
15 These are the services which every state may be said to
need. For a state is not a mere aggregate of persons, but
a union of them sufficing for the purposes of life ; and
if any of these things be wanting, it is as we maintain [2]
impossible that the community can be absolutely self-
sufficing. A state then should be framed with a view to
the fulfilment of these functions. There must be husband-
20 men to procure food, and artisans, and a warlike and a
wealthy class, and priests, and judges to decide what is
necessary [3] and expedient.

Having determined these points, we have in the next **9**
place to consider whether all ought to share is every sort

---

[1] Reading ἐν τούτοις ἂν εἴη ἃ ἀναγκαῖον ὑπάρχειν in l. 4, with Newman.
[2] Cp. ii. 1261ᵇ 12, iii. 1275ᵇ 20, v. 1303ᵃ 26.
[3] Reading ἀναγκαίων καὶ συμφερόντων in l. 23, with the MSS.

of occupation. Shall every man be at once husbandman, 25
artisan, councillor, judge, or shall we suppose the several
occupations just mentioned assigned to different persons ?
or, thirdly, shall some employments be assigned to individuals and others common to all ? The same arrangement, however, does not occur in every constitution ; as
we were saying, all may be shared by all, or not 30
all by all, but only some by some ; and hence arise
the differences of constitutions, for in democracies all
share in all, in oligarchies the opposite practice prevails.
Now, since we are here speaking of the best form of
government, i. e. that under which the state will be most
happy (and happiness, as has been already said, cannot 35
exist without virtue[1]), it clearly follows that in the state
which is best governed and possesses men who are just
absolutely, and not merely relatively to the principle of
the constitution, the citizens must not lead the life of
mechanics or tradesmen, for such a life is ignoble and 40
inimical to virtue.[2] Neither must they be husbandmen,
since leisure is necessary both for the development of 1329^a
virtue and the performance of political duties.

Again, there is in a state a class of warriors, and
another of councillors, who advise about the expedient
and determine matters of law, and these seem in an
especial manner parts of a state. Now, should these 5
two classes be distinguished,[3] or are both functions to be
assigned to the same persons? Here again there is no
difficulty in seeing that both functions will in one way
belong to the same, in another, to different persons. To
different persons in so far as these employments are
suited to different primes of life,[4] for the one requires
wisdom and the other strength. But on the other hand,
since it is an impossible thing that those who are able
to use or to resist force should be willing to remain 10
always in subjection, from this point of view the persons
are the same; for those who carry arms can always

---

[1] Cp. 1323^a 21–1324^a 4, 1328^a 37 sq.
[2] Cp. Plato, *Laws*, xi. 919 C–E.   [3] Omitting ἑτέροις in l. 5.
[4] i. e. the physical and the mental.

determine the fate of the constitution. It remains therefore that both functions should be entrusted by the ideal
constitution to the same persons,[1] not, however, at the same
time, but in the order prescribed by nature, who has given
15 to young men strength and to older men wisdom. Such
a distribution of duties will be expedient and also just,
and is founded upon a principle of conformity to merit.
Besides, the ruling class should be the owners of property,
for they are citizens, and the citizens of a state should be
20 in good circumstances; whereas mechanics or any other
class which is not a producer of virtue have no share
in the state. This follows from our first principle,[2] for
happiness cannot exist without virtue, and a city is not
to be termed happy in regard to a portion of the citizens,
but in regard to them all.[3] And clearly property should
25 be in their hands, since the husbandmen will of necessity be slaves or barbarian Perioeci.[4]

Of the classes enumerated there remain only the
priests, and the manner in which their office is to be
regulated is obvious. No husbandman or mechanic
should be appointed to it; for the Gods should receive
30 honour from the citizens only. Now since the body of
the citizens is divided into two classes, the warriors
and the councillors, and it is beseeming that the worship
of the Gods should be duly performed, and also a rest
provided in their service for those who from age have given
up active life, to the old men of these two classes should
be assigned the duties of the priesthood.[5]

We have shown what are the necessary conditions,
35 and what the parts of a state: husbandmen, craftsmen,
and labourers of all kinds are necessary to the existence
of states, but the parts of the state are the warriors and
councillors. And these are distinguished severally from
one another, the distinction being in some cases permanent, in others not.

40 It is no new or recent discovery of political philo- **10**

---

[1] Reading ἀμφότερα in l. 13, as suggested by Susemihl.
[2] Cp. 1328[b] 35.   [3] Cp. ii. 1264[b] 17-24.   [4] Cp. *infra*, 1330[a] 25-31.
[5] Reading τούτοις, with the MSS., and τὰς ἱερωσύνας (with the third Basel edition) in ll. 33, 34.

sophers that the state ought to be divided into classes, **1329^b** and that the warriors should be separated from the husbandmen. The system has continued in Egypt and in Crete to this day, and was established, as tradition says, by a law of Sesostris in Egypt and of Minos in Crete. The institution of common tables also appears 5 to be of ancient date, being in Crete[1] as old as the reign of Minos, and in Italy far older. The Italian historians say that there was a certain Italus king of Oenotria, from whom the Oenotrians were called Italians, and 10 who gave the name of Italy to the promontory of Europe lying within the Scylletic and Lametic Gulfs,[2] which are distant from one another only half a day's journey. They say that this Italus converted the Oenotrians from shepherds into husbandmen, and besides 15 other laws which he gave them, was the founder of their common meals; even in our day some who are derived from him retain this institution and certain other laws of his. On the side of Italy towards Tyrrhenia dwelt the Opici, who are now, as of old, called Ausones; and on the 20 side towards Iapygia and the Ionian Gulf, in the district called Siritis, the Chones, who are likewise of Oenotrian race. From this part of the world originally came the institution of common tables; the separation into castes from Egypt, for the reign of Sesostris is of far greater antiquity than that of Minos. It is true indeed that these and many other things have been invented several 25 times over[3] in the course of ages, or rather times without number; for necessity may be supposed to have taught men the inventions which were absolutely required, and when these were provided, it was natural that other things which would adorn and enrich life should grow up by degrees. And we may infer that in political 30 institutions the same rule holds. Egypt[4] witnesses to

---

[1] Omitting the comma after Κρήτην in l. 6.
[2] i. e. between these gulfs and the Strait of Messina.
[3] Cp. Plato, *Laws*, iii. 676; Aristotle, *Metaph*. xii. 1074^b 10; and *Pol*. ii. 1264^a 3.
[4] Cp. *Metaph*. i. 981^b 23; *Meteor*. i. 14. 352^b 19; Plato, *Timaeus*, 22 B; *Laws*, ii. 656, 657.

the antiquity of all these things, for the Egyptians appear to be of all people the most ancient; and they have laws and a regular constitution existing from time immemorial. We should therefore make the best use of what has 35 been already discovered, and try to supply defects.

I have already remarked that the land ought to belong to those who possess arms and have a share in the government,[1] and that the husbandmen ought to be a class distinct from them; and I have determined what should be the extent and nature of the territory. Let me proceed to discuss the distribution of the land, and the 40 character of the agricultural class; for I do not think that **1330**ᵃ property ought to be common, as some maintain,[2] but only that by friendly consent there should be a common use of it; and that no citizen should be in want of subsistence.

As to common meals, there is a general agreement that a well-ordered city should have them; and we will hereafter explain what are our own reasons for taking 5 this view.[3]   They ought, however, to be open to all the citizens.[4]   And yet it is not easy for the poor to contribute the requisite sum out of their private means, and to provide also for their household. The expense of religious worship should likewise be a public charge. 10 The land must therefore be divided into two parts, one public and the other private, and each part should be subdivided, part of the public land being appropriated to the service of the Gods, and the other part used to defray the cost of the common meals; while of the 15 private land, part should be near the border, and the other near the city, so that, each citizen having two lots, they may all of them have land in both places; there is justice and fairness in such a division,[5] and it tends to inspire unanimity among the people in their border

---

[1] 1328ᵇ 33-1329ᵃ 2, 1329ᵃ 17-26, 1326ᵇ 26-32.
[2] Cp. ii. 5, *Rep.* iii. 416 D.
[3] Aristotle does not give any explanation in the *Politics.*
[4] Cp. ii. 1271ᵃ 28.
[5] Cp. Plato, *Laws,* v. 745, where the same proposal is found. Aristotle, in Book ii. 1265ᵇ 24, condemns the division of lots which he here adopts.

wars. Where there is not this arrangement, some of
them are too ready to come to blows with their neighbours, while others are so cautious that they quite lose 20
the sense of honour. Wherefore there is a law in some
places which forbids those who dwell near the border to
take part in public deliberations about wars with neighbours, on the ground that their interests will pervert
their judgement. For the reasons already mentioned,
then, the land should be divided in the manner described. The very best thing of all would be that the 25
husbandmen should be slaves taken from among men
who are not all of the same race[1] and not spirited, for if
they have no spirit they will be better suited for their
work, and there will be no danger of their making a
revolution. The next best thing would be that they
should be perioeci of foreign race,[2] and of a like inferior 30
nature ; some of them should be the slaves of individuals,
and employed on the private estates of men of property,
the remainder should be the property of the state and
employed on the common land.[3] I will hereafter explain[4] what is the proper treatment of slaves, and why it
is expedient that liberty should be always held out to
them as the reward of their services.

11   We have already said that the city should be open to
the land and to the sea,[5] and to the whole country as 35
far as possible. In respect of the place itself[6] our wish
would be that its situation should be fortunate in four
things. The first, health—this is a necessity : cities which
lie towards the east, and are blown upon by winds
coming from the east, are the healthiest ; next in health- 40
fulness are those which are sheltered from the north
wind, for they have a milder winter. The site of the
city should likewise be[7] convenient both for political **1330ᵇ**

---

[1] Cp. Plato, *Laws*, vi. 777 C, D.   [2] Cp. 1329ᵃ 26.
[3] Cp. ii. 1267ᵇ 16.
[4] A. does not do so in the *Politics*, but cp. *Oec.* 1344ᵇ 15.
[5] 1327ᵃ 4–40.
[6] Reading πρὸς αὐτήν in l. 36 with the MSS., and omitting εἶναι
with one MS. and apparently with William of Moerbeke.
[7] Reading ἔχειν in l. 2, with the MSS.

administration and for war. With a view to the latter it should afford easy egress to the citizens, and at the same time be inaccessible and difficult of capture to enemies.[1] There should be a natural abundance of springs
5 and fountains in the town, or, if there is a deficiency of them, great reservoirs may be established for the collection of rain-water, such as will not fail when the inhabitants are cut off from the country by war. Special care should be taken of the health of the inhabitants, which will depend chiefly on the healthiness of the locality and of the quarter to which they are exposed,
10 and secondly, on the use of pure water; this latter point is by no means a secondary consideration. For the elements which we use most and oftenest for the support of the body contribute most to health, and among these are water and air. Wherefore, in all wise states,
15 if there is a want of pure water, and the supply is not all equally good, the drinking water ought to be separated from that which is used for other purposes.

As to strongholds, what is suitable to different forms of government varies: thus an acropolis is suited to an
20 oligarchy or a monarchy, but a plain to a democracy; neither to an aristocracy, but rather a number of strong places. The arrangement of private houses is considered to be more agreeable and generally more convenient, if the streets are regularly laid out after the modern fashion which Hippodamus[2] introduced, but for
25 security in war the antiquated mode of building, which made it difficult for strangers to get out of a town and for assailants to find their way in, is preferable. A city should therefore adopt both plans of building: it is possible to arrange the houses irregularly, as husbandmen plant their vines in what are called 'clumps'. The whole
30 town should not be laid out in straight lines, but only certain quarters and regions; thus security and beauty will be combined.

As to walls, those who say[3] that cities making any

---

[1] Repetition of 1326ᵇ 40.   [2] Cp. ii. 1267ᵇ 22.
[3] Cp. Plato, *Laws*, vi. 778 D.

pretension to military virtue should not have them, are
quite out of date in their notions ; and they may see the
cities which prided themselves on this fancy confuted
by facts. True, there is little courage shown in seeking 35
for safety behind a rampart when an enemy is similar in
character and not much superior in number ; but the
superiority of the besiegers may be and often is too much
both for ordinary human valour and for that which is
found only in a few ; and if they are to be saved and to 40
escape defeat and outrage, the strongest wall will be the 1331ᵃ
truest soldierly precaution, more especially now that
missiles and siege engines have been brought to such
perfection. To have no walls would be as foolish as to
choose a site for a town in an exposed country, and to
level the heights ; or as if an individual were to leave his 5
house unwalled, lest the inmates should become cowards.
Nor must we forget that those who have their cities sur-
rounded by walls may either take advantage of them or
not, but cities which are unwalled have no choice.

If our conclusions are just, not only should cities 10
have walls, but care should be taken to make them
ornamental, as well as useful for warlike purposes, and
adapted to resist modern inventions. For as the assailants of a city do all they can to gain an advantage, 15
so the defenders should make use of any means of
defence which have been already discovered, and should
devise and invent others, for when men are well prepared no enemy even thinks of attacking them.

12   As the walls are to be divided by guard-houses and
towers built at suitable intervals, and the body of citizens 20
must be distributed at common tables,[1] the idea will
naturally occur that we should establish some of the
common tables in the guard-houses. These might be
arranged as has been suggested ; while the principal
common tables of the magistrates will occupy a suitable 25
place, and there also will be the buildings appropriated to
religious worship except in the case of those rites which

[1] Cp. 1330ᵃ 3.

the law or the Pythian oracle has restricted to a special locality.¹ The site should be a spot seen far and wide, which gives due elevation to virtue ² and towers over the 30 neighbourhood. Below this spot should be established an agora, such as that which the Thessalians call the ' freemen's agora ' ; from this all trade should be excluded, and no mechanic, husbandman, or any such person allowed 35 to enter, unless he be summoned by the magistrates. It would be a charming use of the place, if the gymnastic exercises of the elder men were performed there. For in this noble practice different ages should be separated, and some of the magistrates should stay with the boys, while the grown-up men remain with the magis- 40 trates ; for the presence of the magistrates is the best mode of inspiring true modesty and ingenuous fear. There **1331ᵇ** should also be a traders' agora, distinct and apart from the other, in a situation which is convenient for the reception of goods both by sea and land.

But in speaking of the magistrates we must not forget 5 another section of the citizens,³ viz. the priests, for whom public tables should likewise be provided in their proper place near the temples. The magistrates who deal with contracts, indictments, summonses, and the like, and those who have the care of the agora and of the city re- 10 spectively, ought to be established near an agora and some public place of meeting ; the neighbourhood of the traders' agora will be a suitable spot ; the upper agora we devote to the life of leisure, the other is intended for the necessities of trade.

The same order should prevail ⁴ in the country, for 15 there too the magistrates, called by some 'Inspectors of Forests' and by others 'Wardens of the Country', must have guard-houses and common tables while they are on duty ; temples should also be scattered throughout the country, dedicated, some to Gods, and some to heroes.

¹ Cp. Plato, *Laws*, v. 738 B-D, vi. 759 C, 778 C, viii. 848 D-E.
² Reading πρὸς τὴν τῆς ἀρετῆς θέσιν in l. 29, with the MSS.
³ Reading in l. 4 τὸ πλῆθος, with the MSS.
⁴ Reading νενεμῆσθαι in l. 13 with some MSS.

But it would be a waste of time for us to linger over details like these. The difficulty is not in imagining but in carrying them out. We may talk about them as 20 much as we like, but the execution of them will depend upon fortune. Wherefore let us say no more about these matters for the present.

13 Returning to the constitution itself, let us seek to determine out of what and what sort of elements the state 25 which is to be happy and well-governed should be composed. There are two things in which all well-being consists: one of them is the choice of a right end and aim of action, and the other the discovery of the actions which are means towards it; for the means and the end may agree or disagree. Sometimes the right end is set 30 before men, but in practice they fail to attain it; in other cases they are successful in all the means, but they propose to themselves a bad end; and sometimes they fail in both. Take, for example, the art of medicine; physicians do not always understand the nature of health, 35 and also the means which they use may not effect the desired end. In all arts and sciences both the end and the means should be equally within our control.

The happiness and well-being which all men manifestly desire, some have the power of attaining, but 40 to others, from some accident or defect of nature, the attainment of them is not granted; for a good life requires a supply of external goods, in a less degree 1332^{a} when men are in a good state, in a greater degree when they are in a lower state. Others again, who possess the conditions of happiness, go utterly wrong from the first in the pursuit of it. But since our object is to discover the best form of government, that, namely, under which a city will be best governed, and 5 since the city is best governed which has the greatest opportunity of obtaining happiness, it is evident that we must clearly ascertain the nature of happiness.

We maintain, and have said in the *Ethics*,[1] if the

------

[1] *Nic. Eth.* i. 1098^{a} 16, x. 1176^{b} 4; and cp. 1328^{a} 37.

arguments there adduced are of any value, that happiness
is the realization and perfect exercise of virtue, and this
10 not conditional, but absolute. And I used the term 'conditional' to express that which is indispensable, and
'absolute' to express that which is good in itself. Take
the case of just actions; just punishments and chastisements
do indeed spring from a good principle, but they are
good only because we cannot do without them—it would be
better that neither individuals nor states should need any-
15 thing of the sort—but actions which aim at honour and
advantage are absolutely the best. The conditional action
is only the choice[1] of a lesser evil; whereas these are
the foundation and creation of good. A good man may
make the best even of poverty and disease, and the other
20 ills of life; but he can only attain happiness under the
opposite conditions[2] (for this also has been determined in
accordance with ethical arguments,[3] that the good man
is he for whom, because he is virtuous, the things that are
absolutely good are good; it is also plain that his use of these
25 goods must be virtuous and in the absolute sense good).
This makes men fancy that external goods are the cause of
happiness, yet we might as well say that a brilliant performance on the lyre was to be attributed to the instrument
and not to the skill of the performer.

It follows then from what has been said that some
things the legislator must find ready to his hand in a
state, others he must provide. And therefore we can
only say: May our state be constituted in such a manner
as to be blessed with the goods of which fortune dis-
30 poses (for we acknowledge her power): whereas virtue
and goodness in the state are not a matter of chance
but the result of knowledge and purpose. A city can
be virtuous only when the citizens who have a share
in the government are virtuous, and in our state all the
citizens share in the government; let us then inquire
35 how a man becomes virtuous. For even if we could

---

[1] Retaining the MS. reading αἵρεσις in l. 17.
[2] *Nic. Eth.* i. 1100^b 22, 1101^a 13.
[3] *Nic. Eth.* iii. 1113^a 22-^b 1 ; *E. E.* vii. 1248^b 26; *M. M.* ii. 1207^h 31.

suppose the citizen body to be virtuous, without each of them being so, yet the latter would be better, for in the virtue of each the virtue of all is involved.

There are three things which make men good and virtuous; these are nature, habit, rational principle.[1] In 40 the first place, every one must be born a man and not some other animal;[2] so, too, he must have a certain character, both of body and soul. But some qualities there is no use in having at birth, for they are altered 1332^b by habit, and there are some gifts which by nature are made to be turned by habit to good or bad. Animals lead for the most part a life of nature, although in lesser particulars some are influenced by habit as well. Man has rational principle, in addition, and man only. Where- 5 fore nature, habit, rational principle must be in harmony with one another; for they do not always agree; men do many things against habit and nature, if rational principle persuades them that they ought. We have already determined what natures are likely to be most easily moulded by the hands of the legislator.[3] All else is the work of education; we learn some things by habit and 10 some by instruction.

14 Since every political society is composed of rulers and subjects, let us consider whether the relations of one to the other should interchange or be permanent.[4] For 15 the education of the citizens will necessarily vary with the answer given to this question. Now, if some men excelled others in the same degree in which gods and heroes are supposed to excel mankind in general (having in the first place a great advantage even in their bodies, and secondly in their minds), so that the superiority of the 20 governors was undisputed and patent to their subjects, it would clearly be better that once for all the one class should rule and the others serve.[5] But since this is unattainable, and kings have no marked superiority over their

[1] Cp. *N. Eth.* x. 1179^b 20.
[2] Reading a comma after ζῷον in l. 41.   [3] 1327^b 36.
[4] Cp. iii. 1279^a 8.   [5] Cp. i. 1254^b 16, 1284^a 3.

subjects, such as Scylax affirms to be found among the
25 Indians, it is obviously necessary on many grounds that
all the citizens alike should take their turn of governing
and being governed. Equality consists in the same
treatment of similar persons, and no government can
stand which is not founded upon justice. For if the
government be unjust every one in the country unites
with the governed in the desire to have a revolution,
30 and it is an impossibility that the members of the government can be so numerous as to be stronger than all their
enemies put together. Yet that governors should excel
their subjects is undeniable. How all this is to be effected,
and in what way they will respectively share in the
35 government, the legislator has to consider. The subject
has been already mentioned.[1] Nature herself has
provided the distinction when she made a difference
between old and young within the same species,
of whom she fitted the one to govern and the
other to be governed. No one takes offence at being
governed when he is young, nor does he think himself
40 better than his governors, especially if he will enjoy the
same privilege when he reaches the required age.

We conclude that from one point of view governors and
governed are identical, and from another different. And
1333[a] therefore their education must be the same and also different. For he who would learn to command well must,
as men say, first of all learn to obey.[2] As I observed
in the first part of this treatise, there is one rule which
is for the sake of the rulers and another rule which is for
5 the sake of the ruled;[3] the former is a despotic, the
latter a free government. Some commands differ not in
the thing commanded, but in the intention with which
they are imposed. Wherefore, many apparently menial
offices are an honour to the free youth by whom they
are performed; for actions do not differ as honourable
10 or dishonourable in themselves so much as in the end
and intention of them. But since we say[4] that the virtue

[1] 1329[a] 2-17.   [2] Cp. iii. 1277[b] 9.
[3] iii. 1278[b] 32-1279[a] 8, cp. 1277[a] 33-[b] 30.   [4] Cp. iii. 4, 5.

of the citizen and ruler is the same as that of the good
man, and that the same person must first be a subject
and then a ruler, the legislator has to see that they
become good men, and by what means this may be 15
accomplished, and what is the end of the perfect life.

Now the soul of man is divided into two parts, one of
which has a rational principle in itself, and the other, not
having a rational principle in itself, is able to obey such
a principle.[1] And we call a man in any way good
because he has the virtues of these two parts. In which
of them the end is more likely to be found is no matter 20
of doubt to those who adopt our division ; for in the
world both of nature and of art the inferior always exists
for the sake of the better or superior, and the better or
superior is that which has a rational principle. This
principle, too, in our ordinary way of speaking, is divided
into two kinds, for there is a practical and a speculative 25
principle.[2] This part, then, must evidently be similarly
divided. And there must be a corresponding division of
actions ; the actions of the naturally better part are to
be preferred by those who have it in their power to attain
to two out of the three or to all, for that is always to
every one the most eligible which is the highest
attainable by him. The whole of life is further divided 30
into two parts, business and leisure,[3] war and peace, and
of actions some aim at what is necessary and useful, and
some at what is honourable. And the preference given
to one or the other class of actions must necessarily be
like the preference given to one or other part of the soul
and its actions over the other ; there must be war for the 35
sake of peace, business for the sake of leisure, things useful and necessary for the sake of things honourable. All
these points the statesman should keep in view when he
frames his laws ; he should consider the parts of the soul
and their functions, and above all the better and the end ;
he should also remember the diversities[4] of human lives 40

[1] Cp. *Nic. Eth.* i. 1102ᵇ 28.   [2] Cp. *Nic. Eth.* vi. 1139ᵃ 6.
[3] *Nic. Eth.* x. 1177ᵇ 4.
[4] Reading διαιρέσεις in l. 41 with the MSS.

and actions. For men must be able to engage in
1333^b business and go to war, but leisure and peace are better ;
they must do what is necessary and indeed what is use-
ful, but what is honourable is better. On such principles
children and persons of every age which requires edu-
5 cation should be trained. Whereas even the Hellenes
of the present day who are reputed to be best governed,
and the legislators who gave them their constitutions,
do not appear to have framed their governments
with a regard to the best end, or to have given them
laws and education with a view to all the virtues, but in
a vulgar spirit have fallen back on those which promised
10 to be more useful and profitable. Many modern writers
have taken a similar view: they commend the Lacedaemonian constitution, and praise the legislator for
making conquest and war his sole aim,[1] a doctrine
15 which may be refuted by argument and has long ago
been refuted by facts. For most men desire empire
in the hope of accumulating the goods of fortune ; and
on this ground Thibron and all those who have written
about the Lacedaemonian constitution have praised their
20 legislator, because the Lacedaemonians, by being trained
to meet dangers, gained great power. But surely they
are not a happy people now that their empire has passed
away, nor was their legislator right. How ridiculous is
the result, if, while they are continuing in the observance
of his laws and no one interferes with them, they have
25 lost the better part of life ! These writers further err
about the sort of government which the legislator should
approve, for the government of freemen is nobler and
implies more virtue than despotic government.[2] Neither
is a city to be deemed happy or a legislator to be praised
30 because he trains his citizens to conquer and obtain
dominion over their neighbours, for there is great evil in
this. On a similar principle any citizen who could,
should obviously try to obtain the power in his own
state,—the crime which the Lacedaemonians accuse king

---

[1] Cp. Plato, *Laws*, i. 628, 638.   [2] Cp. i. 1254^a 25.

Pausanias of attempting,[1] although he had so great
honour already. No such principle and no law having 35
this object is either statesmanlike or useful or right.
For the same things are best both for individuals and for
states, and these are the things which the legislator ought
to implant in the minds of his citizens. Neither should
men study war with a view to the enslavement of those
who do not deserve to be enslaved ; but first of all they 40
should provide against their own enslavement, and in the
second place obtain empire for the good of the governed,
and not for the sake of exercising a general despotism, 1334^a
and in the third place they should seek to be masters
only over those who deserve to be slaves. Facts, as
well as arguments, prove that the legislator should direct
all his military and other measures to the provision of 5
leisure and the establishment of peace. For most of
these military states are safe only while they are at war,[2]
but fall when they have acquired their empire ; like unused iron they lose their temper in time of peace. And
for this the legislator is to blame, he never having taught 10
them how to lead the life of peace.

15   Since the end of individuals and of states is the same,
the end of the best man and of the best constitution
must also be the same ; it is therefore evident that there
ought to exist in both of them the virtues of leisure ; for
peace, as has been often. repeated,[3] is the end of war, 15
and leisure of toil. But leisure and cultivation may be
promoted, not only by those virtues which are practised
in leisure, but also by some of those which are useful to
business.[4] For many necessaries of life have to be
supplied before we can have leisure. Therefore a city
must be temperate and brave, and able to endure : for 20
truly, as the proverb says, ' There is no leisure for slaves,'
and those who cannot face danger like men are the slaves
of any invader. Courage and endurance are required for

---

[1] Cp. v. 1301^b 20, 1307^a 3.   [2] Cp. ii. 1271^b 3.
[3] 1333^a 35, 1334^a 2.
[4] i.e. ' not only by some of the speculative but also by some of
the practical virtues '.

business and philosophy for leisure, temperance and
25 justice for both, and more especially in times of peace and
leisure, for war compels men to be just and temperate,
whereas the enjoyment of good fortune and the leisure
which comes with peace tend to make them insolent.
Those then who seem to be the best-off and to be in the
possession of every good, have special need of justice
30 and temperance,—for example, those (if such there be,
as the poets say ¹) who dwell in the Islands of the Blest;
they above all will need philosophy and temperance and
justice, and all the more the more leisure they have, living
in the midst of abundance. There is no difficulty in
35 seeing why the state that would be happy and good
ought to have these virtues. If it be disgraceful in men
not to be able to use the goods of life, it is peculiarly
disgraceful nôt to be able to use them in time of leisure,
—to show excellent qualities in action and war, and when
they have peace and leisure to be no better than slaves.
40 Wherefore we should not practise virtue after the manner
of the Lacedaemonians.² For they, while agreeing with
1334ᵇ other men in their conception of the highest goods, differ
from the rest of mankind in thinking that they are to be
obtained by the practice of a single virtue. And since
⟨they think⟩ these goods and the enjoyment of them
5 greater than the enjoyment derived from the virtues . . .
and that ⟨it should be practised⟩ for its own sake,³ is
evident from what has been said ; we must now consider
how and by what means it is to be attained.

We have already determined that nature and habit
and rational principle are required,⁴ and, of these, the
proper *nature* of the citizens has also been defined by us.⁵
But we have still to consider whether the training of early
life is to be that of rational principle or habit, for these
two must accord, and when in accord they will then

---

¹ Cp. Hes. *Op. et Dies*, 170; Pind. *Olymp.* ii. 53.
² Cp. ii. 1271ᵃ 41.
³ Newman suggests that the lacuna in l. 4 may be filled as
follows : ' they practise only the virtue which is thought to be useful
as a means to these. Now, that the whole of virtue should be practised '.
⁴ 1332ᵃ 39 sqq.   ⁵ c. 7.

form the best of harmonies. The rational principle may 10
be mistaken and fail in attaining the highest ideal of life,
and there may be a like evil influence of habit. Thus much
is clear in the first place, that, as in all other things, birth
implies an antecedent beginning,[1] and that there are
beginnings whose end is relative to a further end.
Now, in men rational principle and mind are the end
towards which nature strives,[2] so that the birth and moral 15
discipline of the citizens ought to be ordered with a view
to them. In the second place, as the soul and body are
two, we see also that there are two parts of the soul, the
rational and the irrational, and two corresponding states—
reason and appetite. And as the body is prior in order of 20
generation to the soul, so the irrational is prior to the
rational. The proof is that anger and wishing and desire
are implanted in children from their very birth, but reason
and understanding are developed as they grow older.
Wherefore, the care of the body ought to precede that of 25
the soul, and the training of the appetitive part should
follow : none the less our care of it must be for the sake of
the reason, and our care of the body for the sake of the soul.

16   Since the legislator should begin by considering how
the frames of the children whom he is rearing may be as
good as possible, his first care will be about marriage— 30
at what age should his citizens marry, and who are fit to
marry ? In legislating on this subject he ought to consider the persons and the length of their life, that their
procreative life may terminate at the same period, and 35
that they may not differ in their bodily powers, as will
be the case if the man is still able to beget children while
the woman is unable to bear them, or the woman able to
bear while the man is unable to beget, for from these
causes arise quarrels and differences between married
persons. Secondly, he must consider the time at which
the children will succeed to their parents ; there ought
not to be too great an interval of age, for then the 40

[1] i. e. the union of the parents.
[2] i. e. the birth of the offspring, which is the end of the union of
the parents, points to a further end, the development of mind.

parents will be too old to derive any pleasure from their
1335^a affection, or to be of any use to them. Nor ought they
to be too nearly of an age ; to youthful marriages there
are many objections—the children will be wanting in
respect to the parents, who will seem to be their contem-
poraries, and disputes will arise in the management of the
household. Thirdly, and this is the point from which
5 we digressed,[1] the legislator must mould to his will the
frames of newly-born children. Almost all these objects
may be secured by attention to one point. Since the
time of generation is commonly limited within the age
of seventy years in the case of a man, and of fifty in the
10 case of a woman, the commencement of the union should
conform to these periods. The union of male and female
when too young is bad for the procreation of children ;
in all other animals the offspring of the young are small
and ill-developed, and with a tendency to produce female
15 children, and therefore also in man, as is proved by the
fact that in those cities in which men and women are
accustomed to marry young, the people are small and
weak ; in childbirth also younger women suffer more,
and more of them die ; some persons say that this was
the meaning of the response once given to the
20 Troezenians[2]—the oracle really meant that many died
because they married too young ; it had nothing to do
with the ingathering of the harvest. It also conduces
to temperance not to marry too soon ; for women who
marry early are apt to be wanton ; and in men too the
25 bodily frame is stunted if they marry while the seed is
growing (for there is a time when the growth of the seed,
also, ceases, or continues to but a slight extent).[3]
Women should marry when they are about eighteen
years of age, and men at seven and thirty ; then they
30 are in the prime of life, and the decline in the powers of
both will coincide. Further, the children, if their birth
takes place soon, as may reasonably be expected, will
succeed in the beginning of their prime, when the fathers

---

[1] 1334^b 29 sqq.   [2] 'Plough not the young field'.
[3] Transferring ἢ μικρόν from l. 29 to l. 27 after ἔτι, with Göttling.

are already in the decline of life, and have nearly reached their term of three-score years and ten.

Thus much of the age proper for marriage : the season 35 of the year should also be considered ; according to our present custom, people generally limit marriage to the season of winter, and they are right. The precepts of physicians and natural philosophers about generation 40 should also be studied by the parents themselves ; the physicians give good advice about the favourable conditions of the body, and the natural philosophers about 1335ᵇ the winds ; of which they prefer the north to the south.

What constitution in the parent is most advantageous to the offspring is a subject which we will consider more carefully [1] when we speak of the education of children, and we will only make a few general remarks at present. The constitution of an athlete is not suited to the life 5 of a citizen, or to health, or to the procreation of children, any more than the valetudinarian or exhausted constitution, but one which is in a mean between them. A man's constitution should be inured to labour, but not to labour which is excessive or of one sort only, such as is practised by athletes ; he should be capable of all the 10 actions of a freeman. These remarks apply equally to both parents.

Women who are with child should be careful of themselves ; they should take exercise and have a nourishing diet. The first of these prescriptions the legislator will easily carry into effect by requiring that they shall take 15 a walk daily to some temple, where they can worship the gods who preside over birth.[2] Their minds, however, unlike their bodies, they ought to keep quiet, for the offspring derive their natures from their mothers as plants do from the earth.

As to the exposure and rearing of children, let there 20 be a law that no *deformed* child shall live, but that on the ground of an *excess* in the number of children, if the established customs [3] of the state forbid this (for in our

---

[1] A. does not actually do so.   [2] Cp. Plato, *Laws*, vii. 789 E.
[2] Reading ἐθῶν in l. 21 with the MSS.

state population has a limit), no child is to be exposed, but when couples have children in excess, let abortion be
25 procured before sense and life have begun; what may or may not be lawfully done in these cases depends on the question of life and sensation.

And now, having determined at what ages men and women are to begin their union, let us also determine how long they shall continue to beget and bear offspring for the state; men who are too old, like men who are
30 too young, produce children who are defective in body and mind; the children of very old men are weakly. The limit, then, should be the age which is the prime of their intelligence, and this in most persons, according to the notion of some poets who measure life by periods of
35 seven years, is about fifty;[1] at four or five years later, they should cease from having families; and from that time forward only cohabit with one another for the sake of health, or for some similar reason.

As to adultery, let it be held disgraceful, in general,
40 for any man or woman to be found in any way unfaithful
1336^a when they are married, and called husband and wife. If during the time of bearing children anything of the sort occur, let the guilty person be punished with a loss of privileges in proportion to the offence.[2]

After the children have been born, the manner of **17** rearing them may be supposed to have a great effect
5 on their bodily strength. It would appear from the example of animals, and of those nations who desire to create the military habit, that the food which has most milk in it is best suited to human beings; but the less wine the better, if they would escape diseases. Also all the motions to which children can be subjected at their
10 early age are very useful. But in order to preserve their tender limbs from distortion, some nations have had recourse to mechanical appliances which straighten their bodies. To accustom children to the cold from their

[1] Cp. Solon Fragm. 27 Bergk[4].
[2] Cp. *Laws*, viii. 841 D, E.

earliest years is also an excellent practice, which greatly
conduces to health, and hardens them for military service. Hence many barbarians have a custom of plunging 15
their children at birth into a cold stream ; others, like
the Celts, clothe them in a light wrapper only. For
human nature should be early habituated to endure all
which by habit it can be made to endure ; but the process must be gradual. And children, from their natural 20
warmth, may be easily trained to bear cold   Such care
should attend them in the first stage of life.

The next period lasts to the age of five ; during this
no demand should be made upon the child for study or
labour, lest its growth be impeded ; and there should 25
be sufficient motion to prevent the limbs from being
inactive. This can be secured, among other ways, by
amusement, but the amusement should not be vulgar
or tiring or effeminate. The Directors of Education, as 30
they are termed, should be careful what tales or stories
the children hear,[1] for all such things are designed
to prepare the way for the business of later life, and
should be for the most part imitations of the occupations which they will hereafter pursue in earnest.[2]
Those are wrong who in their laws attempt to check
the loud crying and screaming of children, for these con- 35
tribute towards their growth, and, in a manner, exercise
their bodies.[3]   Straining the voice has a strengthening
effect similar to that produced by the retention of the
breath in violent exertions. The Directors of Education 40
should have an eye to their bringing up, and in particular
should take care that they are left as little as possible
with slaves.   For until they are seven years old they 1336^b
must live at home ; and therefore, even at this early age,
it is to be expected that they should acquire a taint of
meanness from what they hear and see. Indeed, there
is nothing which the legislator should be more careful to
drive away than indecency of speech ; for the light 5
utterance of shameful words leads soon to shameful

---

[1] Plato, *Rep.* ii. 377 ff.   [2] Plato, *Laws*, i. 643.
[3] Plato, *Laws*, vii. 792 A.

actions. The young especially should never be allowed
to repeat or hear anything of the sort. A freeman who
is found saying or doing what is forbidden, if he be too
young as yet to have the privilege of reclining at the
10 public tables, should be disgraced[1] and beaten, and an
elder person degraded as his slavish conduct deserves.
And since we do not allow improper language, clearly we
should also banish pictures or speeches from the stage
which are indecent. Let the rulers take care that there
15 be no image or picture representing unseemly actions,
except in the temples of those Gods at whose festivals
the law permits even ribaldry, and whom the law also
permits to be worshipped by persons of mature age on
behalf of themselves, their children, and their wives. But
20 the legislator should not allow youth to be spectators
of iambi or of comedy until they are of an age to sit at
the public tables and to drink strong wine; by that time
education will have armed them against the evil influences
of such representations.

We have made these remarks in a cursory manner,—
25 they are enough for the present occasion; but hereafter[2]
we will return to the subject and after a fuller discussion determine whether such liberty should or should
not be granted, and in what way granted, if at all.
Theodorus, the tragic actor, was quite right in saying
that he would not allow any other actor, not even if he
30 were quite second-rate, to enter before himself, because
the spectators grew fond of the voices which they first
heard. And the same principle applies universally to
association with things as well as with persons, for we
always like best whatever comes first. And therefore
youth should be kept strangers to all that is bad, and
35 especially to things which suggest vice or hate. When the
five years have passed away, during the two following years
they must look on at the pursuits which they are hereafter
to learn. There are two periods of life with reference to
which education has to be divided, from seven to the age
of puberty, and onwards to the age of one and twenty.

---

[1] Retaining ἀτιμίαις in l. 10.   [2] An unfulfilled promise.

The poets who divide ages by sevens[1] are in the main 40
right: but we should observe the divisions actually 1337^{a}
made by nature; for the deficiencies of nature are what
art and education seek to fill up.

Let us then first inquire if any regulations are to be
laid down about children, and secondly, whether the
care of them should be the concern of the state or of
private individuals, which latter is in our own day the 5
common custom, and in the third place, what these regulations should be.

[1] Cp. 1335^{b} 33.

BOOK VIII

NO one will doubt that the legislator should direct his **1**
attention above all to the education of youth; for the
neglect of education does harm to the constitution. The
citizen should be moulded to suit the form of government
under which he lives.[1] For each government has a
15 peculiar character which originally formed and which
continues to preserve it. The character of democracy
creates democracy, and the character of oligarchy creates
oligarchy; and always the better the character, the
better the government.

Again, for the exercise of any faculty or art a previous
20 training and habituation are required; clearly therefore
for the practice of virtue. And since the whole city has
one end, it is manifest that education should be one and
the same for all, and that it should be public, and not
private,—not as at present, when every one looks after
25 his own children separately, and gives them separate instruction of the sort which he thinks best; the training
in things which are of common interest should be the
same for all. Neither must we suppose that any one
of the citizens belongs to himself,[2] for they all belong to
the state, and are each of them a part of the state, and
30 the care of each part is inseparable from the care of the
whole. In this particular as in some others [3] the Lacedaemonians are to be praised, for they take the greatest
pains about their children, and make education the
business of the state.[4]

That education should be regulated by law and should **2**
be an affair of state is not to be denied, but what should
be the character of this public education, and how young

---

[1] Cp. v. 1310^a 12–36. [2] Reading αὐτὸν αὑτοῦ in l. 28.
[3] Reading καὶ τοῦτο in l. 31 with the MSS.
[4] Cp. *Nic. Eth.* x. 1180^a 24.

persons should be educated, are questions which remain
to be considered. As things are, there is disagreement
about the subjects. For mankind are by no means 35
agreed about the things to be taught, whether we look
to virtue or the best life. Neither is it clear whether
education is more concerned with intellectual or with
moral virtue. The existing practice is perplexing ; no
one knows on what principle we should proceed—should 40
the useful in life, or should virtue, or should the higher
knowledge, be the aim of our training ; all three opinions
have been entertained. Again, about the means there is 1337ᵇ
no agreement ; for different persons, starting with different
ideas about the nature of virtue, naturally disagree about
the practice of it. There can be no doubt that children
should be taught those useful things which are really
necessary, but not all useful things ; for occupations are 5
divided into liberal and illiberal ; and to young children
should be imparted only such kinds of knowledge as will
be useful to them without vulgarizing them. And any
occupation, art, or science, which makes the body or soul 10
or mind of the freeman less fit for the practice or exercise
of virtue, is vulgar ; wherefore we call those arts vulgar
which tend to deform the body, and likewise all paid
employments, for they absorb and degrade the mind.
There are also some liberal arts quite proper for a freeman 15
to acquire, but only in a certain degree, and if he attend
to them too closely, in order to attain perfection in them,
the same evil effects will follow. The object also which
a man sets before him makes a great difference ; if he
does or learns anything for his own sake [1] or for the sake
of his friends, or with a view to excellence, the action
will not appear illiberal ; but if done for the sake of 20
others, the very same action will be thought menial and
servile. The received subjects of instruction, as I have
already remarked,[2] are partly of a liberal and partly of
an illiberal character.

3   The customary branches of education are in number four;

[1] Cp. iii. 1277ᵇ 3.   [2] ª 39–ᵇ 3.

645·17   R

they are—(1) reading and writing, (2) gymnastic exercises,
25 (3) music, to which is sometimes added (4) drawing. Of
these, reading and writing and drawing are regarded as
useful for the purposes of life in a variety of ways, and
gymnastic exercises are thought to infuse courage. Concerning music a doubt may be raised—in our own day most
men cultivate it for the sake of pleasure, but originally
30 it was included in education, because nature herself, as
has been often said,[1] requires that we should be able, not
only to work well, but to use leisure well ; for, as I must
repeat once again, the first principle of all action is
leisure. Both are required, but leisure is better than
occupation and is its end ; and therefore the question
must be asked, what ought we to do when at leisure ?
35 Clearly we ought not to be amusing ourselves, for then
amusement would be the end of life. But if this is incon-
ceivable, and amusement is needed more amid serious
occupations than at other times (for he who is hard at
work has need of relaxation, and amusement gives relaxation, whereas occupation is always accompanied with
40 exertion and effort), we should introduce amusements
only at suitable times, and they should be our medicines,
for the emotion which they create in the soul is a relaxa-
1338^a tion, and from the pleasure we obtain rest. But leisure
of itself gives pleasure and happiness and enjoyment of
. life, which are experienced, not by the busy man, but by
those who have leisure. For he who is occupied has
5 in view some end which he has not attained ; but happiness is an end, since all men deem it to be accompanied
with pleasure and not with pain. This pleasure, however, is regarded differently by different persons, and
varies according to the habit of individuals ; the pleasure of the best man is the best, and springs from the
noblest sources. It is clear then that there are branches of
10 learning and education which we must study merely with
a view to leisure spent in intellectual activity, and these
are to be valued for their own sake ; whereas those kinds of
knowledge which are useful in business are to be deemed

ii. 1271^a 41 sqq., vii. 1333^a 16–1334^b 3 ; *N. Eth.* x. 6.

necessary, and exist for the sake of other things. And
therefore our fathers admitted music into education, not
on the ground either of its necessity or utility, for it is not
necessary, nor indeed useful in the same manner as read- 15
ing and writing, which are useful in money-making, in the
management of a household, in the acquisition of knowledge and in political life, nor like drawing, useful for a
more correct judgement of the works of artists, nor again
like gymnastic, which gives health and strength; for 20
neither of these is to be gained from music. There remains, then, the use of music for intellectual enjoyment
in leisure; which is in fact evidently the reason of its
introduction, this being one of the ways in which it is
thought that a freeman should pass his leisure; as Homer
says—

'But he who alone should be called [1] to the pleasant 25
feast',
and afterwards he speaks of others whom he describes as
inviting

'The bard who would delight them all'.[2]
And in another place Odysseus says there is no better
way of passing life than when men's hearts are merry and

'The banqueters in the hall, sitting in order, hear the
voice of the minstrel'.[3]

It is evident, then, that there is a sort of education in 30
which parents should train their sons, not as being useful
or necessary, but because it is liberal or noble. Whether
this is of one kind only, or of more than one, and if
so, what they are, and how they are to be imparted,
must hereafter be determined.[4] Thus much we are
now in a position to say, that the ancients witness to us; 35
for their opinion may be gathered from the fact that
music is one of the received and traditional branches of
education. Further, it is clear that children should be
instructed in some useful things,—for example, in reading

---

[1] Reading ἀλλ' οἶον μόνον in l. 25, with Newman. The line
does not occur in our text of Homer, but in Aristotle's text it
probably came instead of, or after, *Od.* xvii. 383.
[2] *Od.* xvii. 385.   [3] *Od.* ix. 7.   [4] An unfulfilled promise.

and writing,—not only for their usefulness, but also because many other sorts of knowledge are acquired
40 through them. With a like view they may be taught
drawing, not to prevent their making mistakes in their
own purchases, or in order that they may not be im-
1338ᵇ posed upon in the buying or selling of articles, but perhaps
rather because it makes them judges of the beauty of the
human form. To be always seeking after the useful does
not become free and exalted souls.[1] Now it is clear
5 that in education practice must be used before theory,
and the body be trained before the mind ; and therefore
boys should be handed over to the trainer, who creates
in them the proper habit of body, and to the wrestling-
master, who teaches them their exercises.

Of those states which in our own day seem to take the 4
greatest care of children, some aim at producing in them
10 an athletic habit, but they only injure their forms and
stunt their growth. Although the Lacedaemonians have
not fallen into this mistake, yet they brutalize their children by laborious exercises which they think will make
them courageous. But in truth, as we have often re-
15 peated,[2] education should not be exclusively, or princi-
pally, directed to this end. And even if we suppose
the Lacedaemonians to be right in their end, they do
not attain it. For among barbarians and among animals
courage is found associated, not with the greatest ferocity,
but with a gentle and lion-like temper. There are
20 many races who are ready enough to kill and eat men,
such as the Achaeans and Heniochi, who both live about
the Black Sea ;[3] and there are other mainland tribes, as
bad or worse, who all live by plunder, but have no courage.
25 It is notorious that the Lacedaemonians themselves, while
they alone were assiduous in their laborious drill, were
superior to others, but now they are beaten both in
war and gymnastic exercises. For their ancient supe-

---

[1] Cp. Plato, *Rep.* vii. 525 ff.
[2] ii. 1271ᵃ 41–ᵇ 10, vii. 1333ᵇ 5 sqq., 1334ᵃ 40 sqq.
[3] Cp. *N. Eth.* vii. 1148ᵇ 21.

riority did not depend on their mode of training their youth, but only on the circumstance that they trained them when their only rivals did not. Hence we may infer that what is noble, not what is brutal, should have the first place; no wolf or other wild animal will face 30 a really noble danger; such dangers are for the brave man.[1] And parents who devote their children to gymnastics while they neglect their necessary education, in reality vulgarize them; for they make them useful to the art of statesmanship in one quality only, and even in 35 this the argument proves them to be inferior to others. We should judge the Lacedaemonians not from what they have been, but from what they are; for now they have rivals who compete with their education; formerly they had none.

It is an admitted principle, that gymnastic exercises should be employed in education, and that for children 40 they should be of a lighter kind, avoiding severe diet or painful toil, lest the growth of the body be impaired. The evil of excessive training in early years is strikingly proved by the example of the Olympic victors; for not **1339^{a}** more than two or three of them have gained a prize both as boys and as men; their early training and severe gymnastic exercises exhausted their constitutions. When boyhood is over, three years should be spent in other studies; the period of life which follows may then be 5 devoted to hard exercise and strict diet. Men ought not to labour at the same time with their minds and with their bodies;[2] for the two kinds of labour are opposed to one another; the labour of the body impedes the mind, and the labour of the mind the body.   10

5   Concerning music there are some questions which we have already raised;[3] these we may now resume and carry further; and our remarks will serve as a prelude to this or any other discussion of the subject. It is not easy to determine the nature of music, or why any one 15

[1] Cp. *N. Eth.* iii. 1115^{a} 29.   [2] Cp. Plato, *Rep.* vii. 537 B.
[3] 1337^{b} 27–1338^{a} 30.

should have a knowledge of it. Shall we say, for the sake
of amusement and relaxation, like sleep or drinking,
which are not good in themselves, but are pleasant, and
at the same time 'make care to cease', as Euripides[1]
says? And for this end men also appoint music, and
20 make use of all three alike,—sleep, drinking, music,—to
which some add dancing. Or shall we argue that music
conduces to virtue, on the ground that it can form our
minds and habituate us to true pleasures as our bodies
are made by gymnastic to be of a certain character?
25 Or shall we say that it contributes to the enjoyment of
leisure and mental cultivation, which is a third alternative?
Now obviously youths are not to be instructed with a view
to their amusement, for learning is no amusement, but is
accompanied with pain. Neither is intellectual enjoyment
30 suitable to boys of that age, for it is the end, and that
which is imperfect cannot attain the perfect or end. But
perhaps it may be said that boys learn music for the sake
of the amusement which they will have when they are
grown up. If so, why should they learn themselves,
35 and not, like the Persian and Median kings, enjoy the
pleasure and instruction which is derived from hearing
others? (for surely persons who have made music the
business and profession of their lives will be better
performers than those who practise only long enough to
learn). If they must learn music, on the same principle
40 they should learn cookery, which is absurd. And even
granting that music may form the character, the
objection still holds: why should we learn ourselves?
1339[b] Why cannot we attain true pleasure and form a correct
judgement from hearing others, like the Lacedaemonians?—for they, without learning music, nevertheless
can correctly judge, as they say, of good and bad
melodies. Or again, if music should be used to promote
5 cheerfulness and refined intellectual enjoyment, the
objection still remains—why should we learn ourselves
instead of enjoying the performances of others? We
may illustrate what we are saying by our conception of

[1] *Bacchae*, 381.

the Gods; for in the poets Zeus does not himself sing or
play on the lyre. Nay, we call professional performers
vulgar ; no freeman would play or sing unless he were
intoxicated or in jest. But these matters may be left
for the present.[1]   10
   The first question is whether music is or is not to be
a part of education. Of the three things mentioned in our
discussion, which does it produce ?—education or amusement or intellectual enjoyment, for it may be reckoned
under all three, and seems to share in the nature of all of
them. Amusement is for the sake of relaxation, and relax- 15
ation is of necessity sweet, for it is the remedy of pain
caused by toil ; and intellectual enjoyment is universally
acknowledged to contain an element not only of the noble
but of the pleasant, for happiness is made up of both. All 20
men agree that music is one of the pleasantest things,
whether with or without song ; as Musaeus says,

   ' Song is to mortals of all things the sweetest.'

Hence and with good reason it is introduced into social
gatherings and entertainments, because it makes the
hearts of men glad : so that on this ground alone we
may assume that the young ought to be trained in it. 25
For innocent pleasures are not only in harmony with
the perfect end of life, but they also provide relaxation.
And whereas men rarely attain the end, but often rest
by the way and amuse themselves, not only with a view
to a further end, but also for the pleasure's sake, it may be 30
well at times to let them find a refreshment in music.
It sometimes happens that men make amusement the
end, for the end probably contains some element of
pleasure, though not any ordinary or lower pleasure;
but they mistake the lower for the higher, and in seeking for the one find the other, since every pleasure has
a likeness to the end of action.[2] For the end is not 35
eligible for the sake of any future good, nor do the
pleasures which we have described exist for the sake of
any future good but of the past, that is to say, they are

[1] Cp. c. 6.   [2] Cp. *N. Eth.* vii. 1153^b 33.

the alleviation of past toils and pains. And we may infer this to be the reason why men seek happiness from 40 these pleasures. But music is pursued, not only as an alleviation of past toil, but also as providing recreation. And who can say whether, having this use, it may not 1340^a also have a nobler one? In addition to this common pleasure, felt and shared in by all (for the pleasure given by music is natural, and therefore adapted to all ages 5 and characters), may it not have also some influence over the character and the soul? It must have such an influence if characters are affected by it. And that they are so affected is proved in many ways, and not least 10 by the power which the songs of Olympus exercise ; for beyond question they inspire enthusiasm, and enthusiasm is an emotion of the ethical part of the soul. Besides, when men hear imitations, even apart from the rhythms and 15 tunes themselves, their feelings move in sympathy. Since then music is a pleasure, and virtue consists in rejoicing and loving and hating aright, there is clearly nothing which we are so much concerned to acquire and to cultivate as the power of forming right judgements, and of taking delight in good dispositions and noble actions.[1] Rhythm and melody supply imitations of anger and 20 gentleness, and also of courage and temperance, and of all the qualities contrary to these, and of the other qualities of character, which hardly fall short of the actual affections, as we know from our own experience, for in listening to such strains our souls undergo a change. The habit of feeling pleasure or pain at mere representations is not far removed from the same feeling 25 about realities ; [2] for example, if any one delights in the sight of a statue for its beauty only, it necessarily follows that the sight of the original will be pleasant to him. The objects of no other sense, such as taste or touch, 30 have any resemblance to moral qualities; in visible objects there is only a little, for there are figures which are of a moral character, but only to a slight extent, and

[1] Cp. Plato, *Rep.* iii. 401, 402 ; *Laws*, ii. 659 C-E.
[2] Cp. Plato, *Rep.* iii. 395.

all do not participate in the feeling about them. Again, figures and colours are not imitations, but signs, of moral habits, indications which the body gives of states of feeling. The connexion of them with morals is slight, 35 but in so far as there is any, young men should be taught to look, not at the works of Pauson, but at those of Polygnotus,[1] or any other painter or sculptor who expresses moral ideas. On the other hand, even in mere melodies there is an imitation of character, for the 40 musical modes differ essentially from one another, and those who hear them are differently affected by each. Some of them make men sad and grave, like the 1340ᵇ so-called Mixolydian, others enfeeble the mind, like the relaxed modes, another, again, produces a moderate and settled temper, which appears to be the peculiar effect of the Dorian; the Phrygian inspires enthusiasm. The whole subject has been well treated by philosophical 5 writers[2] on this branch of education, and they confirm their arguments by facts. The same principles apply to rhythms;[3] some have a character of rest, others of motion, and of these latter again, some have a more vulgar, others a nobler movement. Enough has been 10 said to show that music has a power of forming the character, and should therefore be introduced into the education of the young. The study is suited to the stage of youth, for young persons will not, if they 15 can help, endure anything which is not sweetened by pleasure, and music has a natural sweetness. There seems to be in us a sort of affinity to musical modes and rhythms, which makes some philosophers say that the soul is a tuning, others, that it possesses tuning.

6   And now we have to determine the question which 20 has been already raised,[4] whether children should be themselves taught to sing and play or not. Clearly there is a considerable difference made in the character by the actual practice of the art. It is difficult, if not

---

[1] Cp. *Poet.* 1448ᵃ 5, 1450ᵃ 26.   [2] Cp. *Rep.* 398 E sqq.
[3] *Rep.* iii. 399 E, 400.   [4] 1339ᵃ 33-ᵇ 10.

impossible, for those who do not perform to be good
25 judges of the performance of others.[1] Besides, children
should have something to do, and the rattle of Archytas,
which people give to their children in order to amuse
them and prevent them from breaking anything in the
house, was a capital invention, for a young thing cannot
be quiet. The rattle is a toy suited to the infant mind,
30 and education is a rattle or toy for children of a larger
growth. We conclude then that they should be taught
music in such a way as to become not only critics but
performers.

The question what is or is not suitable for different ages
may be easily answered ; nor is there any difficulty in
meeting the objection of those who say that the study of
35 music is vulgar.[2] We reply (1) in the first place, that
they who are to be judges must also be performers, and
that they should begin to practise early, although when
they are older they may be spared the execution ; they
must have learned to appreciate what is good and to
delight in it, thanks to the knowledge which they
40 acquired in their youth. As to (2) the vulgarizing effect
which music is supposed to exercise, this is a question
which we shall have no difficulty in determining, when
we have considered to what extent freemen who are
being trained to political virtue should pursue the art,
1341^a what melodies and what rhythms they should be allowed
to use, and what instruments should be employed in
teaching them to play ; for even the instrument makes a
difference. The answer to the objection turns upon these
distinctions ; for it is quite possible that certain methods
of teaching and learning music do really have a
5 degrading effect. It is evident then that the learning of
music ought not to impede the business of riper years, or
to degrade the body or render it unfit for civil or
military training, whether for bodily exercises at the
time or for later studies.
10   The right measure will be attained if students of
music stop short of the arts which are practised in pro-

[1] Cp. 1339^a 42.   [2] Cp. 1339^b 8, 1341^b 14.

fessional contests, and do not seek to acquire those fantastic marvels of execution which are now the fashion in such contests, and from these have passed into education. Let the young practise even such music as we have prescribed,[1] only until they are able to feel delight in noble melodies and rhythms, and not merely in that common part of music in which every slave or child and even some animals find pleasure.

From these principles we may also infer what instruments should be used. The flute, or any other instrument which requires great skill, as for example the harp, ought not to be admitted into education, but only such as will make intelligent students of music or of the other parts of education. Besides, the flute is not an instrument which is expressive of moral character; it is too exciting. The proper time for using it is when the performance aims not at instruction, but at the relief of the passions.[2] And there is a further objection; the impediment which the flute presents to the use of the voice detracts from its educational value. The ancients therefore were right in forbidding the flute to youths and freemen, although they had once allowed it. For when their wealth gave them a greater inclination to leisure, and they had loftier notions of excellence, being also elated with their success, both before and after the Persian War, with more zeal than discernment they pursued every kind of knowledge, and so they introduced the flute into education. At Lacedaemon there was a choragus who led the chorus with a flute, and at Athens the instrument became so popular that most freemen could play upon it. The popularity is shown by the tablet which Thrasippus dedicated when he furnished the chorus to Ecphantides. Later experience enabled men to judge what was or was not really conducive to virtue, and they rejected both the flute and several other old-fashioned instruments, such as the Lydian harp, the many-stringed lyre, the 'heptagon', 'triangle', 'sambuca', and the like —which are intended only to give pleasure to the hearer, 1341ᵇ

[1] Omitting μή in l. 13. [2] Cp. 1341ᵇ 38.

and require extraordinary skill of hand.[1]   There is a
meaning also in the myth of the ancients, which tells
how Athene invented the flute and then threw it away.
5 It was not a bad idea of theirs, that the Goddess disliked
the instrument because it made the face ugly; but with
still more reason may we say that she rejected it because
the acquirement of flute-playing contributes nothing to
the mind, since to Athene we ascribe both knowledge
and art.

Thus then we reject the professional instruments and
also the professional mode of education in music (and
10 by professional we mean that which is adopted in contests), for in this the performer practises the art, not for
the sake of his own improvement, but in order to give
pleasure, and that of a vulgar sort, to his hearers.   For
this reason the execution of such music is not the part of
a freeman but of a paid performer, and the result is that
the performers are vulgarized, for the end at which they
15 aim is bad.[2]   The vulgarity of the spectator tends to
lower the character of the music and therefore of the performers; they look to him—he makes them what they
are, and fashions even their bodies by the movements
which he expects them to exhibit.

We have also to consider rhythms and modes, and 7
20 their use in education.   Shall we use them all or make a
distinction? and shall the same distinction be made for
those who practise music with a view to education, or
shall it be some other?[3]   Now we see that music is
produced by melody and rhythm, and we ought to know
25 what influence these have respectively on education, and
whether we should prefer excellence in melody or
excellence in rhythm.   But[4] as the subject has been
very well treated by many musicians of the present day,
and also by philosophers[5] who have had considerable

---

[1] Cp. Plato, *Rep.* iii. 399 c, D.   [2] Cp. Plato, *Laws*, iii. 700.
[3] Omitting τρίτον δεῖ in l. 23.
[4] Reading in ll. 23-27, with Bonitz, τινα ἕτερον. ἐπεὶ δή . . .
παιδείαν, καὶ πότερον . . . εὔρυθμον, νομίσαντες κτλ.
[5] Cp. *Rep.* iii. 398 D sqq.

experience of musical education, to these we would refer 30
the more exact student of the subject; we shall only
speak of it now after the manner of the legislator, stating
the general principles.

We accept the division of melodies proposed by certain philosophers into ethical melodies, melodies of
action, and passionate or inspiring melodies, each having,
as they say, a mode corresponding to it. But we main- 35
tain further that music should be studied, not for the
sake of one, but of many benefits, that is to say, with
a view to (1) education, (2) purgation (the word 'purgation'
we use at present without explanation, but when hereafter
we speak of poetry,[1] we will treat the subject with more
precision); music may also serve (3) for intellectual en- 40
joyment, for relaxation and for recreation after exertion.
It is clear, therefore, that all the modes must be employed 1342^a
by us, but not all of them in the same manner. In
education the most ethical modes are to be preferred,
but in listening to the performances of others we may
admit the modes of action and passion also. For feelings 5
such as pity and fear, or, again, enthusiasm, exist very
strongly in some souls, and have more or less influence
over all. Some persons fall into a religious frenzy, whom
we see as a result of the sacred melodies—when they
have used the melodies that excite the soul to mystic 10
frenzy—restored as though they had found healing and
purgation. Those who are influenced by pity or fear,
and every emotional nature, must have a like experience, and others [2] in so far as each is susceptible to such 15
emotions, and all are in a manner purged and their
souls lightened and delighted. The purgative melodies
likewise give an innocent pleasure to mankind. Such
are the modes and the melodies in which those who
perform music at the theatre should be invited to compete. But since the spectators are of two kinds—the
one free and educated, and the other a vulgar crowd

---

[1] Cp. *Poet.* 1449^b 27, though the promise ·is really unfulfilled
The reference is probably to a lost part of the *Poetics*.
[2] Retaining δ' in l. 13.

20 composed of mechanics, labourers, and the like—there
ought to be contests and exhibitions instituted for the
relaxation of the second class also. And the music will
correspond to their minds ; for as their minds are perverted
from the natural state, so there are perverted modes and
25 highly strung and unnaturally coloured melodies. A
man receives pleasure from what is natural to him, and
therefore professional musicians may be allowed to practise
this lower sort of music before an audience of a lower
type. But, for the purposes of education, as I have
already said,[1] those modes and melodies should be
employed which are ethical, such as the Dorian, as we
30 said before ;[2] though we may include any others which
are approved by philosophers who have had a musical
education. The Socrates of the *Republic*[2] is wrong
in retaining only the Phrygian mode along with the
1342ᵇ Dorian, and the more so because he rejects the flute ;
for the Phrygian is to the modes what the flute is
to musical instruments—both of them are exciting and
emotional. Poetry proves this, for Bacchic frenzy and
5 all similar emotions are most suitably expressed by the
flute, and are better set to the Phrygian than to any
other mode. The dithyramb, for example, is acknowledged to be Phrygian, a fact of which the connoisseurs
of music offer many proofs, saying, among other things,
that Philoxenus, having attempted to compose his
10 *Mysians*[4] as a dithyramb in the Dorian mode, found
it impossible, and fell back by the very nature of things
into the more appropriate Phrygian. All men agree
that the Dorian music is the gravest and manliest. And
15 whereas we say that the extremes should be avoided and
the mean followed, and whereas the Dorian is a mean
between the other modes,[5] it is evident that our youth
should be taught the Dorian music.

Two principles have to be kept in view, what is
possible, what is becoming : at these every man ought

---

[1] 1342ª 2.   [2] 1340ᵇ 3 sq.   [3] Plato, *Rep.* iii. 399 A.
[4] Reading διθύραμβον τοὺς Μυσοὺς in l. 10, with Schneider.
[5] Cp. 1340ª 42.

to aim. But even these are relative to age; the old, 20 who have lost their powers, cannot very well sing the high-strung modes, and nature herself seems to suggest that their songs should be of the more relaxed kind. Wherefore the musicians likewise blame Socrates,[1] and with justice, for rejecting the relaxed modes in education under the idea that they are intoxicating, not in the 25 ordinary sense of intoxication (for wine rather tends to excite men), but because they have no strength in them. And so, with a view also to the time of life when men begin to grow old, they ought to practise the gentler modes and melodies as well as the others, and, further, any mode, such as the Lydian above all others appears 30 to be, which is suited to children of tender age, and possesses the elements both of order and of education. Thus it is clear [2] that education should be based upon three principles—the mean, the possible, the becoming, these three.

---

[1] *Rep.* iii. 398 E sqq.
[2] Reading ἢ δῆλον in l. 33, with Göttling ; cf. ii. 1272^b 9.

INDEX

S

T

INDEX

INDEX

should be helped by the rich, 20^a 32-^b 16.

Population, decline of, at Sparta, 70^a 29 ; importance of regulating, 65^a 38-^b16, 66^b 8, 70^a 29 -^b 6, 35^b 21 ; changes of government brought about by the natural increase of population in Hellas, 86^b 20, 93^a 1, 97^b 22, 20^a 17, cf. 21^a 1 ; a limit of population necessary to good government, 65^a 13, 38, 66^b 8, 70^b 4, 26^a 5-^b 7, ^b 20, 27^a 15, 35^b 21.

Possession, a, may be called an instrument for maintaining life, 53^b 31 ; is an instrument of action, 54^a 2.

Poverty, not the cause of the worst crimes, 66^b 38 ; always antagonistic to riches, 91^b 9 ; the parent of revolution and crime, 65^b 12 (but cp. 16^b 14) ; one of the essential characteristics of democracy, 17^b 40.

Pre-eminence in virtue; the preeminently good man or family should be supreme, 83^b 21, 84^a 3-^b 34, 88^a 15-29, 1^a 39, 25^b 10.

Preservation, the general causes of, in states, 7^b 26-10^a 38 ; the causes which affect monarchies, 13^a 18-33 ; tyrannies, ^a 34 -15^b 10 ; democracies, 19^b 33 -20^b 17, 21^a 1 ; oligarchies, ^a 3 -^b 1.

Presidents ; name given to certain magistrates, 21^b 39, 31^b 6.

Priests, are not political officers, 99^a 17 ; necessary to the state, 28^b 11, 22 ; should be taken from the aged citizens who are past state service, 29^a 27 ; their duties, 22^b 18-29 ; required to take their meals at common tables, 31^b 5.

Prior and posterior ; the state prior to the family or the individual, 53^a 18 ; the whole prior to the part, ^a 20 ; true forms of government prior to perversions, 75^b 1 ; the body prior in order of generation to the soul, 34^b 20 ; the irrational element prior to the rational, ^b 21.

Prisoners of war, usually made slaves, 55^a 6, 23.

Probuli, or senators, the head of the state in oligarchies, 98^b 29, 99^b 31-38, 22^b 16, 23^a 7.

Production, instruments of, 54^a 1.

Property, a part of the household, 53^b 23, 56^a 3 ; a condition but not a part of the state, 28^a 34 ; in the sense of food, provided by nature for all, 56^b 7, 58^a 34 ;—the pleasure of property, 63^a 40 ;-- Plato's limit of property unsatisfactory, 65^a 29 ; the limit should be such as to enable a man to live both temperately and liberally, ^a 32, 26^b 30 ;-- inequality of property at Sparta, 70^a 15-^b 6, 6^b 36, 7^a 35, 16^b 8 ;—a great cause of revolutions, 66^a 37-^b21.

Property, community of; criticism of Plato's scheme, 62^b 37-64^b 25 (see Plato); common property opposed to human nature, 63^a 15, 64^a 1 ; exists in a modified degree among friends, 63^a 29-37, 30^a 1 ; found to some extent at Sparta and Tarentum, 63^a 35, 20^b 9 ; would destroy the virtues of temperance and liberality, 63^b 5-14 ; would not produce the marvellous results which Plato expects, ^b 15 ;—equalization of, proposed by Phaleas, 66^a 39-67^b 19, 74^b 9 ; would not remedy the deeper evils of human nature, 66^b 28-67^a 17, 67^a 39.

Property qualification, required in the holders of various offices, 82^a 29, 91^b 39, 92^a 39, ^b29, 93^a 14, 18^b 30 ; ought not to be excessive, 97^b 2 ; in oligarchies should be fixed according to two standards, 20^b 22 ; changes in, a cause of revolutions, 3^a 12, 23, 6^b 6-16, 7^a 27 ; the evil may be remedied by periodical revisions of the census, 8^a 35-^b6.

Property taxes, in democracies, 20^a 20.

INDEX

family, 52^b 16; the state a union of villages, ^{b}27.

Violence, often associated with virtue, 55^a 13.

Virtue, the especial characteristic of aristocratical governments, 73^a 26, 93^a 35-^{b}21, 7^a 9; often allied to force, 55^a 13; more a concern of household management than wealth, 59^b 20; depends upon the supremacy of the rational principle in the soul, 33^a 18; cannot be included under a general definition, 60^a 25; must be taught to the slave by his master, ^{b}3; ought to be the aim and care of the state, 80^b 5, 32^a 31 (cp. 93^b 12); gives a claim to superiority in the state, 81^a 4, 83^a 24; has many kinds, 79^b 1; cannot ruin those who possess her, 81^a 19; is a mean, 95^a 37; how far required in the great officers of state, 9^a 33-^{b} 14; must be at least pretended by the tyrant, 15^a 14, ^{b} 8; is regarded as a secondary object by mankind, 23^a 36 :— cannot be separated from happiness, 23^a 27, 24^a 12, 25^a 16, 28^a 37, ^{b}35, 32^a 7; results from nature, habit, and reason, 32^a 38-^{b} 11, 34^b 6-28; is not a matter of chance, 32^a 31; how far consistent with the political life, 24^a 5-25^b 32; should it be made the aim of education? 37^a 33-^{b}23; consists in hating and loving and rejoicing aright, 40^a 15 :—should not (as is done by the Lacedaemonians) be supposed inferior to external goods, 71^b 9 (cp. 23^a 36); nor be practised with a view to the single object of success in war, 71^a 41, 24^b 5, 33^b 12, 34^a 40;—the virtue proper to the slave, the woman, the child, 59^b 21-32; of the ruler and the subject different, ^{b} 33-60^a 9, 77^a 13-^{b} 30; of the ruler, practical wisdom, of the subject, true opinion, ^{b} 25; of men and women not the same, 59^b 28, 60^a 20-31,

77^b 20; less required in the artisan than the slave, 60^a 36 (cp. 29^a 19); of the citizen relative to the constitution, 76^b 16-77^a 13, 93^b 3, 9^a 36; of the good man absolute, 76^b 16-77^a 13, 32^a 22; of the good citizen :—is it identical with that of the good man? 76^b 16 -77^b 30, 78^a 40, 88^a 32-^{b} 2, 33^a 11; of the citizen in the perfect state, 76^b 35, 84^a 1, 93^b 3.

Virtue, military, is found in the masses, 79^b 1; the social, is justice, 53^a 37, 83^a 38.

Virtues, the, of women and children important to the state, 60^b 16, 69^b 12; of the state and the individual the same, 23^b 33; of the military life, 70^a 5, 34^a 25; of leisure, ^{a} 14.

Viviparous animals, the, 56^b 13.

Vote, election by, modes in which it can be employed, 66^a 9, 0^a 9-^{b} 5.

W

Walls, are not, as Plato supposes (*Laws*, vi. 778), unnecessary, 30^b 32.

Walls, officers appointed to take charge of the, 21^b 26, 22^a 35.

War, a part of the art of acquisition when directed against wild beasts and against men who are intended by nature to be slaves, 55^b 37, 56^b 23, 33^b 38; exists for the sake of peace, 33^a 35, 34^a 2-16; a school of virtue, 70^a 5; a remedy against the dangers of prosperity, 34^a 25; constant war a part of tyrannical policy, 13^b 28; success in war the sole object of the Lacedaemonian and Cretan constitutions, 71^a 41-^{b}10, 24^b 5, 33^b 12, 34^a 40; progress in war: — invention of tactics, 97^b 20; — of siege machines, 31^a 1; improvement of fortifications, ^{a}16.

War, captives taken in, ought they to be made slaves? 55^a 3 -^{b} 4.

INDEX

pursuits as men, 64^{b}4 ; said to have been common among certain Libyan tribes, 62^a 20 ; have great influence among warlike races, 69^b 24 ; caused great harm to Sparta by their disorder and licence, ^{b}12–70^a 15 ; possessed two-fifths of the land in Laconia, 70^a 23 ; too proud in oligarchies to be controlled, 0^{a}7 ; have often ruined tyrannies by their insolence, 14^b 27; are allowed great licence in democracies and tyrannies, 13^{b}33, 19^{b}28 ; commonly cease to bear children after fifty, 35^{a}9 ; should not marry too young, ^{a}11 ; impart their nature to their offspring, ^{b}18 ; guardians of, 99^{a}22, 0^{a}4, 22^{b}39.

Women and children, the community of, proposed by Plato, 61^{a}4, 74^{b}9 ; he has not explained whether he would extend it to the dependent classes, 64^{a}11–^{b}4 ; — objections of Aristotle : (1) unity would not be promoted, 61^{b}16 ; (2) there would be a general neglect of the children, ^{b}32 ; (3) the parentage of the children could not be concealed, 62^{a}14 ; (4) expiations would be impossible, ^{a}31 ; (5) the concealment of relationship would lead to unnatural crimes, ^{a}25–40, ^{b}29 ; (6) affection would be weakened, ^{a}40–^{b}24 ; (7) the transfer of children to another rank would be found impracticable, ^{b}24 ; (8) the household would be neglected, 64^{a}40.

X

Xenelasia : *see* Strangers.
Xerxes, King of Persia, conspiracy of Artapanes against, 11^{b}38.

Z

Zaleucus, the Locrian legislator, 74^{a}22 ; said to have been a disciple of Thales, ^{a}29.
Zancle, seizure of, by the Samians, 3^{a}35.
Zeugitae, the (in Solon's legislation), 74^{a}20.
Zeus, 84^{b}31 ; 'the father of gods and men,' 59^{b}13 ; never represented by the poets as singing or playing, 39^{b}8 : — Olympian, temple of (at Athens), built by the Peisistratidae, 13^{b}23.

OECONOMICA

BY

E. S. FORSTER

M.A., LECTURER IN GREEK IN THE UNIVERSITY OF SHEFFIELD
FORMERLY SCHOLAR OF ORIEL COLLEGE

FIRST EDITION 1920

Reprinted lithographically in Great Britain
by LOWE & BRYDONE, PRINTERS LTD., LONDON
from sheets of the first edition
1938, 1946, 1952, 1961

PREFACE

THE text used for this translation is that of F. Susemihl (*Aristotelis quae feruntur Oeconomica*, Leipzig, Teubner, 1887). Mr. W. D. Ross has read through the translation both in manuscript and in proof and has made a number of valuable suggestions which have all been adopted.

Of the two Books of *Oeconomica* which have come down to us in the Aristotelian Corpus neither can be regarded as the work of Aristotle himself. The First Book contains elements derived from Aristotle, but it also owes a good deal to the *Oeconomicus* of Xenophon.[1] It appears to be the work of a Peripatetic writer who was a pupil either of Aristotle himself or of a disciple of that philosopher.[2] The writer was clearly well acquainted with the writings of Aristotle and, though his doctrines are not purely Aristotelian,[3] he certainly wrote at a date before the Peripatetic school had become eclectic and coloured by Stoic influence in the second century B. C.

The Second Book is evidently of a different character and the work of a different writer. It consists of an Introduction, which divides Economics into four kinds, Royal, Satrapic, Political, and Personal—a division quite unknown to Aristotle—and then proceeds to relate a series of anecdotes which have no logical connexion with the introduction and are mainly concerned with questionable methods of raising money. Several of those about whom the anecdotes are related lived after the time of Aristotle,[4] and the style of the writer is certainly Hellenistic. That the author lived outside Greece proper is indicated by the fact that his examples are mainly derived from Asia Minor, Syria, and Egypt.

Susemihl in his edition adds as a Third Book a treatise

---

[1] A list of parallels with Aristotle's *Politics* and Xenophon's *Oeconomicus* is given by Susemihl, *op. cit.*, pp. vi and vii.

[2] Possibly Eudemus, see Zeller, *Aristotle and the Later Peripatetics* (Engl. Trans.), vol. ii, p. 498.

[3] e. g. Economics is regarded as a separate science from Politics.

[4] See Susemihl, *op. cit.*, pp. xi and xii.

PREFACE

preserved only in Latin translations dealing with the position and duties of a wife in the household. The author of the original was certainly not Aristotle, but it has been conjectured by Rose[1] that it is the treatise entitled Νόμοι ἀνδρὸς καὶ γαμετῆς, which figures in the appendix of an anonymous index of Aristotelian works extracted from Hesychius Milesius. This treatise has not been translated for the present work.

E. S. F.

THE UNIVERSITY, SHEFFIELD.
June 20, 1919.

[1] *Aristoteles pseudepigr.*, p. 180 ff.

CONTENTS

OECONOMICA

BOOK I

1   THE sciences of politics and economics differ not only as 1343ᵃ
widely as a household and a city (the subject-matter with
which they severally deal), but also in the fact that the
science of politics involves a number of rulers, whereas the
sphere of economics is a monarchy.

Now certain of the arts fall into sub-divisions, and it does 5
not pertain to the same art to manufacture and to use the
article manufactured, for instance, a lyre or pipes; but the
function of political science is both to constitute a city in
the beginning and also when it has come into being to make
a right use of it.   It is clear, therefore, that it must be the
function of economic science too both to found a household
and also to make use of it.

Now a city is an aggregate made up of households and land 10
and property, possessing in itself the means to a happy life.
This is clear from the fact that, if men cannot attain this
end, the community is dissolved.   Further, it is for this end
that they associate together; and that for the sake of which
any particular thing exists and has come into being is its
essence.   It is evident, therefore, that economics is prior in
origin to politics; for its function is prior, since a household 15
is part of a city.   We must therefore examine economics
and see what its function is.

2   The component parts of a household are man and
property.   But since the nature of any given thing is most
quickly seen by taking its smallest parts, this would apply
also to a household.   So, according to Hesiod, it would be 20
necessary that there should be

> First and foremost a house, a woman, and an ox for
> the plough [1] . . . ,

[1] *Works and Days*, 405.

645·19

for the former is the first condition of subsistence, the latter is the proper possession of all freemen. We should have, therefore, as a part of economics to make proper rules for the association of husband and wife; and this involves providing what sort of a woman she ought to be.

25 In regard to property the first care is that which comes naturally. Now in the course of nature the art of agriculture is prior, and next come those arts which extract the products of the earth, mining and the like. Agriculture ranks first because of its justice; for it does not take anything away from men, either with their consent, as do retail trading and the mercenary arts, or against their will, as do the 30 warlike arts. Further, agriculture is natural; for by nature 1343ᵇ all derive their sustenance from their mother, and so men derive it from the earth. In addition to this it also conduces greatly to bravery; for it does not make men's bodies unserviceable, as do the illiberal arts, but it renders them 5 able to lead an open-air life and work hard; furthermore it makes them adventurous against the foe, for husbandmen are the only citizens whose property lies outside the fortifications.

As regards the human part of the household, the first care 3 is concerning a wife; for a common life is above all things natural to the female and to the male. For we have else-10 where[1] laid down the principle that nature aims at producing many such forms of association, just as also it produces the various kinds of animals. But it is impossible for the female to accomplish this without the male or the male without the female, so that their common life has necessarily arisen. Now in the other animals this intercourse is not based on reason, but depends on the amount of natural instinct which 15 they possess and is entirely for the purpose of procreation. But in the civilized and more intelligent animals the bond of unity is more perfect (for in them we see more mutual help and goodwill and co-operation), above all in the case of man, because the female and the male co-operate 20 to ensure not merely existence but a good life. And the

[1] Cp. *Eth. Nic.* 1162ᵃ 16 ff.; *Pol.* 1252ᵃ 26 ff.

production of children is not only a way of serving nature
but also of securing a real advantage ; for the trouble which
parents bestow upon their helpless children when they are
themselves vigorous is repaid to them in old age when they
are helpless by their children, who are then in their full
vigour. At the same time also nature thus periodically
provides for the perpetuation of mankind as a species, since 25
she cannot do so individually. Thus the nature both of the
man and of the woman has been preordained by the will of
heaven to live a common life. For they are distinguished
in that the powers which they possess are not applicable to
purposes in all cases identical, but in some respects their
functions are opposed to one another though they all tend
to the same end. For nature has made the one sex stronger, 30
the other weaker, that the latter through fear may be the
more cautious, while the former by its courage is better 1344ᵃ
able to ward off attacks ; and that the one may acquire
possessions outside the house, the other preserve those
within. In the performance of work, she made one sex able
to lead a sedentary life and not strong enough to endure
exposure, the other less adapted for quiet pursuits but well 5
constituted for outdoor activities ; and in relation to offspring
she has made both share in the procreation of children, but
each render its peculiar service towards them, the woman by
nurturing, the man by educating them.

4   First, then, there are certain laws to be observed towards
a wife, including the avoidance of doing her any wrong ; for
thus a man is less likely himself to be wronged. This is
inculcated by the general law, as the Pythagoreans say, 10
that one least of all should injure a wife as being 'a
supplant and seated at the hearth'.[1] Now wrong inflicted by a husband is the formation of connexions outside
his own house. As regards sexual intercourse, a man
ought not to accustom himself not to need it at all nor
to be unable to rest when it is lacking,[2] but so as to be

---

[1] Reading in l. 11 with Scaliger and Wilamowitz ἐφ' ἑστίας ἡμένην.
The κοινὸς νόμος will then be that which forbids injury to suppliants,
which, says the author, includes injury to a wife. ἀφ' ἑστίας ἡγμένην
can scarcely mean ' torn from the hearth '.

[2] Reading in l. 14 with some MSS. ἀπόντος.

¹⁵ content with or without it. The saying of Hesiod is a good one:

> A man should marry a maiden, that habits discreet he may teach her.¹

For dissimilarity of habits tends more than anything to destroy affection. As regards adornment, husband and wife ought not to approach one another with false affecta-²⁰ tion in their person any more than in their manners ; for if the society of husband and wife requires such embellishment, it is no better than play-acting on the tragic stage.

Of possessions, that which is the best and the worthiest 5 subject of economics comes first and is most essential— I mean, man. It is necessary therefore first to provide one-²⁵ self with good slaves. Now slaves are of two kinds, the overseer and the worker. And since we see that methods of education produce a certain character in the young, it is necessary when one has procured slaves to bring up care-fully those to whom the higher duties are to be entrusted. The intercourse of a master with his slaves should be such as not either to allow them to be insolent or to irritate them. ³⁰ To the higher class of slaves he ought to give some share of honour, and to the workers abundance of nourishment. And since the drinking of wine makes even freemen inso-lent, and many nations even of freemen abstain therefrom (the Carthaginians, for instance, when they are on military service), it is clear that wine ought never to be given to ³⁵ slaves, or at any rate very seldom. Three things make up the life of a slave, work, punishment, and food. To give them food but no punishment and no work makes them ¹³⁴⁴ᵇ insolent ; and that they should have work and punishment but no food is tyrannical and destroys their efficiency. It remains therefore to give them work and sufficient food ; for it is impossible to rule over slaves without offering rewards, and a slave's reward is his food. And just as all other men ⁵ become worse when they get no advantage by being better and there are no rewards for virtue and punishments for

---

¹ *Works and Days*, 699.

vice, so also is it with slaves. Therefore we must take careful notice and bestow or withhold everything, whether food or clothing or leisure or punishments, according to merit, in word and deed following the practice adopted by physicians in the matter of medicine, remembering at the 10 same time that food is not medicine because it must be given continually.

The slave who is best suited for his work is the kind that is neither too cowardly nor too courageous. Slaves who have either of these characteristics are injurious to their owners ; those who are too cowardly lack endurance, while the high-spirited are not easy to control. All ought to have 15 a definite end in view ; for it is just and beneficial to offer slaves their freedom as a prize, for they are willing to work when a prize is set before them and a limit of time is defined. One ought to bind slaves to one's service by the pledges of wife and children, and not to have many persons of the same race in a household, any more than in a state. One ought to provide sacrifices and pleasures more for the 20 sake of slaves than for freemen ; for in the case of the former there are present more of the reasons why such things have been instituted.

6   The economist ought to possess four qualities in relation to wealth. He ought to be able to acquire it, and to guard it ; otherwise there is no advantage in acquiring it, but it is a case of drawing water with a sieve, or the proverbial jar 25 with a hole in it. Further, he ought to be able to order his possessions aright and make a proper use of them ; for it is for these purposes that we require wealth. The various kinds of property ought to be distinguished, and those which are productive ought to be more numerous than the unpro-ductive, and the sources of income ought to be so distributed that they may not run a risk with all their possessions at the same time. For the preservation of wealth it is best to 30 follow both the Persian and the Laconian methods. The Attic system of economy is also useful ; for they sell their produce and buy what they want, and thus there is not the need of a storehouse in the smaller establishments. The Persian

B

system was that everything should be organized and that
35 the master should superintend everything personally, as Dio
said of Dionysius; for no one looks after the property of
others as well as he looks after his own, so that, as far as
1345ᵃ possible, a man ought to attend to everything himself. The
sayings of the Persian and the Libyan may not come
amiss; the former of whom, when asked what was the best
thing to fatten a horse, replied, ' His master's eye ', while
the Libyan, when asked what was the best manure, answered,
5 'The landowner's foot-prints'. Some things should be
attended to by the master, others by his wife, according to
the sphere allotted to each in the economy of the household. Inspections need only be made occasionally in small
establishments, but should be frequent where overseers are
employed. For perfect imitation is impossible unless a
good example is set, especially when trust is delegated to
10 others; for unless the master is careful, it is impossible for
his overseers to be careful. And since it is good for the
formation of character and useful in the interests of economy,
masters ought to rise earlier than their slaves and retire to
rest later, and a house should never be left unguarded any
15 more than a city, and when anything needs doing it ought
not to be left undone, whether it be day or night. There
are occasions when ¹ a master should rise while it is still
night; for this helps to make a man healthy and wealthy
and wise. On small estates the Attic system of disposing
of the produce ² is a useful one; but on large estates, where
20 a distinction is made between yearly and monthly expenditure and likewise between the daily and the occasional use
of household appliances, such matters must be entrusted to
overseers. Furthermore, a periodical inspection should be
made, in order to ascertain what is still existing and what
is lacking.

The house must be arranged both with a view to one's
25 possessions ³ and for the health and well-being of its inhabitants. By possessions I mean the consideration of

---

¹ Reading in l. 16 τοτέ τε as suggested by Sylburg.
² Cp. 1344ᵇ 31–3.
³ κτήματα is here used in a very wide sense since it includes not only
produce of the land and clothing, but also slaves and even guests.

what is suitable for produce and clothing, and in the case of
produce what is suitable for dry and what for moist produce,
and amongst other possessions what is suitable for property
whether animate or inanimate, for slaves and freemen,
women and men, strangers and citizens. With a view to 30
well-being and health, the house ought to be airy in
summer and sunny in winter. This would be best secured
if it faces north and is not as wide as it is long. In large
establishments a man who is no use for other purposes
seems to be usefully employed as a doorkeeper to safe- 35
guard what is brought into and out of the house. For the 1345^b
ready use of household appliances the Laconian method
is a good one; for everything ought to have its own
proper place and so be ready for use and not require to be
searched for.

BOOK II

7 HE who intends to practise economy aright ought to be ɪ
fully acquainted with the places in which his labour lies
and to be naturally endowed with good parts and deliber-
10 ately industrious and upright ; for if he is lacking in any
of these respects, he will make many mistakes in the
business which he takes in hand.

Now there are four kinds of economy, that of the king
(Royal Economy), that of the provincial governor (Satrapic
Economy), that of the city (Political Economy), and that
of the individual (Personal Economy). This is a broad
method of division ; and we shall find that the other forms
of economy fall within it.

Of these the Royal is the most important and the
15 simplest, the Political is the most varied and the easiest,
the Personal the least important and the most varied.[1]
They must necessarily have most of their characteristics in
common ; but it is the points which are peculiar to each
kind that we must consider. Let us therefore examine
20 Royal Economy first. It is universal in its scope, but has
four special departments—the coinage, exports, imports,
and expenditure. To take each of these separately : in
regard to the coinage,[2] I mean the question as to what
coin should be struck and when it should be of a high and
when of a low value ; in the matter of exports and imports,
what commodities it will be advantageous to receive from
25 the satraps under the Royal rule[3] and dispose of and when ;
in regard to expenditure, what expenses ought to be curtailed and when, and whether one should pay what is

---

[1] This sentence is clearly corrupt. No mention is made of ἡ σατρα-
πική, and ποικιλωτάτη cannot be applied both to ἡ πολιτική and ἡ ἰδιωτική :
it is probably right as applied to ἡ ἰδιωτική, being equivalent to ἀνώμαλος
in 1346ᵃ 9.

[2] Reading as suggested by Bekker ἕκαστον περὶ μὲν τὸ νόμισμα in l. 22.

[3] ἐν τῇ ταγῇ in l. 25 is probably corrupt.

expended in coin or in commodities which have an equivalent value.

Let us next take Satrapic Economy. Here we find six kinds of revenue : from land, from the peculiar products of the district, from merchandise, from taxes, from cattle, 30 and from all other sources. Of these the first and most important is that which comes from land (which some call tax on land-produce, others tithe) ; next in importance is the revenue from peculiar products, from gold, or silver, or copper, or anything else which is found in a particular 35 locality ; thirdly comes that derived from merchandise ; fourthly, the revenue from the cultivation of the soil and 1346$^\mathrm{a}$ from market-dues ; fifthly, that which comes from cattle, which is called tax on animal produce or tithe ; and sixthly, that which is derived from other sources, which is called the poll-tax or tax on handicraft.

Thirdly, let us examine the economy of the city. 5 Here the most important source of revenue is from the peculiar products of the country, next comes that derived from merchandise and customs,[1] and lastly that which comes from the ordinary taxes.

Fourthly and lastly, let us take Personal Economy. Here we find wide divergences, because economy is not necessarily always practised with one aim in view. It is 10 the least important kind of economy, because the incomings and expenses are small. Here the main source of revenue is the land, next other kinds of property,[2] and thirdly investments of money.

Further, there is a consideration which is common to all branches of economy and which calls for the most careful attention, especially in personal economy, namely, that the 15 expenditure must not exceed the income.

Now that we have mentioned the divisions of the subject, we must next consider whether, if the satrapy or city with which we are dealing can produce all,[3] or the most important revenues which we have just distinguished, some

[1] ἡ πρόσοδος ἡ ἀπὸ τῶν διαγωγῶν is apparently equivalent to the διαγώγιον (*portorium*) of Polyb. 26. 7. 7.
[2] Reading with Spengel κτημάτων in l. 13.
[3] Reading with Schneider and Bekker ἅπαντα ⟨ἁ⟩ in l. 19.

20 rather than others¹ ought to be employed. Next we must consider which sources of revenue do not exist at all but can be introduced, or are at present small but can be augmented ; and which of the expenses at present incurred, and to what amount, can be entirely² dispensed with without 25 doing any harm.

We have now mentioned the various kinds of economy and their constituent parts. We have further made a collection of all the methods that we conceived to be worth mentioning, which men of former days have employed or cunningly devised in order to provide themselves with 30 money. For we conceived that this information also might be useful ; for a man will be able to apply some of these instances to such business³ as he himself takes in hand.

Cypselus, the Corinthian, having vowed to Zeus that, if **2** he made himself master of the city, he would dedicate to him all the property of the Corinthians, ordered them to 1346ᵇ draw up a list of their possessions. When they had done so, he took a tenth part from each citizen and told them to trade with the remainder. As each year came round, he did the same thing again, with the result that in ten years 5 he had all that he had consecrated to the god, while the Corinthians had acquired other property.

Lygdamis, the Naxian, having driven certain men into exile, when no one was willing to buy their possessions except at a low price, sold them to the exiles themselves. And offerings belonging to them which were lying⁴ half 10 finished in certain workshops he sold to the exiles and any one else who wished to buy them, allowing the name of the purchaser to be inscribed upon them.

The Byzantines being in need of money sold the sacred enclosures belonging to the state.⁵ Those which

---

¹ Reading as suggested by Susemihl ⟨τούτοις μᾶλλον αὐτῶν ἢ ἐκείνοις, ἢ ἐκείνοις μᾶλλον ἢ⟩ τούτοις in l. 20.

² Omitting τά in l. 24 with the MSS.

³ Reading in l. 30 ἔστι γὰρ ὅτι (Richards) τούτων ἐφαρμόσει τις (Sylburg) οἷς (Schneider) ἂν αὐτὸς πραγματεύηται.

⁴ Reading with Keil ἀποκείμενα in l. 10.

⁵ The *locus classicus* on such enclosures is the speech of Lysias περὶ τοῦ σηκοῦ.

were fertile they sold on lease, and those which were un-
productive in perpetuity. They treated in the same way 15
the enclosures which belonged to associations and clans and
all which were situated on private estates ; for the owners of
the rest of the property bought them at a high price. To
the associations they sold other lands, viz. the public lands
round the gymnasium, or the market-place, or the harbour,
and the places where markets were held at which various 20
commodities were sold, and they gave the rights over the
sea-fisheries and the sale of salt, and the stands¹ where
jugglers, and soothsayers, and druggists, and other such
persons plied their trades ; but they ordered them to pay
over a third of their profits. And they sold the right of
changing money to a single bank, and no one else might 25
either give money in exchange to any one, or receive it in
exchange from any one, under penalty of forfeiting the
money. And whereas there was a law amongst them that
no one should have political rights who was not born of
parents who were both citizens, being in want of money
they passed a decree that a man who was sprung from
a citizen on one side only should become a citizen if he
paid down thirty minae. And as they were suffering from
want of food and lack of money, they made the ships from 30
the Black Sea put in ; but, as time went on, the merchants
protested and so they paid them interest at ten per cent.
and ordered those who purchased anything to pay the
ten per cent. in addition to the price. And whereas
certain resident aliens had lent money on mortgaged 1347ª
property, because these had not the right to hold property,
they passed a decree that any one who wished could obtain
a title to the property by paying a third of the loan to the
state.

Hippias, the Athenian, put up for sale the parts of the
upper rooms which projected into the public streets, and 5
the steps and fences in front of the houses, and the doors
which opened outwards. The owners of the property therefore bought them, and a large sum was thus collected. He

¹ Reading as suggested by Susemihl τοιουτοτρόπων ⟨τοὺς τόπους⟩ in
l. 22.

also declared the coinage then current in Athens to be base,
and fixing a price for it ordered it to be brought to him;
but when they met to consider the striking of a new type
10 of coin, he gave them back the same money again. And
if any one was about to equip a trireme or a division of
cavalry or to provide a tragic chorus or incur expense on
any other such state-service, he fixed a moderate fine and
allowed him, if he liked, to pay this and be enrolled amongst
those who had performed state services. He also ordered
that a measure of barley, and another of wheat, and an
15 obol should be brought to the priestess of Athena-on-the-
Acropolis on behalf of any one who died, and that the
same offering should be made by any one to whom a child
was born.

The Athenians who dwell in Potidaea, being in need
of money to carry on war, ordered all the citizens to draw
20 up a list of their property, each man enrolling not his whole
property collectively in his own deme, but each piece of
property separately in the place where it was situated, in
order that the poor might give in an assessment; any one
who possessed no property was to assess his own person at
two minae. On the basis of this assessment they contributed
each in full to the state the amount enjoined.

25   Sosipolis of Antissa, when the city was in want of
money, since the citizens were wont to celebrate the feast
of Dionysus with great splendour and every year went to
great expense in providing, amongst other things, very costly
victims, persuaded them, when the festival was near at hand,
to vow to Dionysus that they would give double offerings
30 the next year and collect and sell the dedications for the
current year. Thus a substantial sum was collected for the
needs of the moment.

The people of Lampsacus, expecting a large fleet of
triremes to come against them, ordered the dealers to sell
a *medimnus* of barley-meal, of which the market price was
four *drachmae*, at six *drachmae*, and a *chous* of oil, the price
of which was three *drachmae*, at four *drachmae* and a half,
35 and likewise wine and the other commodities. The individual seller thus received the usual price, while the

city gained the surplus and so was well provided with money.

The people of Heraclea, when they were sending forty ships against the tyrants on the Bosporus, not being well provided with money, bought up from the merchants all 5 their corn and oil and wine and the rest of their stores, fixing a date in the future at which they were to make the payment. Now it suited the merchants better to sell their cargoes wholesale rather than retail. So the people of Heraclea, giving the soldiers two months' pay, took the provisions with them[1] on board merchant-vessels and put 10 an official in charge of each of the ships. When they reached the enemies' territory, the soldiers bought up all the provisions from them.[2] Thus money was collected before the generals had to pay the soldiers again, and so the same money was distributed time after time until 15 they returned home.

When the Samians begged for money for their return home, the Lacedaemonians passed a decree that they would fast for one day, themselves and their domestics and their beasts of burden, and would give to the Samians the amount that each of them usually expended.

The Chalcedonians, having a large number of foreign 20 mercenaries in their city, owed them pay which they could not give them. They therefore proclaimed that if any citizen or resident alien had any right of seizure against any state or individual and wished to exercise it, they should give in their names. When many did so, they seized the ships which sailed into the Black Sea on a plausible pretext, 25 and appointed a time at which they promised to give an account of their captures. When a large sum of money had been collected they dismissed the soldiers and submitted themselves to trial for their reprisals, and the state out of its revenues made restitution to those who had been 30 unjustly plundered.

---

[1] Reading with Kirchhoff in l. 9 διδόντες διμήνου μισθὸν παρῆγον ἅμα τὴν ἀγοράν. With this reading we have an example of the common confusion of λλ and μ.

[2] An early example of a Field Force Canteen.

When the people of Cyzicus were at variance and the popular party had gained the upper hand and the wealthy citizens had been imprisoned, they passed a decree, since they owed money to their soldiers, that they would not put their prisoners to death, but would exact money from them and send them into exile.

35   The Chians, who have a law that a public register of debts should be kept, being in want of money decreed that 1348^a debtors should pay their debts to the state and that the state should disburse the interest from its revenues to the creditors until they should reach their former state of prosperity.[1]

5   Mausolus, tyrant of Caria, when the king of Persia sent and ordered him to pay his tribute, collected together the richest men in the country and told them that the king was demanding the tribute, but he himself could not provide it. And certain men, who had been suborned to do so, immediately promised to contribute and named the amount that each would give. Upon this the wealthier men, partly 10 through shame and partly from fear, promised and actually contributed far larger sums.

On another occasion when he was in need of money, he called together the Mylassians and told them that this city of his, though it was their mother-city, was unfortified and that the king of Persia was marching against him. He therefore ordered the Mylassians each to contribute as 15 much money as possible, saying that by what they paid now they would save the rest of their possessions.[2] When a large contribution had been made, he kept the money and told them that at the moment the god would not allow them to build the wall.

Condalus, a governor under Mausolus, whenever during his passage through the country any one brought 20 him a sheep or a pig or a calf, used to make a record of the

---

[1] The meaning seems to be that all debts were repaid to the state by private debtors instead of to their creditors, and the state then paid interest to the creditors, thus virtually raising a loan for itself. Many editors emend in l. 3 to ἕως ἂν καὶ τὸ ἀρχαῖον ἐκπορίσωσιν, 'until they could afford to pay up the capital'.

[2] Reading in l. 15 τὰ λοιπ᾽ ⟨ἂν⟩ σῴζειν (Richards).

donor and the date and order him to take it back home and keep it until he returned. When he thought that sufficient time had elapsed, he used to ask for the animal which was being kept for him, and reckoned up and demanded the produce-tax on it as well. And any trees which projected over or fell into the royal roads he used to sell as profits.[1] And if any soldier died, he demanded [2] a drachma as a toll 25 for the corpse passing the gates; and so he not only received money from this source, but also the officers could not deceive him as to the date of the soldier's death. Also, noticing that the Lycians were fond of wearing their hair long, he pretended that a dispatch had come from the king of Persia ordering him to send hair to make false fringes 30 and that he was therefore commanded by Mausolus to cut off their hair. He therefore said that, if they would pay him a fixed poll-tax, he would send for hair to Greece. They gladly gave him what he asked, and a large sum of money was collected from a great number of them.

Aristotle, the Rhodian, who was governor of Phocaea, 35 was in want of money. Perceiving therefore that there were two parties amongst the Phocaeans, he made secret 1348ᵇ overtures to one party saying that the other faction was offering him money on condition that he would turn the scale in their favour, but that for his own part he would rather receive money from *them* and give the direction of affairs into their hands. When they heard this, those who were present immediately gave him the money, supplying 5 him with all he asked for. He then went to the other party ..nd showed them what he had received from their opponents; whereupon they also professed their willingness to give him an equal sum. So he took the money from both parties and reconciled them one with another. Also, noticing that there was much litigation among the citizens and that there 10 were grievances of long standing among them owing to war, he established a court of law and proclaimed that unless they submitted their cases to judgement within a period [3]

---

[1] ἐπικαρπίας is here used in its wider sense of 'profits'; in l. 23 it has the special sense of 'tax on animal produce', as in 1346ᵃ 2.

[2] Reading in l. 26 διαπύλιον ἔπρατε (Scaliger).

[3] Reading in l. 12 χρόνου (Richards).

which he appointed, there would be no further settlement of their former claims. Then getting control of the deposits paid in a number of suits, and the cases which were subject 15 to appeal with damages[1], and receiving money from both parties by other means, he collected a large sum.

The Clazomenians, when they were suffering from famine and were in want of money, decreed that private individuals who had any olive oil should lend it to the state, which would pay them interest. Now olives are abundant 20 in this country. When the owners had lent them the oil, they hired ships and sent it to the marts from which their corn came, giving the value of the oil as a pledge. And when they owed pay to their soldiers to the amount of twenty talents and could not provide it, they paid the generals four talents a year as interest. But finding that they did not reduce the principal and that they were 25 continually spending money to no purpose, they struck an iron coinage to represent a sum of twenty talents of silver, and then distributing it among the richest citizens in proportion to their wealth they received in exchange an equivalent sum in silver. Thus the individual citizens had money to disburse for their daily needs and the state was 30 freed from debt. They then paid them interest out of their revenues and continually divided it up and distributed it in proper proportions, and called in the iron coinage.

The Selybrians were once in need of money; and so, as they had a law which forbade the export of corn to another state[2] which was suffering from famine, and they 35 had a supply of last season's corn, they passed a decree that private persons should hand over their corn to the state at 1349^a a fixed price, each reserving a year's supply; they then allowed any one who wished to export his supply, fixing a price which they thought would give them a profit.

The people of Abydos, when their land was untilled owing to political dissensions and the resident aliens were paying them nothing because they still owed them money, 5 passed a decree that any one who was willing should lend

---

[1] Reading ὑφ' ἑαυτόν for ἐφ' ἑαυτόν in l. 14.
[2] Reading with Keil ⟨τοῖς ἄλλοις⟩ ἐν in l. 34.

money to the farmers in order that they might till the soil, providing that they should enjoy the first-fruits of the crop and that the others should have what remained.

The Ephesians, being in need of money, made a law that their women should not wear gold ornaments, but 10 should lend to the state what they already possessed ; and fixing the amount which was to be paid they allowed the name of any one who presented that sum to be inscribed as that of the dedicator on certain of the pillars in the temple.

Dionysius of Syracuse, wishing to collect money, called together an assembly and declared that Demeter had 15 appeared to him and bade him bring the ornaments of the women to her temple. He had therefore, he said, done so with the ornaments of the women of his own household ; and he demanded that every one else should do the same, lest vengeance from the goddess should fall upon them. Any one who refused would, he said, be guilty of sacrilege. When all had brought what they possessed through fear of 20 the goddess and dread of Dionysius, after dedicating the ornaments to the goddess he then appropriated them, saying that they were lent to him by her. And when some time had elapsed and the women began wearing ornaments again, he ordered that any woman who wished to wear jewellery of gold should dedicate a fixed sum in the temple.

And when he was intending to build triremes, he knew 25 that he would be in want of money. He therefore called together an assembly and said that a certain city was to be betrayed to him and that he needed money for this purpose. He therefore asked the citizens to contribute two staters each ; and they did so. He then let two or three days elapse, and pretending that he had failed in his attempt, after commending their generosity he gave every man his contribution back again.   By this action he won the hearts of the 30 citizens. And so they again contributed, thinking that they would receive their money back again ; but he took the money and kept it for building his ships.

And when he was in need of money he struck a coinage of tin, and calling an assembly together he spoke at great

35 length in favour of the money which had been coined ; and they, even against their will, decreed that every one [1] should regard any of it that he accepted as silver and not as tin.

On another occasion, being in want of money, he asked 1349ᵇ the citizens to give him contributions ; but they declared that they had nothing to give. Accordingly he brought out his own household goods and offered them for sale, as though compelled to do so by poverty. When the Syracusans bought them, he kept a record of what each had bought, 5 and when they had paid the price, he ordered each of them to bring back the articles which he had bought.

And when the citizens owing to the taxes could not keep cattle, he said that he had enough up to the present ; those therefore who kept cattle should now be free from a tax on them. But since many soon acquired a large number of cattle, thinking that they could keep them without paying 10 a tax on them, when he thought that a fitting moment had come he gave orders that they should assess their value and then imposed a tax. Accordingly the citizens, angry at having been deceived, slew their cattle and sold them. And when, to prevent this, he ordered them to kill only as many as were needed for daily use, they next devoted them for sacrifice to the gods. Dionysius then forbade them to sacrifice any female beast.

On another occasion when he was in need of money, he 15 ordered all families of orphans to enrol themselves ; and when many [2] had done so, he enjoyed their property until each member of such families came of age.

And after he had captured Rhegium he called an assembly of the inhabitants together and informed them that he would be quite justified in enslaving them, but under 20 the circumstances he would let them go free if he received the amount which he had spent on the war and three *minae* a head from all of them. The Rhegians then brought to light the wealth which before had been hidden, and the poor borrowed from the richer citizens and from foreigners and provided 25 the sum which he demanded. When he had received it

---

[1] Reading ἕκαστον (Richards) in l. 35.
[2] Reading with Schneider πολλῶν for ἄλλων in l. 16.

from them he nevertheless sold them all as slaves, and seized all the treasures which had before been hidden and were now brought to light.

Also having borrowed money from the citizens under promise of repayment, when they demanded it back he ordered them to bring him whatever money any of them possessed, threatening them with death as the penalty if they failed to do so. When the money had been brought, he 30 issued it again after stamping it afresh so that each *drachma* had the value of two *drachmae*, and paid back the original debt and the money which they brought him on this occasion.[1]

And when he sailed against Tyrrhenia with a hundred ships he took much gold and silver and a considerable quantity of other ornaments of all kinds from the temple of Leucothea. And knowing that the sailors too were keeping 35 many things for themselves, he made a proclamation that every one should bring him the half of what he had and 1350ᵃ might retain the other half; and he threatened with death any one who failed to deliver up the half. The sailors, supposing that if they gave up the half they would be allowed undisturbed possession of the rest, did so ; but Dionysius, when he had received it, ordered them to go back and bring him the other half.   5

The Mendaeans used the proceeds of their harbour customs and their other dues for the administration of their city, but did not exact the taxes on land and houses ; but they kept a register of property-owners, and whenever they needed money, those who owed taxes paid them. They 10 thus profited during the time which elapsed by having full use of the money without paying interest.

When they were at war with the Olynthians and needed money, seeing that they had slaves they decreed that a female and a male slave should be left to each citizen and the rest sold, so that private individuals might lend money 15 to the state.[2]

Callistratus, when the harbour-dues in Macedonia

---

[1] Reading in l. 32 as suggested by Susemihl ⟨ἀπέδωκε καὶ ὁ νῦν⟩ ἀνήνεγκαν.

[2] Reading ὡς τῇ πόλει for τῇ πόλει ὡς in l. 14.

were usually sold at twenty talents, made them fetch double
that price. For, noticing that the richer men always bought
them because it was necessary that the sureties provided
20 for the twenty talents should be possessed of one talent, he
proclaimed that any one who liked could purchase them and
that sureties should be provided for only a third or any
other proportion which[1] he could persuade them each to
guarantee.

Timotheus, the Athenian, when he was at war with
the Olynthians, and in need of money, struck a bronze
25 coinage and distributed it to the soldiers. When they protested, he told them that the merchants and retailers would
all sell their goods on the same terms as before. He then
told the merchants, if they received any bronze money, to
use it again to buy the commodities sent in for sale from
the country and anything which was brought in as plunder,
and said that, if they brought him any bronze money which
they had left over, they should receive silver for it.
30 When he was making war in the neighbourhood of
Corcyra and was in difficulties, and the soldiers were
demanding their pay and refusing to ⸱obey him and
threatening to go over[2] to the enemy, he called together
an assembly and told them that no money could reach him
35 owing to the stormy weather, for he had, he declared, such
an abundance of supplies that he offered them as a free gift
the three months' rations which they had already received.
1350ᵇ They, supposing that Timotheus would never have made
such a valuable concession unless he really expected the
money, kept silence about the pay; and he meanwhile
achieved the objects which he had in view.

When he was besieging Samos he actually sold to the
5 inhabitants the fruits and the produce of their lands, and
so had abundance of money to pay his soldiers. And when
there was a shortage of provisions in the ⸱camp owing to
the arrival of newcomers, he forbade the sale of corn ready
ground, and of any smaller measure than a *medimnus*, and
10 of any liquid in a smaller quantity than a *metreta*. Accord-

---

[1] Reading καθ' ὁπόσον ⟨ἂν⟩ ἑκάστους (Richards) in l. 21.
[2] Reading ἀποπορεύεσθαι (Richards) in l. 33.

ingly the commanders of divisions and companies bought
up provisions wholesale and distributed them to the soldiers,
while the newcomers brought their own provisions with them
and, when they departed, sold anything that they had left.
The result was that the soldiers had an abundance of
provisions.   15

Didales, the Persian, having soldiers under his command, could supply their daily needs from the enemy's
country, but having no money to give them, and being
requested to pay them, when the time came at which it was
due he devised the following plan. He called together an
assembly and told them that he had no lack of money, but 20
that it was in a certain place which he named. He therefore moved his camp and started to march thither. Then
when he was near the place, he went in advance to it and
took from the temples there all the embossed silver plate
which they contained. He then loaded his mules so that
the silver plate was visible, and they looked as though they
were carrying solid silver. The soldiers, when they saw it, 25
thought that the loads were all solid silver and were encouraged, thinking that they would receive their pay. But
Didales told them that he must go to Amisus and have
the silver minted. Now the journey to Amisus was one of
many days and exposed to the weather. So all this time
he made use of the army, merely giving them their rations.

He kept in his personal service all the skilled artificers 30
in the army and the retailers who carried on traffic in any
commodity; and no one else was permitted to do any of
these things.

Chabrias, the Athenian, advised Taus, king of Egypt,
when he was starting on a warlike expedition and was in
need of money, to say to the priests that owing to the 35
expense some of the temples and the majority of the priests
must be dispensed with. When the priests heard this, each 1351ᵃ
wishing to retain his own temple, they privately offered
him[1] money. And when Taus had accepted money from
all of them, Chabrias advised him to order them to expend

---

[1] Reading in l. 2 ἰδίᾳ (cp. 1352ᵇ 23) with Scaliger and Schneider for
ἴδια, and αὐτῷ with Sylburg and Schneider for αὐτοῖς.

C

a tenth part of the amount which they formerly spent on
5 their temple[1] and to lend the rest to him until the war
against the king of Persia should come to an end. And he
advised him to fix the necessary amount and demand a
contribution from each household and likewise from each
individual; and that, when corn was sold, the buyer and
the seller should give an obol for each *artabe* over and
10 above the price; and that he should demand the payment
of a tenth part of the profits derived from shipping and
manufactures and any other form of industry. And he
advised him, when he was leaving the country on an expedition, to order that any unminted silver or gold which
any one possessed should be brought to him: and when
15 most people brought it, he advised him to make use of it
and to commend the lenders to the provincial governors so
that they might repay them out of the taxes.

Iphicrates, the Athenian, when Cotys had collected
an army, provided him with money in the following way.
20 He advised him to order the men under his command to
sow land for him with three *medimni* of corn. The result
of this was that a great quantity of corn was collected.
Accordingly he brought it down to the markets and sold it,
and thus gained an abundance of money.

Cotys, the Thracian, tried to borrow money from the
25 Peirinthians so that he might collect an army; but the
Peirinthians refused to give him any. He therefore begged
them at any rate to grant him some men from among their
citizens to act as a garrison for certain strongholds, in order
that he might make full use of the soldiers who were at
present on duty there. To this request they promptly
acceded, thinking that they would thus obtain possession of
30 these strongholds. But Cotys threw into prison those who
were sent and ordered the Peirinthians to recover them by
sending him the money which he wished to borrow from
them.

Mentor, the Rhodian, having arrested Hermeias and
seized his estates, allowed the overseers whom Hermeias
35 had appointed to retain their positions. But when they all

---

[1] Omitting καὶ εἰς αὑτόν in l. 4 with Γ and Schneider.

felt secure and took steps to recover anything which had
been hidden or deposited for safety elsewhere, he arrested
them and deprived them of all they had.

Memnon, the Rhodian, after making himself master 1351ᵇ
of Lampsacus, was in need of money. He therefore exacted
a heavy tribute from the richest citizens, telling them that
they could collect it from the rest of the citizens. But when
the latter had contributed, he ordered them to lend him 5
this sum as well, fixing a period [1] within which he would
pay them back.

On another occasion when he was in need of money, he
demanded contributions from them, saying that they should
be repaid out of the revenues. They therefore contributed,
thinking that they would soon receive their money back.
But when the time was at hand for the payment of the
revenues, he told them that he needed these revenues as 10
well, but would repay them later with interest.

He also excused himself from paying the rations and
wages of those who were serving under him for six days in
the year,[2] declaring that on these days they had no watch to
keep, no marching and no expenses, meaning the 'omitted'
days.[3]   As he was already giving the soldiers their rations 15
on the second day of the new month, he thus passed over
three days in the first month and five by the following
month, and so he gradually gained on them till he reached
a total of thirty days.[4]

Charidemus of Orus, who held certain places in
Aeolia, when Artabazus was marching against him needed 20
money to pay his soldiers. At first, then, the citizens gave

---

[1] Reading with Kirchhoff χρόνον for ἐν χρόνῳ in l. 5.

[2] Reading with Richards τοῦ ἐνιαυτοῦ in l. 12.

[3] Memnon's argument seems to have been that of the twelve months
in the year six were 'hollow' months, i. e. had only twenty-nine days,
and that since thirty was the proper number of days in a month, he
would be paying them for six days too much, if he gave them the same
amount for a 'hollow' as for a 'full' month.

[4] The year consisting of twelve months of twenty-nine and thirty
days alternately, in the first month he docked them of three days' pay
(one day on the ground that it was a 'hollow' month, and two days by
paying them in advance on the second day for the rest of the month);
in the second month, which was not a 'hollow' month, he deprived
them of two days' pay by paying them in advance on the second day.
They thus lost five days in each period of two months, i. e. a total of
thirty days in the year.

him contributions, but afterwards they declared that they had nothing left to give. Charidemus then ordered the inhabitants of the place which he thought was richest to send away to another place any coin or other valuable treasure which they possessed, and he promised to give them an
25 escort; at the same time it was clear that he himself was also removing his valuables. When they had obeyed him, he led them a little way outside the city and, after examining what they had, took all that he needed and sent them back again. He also made a proclamation in the cities over which he ruled that no one was to keep any
30 arms in his house, the penalty for so doing being a fine which he specified. He then took no further action and paid no attention to the matter. The citizens, thinking that he had not meant the proclamation to be taken seriously, continued to keep the arms which they happened to possess. But Charidemus suddenly instituted a house to house search and exacted the fine from those in whose
35 houses he found any arms.

A certain Philoxenus, a Macedonian who was satrap of Caria, being in need of money, said that he intended to celebrate the Dionysia, and he nominated the richest of
1352^a the Carians to defray the cost of the choruses and gave directions as to what they had to supply. But seeing that they were annoyed, he sent to them secretly and asked them what they were willing to give to be released from serving. They declared their readiness to give considerably
5 more than they thought it would cost them, in order to be freed from the trouble and the neglect of their private affairs which it would entail. Philoxenus accepted what they offered and put others on the list, until he received from them what he wanted and what each could spare.

Evaeses, the Syrian, being satrap of Egypt, discovering that the provincial governors were on the point of
10 revolting from him, summoned them to the palace and hanged them all, and ordered that their relatives should be told that they were in prison. Their relatives therefore severally began to negotiate on their behalf and tried to buy the release of the captives. Evaeses made an agree-

ment in each case and, after receiving the sums for which ₁₅
he had stipulated, restored them to their relatives—dead.

Cleomenes, an Alexandrian who was satrap of Egypt,
when there was a severe famine everywhere else while
Egypt was less seriously affected, forbade the export of
corn, and when the provincial governors declared that
they would not be able to pay the tribute because corn
could not be exported, he cancelled the prohibition, but ₂₀
put a heavy tax on the corn. The result was that, if he
did not succeed in getting a large tax at the cost of a small
exportation, at least[1] the provincial governors lost their
excuse.

As he was sailing through the district in which the
crocodile is regarded as a deity, one of his slaves was
carried off. He therefore summoned the priests and told ₂₅
them that since he had been injured without provocation he
intended to take vengeance[2] on the crocodiles, and gave
orders to hunt them. The priests, in order that their god
might not be held in contempt, collected all the gold that
they possessed and presented it to him, with the result that
he desisted.

When king Alexander commanded him to found a city
near the Pharos and to establish there the mart which was ₃₀
formerly held at Canopus, he sailed to Canopus and told
the priests and the owners of property there that he had
come to transfer them. The priests and inhabitants collected
and gave him a sum of money to induce him to leave their
mart undisturbed. This he accepted and for the moment ₃₅
left them alone, but afterwards, when he had the material
for building ready, he sailed to Canopus and demanded
an excessive amount of money from them, which he 1352ᵇ
said represented the difference to him between having
the mart near the Pharos and at Canopus. And when they
said that they would not be able to give him the money he
made them move their city.

And when he had sent some one to make a purchase and
discovered that his messenger had got what he wanted

---

[1] Reading γε for τε (W. D. Ross) in l. 22.
[2] Reading with Keil ἀμυνεῖσθαι for ἀμύνεσθαι in l. 25.

5 cheaply but intended to charge him an excessive price, he told the friends of the purchaser that he had heard that he had made his purchases at an excessive price and therefore he should not pay any attention to him; at the same time with assumed wrath he railed against his stupidity. When 10 they heard this they told Cleomenes that he ought not to believe those who spoke against the messenger until he came himself and rendered his account. When the purchaser arrived they told him what Cleomenes had said; and he, wishing to make a good impression on them and on Cleomenes, submitted the prices at which he had actually bought the goods.

When corn was being sold in the country at ten *drachmae*, 15 he summoned the dealers and asked them at what price they would do business with him. They named a lower price than that at which they were selling to the merchants. However, he ordered them[1] to hand over their corn at the same price as they were selling to every one else ; and fixing the price of corn at thirty-two *drachmae* he then sold it himself.

20 He also called the priests together and told them that the expenditure[2] on the temples in the country was excessive ; consequently some of the temples and the majority of the priests must be abolished. The priests individually and collectively gave him the sacred treasures, thinking that he really intended to carry out his threat and because each wished that his own temple should be un-25 disturbed and himself continue to be priest.

Antimenes, the Rhodian, being put by Alexander in charge of the roads[3] round Babylon, raised money in the following way. An ancient law existed in Babylonia that anything which was brought into the country should pay a duty of ten per cent., but no one ever enforced it. Antimenes, waiting till all the satraps and soldiers were 30 expected and no small number of ambassadors and crafts-

---

[1] Reading with Bekker ἐκείνους in l. 17.
[2] Omitting ἀνώμαλον with some MSS. in l. 20.
[3] ἡμιόδιος in l. 26 is corrupt, but the right sense is given by the Latin version, which reads *curatione ei data uiarum.*

men summoned from abroad, bringing others with them,[1] and persons travelling on their own private affairs, and many gifts were being brought up, exacted the ten per cent. duty according to the existing law.

On another occasion, when providing the slaves who were to look after the camp, he commanded that any owner who wished should register the value which he put upon 35 them, and they were to pay eight *drachmae* a year; if the slave ran away the owner was to receive the price which he had registered.[2] Many slaves being registered, he 1353ª amassed a considerable sum of money. And whenever any slave ran away he ordered the satrap of the country [3] in which the camp was situated to recover the runaway or else to pay the price to the owner.

Ophelas, the Olynthian, having appointed a super- 5 intendent over the province of Athribis, when the provincial governors of that district came to him and expressed their willingness to pay of their own accord a much larger sum and begged him to dismiss the superintendent whom he had just appointed, asked them if they would be able to pay what they promised; when they answered in the 10 affirmative he left the superintendent at his post and bade him exact the amount of tribute which they themselves had assessed. Thus he did not think it right either to degrade the official whom he had appointed or to impose a heavier tribute upon them than they themselves had fixed, but at the same time he himself received a far larger amount of money.

Pythocles, the Athenian, recommended to the Athe- 15 nians that the state should take the lead from the mines at Laurium out of private hands at the market price of two *drachmae* and that they should then themselves fix the price at six *drachmae* and so sell it.

Chabrias, when crews had been enrolled for a hundred and twenty ships and Taus only needed sixty, ordered the 20 crews of the sixty ships which remained behind to supply

[1] Omitting in l. 31 τοὺς before ἄγοντας (Aldine), but the whole phrase ἄλλους τοὺς ἄγοντας is probably corrupt.
[2] An early example of insuring employees.
[3] Reading with Schneider τῆς ⟨γῆς⟩ in l. 3.

those who sailed with two months' provisions, or else to sail themselves. They, wishing to attend to their own affairs, complied with his demand.

Antimenes ordered the satraps to keep the storehouses
25 filled along the royal roads according to the custom of the country; but whenever an army or any other body of men unaccompanied by the king passed along, he used to send one of his own men and sell the contents of the storehouses.
1353^b Cleomenes, when the first day of the month was approaching and he had to give his soldiers their rations, purposely put back into harbour, and when the new month was approaching he put out again and distributed the rations; he then left an interval from the beginning of the
5 month until the first day of the next month. The soldiers, therefore, because they had recently received their rations, kept quiet; and Cleomenes by passing over a month deprived them of a month's pay in each year.

Stabelbius, general of the Mysians, when he owed his soldiers pay, called the officers[1] together and told
10 them that he had no need of private soldiers but only of officers, and that, when he did need soldiers, he gave each officer a sum of money and sent him out to collect mercenaries, and that he would rather give the officers the pay which ought to go to the soldiers. He therefore ordered them each to send away their own levies out of the country. The officers, thinking that it would be an
15 opportunity to make money, dismissed the soldiers in accordance with his commands. But after a short interval he collected the officers together and told them that just as a flute player was no use without a chorus, so too officers were useless without private soldiers; he therefore ordered them to leave the country.

20 Dionysius, when he was making a round of the temples, whenever he saw a gold or silver table displayed, ordered that a libation should be poured out 'to good luck' and that the table should be carried off; and whenever he saw amongst the statues one which held out a wine cup, he

---

[1] Reading in l. 8 ὁ Μυσῶν στρατηγὸς (Scaliger) ὀφείλων (Schneider) στρατιώταις μισθόν, συγκαλέσας τοὺς ἡγέμονας (Camerarius) ἔφησεν.

would say, ' I accept your pledge ', and order the statue to
be carried away.   And he used to strip the raiment of gold [1]
and crowns of silver [2] from the statues, saying that he 25
would give [3] them others lighter and more fragrant ; he then
clad them with white garments and crowns of white violets.

[1] Omitting τε between τά and χρυσᾶ in l. 24.
[2] Reading τοὺς στεφάνους ⟨τοὺς ἀργυροῦς⟩ (coni. Susemihl) in l. 24.
[3] Reading εὐωδέστερ' ἂν δοῦναι (Richards) in l. 26.

INDEX

ATHENIENSIUM

RESPUBLICA

BY

SIR FREDERIC G. KENYON

K.C.B., F.B.A.

HON. FELLOW OF MAGDALEN AND NEW COLLEGES

FIRST EDITION 1920

Reprinted lithographically in Great Britain
by LOWE & BRYDONE, PRINTERS LTD., LONDON
from sheets of the first edition
1938, 1946, 1952, 1961

PREFACE

THIS translation of the treatise on the Constitution of Athens is a revision of a translation prepared by me, shortly after the first appearance of the Greek text in 1891, for Messrs. Bell & Son, and is issued with their concurrence. It has been revised throughout, with a view both to improving it in detail and to bringing it into conformity with the text as now established. In particular, the last six chapters, which have been reconstructed out of a large number of fragments and were first printed as a continuous text in the edition prepared by me for the Berlin Academy (1903), are now translated for the first time.

The text taken as the basis is that printed in the Oxford series (*Scriptorum Classicorum Bibliotheca Oxoniensis*), which will be published almost simultaneously. It is almost identical with that of the Berlin edition; indeed the extent of variation between this and all recent editions—Thalheim (1909), Sandys (1912), Hude (1916)—is very slight, and in default of the appearance of another manuscript of the treatise, to set beside the British Museum papyrus, the text may be considered as definitely established within very narrow limits.

In translating it, I have endeavoured to follow the matter-of-fact, unadorned style of the original. In the notes I have confined myself to the indication of possible variations of text and the explanation of passages which appear obscure. I have not undertaken any examination of the credibility of the statements made, or of the historical value of the treatise.

I have to thank Mr. W. D. Ross and Prof. J. A. Smith for suggestions on points of detail.

F. G. K.

Dec. 1, 1919.

CONTENTS

CONTENTS

CONTENTS

CONTENTS

ATHENIENSIUM RESPUBLICA

... [They[1] were tried] by a court empanelled from among **I** the noble families, and sworn upon the sacrifices. The part of accuser was taken by Myron. They were found guilty of the sacrilege, and their bodies were cast out of their graves and their race banished for evermore. In view of this expiation[2], Epimenides the Cretan performed a purification of the city.

After this event there was contention for a long time **2** between the upper classes and the populace. Not only was **2** the constitution at this time oligarchical in every respect, but the poorer classes, men, women, and children, were the serfs of the rich. They were known as Pelătae and also as Hectēmŏri,[3] because they cultivated the lands of the rich at the rent thus indicated. The whole country was in the hands of a few persons, and if the tenants failed to pay their rent they were liable to be haled into slavery, and their children with them. All loans were secured upon the debtor's person, a custom which prevailed until the

[1] The narrative opens with the trial of the Alcmeonidae for sacrilege. Cylon, a young noble, had attempted to seize despotic power by force; but his attempt failed, and his adherents fled to sanctuary, which they were only induced to leave under a safe conduct. This was violated by the archon Megacles, one of the great house of the Alcmeonidae, who caused them all to be put to death; a sacrilege which was supposed to be the cause of the misfortunes which subsequently befell Athens, until the Alcmeonidae submitted themselves to trial. The date of Cylon's attempt to set himself up as tyrant is shown by this treatise to have been before the time of Draco; and, as Cylon was an Olympic victor in 640 B.C., and was apparently still a young man at the time of his attempt, the latter (which took place in an Olympic year) may be assigned to 632 B.C. The expulsion of the Alcmeonidae did not take place till many years afterwards; the visit of Epimenides probably took place about 596 B.C., shortly before the legislation of Solon. Aristotle is here carrying down the story of Cylon's attempt to its conclusion, and he subsequently goes back to the reforms of Draco.

[2] Or 'in addition'; but the order of the words is in favour of the other interpretation.

[3] i.e. those who paid a sixth portion. Some scholars, however, interpret it to mean tenants who received only a sixth part of the produce, and paid five-sixths to their landlords.

time of Solon, who was the first to appear as the champion
3 of the people. But the hardest and bitterest part of the
constitution in the eyes of the masses was their state of
serfdom. Not but what they were also discontented with
every other feature of their lot; for, to speak generally, they
had no part nor share in anything.

3   Now the ancient constitution, as it existed before the time
of Draco, was organized as follows. The magistrates were
elected according to qualifications of birth and wealth. At
first they governed for life, but subsequently for terms
2 of ten years.[1] The first magistrates, both in date and in
importance, were the King, the Polemarch, and the Archon.
The earliest of these offices was that of the King, which
existed from ancestral antiquity. To this was added,
secondly, the office of Polemarch, on account of some of the
kings proving feeble in war; for it was on this account that
Ion [2] was invited to accept the post on an occasion of press-
3 ing need. The last of the three offices was that of the
Archon, which most authorities state to have come into
existence in the time of Medon. Others assign it to the
time of Acastus,[3] and adduce as proof the fact that the nine
Archons swear to execute their oaths 'as in the days of
Acastus', which seems to suggest that it was in his time

[1] The absolute monarchy appears to have ended with Codrus, whose
traditional date is about 1066 B.C. With the accession of his son,
Medon, a change was evidently made in the nature of the kingly
power, which is described in the following sentences. The office of
Polemarch was already in existence; but at this date the third office,
that of Archon, was created, and, according to Aristotle, the descendants
of Codrus agreed to surrender the kingship, taking in exchange the
archonship, to which the more important functions of the king had
been transferred. This agrees with the tradition that the kingship was
abolished after the death of Codrus, though in fact it did not absolutely
cease to exist, but was reduced to the second rank, retaining little
except sacrificial functions. In 752 B.C. the term of the Archon was
limited to ten years, the election being still confined to members of the
royal house. After four Archons had ruled on these conditions, the
office was thrown open to all the Eupatridae, or nobles; and in 682 B.C.
the board of nine annual Archons was substituted for the decennial
Archon.

[2] Ion was said to have come to the assistance of his grandfather
Erechtheus, when the latter was engaged in war with Eumolpus of
Eleusis, and to have been made Polemarch, or commander-in-chief, of
the Athenians.

[3] The successor of Medon.

that the descendants of Codrus retired from the kingship in return for the prerogatives conferred upon the Archon. Whichever way it be, the difference in date is small; but that it was the last of these magistracies to be created is shown by the fact that the Archon has no part in the ancestral sacrifices, as the King and the Polemarch have, but exclusively in those of later origin. So it is only at a comparatively late date that the office of Archon has become of great importance, through the dignity conferred by these later additions. The Thesmothĕtae [1] were appointed many years 4 afterwards, when these offices had already become annual, with the object that they might publicly record all legal decisions, and act as guardians of them with a view to determining the issues between litigants. Accordingly their office, alone of those which have been mentioned, was never of more than annual duration.

Such, then, is the relative chronological precedence of 5 these offices. At that time the nine Archons did not all live together. The King occupied the building now known as the Bucolium, near the Prytanēum, as may be seen from the fact that even to the present day the marriage of the King's wife to Dionysus [2] takes place there. The Archon lived in the Prytaneum, the Polemarch in the Epilycēum. The latter building was formerly called the Polemarchēum, but after Epilycus, during his term of office as Polemarch, had rebuilt it and fitted it up, it was called the Epilyceum. The Thesmothetae occupied the Thesmothetēum. In the time of Solon, however, they all came together into the Thesmotheteum. They had power to decide cases finally on their own authority, not, as now, merely to hold a preliminary hearing. Such then was the arrangement of the magistracies. The Council of Areopagus had as its constitu- 6 tionally assigned duty the protection of the laws; but in point of fact it administered the greater and most important part of the government of the state, and inflicted personal punishments and fines summarily upon all who misbehaved

---

[1] The six junior Archons.
[2] The wife of the King-archon every year went through the ceremony of marriage to the god Dionysus, at the feast of the Anthesteria.

themselves. This was the natural consequence of the facts that the Archons were elected under qualifications of birth and wealth, and that the Areopagus was composed of those who had served as Archons; for which latter reason the membership of the Areopagus is the only office which has continued to be a life-magistracy to the present day.

4 Such was, in outline, the first constitution, but not very long after the events above recorded, in the archonship of Aristaichmus,[1] Draco enacted his ordinances. Now his constitution had the following form. The franchise was given to all who could furnish themselves with a 2 military equipment. The nine Archons and the Treasurers were elected by this body from persons possessing an unencumbered property of not less than ten minas, the less important officials from those who could furnish themselves with a military equipment, and the generals [Stratēgi] and commanders of the cavalry [Hipparchi] from those who could show an unencumbered property of not less than a hundred minas, and had children born in lawful wedlock over ten years of age. These officers were required to hold to bail the Prytănes, the Strategi, and the Hipparchi of the preceding year until their accounts had been au lited, taking four securities of the same class as that to which the Strategi 3 and the Hipparchi belonged. There was also to be a Council, consisting of four hundred and one members, elected by lot from among those who possessed the franchise. Both for this and for the other magistracies[2] the lot was cast among those who were over thirty years of age; and no one might hold office twice until every one else had had his turn, after which they were to cast the lot afresh. If any member of the Council failed to attend when there was a sitting of the Council or of the Assembly, he paid a fine, to the amount of three drachmas if he was a Pentacosiomedimnus,[3] 4 two if he was a Knight, and one if he was a Zeugites. The

[1] The name of this Archon is not otherwise known, but the traditional date of Draco is 621 B.C.

[2] i.e. the other magistracies to which election was made by lot. This does not mean that all the magistrates were at this time elected by lot, which certainly was not the case.

[3] The meanings of these terms are explained in ch. 7, 4.

Council of Areopagus was guardian of the laws, and kept
watch over the magistrates to see that they executed their
offices in accordance with the laws. Any person who felt
himself wronged might lay an information before the Council
of Areopagus, on declaring what law was broken by the
wrong done to him. But, as has been said before,[1] loans 5
were secured upon the persons of the debtors, and the land
was in the hands of a few.

Since such, then, was the organization of the constitu- 5
tion, and the many were in slavery to the few, the people
rose against the upper class. The strife was keen, and 2
for a long time the two parties were ranged in hostile
camps against one another, till at last,[2] by common consent,
they appointed Solon to be mediator and Archon, and committed the whole constitution to his hands. The immediate
occasion of his appointment was his poem, which begins
with the words :

I behold, and within my heart deep sadness has claimed
    its place,
As I mark the oldest home of the ancient Ionian race
Slain by the sword.[3]

In this poem he fights and disputes on behalf of each
party in turn against the other, and finally he advises them
to come to terms and put an end to the quarrel existing
between them. By birth and reputation Solon was one of 3
the foremost men of the day, but in wealth and position he
was of the middle class, as is generally agreed, and is, indeed,
established by his own evidence in these poems, where he
exhorts the wealthy not to be grasping.

But ye who have store of good, who are sated and overflow,
Restrain your swelling soul, and still it and keep it low :
Let the heart that is great within you be trained a
    lowlier way ;
Ye shall not have all at your will, and we will not for
    ever obey.

[1] Ch. 2, 2.
[2] The traditional date for Solon's legislation is 594 B. C.
[3] A passage of considerable length, which evidently comes from the
same poem, is quoted by Demosthenes (*de Fals. Leg.* ch. 255), but this
beginning of it is not otherwise known, nor yet the four lines quoted
just below.

Indeed, he constantly fastens the blame of the conflict on the rich; and accordingly at the beginning of the poem he says that he fears 'the love of wealth and an overweening mind', evidently meaning that it was through these that the quarrel arose.

6 As soon as he was at the head of affairs, Solon liberated the people once and for all, by prohibiting all loans on the security of the debtor's person: and in addition he made laws by which he cancelled all debts, public and private. This measure is commonly called the Seisachtheia [= removal of burdens], since thereby the people had their ₂ loads removed from them. In connexion with it some persons try to traduce the character of Solon. It so happened that, when he was about to enact the Seisachtheia, he communicated his intention to some members of the upper class, whereupon, as the partisans of the popular party say, his friends stole a march on him; while those who wish to attack his character maintain that he too had a share in the fraud himself. For these persons borrowed money and bought up a large amount of land, and so when, a short time afterwards, all debts were cancelled, they became wealthy; and this, they say, was the origin of the families which were afterwards looked on as having been wealthy from primeval times. ₃ However, the story of the popular party is by far the most probable. A man who was so moderate and public-spirited in all his other actions, that when it was within his power to put his fellow-citizens beneath his feet and establish himself as tyrant, he preferred instead to incur the hostility of both parties by placing his honour and the general welfare above his personal aggrandisement, is not likely to have consented to defile his hands by such a petty and palpable fraud. ₄ That he had this absolute power is, in the first place, indicated by the desperate condition of the country; moreover, he mentions it himself repeatedly in his poems, and it is universally admitted. We are therefore bound to consider this accusation to be false.

7 Next Solon drew up a constitution and enacted new laws; and the ordinances of Draco ceased to be used, with

the exception of those relating to murder. The laws were inscribed on the wooden stands,[1] and set up in the King's Porch, and all swore to obey them ; and the nine Archons made oath upon the stone,[2] declaring that they would dedicate a golden statue if they should transgress any of them. This is the origin of the oath to that effect which they take to the present day. Solon ratified his laws for a hundred [2] years ; and the following was the fashion in which he organized the constitution. He divided the population according [3] to property into four classes, just as it had been divided before, namely, Pentacosiomedimni, Knights, Zeugitae, and Thetes.[3] The various magistracies, namely, the nine Archons, the Treasurers, the Commissioners for Public Contracts [Polētae], the Eleven,[4] and the Exchequer Clerks [Colacrĕtae],[5] he assigned to the Pentacosiomedimni, the Knights, and the Zeugitae, giving offices to each class in proportion to the value of their rateable property. To those who ranked among the Thetes he gave nothing but a place in the Assembly and in the juries. A man had to rank as [4] a Pentacosiomedimnus if he made, from his own land, five hundred measures, whether liquid or solid. Those ranked as Knights who made three hundred measures, or, as some say, those who were able to maintain a horse. In support of the latter definition they adduce the name of the class, which may be supposed to be derived from this fact, and also some votive offerings of early times; for in the Acropolis there is a votive offering, a statue of Diphilus,[6] bearing this inscription :

[1] i. e. the well-known pillars, which were formed by joining together four rectangular tablets made of wood.

[2] See ch. 55, 5.

[3] The name Pentacosiomedimnus means one who possesses 500 measures, as explained in the text below ; that of Knight, or Horseman, implies ability to keep a horse ; that of Zeugites, ability to keep a yoke of oxen ; while the Thetes were originally serfs attached to the soil.

[4] The superintendents of the state prison ; see ch. 52, 1.

[5] These officers, whose original function was said to have been to 'collect the pieces after a sacrifice', were the Treasury officials in early times, who received the taxes and handed them over to be kept by the Treasurers. In later times the Colacretae seem to have ceased to exist, and they are not mentioned in Aristotle's enumeration of the officials in his own day.

[6] Mr. A. S. Murray has pointed out that this must be a mistake,

The son of Diphilus, Anthemion hight,
Raised from the Thetes and become a Knight,
Did to the gods this sculptured charger bring,
For his promotion a thank-offering.

And a horse stands in evidence beside the man, implying that this was what was meant by belonging to the rank of Knight. At the same time it seems reasonable to suppose that this class, like the Pentacosiomedimni, was defined by the possession of an income of a certain number of measures. Those ranked as Zeugitae who made two hundred measures, liquid or solid ; and the rest ranked as Thetes, and were not eligible for any office. Hence it is that even at the present day, when a candidate for any office is asked to what class he belongs, no one would think of saying that he belonged to the Thetes.

8   The elections to the various offices Solon enacted should be by lot, out of candidates selected by each of the tribes. Each tribe selected ten candidates for the nine archonships, and among these the lot was cast. Hence it is still the custom for each tribe to choose ten candidates by lot, and then the lot is again cast among these. A proof that Solon regulated the elections to office according to the property classes may be found in the law still in force with regard to the Treasurers, which enacts that they shall be chosen from the Pentacosiomedimni.[1]   Such was Solon's legislation with respect to the nine Archons; whereas in early times the Council of Areopagus[2] summoned suitable persons according to its own judgement and appointed them for the year to the

either of Aristotle, or, more probably, of the copyist. The statue set up by Anthemion must have been his own, not his father's, since the latter, as the inscription proves, could not properly have been repre-sented with a horse, as he was only a member of the Thetes. We should therefore read 'a statue of Anthemion, son of Diphilus'.

[1] That this qualification was, in Aristotle's own time, purely nominal appears from ch. 47, 1, where it is stated that the person on whom the lot falls holds the office, be he ever so poor.

[2] This statement is of great value, as nothing was previously known concerning the way in which the Archons and other magistrates were appointed previous to the time of Solon. The elections by the Areopagus, which may have begun as early as the first successors of Codrus, apparently lasted till the reforms of Draco, by which the franchise was conferred on all who could furnish a military equipment, and the magistrates were presumably thenceforward elected in the general Ecclesia or Assembly.

several offices. There were four tribes, as before, and four
tribe-kings. Each tribe was divided into three Trittyes [3]
[= Thirds], with twelve Naucraries[1] in each ; and the
Naucraries had officers of their own, called Naucrāri, whose
duty it was to superintend the current receipts and expenditure. Hence, among the laws of Solon now obsolete, it is
repeatedly written that the Naucrari are to receive and to
spend out of the Naucraric fund. Solon also appointed a
Council of four hundred, a hundred from each tribe ; but he [4]
assigned to the Council of the Areopagus the duty of superintending the laws, acting as before as the guardian of the
constitution in general. It kept watch over the affairs of the
state in most of the more important matters, and corrected
offenders, with full powers to inflict either fines or personal
punishment. The money received in fines it brought up into
the Acropolis, without assigning the reason for the mulct.
It also tried those who conspired for the overthrow of the
state, Solon having enacted a process of impeachment to deal
with such offenders. Further, since he saw the state often
engaged in internal disputes, while many of the citizens from [5]
sheer indifference accepted whatever might turn up, he made
a law with express reference to such persons, enacting that
any one who, in a time of civil factions, did not take up arms
with either party, should lose his rights as a citizen and
cease to have any part in the state.

Such, then, was his legislation concerning the magistracies.
There are three points in the constitution of Solon which **9**
appear to be its most democratic features : first and most
important, the prohibition of loans on the security of the
debtor's person ; secondly, the right of every person who
so willed to claim redress on behalf of any one to whom
wrong was being done ; thirdly, the institution of the
appeal to the jury-courts ; and it is to this last, they say,
that the masses have owed their strength most of all, since,

---

[1] It appears from ch. 21, 5 that the Naucraries were local divisions,
which, under the constitution of Cleisthenes, were replaced by the
demes. The division of tribes into Trittyes and Naucraries existed
before the time of Solon, as appears from Herodotus (v. 71), and they
are only mentioned here as continuing under Solon's constitution, not
as created by him.

2 when the democracy is master of the voting-power, it is master of the constitution. Moreover, since the laws were not drawn up in simple and explicit terms (but like the one concerning inheritances and wards of state), disputes inevitably occurred, and the courts had to decide in every matter, whether public or private. Some persons in fact believe that Solon deliberately made the laws indefinite, in order that the final decision might be in the hands of the people. This, however, is not probable, and the reason no doubt was that it is impossible to attain ideal perfection when framing a law in general terms; for we must judge of his intentions, not from the actual results in the present day, but from the general tenor of the rest of his legislation.

10 These seem to be the democratic features of his laws; but in addition, before the period of his legislation, he carried through his abolition of debts, and after it his increase in the standards of weights and measures, and of the currency. 2 During his administration the measures were made larger than those of Pheidon, and the mina, which previously had a standard of seventy drachmas, was raised to the full hundred.[1] The standard coin in earlier times was the two-drachma piece. He also made weights corresponding with the coinage, sixty-three minas going to the talent; and the odd three minas were distributed among the staters and the other values.[2]

11 When he had completed his organization of the constitution in the manner that has been described, he found himself beset by people coming to him and harassing him concerning his laws, criticizing here and questioning there, till, as he wished neither to alter what he had decided on nor yet to be an object of ill will to every one by remaining in Athens,

---

[1] This is a somewhat curious way of expressing the fact that Solon substituted the Euboic for the Aeginetan standard of coinage. Each mina had 100 drachmas in its own standard, but the weight of the Aeginetan mina was only equivalent to 70 Euboic drachmas. The object of the change was to encourage trade with the great commercial cities of Euboea and with Corinth.

[2] i.e. the talent was raised by one-twentieth; it still consisted of sixty minas, but these were equal to sixty-three of the old minas, and the increase was distributed proportionately over the smaller values, such as the stater (= four drachmas).

he set off on a journey to Egypt, with the combined objects
of trade and travel, giving out that he should not return for
ten years. He considered that there was no call for him
to expound the laws personally, but that every one should
obey them just as they were written. Moreover, his [2]
position at this time was unpleasant. Many members
of the upper class had been estranged from him on account
of his abolition of debts, and both parties were alienated
through their disappointment at the condition of things
which he had created. The mass of the people had
expected him to make a complete redistribution of all
property, and the upper class hoped he would restore
everything to its former position, or, at any rate, make but
a small change. Solon, however, had resisted both classes.
He might have made himself a despot by attaching himself
to whichever party he chose, but he preferred, though at the
cost of incurring the enmity of both, to be the saviour of his
country and the ideal lawgiver.

The truth of this view of Solon's policy is established [12]
alike by common consent, and by the mention he has
himself made of the matter in his poems. Thus:

I gave to the mass of the people such rank as befitted
    their need,
I took not away their honour, and I granted naught to
    their greed;
While those who were rich in power, who in wealth were
    glorious and great,
I bethought me that naught should befall them unworthy
    their splendour and state;
So I stood with my shield outstretched, and both were
    safe in its sight,
And I would not that either should triumph, when the
    triumph was not with right.

Again he declares how the mass of the people ought to be [2]
treated:

But thus will the people best the voice of their leaders
    obey,
When neither too slack is the rein, nor violence holdeth
    the sway;

For indulgence breedeth a child, the presumption that
　　spurns control,
When riches too great are poured upon men of un-
　　balanced soul.

3 And again elsewhere he speaks about the persons who
wished to redistribute the land:

So they came in search of plunder, and their cravings
　　knew no bound,
Every one among them deeming endless wealth would
　　here be found,
And that I with glozing smoothness hid a cruel mind within.
Fondly then and vainly dreamt they; now they raise an
　　angry din,
And they glare askance in anger, and the light within
　　their eyes
Burns with hostile flames upon me. Yet therein no
　　justice lies.
All I promised, fully wrought I with the gods at hand
　　to cheer,
Naught beyond in folly ventured. Never to my soul
　　was dear
With a tyrant's force to govern, nor to see the good and base
Side by side in equal portion share the rich home of
　　our race.

4 Once more he speaks of the abolition of debts and of those
who before were in servitude, but were released owing to the
Seisachtheia:

Of all the aims for which I summoned forth
The people, was there one I compassed not?
Thou, when slow time brings justice in its train,
O mighty mother of the Olympian gods,
Dark Earth, thou best canst witness, from whose breast
I swept the pillars [1] broadcast planted there,
And made thee free, who hadst been slave of yore.
And many a man whom fraud or law had sold
Far from his god-built land, an outcast slave,
I brought again to Athens; yea, and some,
Exiles from home through debt's oppressive load,
Speaking no more the dear Athenian tongue,
But wandering far and wide, I brought again;

---

[1] These were the pillars set up on mortgaged lands, to record the
fact of the encumbrance.

And those that here in vilest slavery
Crouched 'neath a master's frown, I set them free.
Thus might and right were yoked in harmony,
Since by the force of law I won my ends
And kept my promise. Equal laws I gave
To evil and to good, with even hand
Drawing straight justice for the lot of each.
But had another held the goad as I,
One in whose heart was guile and greediness,
He had not kept the people back from strife.
For had I granted, now what pleased the one,
Then what their foes devised in counterpoise,
Of many a man this state had been bereft.
Therefore I showed my might on every side,
Turning at bay like wolf among the hounds.

And again he reviles both parties for their grumblings in the 5
times that followed :

Nay, if one must lay blame where blame is due,
Wer't not for me, the people ne'er had set
Their eyes upon these blessings e'en in dreams :—
While greater men, the men of wealthier life,
Should praise me and should court me as their friend.

For had any other man, he says, received this exalted post,

He had not kept the people back, nor ceased
Till he had robbed the richness of the milk.
But I stood forth a landmark in the midst,
And barred the foes from battle.

Such, then, were Solon's reasons for his departure from 13
the country. After his retirement the city was still torn by
divisions. For four years, indeed, they lived in peace ; but
in the fifth year after Solon's government they were unable
to elect an Archon on account of their dissensions, and
again four years later they elected no Archon for the same
reason. Subsequently, after a similar period had elapsed, 2
Damasias was elected Archon ;[1] and he governed for two years
and two months, until he was forcibly expelled from his
office. After this it was agreed, as a compromise, to elect
ten Archons, five from the Eupatridae, three from the

---

[1] Probably in 582 B.C. ; but several varieties of calculation are
possible, and some editors omit the words ' after a similar period had
elapsed '.

Agroeci, and two from the Demiurgi;[1] and they ruled for the year following Damasias. It is clear from this that the Archon was at the time the magistrate who possessed the greatest power, since it is always in connexion

3 with this office that conflicts are seen to arise. But altogether they were in a continual state of internal disorder. Some found the cause and justification of their discontent in the abolition of debts, because thereby they had been reduced to poverty; others were dissatisfied with the political constitution, because it had undergone a revolutionary change; while with others the motive was found in

4 personal rivalries among themselves. The parties at this time were three in number. First there was the party of the Shore, led by Megacles the son of Alcmeon, which was considered to aim at a moderate form of government; then there were the men of the Plain, who desired an oligarchy and were led by Lycurgus; and thirdly there were the men of the Highlands, at the head of whom was Pisistratus, who

5 was looked on as an extreme democrat. This latter party was reinforced by those who had been deprived of the debts due to them, from motives of poverty, and by those who were not of pure descent, from motives of personal apprehension.[2] A proof of this is seen in the fact that after the tyranny was overthrown a revision was made of the citizen-roll, on the ground that many persons were partaking in the franchise without having a right to it. The names given to the respective parties were derived from the districts in which they held their lands.

14 Pisistratus had the reputation of being an extreme democrat, and he also had distinguished himself greatly in the war with Megara. Taking advantage of this, he wounded himself, and by representing that his injuries had been inflicted on him by his political rivals, he persuaded the people, through a motion proposed by Aristion, to grant him a bodyguard. After he had got these 'club-bearers',

[1] Eupatridae=the aristocrats, Agroeci=the country, or agricultural, party, Demiurgi=the handworkers, or labour party.
[2] Sc., lest their right to the franchise should be disputed, as it in fact was after the fall of the Pisistratidae.

as they were called, he made an attack with them on the people and seized the Acropolis. This happened in the archonship of Comeas, thirty-one years after the legislation of Solon. It is related that, when Pisistratus asked for his 2 bodyguard, Solon opposed the request, and declared that in so doing he proved himself wiser than half the people and braver than the rest,—wiser than those who did not see that Pisistratus designed to make himself tyrant, and braver than those who saw it and kept silence. But when all his words availed nothing he carried forth his armour and set it up in front of his house, saying that he had helped his country so far as lay in his power (he was already a very old man), and that he called on all others to do the same. Solon's exhortations, however, proved fruitless, and Pisistratus 3 assumed the sovereignty. His administration was more like a constitutional government than the rule of a tyrant ; but before his power was firmly established, the adherents of Megacles and Lycurgus made a coalition and drove him out. This took place in the archonship of Hegesias, five years after the first establishment of his rule. Eleven years 4 later [1] Megacles, being in difficulties in a party struggle, again opened negotiations with Pisistratus, proposing that the latter should marry his daughter ; and on these terms he brought him back to Athens, by a very primitive and simple-minded device. He first spread abroad a rumour that Athena was bringing back Pisistratus, and then, having found a woman of great stature and beauty, named Phyë

---

[1] There is some error in Aristotle's chronology of the life of Pisistratus, for while he states below that, of the thirty-three years between his first accession and his death, nineteen were spent in possession of the tyranny and fourteen in exile, in the actual enumeration of years he gives twenty-one years of exile and consequently only twelve of rule, of which only one can be assigned to his last period of government, which is always spoken of as the longest. It is therefore tolerably certain that one of the periods of exile is wrongly dated ; and as the ten years of the second exile are confirmed by Herodotus, it may be concluded that the eleven years here assigned to the first exile are wrong, and should be reduced to four. It should be noticed that in the *Politics* it is stated that Pisistratus was actually in power only seventeen years out of the thirty-three ; but this would reduce the duration of his third tenure of power lower than is at all probable, unless we suppose that the length of the two earlier terms is wrongly given here. For a statement of the various solutions offered by different commentators, see Sandys *ad loc.*

(according to Herodotus, of the deme of Paeānia, but as others say a Thracian flower-seller of the deme of Collytus), he dressed her in a garb resembling that of the goddess and brought her into the city with Pisistratus. The latter drove in on a chariot with the woman beside him, and the inhabitants of the city, struck with awe, received him with adoration.

15 In this manner did his first return take place. He did not, however, hold his power long, for about six years after his return he was again expelled. He refused to treat the daughter of Megacles as his wife, and being afraid, in consequence, of a combination of the two opposing parties, he 2 retired from the country. First he led a colony to a place called Rhaicēlus, in the region of the Thermaic gulf; and thence he passed to the country in the neighbourhood of Mt. Pangaeus. Here he acquired wealth and hired mercenaries; and not till ten years had elapsed did he return to Eretria and make an attempt to recover the government by force. In this he had the assistance of many allies, notably the Thebans and Lygdămis of Naxos, and also the Knights who held the supreme power in the constitution of 3 Eretria. After his victory in the battle at Pallēnē he captured Athens, and when he had disarmed the people he at last had his tyranny securely established, and was able 4 to take Naxos and set up Lygdamis as ruler there. He effected the disarmament of the people in the following manner. He ordered a parade in full armour in the Thesēum, and began to make a speech to the people. He spoke for a short time, until the people called out that they could not hear him, whereupon he bade them come up to the entrance of the Acropolis, in order that his voice might be better heard. Then, while he continued to speak to them at great length, men whom he had appointed for the purpose collected the arms and locked them up in the chambers of the Theseum hard by, and came and made 5 a signal to him that it was done. Pisistratus accordingly, when he had finished the rest of what he had to say, told the people also what had happened to their arms; adding that they were not to be surprised or alarmed, but go home

and attend to their private affairs, while he would himself for the future manage all the business of the state.

Such was the origin and such the vicissitudes of the **16** tyranny of Pisistratus. His administration was temperate, **2** as has been said before, and more like constitutional government than a tyranny. Not only was he in every respect humane and mild and ready to forgive those who offended, but, in addition, he advanced money to the poorer people to help them in their labours, so that they might make their living by agriculture. In this he had two **3** objects, first that they might not spend their time in the city but might be scattered over all the face of the country, and secondly that, being moderately well off and occupied with their own business, they might have neither the wish nor the time to attend to public affairs. At the same time **4** his revenues were increased by the thorough cultivation of the country, since he imposed a tax of one tenth on all the produce. For the same reasons he instituted the local **5** justices,[1] and often made expeditions in person into the country to inspect it and to settle disputes between individuals, that they might not come into the city and neglect their farms. It was in one of these progresses that, as the **6** story goes, Pisistratus had his adventure with the man of Hymettus, who was cultivating the spot afterwards known as 'Tax-free Farm'. He saw a man digging and working at a very stony piece of ground, and being surprised he sent his attendant to ask what he got out of this plot of land. 'Aches and pains', said the man; 'and that's what Pisistratus ought to have his tenth of'. The man spoke without knowing who his questioner was; but Pisistratus was so pleased with his frank speech and his industry that he granted him exemption from all taxes. And so in **7** matters in general he burdened the people as little as possible with his government, but always cultivated peace and kept them in all quietness. Hence the tyranny of Pisistratus was often spoken of proverbially as 'the age of gold'; for when his sons succeeded him the government

---

[1] See ch. 53, 1, where it is stated that their number was at first thirty, but was subsequently increased to forty.

8 became much harsher. But most important of all in this respect was his popular and kindly disposition. In all things he was accustomed to observe the laws, without giving himself any exceptional privileges. Once he was summoned on a charge of homicide before the Areopagus, and he appeared in person to make his defence; but the prosecutor was afraid to present himself and abandoned the
9 case. For these reasons he held power long, and whenever he was expelled he regained his position easily. The majority alike of the upper class and of the people were in his favour; the former he won by his social intercourse with them, the latter by the assistance which he gave to their private purses, and his nature fitted him to win the hearts
10 of both. Moreover, the laws in reference to tyrants at that time in force at Athens were very mild, especially the one which applies more particularly to the establishment of a tyranny. The law ran as follows: 'These are the ancestral statutes of the Athenians; if any persons shall make an attempt to establish a tyranny, or if any person shall join in setting up a tyranny, he shall lose his civic rights, both himself and his whole house.'

17 Thus did Pisistratus grow old in the possession of power, and he died a natural death in the archonship of Philoneos,[1] three and thirty years from the time at which he first established himself as tyrant, during nineteen of which he
2 was in possession of power; the rest he spent in exile. It is evident from this that the story is mere gossip which states that Pisistratus was the youthful favourite of Solon and commanded in the war against Megara for the recovery of Salamis. It will not harmonize with their respective ages, as any one may see who will reckon up the years of the life
3 of each of them, and the dates at which they died. After the death of Pisistratus his sons took up the government, and conducted it on the same system. He had two sons by his first and legitimate[2] wife, Hippias and Hipparchus, and two by his Argive consort, Iophon and Hegesistratus, who

---

[1] 527 B.C.
[2] Pisistratus's second wife was a foreigner, and therefore not legitimate according to strict Athenian law.

was surnamed Thessalus. For Pisistratus took a wife from 4
Argos, Timonassa, the daughter of a man of Argos, named
Gorgĭlus ; she had previously been the wife of Archīnus of
Ambracia, one of the descendants of Cypsĕlus. This was
the origin of his friendship with the Argives, on account of
which a thousand of them were brought over by Hegesistratus
and fought on his side in the battle at Pallene. Some
authorities say that this marriage took place after his first
expulsion from Athens, others while he was in possession
of the government.

Hippias and Hipparchus assumed the control of affairs on 18
grounds alike of standing and of age ; but Hippias, as being
also naturally of a statesmanlike and shrewd disposition,
was really the head of the government. Hipparchus was
youthful in disposition, amorous, and fond of literature (it
was he who invited to Athens Anacreon, Simonides, and
the other poets), while Thessalus was much junior in age, and 2
was violent and headstrong in his behaviour. It was from
his character that all the evils arose which befell the house.[1]
He became enamoured of Harmodius, and, since he failed
to win his affection, he lost all restraint upon his passion, and
in addition to other exhibitions of rage he finally prevented
the sister of Harmodius from taking the part of a basket-
bearer in the Panathenaic procession, alleging as his reason
that Harmodius was a person of loose life.   Thereupon, in a
frenzy of wrath, Harmodius and Aristogeiton did their celebrated deed, in conjunction with a number of confederates.[2]
But while they were lying in wait for Hippias in the Acropolis 3
at the time of the Panathenaea (Hippias, at this moment,
was awaiting the arrival of the procession, while Hipparchus
was organizing its dispatch) they saw one of the persons.

[1] This is a direct contradiction of the narrative of Thucydides (vi. 54),
who makes Hipparchus responsible for the outrage which provoked the
plot of Harmodius and Aristogeiton. It is impossible to say positively
which is right.   The exact details would be known to few, and the
fact that it was Hipparchus who was killed (though Hippias, and not
he, was the person aimed at) would cause men to believe that he was
the person to blame.
[2] Thucydides states expressly (vi. 56) that the conspirators were few in
number.   Aristotle probably again intends to correct him, silently
but pointedly.

privy to the plot talking familiarly with him. Thinking
that he was betraying them, and desiring to do something
before they were arrested, they rushed down and made their
attempt without waiting for the rest of their confederates.
They succeeded in killing Hipparchus near the Leocorēum
while he was engaged in arranging the procession, but ruined
4 the design as a whole; of the two leaders, Harmodius
was killed on the spot by the guards, while Aristogeiton was
arrested, and perished later after suffering long tortures.
While under the torture he accused many persons who
belonged by birth to the most distinguished families and
were also personal friends of the tyrants. At first the
government could find no clue to the conspiracy; for the
current story,[1] that Hippias made all who were taking part
in the procession leave their arms, and then detected those
who were carrying secret daggers, cannot be true, since at
that time they did not bear arms in the processions, this being
a custom instituted at a later period by the democracy.
5 According to the story of the popular party, Aristogeiton
accused the friends of the tyrants with the deliberate intention that the latter might commit an impious act, and at the
same time weaken themselves, by putting to death innocent
men who were their own friends; others say that he told no
6 falsehood, but was betraying the actual accomplices. At
last, when for all his efforts he could not obtain release by
death, he promised to give further information against a
number of other persons; and, having induced Hippias to
give him his hand to confirm his word, as soon as he had
hold of it he reviled him for giving his hand to the murderer
of his brother, till Hippias, in a frenzy of rage, lost control of
himself and snatched out his dagger and dispatched him.

19   After this event the tyranny became much harsher. In
consequence of his vengeance for his brother, and of the
execution and banishment of a large number of persons,
Hippias became a distrusted and an embittered man.
2 About three years after the death of Hipparchus, finding his

---

[1] This is the version given by Thucydides (vi. 58), which Aristotle
evidently again wishes to correct.

position in the city insecure, he set about fortifying Munichia, with the intention of establishing himself there. While he was still engaged on this work, however, he was expelled by Cleomenes, king of Lacedaemon, in consequence of the Spartans being continually incited by oracles to overthrow the tyranny. These oracles were obtained in the following way. The Athenian exiles, headed by the 3 Alcmeonidae, could not by their own power effect their return, but failed continually in their attempts. Among their other failures, they fortified a post in Attica, Lipsydrium, above Mt. Parnes, and were there joined by some partisans from the city ; but they were besieged by the tyrants and reduced to surrender. After this disaster the following became a popular drinking song :

> Ah ! Lipsydrium, faithless friend !
> Lo, what heroes to death didst send,
> Nobly born and great in deed !
> Well did they prove themselves at need
> Of noble sires a noble seed.

Having failed, then, in every other method, they took the 4 contract for rebuilding the temple at Delphi,[1] thereby obtaining ample funds, which they employed to secure the help of the Lacedaemonians. All this time the Pythia kept continually enjoining on the Lacedaemonians who came to consult the oracle, that they must free Athens ; till finally she succeeded in impelling the Spartans to that step, although the house of Pisistratus was connected with them by ties of hospitality. The resolution of the Lacedaemonians was, however, at least equally due to the friendship which had been formed between the house of Pisistratus and Argos. Accordingly they first sent Anchimolus by sea 5 at the head of an army ; but he was defeated and killed, through the arrival of Cineas of Thessaly to support the sons of Pisistratus with a force of a thousand horsemen. Then, being roused to anger by this disaster, they sent their king, Cleomenes, by land at the head of a larger force ; and he, after defeating the Thessalian cavalry when they

---

[1] The temple at Delphi had been burnt, as is recorded by Herodotus (ii. 180).

attempted to intercept his march into Attica, shut up Hippias within what was known as the Pelargic wall and blockaded him there with the assistance of the Athenians. 6 While he was sitting down before the place, it so happened that the sons of the Pisistratidae were captured in an attempt to slip out ; upon which the tyrants capitulated on condition of the safety of their children, and surrendered the Acropolis to the Athenians, five days being first allowed them to remove their effects. This took place in the archonship of Harpactides,[1] after they had held the tyranny for about seventeen years since their father's death, or in all, including the period of their father's rule, for nine-and-forty years.

20   After the overthrow of the tyranny, the rival leaders in the state were Isagoras son of Tisander, a partisan of the tyrants, and Cleisthenes, who belonged to the family of the Alcmeonidae. ' Cleisthenes, being beaten in the political clubs, called in the people by giving the franchise to the 2 masses.   Thereupon Isagoras, finding himself left inferior in power, invited Cleomenes, who was united to him by ties of hospitality, to return to Athens, and persuaded him to 'drive out the pollution ',[2] a plea derived from the fact that the Alcmeonidae were supposed to be under the 3 curse of pollution.   On this Cleisthenes retired from the country, and Cleomenes, entering Attica with a small force, expelled, as polluted, seven hundred Athenian families. Having effected this, he next attempted to dissolve the Council, and to set up Isagoras and three hundred of his partisans as the supreme power in the state.   The Council, however, resisted, the populace flocked together, and Cleomenes and Isagoras, with their adherents, took refuge in the Acropolis.   Here the people sat down and besieged them for two days ; and on the third they agreed to let Cleomenes and all his followers depart, while they summoned Cleisthenes 4 and the other exiles back to Athens.   When the people had

---

[1] The Archon's name was not previously known, but the date is established independently as the year 511–10 B.C. (the Athenian official year beginning in July), apparently in the spring of 510 B.C.

[2] i. e. to expel the house of the Alcmeonidae, which was still supposed to be polluted by the sacrilege in the the affair of Cylon.

thus obtained the command of affairs, Cleisthenes was their
chief and popular leader. And this was natural; for the
Alcmeonidae were perhaps the chief cause of the expulsion
of the tyrants, and for the greater part of their rule were
at perpetual war with them. But even earlier than the 5
attempts of the Alcmeonidae, one Cedon made an attack
on the tyrants; whence there came another popular drinking
song, addressed to him:

Pour a health yet again, boy, to Cedon; forget not this
    duty to do,
If a health is an honour befitting the name of a good
    man and true.

The people, therefore, had good reason to place confidence **21**
in Cleisthenes. Accordingly, now that he was the popular
leader, three years after the expulsion of the tyrants, in the
archonship of Isagoras,[1] his first step was to distribute the 2
whole population into ten tribes in place of the existing
four, with the object of intermixing the members of the
different tribes, and so securing that more persons might
have a share in the franchise.[2] From this arose the saying
'Do not look at the tribes', addressed to those who wished
to scrutinize the lists of the old families.[3] Next he made 3
the Council to consist of five hundred members instead of
four hundred, each tribe now contributing fifty, whereas

---

[1] 508 B. C.

[2] It is not at first sight evident why a mere redistribution of the
population into ten tribes instead of four should give more persons
a share in the franchise. But the object of Cleisthenes was to break
down the old family and tribal feelings on which political contests had
hitherto been based. To do this, he established a new division into
tribes, which corresponded to no existing subdivision of the old ones,
and at the same time he introduced a large number of new citizens by
the enfranchisement of emancipated slaves and resident aliens.
There would have been endless difficulties in the way of introducing
them into the old tribes, which were organized into clans and families
on the old aristocratic basis; but they were easily included in the new
tribes, which had no such associations connected with them.

[3] Apparently this means that since the tribes now bore no relation
to the ancient families, it was useless to look at the lists of the tribes
if any one wished to examine the rolls of the families. Hence the
phrase seems to have become a proverbial one for making useless
distinctions or refinements. The families (together with the larger
units known as phratries or clans) were ancient divisions of the four old
tribes, on the basis of kinship, and mainly for social and religious
purposes.

formerly each had sent a hundred. The reason why he did not organize the people into twelve tribes was that he might not have to use the existing division into trittyes; for the four tribes had twelve trittyes, so that he would not have achieved his object of redistributing the population in 4 fresh combinations. Further, he divided the country into thirty groups of demes,[1] ten from the districts about the city, ten from the coast, and ten from the interior. These he called trittyes; and he assigned three of them by lot to each tribe, in such a way that each should have one portion in each of these three localities. All who lived in any given deme he declared fellow-demesmen, to the end that the new citizens might not be exposed by the habitual use of family names, but that men might be officially described by the names of their demes;[2] and accordingly it is by the names of their demes that the Athenians speak of one another.

5 He also instituted Demarchs, who had the same duties as the previously existing Naucrari,—the demes being made to take the place of the naucraries. He gave names to the demes, some from the localities to which they belonged, some from the persons who founded them, since some of the areas no longer corresponded to localities possessing names.

6 On the other hand he allowed every one to retain his family and clan and religious rites according to ancestral custom. The names given to the tribes were the ten which the Pythia appointed out of the hundred selected national heroes.

22 By these reforms the constitution became much more

---

[1] The total number of demes, or parishes, is not given, but from Herodotus it appears to have been a hundred. It gradually increased with the growth of population, and in the third century B.C. there were 176 demes. The demes composing each trittys appear to have been contiguous, but each trittys was separate from its two fellows, so that the party feeling of the tribe was spread over three local divisions, and the old feuds between the different districts of Attica became impossible.

[2] If the people continued to speak of one another by their family names as hitherto, newly enfranchised citizens, whose fathers had been slaves or aliens, would be markedly distinguished from the older citizens who belonged to ancient families; but by making the name of the deme part of the necessary description of every citizen he broke down the family tradition; moreover, it was easy for any man to establish his claim to citizenship by naming the deme to which he belonged, even though his father's name might be foreign or unfamiliar.

democratic than that of Solon. The laws of Solon had been obliterated by disuse during the period of the tyranny, while Cleisthenes substituted new ones with the object of securing the goodwill of the masses. Among these was the law concerning ostracism. Four years[1] after the establish- 2 ment of this system, in the archonship of Hermocreon, they first imposed upon the Council of Five Hundred the oath which they take to the present day. Next they began to elect the generals by tribes, one from each tribe, while the Polemarch was the commander of the whole army. Then, 3 eleven years later, in the archonship of Phaenippus they won the battle of Marathon; and two years after this victory, when the people had now gained self-confidence, they for the first time made use of the law of ostracism. This had originally been passed as a precaution against men in high office, because Pisistratus took advantage of his position as a popular leader and general to make himself tyrant; and 4 the first person ostracized was one of his relatives, Hipparchus son of Charmus, of the deme of Collytus, the very person on whose account especially Cleisthenes had enacted the law, as he wished to get rid of him. Hitherto, however, he had escaped; for the Athenians, with the usual leniency of the democracy, allowed all the partisans of the tyrants, who had not joined in their evil deeds in the time of the troubles, to remain in the city; and the chief and leader of these was Hipparchus. Then in the very next year, in the archonship 5 of Telesinus,[2] they for the first time since the tyranny elected,

---

[1] This, if correct, would place this event in 504 B. C. But, in the first place, that year belongs to another Archon; and secondly, it is inconsistent with the statement below, that the battle of Marathon occurred eleven years later. Marathon was fought in 490 B. C., there-fore the archonship of Hermocreon should be assigned to 501 B. C., for which year no name occurs in the extant lists of Archons. Whether the mistake in the present passage is due to the author or a copyist it is impossible to say.

[2] 487 B. C. The date here given is valuable, because it had hitherto been a matter of doubt whether Callimachus, the polemarch at Marathon, on whose casting vote the fighting of that battle depended, was elected by lot or by open vote. The words of Herodotus (vi. 109), strictly interpreted, imply the former; but it is repugnant to common sense to suppose that an officer holding so important a position was elected by lot, and it is now clear that, until three years after Marathon, the Archons were still elected by direct vote, and, as stated above in this

C

tribe by tribe, the nine Archons by lot out of the five hundred[1] candidates selected by the demes, all the earlier ones having been elected by vote;[2] and in the same year Megacles son of Hippocrates, of the deme of Alopĕcē, was 6 ostracized. Thus for three years they continued to ostracize the friends of the tyrants, on whose account the law had been passed; but in the following year they began to remove others as well, including any one who seemed to be more powerful than was expedient. The first person unconnected with the tyrants who was ostracized was 7 Xanthippus son of Ariphron. Two years later, in the archonship of Nicodemus,[3] the mines of Maroneia were discovered, and the state made a profit of a hundred talents from the working of them. Some persons advised the people to make a distribution of the money among themselves, but this was prevented by Themistocles. He refused to say on what he proposed to spend the money, but he bade them lend it to the hundred richest men in Athens, one talent to each, and then, if the manner in which it was employed pleased the people, the expenditure should be charged to the state, but otherwise the state should receive the sum back from those to whom it was lent. On these terms he received the money and with it he had a hundred triremes built, each of the hundred individuals building one; and it was with these ships that they fought the battle of Salamis against the barbarians. About this time Aristides 8 the son of Lysimachus was ostracized. Three years later, however, in the archonship of Hypsichides,[4] all the

same chapter, the polemarch was the chief of the army, the ten generals (who subsequently became the chief military commanders) being his subordinates.

[1] It is probable that there is a mistake in this number. It appears from ch. 8, 1 that under the Solonian constitution the number of candidates nominated by each tribe was ten, and that the same was the number in the writer's own day; and it is hardly likely that the higher number of fifty ever prevailed at an intermediate period. The Greek numerals for 100 and 500 are easily confused.

[2] This statement can only apply to the period after the expulsion of the tyrants and the reforms of Cleisthenes, since under the Solonian constitution (ch. 8, 1) the Archons were elected by lot out of forty candidates selected by the tribes.

[3] 483 B.C.   [4] 481 B.C.   The name of this Archon is new.

ostracized persons were recalled, on account of the advance
of the army of Xerxes ; and it was laid down for the future
that persons under sentence of ostracism must live between
Geraestus and Scyllaeum,[1] on pain of losing their civic rights
irrevocably.

So far, then, had the city progressed by this time, growing 23
gradually with the growth of the democracy ; but after the
Persian wars the Council of Areopagus once more developed
strength and assumed the control of the state. It did not
acquire this supremacy by virtue of any formal decree, but
because it had been the cause of the battle of Salamis being
fought. When the generals were utterly at a loss how to
meet the crisis and made proclamation that every one
should see to his own safety, the Areopagus provided a
donation of money, distributing eight drachmas to each
member of the ships' crews, and so prevailed on them to go
on board. On these grounds people bowed to its prestige ; 2
and during this period Athens was well administered. At this
time they devoted themselves to the prosecution of the war
and were in high repute among the Greeks, so that the command by sea was conferred upon them, in spite of the
opposition of the Lacedaemonians. The leaders of the 3
people during this period were Aristides, son of Lysimachus,
and Themistocles, son of Neocles, of whom the latter
appeared to devote himself to the conduct of war, while the
former had the reputation of being a clever statesman and
the most upright man of his time. Accordingly the one
was usually employed as general, the other as political
adviser. The rebuilding of the fortifications they conducted 4
in combination, although they were political opponents ; but
it was Aristides who, seizing the opportunity afforded by the
discredit brought upon the Lacedaemonians by Pausanias,
guided the public policy in the matter of the defection

---

[1] So the MS., but one of the grammarians, who probably drew from
this passage, says that ostracized persons were compelled to live *outside*
these boundaries ; and it is possible that the MS. reading here should
be altered by the insertion of μή or the substitution of ἐκτός for ἐντός.
Certainly in later times we find ostracized persons living beyond these
limits ; and the balance of probability perhaps leans this way. Geraestus
is at the extreme south of Euboea, and Scyllaeum at the extreme east
of Argolis.

₅ of the Ionian states from[1] the alliance with Sparta. It follows that it was he who made the first assessment of tribute from the various allied states, two years after the battle of Salamis, in the archonship of Timosthenes;[2] and it was he who took the oath of offensive and defensive alliance with the Ionians, on which occasion they cast the masses of iron into the sea.[3]

24 After this, seeing the state growing in confidence and much wealth accumulated, he advised the people to lay hold of the leadership of the league, and to quit the country districts and settle in the city. He pointed out to them that all would be able to gain a living there, some by service in the army, others in the garrisons, others by taking a part in public affairs; and in this way they would secure the
₂ leadership. This advice was taken; and when the people had assumed the supreme control they proceeded to treat their allies in a more imperious fashion, with the exception of the Chians, Lesbians, and Samians. These they maintained to protect their empire, leaving their constitutions untouched, and allowing them to retain whatever dominion
₃ they then possessed. They also secured an ample maintenance for the mass of the population in the way which Aristides had pointed out to them. Out of the proceeds of the tributes and the taxes and the contributions of the allies more than twenty thousand persons were maintained. There were 6,000 jurymen, 1,600 bowmen, 1,200 Knights, 500 members of the Council, 500 guards of the dockyards, besides fifty guards in the Acropolis. There were some 700 magistrates at home, and some 700[4] abroad. Further, when they subsequently went to war, there were in addition 2,500 heavy-armed troops, twenty guard-ships,[5] and other

---

[1] The MS. has 'and'; but the sense of the passage requires the alteration, since there is no indication of Athens having made an alliance with Sparta at this time.

[2] 478 B.C.

[3] For this ceremony, as a sign of a determination which should last until the metal floated to the top of the sea, cf. Herodotus (i. 165) and Horace (*Epod.* xvi. 25, 26).

[4] The number seems to be repeated by mistake on the part of the copyist.

[5] The normal crew of a trireme was 200 men. At that rate these

ships which collected the tributes, with crews amounting
to 2,000 men, selected by lot; and besides these there were
the persons maintained at the Prytanēum, and orphans, and
gaolers, since all these were supported by the state.

Such was the way in which the people earned their 25
livelihood. The supremacy of the Areopagus lasted for
about seventeen years after the Persian wars, although
gradually declining. But as the strength of the masses
increased, Ephialtes, son of Sophonides, a man with a
reputation for incorruptibility and public virtue, who had
become the leader of the people, made an attack upon that
Council. First of all he ruined many of its members by 2
bringing actions against them with reference to their administration. Then, in the archonship of Conon,[1] he
stripped the Council of all the acquired prerogatives from
which it derived its guardianship of the constitution, and
assigned some of them to the Council of Five Hundred, and
others to the Assembly and the law-courts. In this 3
revolution he was assisted by Themistocles,[2] who was
himself a member of the Areopagus, but was expecting to
be tried before it on a charge of treasonable dealings with
Persia. This made him anxious that it should be overthrown, and accordingly he warned Ephialtes that the
Council intended to arrest him, while at the same time he
informed the Areopagites that he would reveal to them

twenty guard-ships represent 4,000 men, and the 2,000 men mentioned
in the next clause presumbly represent ten ships.

[1] 462 B.C.

[2] This is one of the most striking of the new views of history brought
to light by the reappearance of Aristotle's work. The current opinion
(based mainly on Thucydides) is that Themistocles was ostracized
about 471 B.C., that the charge of complicity with Pausanias in his
intrigues with Persia was brought agai..st him about 466 B.C., and
that he reached Persia in his flight about 465 B.C., the year in which
Artaxerxes succeeded Xerxes. It now appears (if the evidence of this
work is to be accepted) that he was in Athens in 462 B.C., and his
ostracism cannot, therefore, be placed earlier than 461 B.C., and his
flight to Persia may have occurred in 460 B.C. This statement is
irreconcilable with the narrative of Thucydides (i. 137) that in his
flight he was nearly captured by the Athenian fleet then engaged in
the siege of Naxos, which is generally assigned to the year 466 B.C.;
and most critics reject it. It is evident, however, that Thucydides'
system of chronology for this period was not the only one current in
antiquity.

certain persons who were conspiring to subvert the constitution. He then conducted the representatives delegated by the Council to the residence of Ephialtes, promising to show them the conspirators who assembled there, and proceeded to converse with them in an earnest manner. Ephialtes, seeing this, was seized with alarm and took 4 refuge in suppliant guise at the altar. Every one was astounded at the occurrence, and presently, when the Council of Five Hundred met, Ephialtes and Themistocles together proceeded to denounce the Areopagus to them. This they repeated in similar fashion in the Assembly, until they succeeded in depriving it of its power. Not long afterwards, however, Ephialtes was assassinated by Aristodïcus of Tanagra. In this way was the Council of Areopagus deprived of its guardianship of the state.

26 After this revolution the administration of the state became more and more lax, in consequence of the eager rivalry of candidates for popular favour. During this period the moderate party, as it happened, had no real chief, their leader being Cimon son of Miltiades, who was a comparatively young man [1], and had been late in entering public life; and at the same time the general populace suffered great losses by war. The soldiers for active service were selected at that time from the roll of citizens, and as the generals were men of no military experience, who owed their position solely to their family standing, it continually happened that some two or three thousand of the troops perished on an expedition; and in this way the best men alike of the lower and the upper classes were exhausted. 2 Consequently in most matters of administration less heed was paid to the laws than had formerly been the case. No alteration, however, was made in the method of election of the nine Archons, except that five years after the death of Ephialtes it was decided that the candidates to be submitted to the lot for that office might be selected from

---

[1] This is inconsistent with the received chronology, and also with the words which immediately follow; hence various conjectures (e. g. νωθρόν, 'sluggish', for νεώτερον) have been proposed, none wholly satisfactory.

the Zeugitae as well as from the higher classes.[1] The first
Archon from that class was Mnesitheides.[2] Up to this
time all the Archons had been taken from the Pentacosiomedimni and Knights, while the Zeugitae were confined to
the ordinary magistracies, save where an evasion of the law
was overlooked. Four years later, in the archonship of [3]
Lysicrates,[3] the thirty 'local justices',[4] as they were called,
were re-established; and two years afterwards, in the
archonship of Antidotus,[5] in consequence of the great [4]
increase in the number of citizens, it was resolved, on the
motion of Pericles, that no one should be admitted to the
franchise who was not of citizen birth by both parents.

After this Pericles came forward as popular leader, **27**
having first distinguished himself while still a young
man by prosecuting Cimon on the audit of his official
accounts as general. Under his auspices the constitution
became still more democratic. He took away some of the
privileges of the Areopagus, and, above all, he turned the
policy of the state in the direction of sea power, which
caused the masses to acquire confidence in themselves and
consequently to take the conduct of affairs more and more
into their own hands. Moreover, forty-eight years after the [2]
battle of Salamis, in the archonship of Pythodōrus,[6] the
Peloponnesian war broke out, during which the populace
was shut up in the city and became accustomed to gain its
livelihood by military service, and so, partly voluntarily and
partly involuntarily, determined to assume the administration
of the state itself. Pericles was also the first to institute [3]
pay for service in the law-courts, as a bid for popular favour
to counterbalance the wealth of Cimon. The latter, having

---

[1] It is evident from ch. 7, 4 that the eligibility to the archonship was
never, strictly speaking, extended beyond this, though in practice
members of the lowest order, the Thetes, often held the office.

[2] The archonship of Mnesitheides was in 457 B.C.; and as the death
of Ephialtes was in 462 B.C., and it has just been stated that the
alteration in the law was made five years later, it follows that a
Zeugites was elected for the first year in which the members of that
order were eligible.

[3] 453 B.C.   [4] See chapters 16, 5 and 53, 1.   [5] 451 B.C.

[6] 432–1 B.C.; and as the war broke out four months before the end
of Pythodorus' year of office (Thuc. ii. 2), the actual date falls in
the spring of 431 B.C.

private possessions on a regal scale, not only performed the regular public services magnificently, but also maintained a large number of his fellow-demesmen. Any member of the deme of Laciădae could go every day to Cimon's house and there receive a reasonable provision; while his estate was guarded by no fences, so that any one who liked might
4 help himself to the fruit from it. Pericles' private property was quite unequal to this magnificence and accordingly he took the advice of Damonides of Oia (who was commonly supposed to be the person who prompted Pericles in most of his measures, and was therefore subsequently ostracized), which was that, as he was beaten in the matter of private possessions, he should make gifts to the people from their own property; and accordingly he instituted pay for the members of the juries. Some critics accuse him of thereby causing a deterioration in the character of the juries, since it was always the common people who put themselves forward for selection as jurors, rather than the men of better
5 position. Moreover, bribery came into existence after this, the first person to introduce it being Anytus, after his command at Pylos.[1] He was prosecuted by certain individuals on account of his loss of Pylos, but escaped by bribing the jury.

28 So long, however, as Pericles was leader of the people, things went tolerably well with the state; but when he was dead there was a great change for the worse. Then for the first time did the people choose a leader who was of no reputation among men of good standing, whereas up to this time such men had always been found as leaders of the
2 democracy. The first leader of the people,[2] in the very beginning of things, was Solon, and the second was

---

[1] Pylos was recaptured by the Spartans, owing to the neglect of Anytus to relieve it, in 411 B.C. Anytus was one of the leaders of the moderate aristocratic party (ch. 34, 3), and one of the prosecutors of Socrates.

[2] It is evident that this designation 'leader of the people' became a sort of semi-official title. There is no sufficient evidence that there was ever a regular process of appointment to the post; but there was always some recognized chief of the democratic party to whom the name was given. The leader of the aristocratic party does not seem to have had any equally well recognized designation.

Pisistratus, both of them men of birth and position. After the overthrow of the tyrants there was Cleisthenes, a member of the house of the Alcmeonidae; and he had no rival opposed to him after the expulsion of the party of Isagoras. After this Xanthippus was the leader of the people, and Miltiades of the upper class. Then came Themistocles and Aristides,[1] and after them Ephialtes as leader of the people, and Cimon son of Miltiades of the wealthier class. Pericles followed as leader of the people, and Thucydides, who was connected by marriage with Cimon, of the opposition. After the death of Pericles, Nicias, who sub- 3 sequently fell in Sicily, appeared as leader of the aristocracy, and Cleon son of Cleaenetus of the people. The latter seems, more than any one else, to have been the cause of the corruption of the democracy by his wild undertakings; and he was the first to use unseemly shouting and coarse abuse on the Bema,[2] and to harangue the people with his cloak girt up short about him, whereas all his predecessors had spoken decently and in order. These were succeeded by Theramenes son of Hagnon as leader of the one party, and the lyre-maker Cleophon of the people. It was Cleophon who first granted the two-obol donation for the theatrical performances,[3] and for some time it continued to be given; but then Callicrates of Paeania ousted him by promising to add a third obol to the sum. Both of these persons were subsequently condemned to death; for the people, even if they are deceived for a time, in the end generally come to detest those who have beguiled them into any unworthy action. After Cleophon the popular leader- 4 ship was occupied successively by the men who chose to talk the biggest and pander the most to the tastes of the majority, with their eyes fixed only on the interests of the moment.

---

[1] Themistocles and Aristides were both of them leaders of the democracy, as is stated in ch. 23, 3. It is a mistake to regard Aristides as an aristocratic leader.

[2] The Bema was the platform or tribune from which orators spoke in the Athenian Assembly.

[3] Two obols was the price of a seat in the theatre; and after the time of Cleophon (the date had hitherto been placed earlier, Plutarch appearing to assign the measure to Pericles) the necessary sum was provided, for all citizens who chose to apply for it, by the state.

5 The best statesmen at Athens, after those of early times, seem to have been Nicias, Thucydides, and Theramenes. As to Nicias and Thucydides, nearly every one agrees that they were not merely men of birth and character, but also statesmen, and that they ruled the state with paternal care. On the merits of Theramenes opinion is divided, because it so happened that in his time public affairs were in a very stormy state. But those who give their opinion deliberately find him, not, as his critics falsely assert, overthrowing every kind of constitution, but supporting every kind so long as it did not transgress the laws ; thus showing that he was able, as every good citizen should be, to live under any form of constitution, while he refused to countenance illegality and was its constant enemy.

29 So long as the fortune of the war continued even, the Athenians preserved the democracy ; but after the disaster in Sicily, when the Lacedaemonians had gained the upper hand through their alliance with the king of Persia, they were compelled to abolish the democracy and establish in its place the constitution of the Four Hundred. The speech recommending this course before the vote was made by Melobius, and the motion was proposed by Pythodorus of Anaphlystus; but the real argument which persuaded the majority was the belief that the king of Persia was more likely to form an alliance with them if the constitution were on an oligarchical basis. The motion of Pytho-
2 dorus was to the following effect. The popular Assembly was to elect twenty persons, over forty years of age, who, in conjunction with the existing ten members of the Committee of Public Safety,[1] after taking an oath that they would frame such measures as they thought best for the state, should then prepare proposals for the public safety. In addition, any other person might make proposals, so that of all the schemes before them the people might choose the
3 best. Cleitophon concurred with the motion of Pythodorus, but moved that the committee should also investigate the

---

[1] This committee is probably the same as that which we know from Thucydides to have been appointed immediately after the news of the Sicilian disaster was received in Athens.

ancient laws enacted by Cleisthenes when he created the democracy, in order that they might have these too before them and so be in a position to decide wisely; his suggestion being that the constitution of Cleisthenes was not really democratic, but closely akin to that of Solon. When the 4 committee was elected, their first proposal was that the Prytanes[1] should be compelled to put to the vote any motion that was offered on behalf of the public safety. Next they abolished all indictments for illegal proposals, all impeachments and public prosecutions, in order that every Athenian should be free to give his counsel on the situation, if he chose; and they decreed that if any person imposed a fine on any other for his acts in this respect, or prosecuted him or summoned him before the courts, he should, on an information being laid against him, be summarily arrested and brought before the generals, who should deliver him to the Eleven[2] to be put to death. After these preliminary 5 measures, they drew up the constitution in the following manner. The revenues of the state were not to be spent on any purpose except the war. All magistrates should serve without remuneration for the period of the war, except the nine Archons and the Prytanes for the time being, who should each receive three obols a day. The whole of the rest of the administration was to be committed, for the period of the war, to those Athenians who were most capable of serving the state personally or pecuniarily, to the number of not less than five thousand. This body was to have full powers, to the extent even of making treaties with whomsoever they willed; and ten representatives, over forty years of age, were to be elected from each tribe to draw up the list of the Five Thousand, after taking an oath on a full and perfect sacrifice.

These were the recommendations of the committee; and **30** when they had been ratified the Five Thousand[3] elected

---

[1] See ch. 43, 4.　　[2] See ch. 52, 1.

[3] This mention of the Five Thousand appears to be in direct contradiction to the statement in ch. 32, 3, that the Five Thousand were only nominally selected, which is also in accordance with the statement of Thucydides (viii. 92). There are two possible explanations: either all

from their own number a hundred commissioners to draw up the constitution. They, on their appointment, drew up 2 and produced the following recommendations. There should be a Council, holding office for a year, consisting of men over thirty years of age, serving without pay. To this body should belong the Generals, the nine Archons, the Amphictyonic Registrar [Hieromnemon],[1] the Taxiarchs, the Hipparchs, the Phylarchs,[2] the commanders of garrisons, the Treasurers of Athena and the other gods, ten in number, the Hellenic Treasurers [Hellenotamiae],[3] the Treasurers of the other non-sacred moneys, to the number of twenty, the ten Commissioners of Sacrifices [Hieropoei], and the ten Superintendents of the mysteries. All these were to be appointed by the Council from a larger number of selected candidates, chosen from its members for the time being. The other offices were all to be filled by lot, and not from the members of the Council. The Hellenic Treasurers who actually administered the funds should not sit with the 3 Council.[4] As regards the future, four Councils were to be created, of men of the age already mentioned, and one of these was to be chosen by lot to take office at once, while the others were to receive it in turn, in the order decided by the lot. For this purpose the hundred commissioners were

persons possessing the necessary qualification of being able to furnish arms were temporarily called the Five Thousand until the list of that body could be properly drawn up (thus the so-called Five Thousand which took over the government after the fall of the Four Hundred actually included all persons able to furnish arms) ; or the Five Thousand nominated by the hundred persons mentioned at the end of the last chapter was only a provisional body, and a fresh nomination was to be made when the constitution had been finally drawn up.

[1] This is the title of one of the two members sent by each Amphictyonic state to the general councils. He served as secretary, while the other, the Pylagoras, was the actual representative of his state.

[2] For these military officers see ch. 61, 3-6.

[3] These were the officers appointed to receive the contribution of the allied states of the Confederacy of Delos, or, as these states subsequently became, the subject-allies of the Athenian empire. After the loss of the empire by the result of the Poloponnesian war these officers were no longer required, and consequently ceased to exist.

[4] If this is not to be taken as directly contradicting the statement made just above, it must be supposed that the actual handling of the money was confined to a few of the Hellenotamiae (probably in rotation), the duties of the rest being to advise and superintend.

to distribute themselves and all the rest[1] as equally as possible into four parts, and cast lots for precedence, and the selected body should hold office for a year. They[2] were 4 to administer that office as seemed to them best, both with reference to the safe custody and due expenditure of the finances, and generally with regard to all other matters to the best of their ability. If they desired to take a larger number of persons into counsel, each member might call in one assistant of his own choice, subject to the same qualification of age. The Council was to sit once every five days, unless there was any special need for more frequent sittings. The casting of the lot for the Council was to be held by the nine Archons ; votes on divisions were to be counted by five tellers chosen by lot from the members of the Council, and of these one was to be selected by lot every day to act as president. These 5 five persons were to cast lots for precedence between the parties wishing to appear before the Council, giving the first place to sacred matters, the second to heralds, the third to embassies, and the fourth to all other subjects ; but matters concerning the war might be dealt with, on the motion of the generals, whenever there was need, without balloting. Any member of the Council who did not enter 6 the Council-house at the time named should be fined a drachma for each day, unless he was away on leave of absence from the Council.

Such was the constitution which they drew up for the 31 time to come, but for the immediate present they devised the following scheme. There should be a Council of Four Hundred, as in the ancient constitution,[3] forty from each tribe, chosen out of candidates of more than thirty years of age, selected by the members of the tribes. This Council should appoint the magistrates and draw up the form of oath which they were to take ; and in all that concerned the laws, in the

---

[1] i.e., apparently, all the rest of the Five Thousand who were over thirty years of age.

[2] Mr. J. A. R. Munro (*Classical Quarterly*) proposes to transfer this sentence and the next, so as to make them precede the two previous sentences, and relate to the Hellenic Treasurers. This transposition would make the sense much clearer.

[3] i.e. as in the constitution of Solon.

examination of official accounts, and in other matters generally, they might act according to their discretion. They
must, however, observe the laws that might be enacted with
reference to the constitution of the state, and had no power to
alter them nor to pass others. The generals should be provi-
sionally elected from the whole body of the Five Thousand,
but so soon as the Council came into existence it was to hold
an examination of military equipments, and thereon elect
ten persons, together with a secretary, and the persons thus
elected should hold office during the coming year with full
powers, and should have the right, whenever they desired it, of
joining in the deliberations of the Council. The Five Thousand[1] was also to elect a single Hipparch and ten Phylarchs;
but for the future the Council was to elect these officers
according to the regulations above laid down. No office,
except those of member of the Council and of general, might
be held more than once, either by the first occupants or by
their successors. With reference to the future distribution[2]
of the Four Hundred into the four successive sections, the
hundred commissioners must divide them whenever the time
comes for the citizens to join in the Council along with the rest.

32 The hundred commissioners appointed by the Five
Thousand drew up the constitution as just stated; and after
it had been ratified by the people, under the presidency of
Aristomachus, the existing Council, that of the year of
Callias,[3] was dissolved before it had completed its term of
office. It was dissolved on the fourteenth day of the month

---

[1] The subject is not expressed in the original, but as it is stated that
in the future the Council was to elect these officers, it seems certain
that the provisional arrangement was that the Five Thousand should
elect them, as in the case of the generals, the Council not being
yet properly constituted.

[2] i.e. the distribution mentioned in the preceding chapter. Apparently the sense intended is that the division into the four sections
should take place so soon as the remaining citizens from whom the four
Councils were to be drawn up (viz. the members of the Five Thousand
over thirty years of age) had been associated with the Four Hundred
who formed the provisional Council. i.e., practically, so soon as the list
of the qualified members of the Five Thousand was ready.

[3] Callias' year of office began in 412 B.C., and was now within two
months of its end. The date of the entry of the Four Hundred into
office is consequently in May, 411 B.C.

Thargelion, and the Four Hundred entered into office on the twenty-first; whereas the regular Council, elected by lot, ought to have entered into office on the fourteenth of Scirophorion.[1] Thus was the oligarchy established, in the 2 archonship of Callias, just about a hundred years after the expulsion of the tyrants. The chief promoters of the revolution were Pisander, Antiphon, and Theramenes, all of them men of good birth and with high reputations for ability and judgement. When, however, this constitution 3 had been established, the Five Thousand were only nominally selected, and the Four Hundred, together with the ten officers on whom full powers had been conferred,[2] occupied the Council-house and really administered the government. They began by sending ambassadors to the Lacedaemonians proposing a cessation of the war on the basis of the existing position; but as the Lacedaemonians refused to listen to them unless they would also abandon the command of the sea, they broke off the negotiations.

For about four months the constitution of the Four 33 Hundred lasted, and Mnasilochus held office as Archon of their nomination for two months of the year of Theopompus, who was Archon for the remaining ten. On the loss of the naval battle of Eretria, however, and the revolt of the whole of Euboea except Orĕum, the indignation of the people was greater than at any of the earlier disasters, since they drew far more supplies at this time from Euboea than from Attica itself. Accordingly they deposed the Four Hundred and committed the management of affairs to the Five Thousand, consisting of persons possessing a military equipment. At the same time they voted that pay should not be given for any public office. The persons chiefly 2 responsible for the revolution were Aristocrates and Thera- menes, who disapproved of the action of the Four Hundred in retaining the direction of affairs entirely in their own hands, and referring nothing to the Five Thousand. During

[1] Roughly equivalent to June, the last month of the official year at Athens. The 'regular Council' means the Council which, in the ordinary course of things under the democracy, should have been elected by lot to succeed that belonging to the year of Callias.
[2] i. e. the ten Generals appointed as provided for in ch. 31, 2.

this period the constitution of the state seems to have been admirable, since it was a time of war and the franchise was in the hands of those who possessed a military equipment.[1]

34   The people, however, in a very short time deprived the Five Thousand of their monopoly of the government.[2] Then, six years after the overthrow of the Four Hundred, in the archonship of Callias of Angĕlē,[3] the battle of Arginusae took place, of which the results were, first, that the ten generals who had gained the victory were all[4] condemned by a single decision, owing to the people being led astray by persons who aroused their indignation ; though, as a matter of fact, some of the generals had actually taken no part in the battle, and others were themselves picked up by other vessels.[5]   Secondly, when the Lacedaemonians proposed to evacuate Decelēa and make peace on the basis of the existing position, although some of the Athenians supported this proposal, the majority refused to listen to them.   In this they were led astray by Cleophon, who appeared in the Assembly drunk and wearing his breastplate,[6] and prevented peace being made, declaring that he would never accept peace unless the Lacedaemonians abandoned their claims on all the cities allied with them.[7]   They mismanaged their

[1] This is an echo of the commendation which Thucydides expresses at greater length (viii. 97).

[2] Probably after the battle of Cyzicus, in 410 B.C., when the fleet, which was democratic in its sympathies, returned to Athens.

[3] 406 B.C. This was, however, five years after the overthrow of the oligarchy, not six, so that either Aristotle calculated from the beginning and not the end of the rule of the Four Hundred, or the numeral must be altered in the MS.

[4] This is probably inexact. Two of the generals, Conon and Leon, can hardly have been included in the accusation, as Conon was blockaded in Mytilene and Leon is never mentioned in connexion with either the battle or the trial. It is true that Aristotle says below that some of the condemned generals had not taken part in the battle, but if this had actually been the case, Xenophon could hardly have helped noticing it.   Xenophon does expressly name the eight generals who were present at the battle, and states their positions in the Athenian line ; and, of these eight, six stood their trial and were executed, while the remaining two declined to return to Athens and were, no doubt, condemned in absence.

[5] And therefore were in no condition to be picking up the survivors on other disabled ships, for neglecting which they were condemned.

[6] As a warlike demonstration, like a politician appearing in khaki.

[7] Cleophon retorted against the Lacedaemonians the ground on which they had refused to accept the Athenian overtures in 411 B.C.

opportunity then, and in a very short time they learnt their mistake. The next year, in the archonship of Alexias, they suffered the disaster of Aegospotami, the consequence of which was that Lysander became master of the city, and set up the Thirty as its governors. He did so in the following manner. One of the terms of peace stipulated 3 that the state should be governed according to 'the ancient constitution'. Accordingly the popular party tried to preserve the democracy, while that part of the upper class which belonged to the political clubs,[1] together with the exiles who had returned since the peace, aimed at an oligarchy, and those who were not members of any club, though in other respects they considered themselves as good as any other citizens, were anxious to restore the ancient constitution. The latter class included Archīnus, Anytus, Cleitophon, Phormisius, and many others, but their most prominent leader was Theramenes. Lysander, however, threw his influence on the side of the oligarchical party, and the popular Assembly was compelled by sheer intimidation to pass a vote establishing the oligarchy. The motion to this effect was proposed by Dracontides of Aphidna.

In this way were the Thirty established in power, in the 35 archonship of Pythodorus.[2] As soon, however, as they were masters of the city, they ignored all the resolutions which had been passed relating to the organization of the constitution,[3] but after appointing a Council of Five Hundred and the other magistrates out of a thousand selected candidates,[4] and associating with themselves ten Archons in Piraeus, eleven superintendents of the prison, and three hundred 'lash-bearers' as attendants, with the help of these they kept the city under their own control. At 2 first, indeed, they behaved with moderation towards the citizens and pretended to administer the state according to the ancient constitution. In pursuance of this policy they

[1] i. e. the extreme oligarchs.   [2] The year 404–403 B.C.

[3] The Thirty were appointed avowedly to draw up a scheme for the constitution, like the hundred commissioners mentioned in ch. 30.

[4] MS. 'out of candidates selected from the thousand'; but nothing is known about any such body. The other magistrates were probably included in the Council (cf. ch. 30, 2), so that 500 names had to be chosen from 1000.

D

took down from the hill of Areopagus the laws of Ephialtes and Archestratus relating to the Areopagite Council; they also repealed such of the statutes of Solon as were obscure,[1] and abolished the supreme power of the law-courts. In this they claimed to be restoring the constitution and freeing it from obscurities; as, for instance, by making the testator free once for all to leave his property as he pleased, and abolishing the existing limitations in cases of insanity, old age, and undue female influence, in order that no opening might be left for professional accusers.[2] In other 3 matters also their conduct was similar. At first, then, they acted on these lines, and they destroyed the professional accusers and those mischievous and evil-minded persons who, to the great detriment of the democracy, had attached themselves to it in order to curry favour with it. With all of this the city was much pleased, and thought that the 4 Thirty were doing it with the best of motives. But so soon as they had got a firmer hold on the city, they spared no class of citizens, but put to death any persons who were eminent for wealth or birth or character. Herein they aimed at removing all whom they had reason to fear, while they also wished to lay hands on their possessions; and in a short time they put to death not less than fifteen hundred persons.

36 Theramenes, however, seeing the city thus falling into ruin, was displeased with their proceedings, and counselled them to cease such unprincipled conduct and let the better classes have a share in the government. At first they resisted his advice, but when his proposals came to be known abroad, and the masses began to associate themselves with him, they were seized with alarm lest he should make himself the

---

[1] See ch. 9, 2.

[2] Solon's law allowed a man who had no legitimate children to leave his property as he chose, provided his will was made while he was of sound mind and subject to no undue influence. These provisions were reasonable enough in themselves, but a class of hangers-on of the law-courts had sprung up, who made a profession of challenging the legality of testamentary dispositions on these grounds, no doubt in the hope of extorting money. In order to put an end to this trade the Thirty abolished the qualifications in the law of Solon on which it was based.

leader of the people and destroy their despotic power. Accordingly they drew up a list of three thousand [1] citizens, to whom they announced that they would give a share in the constitution. Theramenes, however, criticized this scheme also, first on the ground that, while proposing to give all respectable citizens a share in the constitution, they were actually giving it only to three thousand persons, as though all merit were confined within that number; and secondly because they were doing two inconsistent things, since they made the government rest on the basis of force, and yet made the governors inferior in strength to the governed. However, they took no notice of his criticisms, and for a long time put off the publication of the list of the Three Thousand and kept to themselves the names of those who had been placed upon it; and every time they did decide to publish it they proceeded to strike out some of those who had been included in it, and insert others who had been omitted.

Now when winter had set in, Thrasybūlus and the exiles **37** occupied Phylē, and the force which the Thirty led out to attack them met with a reverse. Thereupon the Thirty decided to disarm the bulk of the population and to get rid of Theramenes; which they did in the following way. They introduced two laws into the Council, which they commanded it to pass; the first of them gave the Thirty absolute power to put to death any citizen who was not included in the list of the Three Thousand, while the second disqualified all persons from participation in the franchise who should have assisted in the demolition of the fort of Eëtioneia,[2] or have acted in any way against the Four Hundred who had organized the previous oligarchy. Theramenes had done both, and accordingly, when these

---

[1] The MS. says two thousand, but this must be a copyist's error, as the Three Thousand is mentioned immediately below, and that number is confirmed by the other authorities.

[2] The Four Hundred had begun to build this fort, which commanded the entrance to the Piraeus, in the later days of their rule; but Theramenes and others of the moderate party, suspecting that it was intended to enable the oligarchs to betray the port to the Spartans, incited the populace to destroy it. This was one of the most serious blows dealt to the power of the Four Hundred.

laws were ratified, he became excluded from the franchise and
2 the Thirty had full power to put him to death.[1] Theramenes
having been thus removed, they disarmed all the people
except the Three Thousand, and in every respect showed a
great advance in cruelty and crime. They also sent
ambassadors to Lacedaemon to blacken the character of
Theramenes and to ask for help; and the Lacedaemonians,
in answer to their appeal, sent Callibius as military governor
with about seven hundred troops, who came and occupied
the Acropolis.

38 These events were followed by the occupation of Munichia
by the exiles from Phyle, and their victory over the Thirty
and their partisans. After the fight the party of the city
retreated, and next day they held a meeting in the market-
place and deposed the Thirty, and elected ten citizens with
full powers to bring the war to a termination. When, however, the Ten had taken over the government they did
nothing towards the object for which they were elected, but
sent envoys to Lacedaemon to ask for help and to borrow
2 money. Further, finding that the citizens who possessed the
franchise were displeased at their proceedings, they were
afraid lest they should be deposed, and consequently, in
order to strike terror into them (in which design they succeeded), they arrested Demarĕtus, one of the most eminent
citizens, and put him to death. This gave them a firm hold
on the government, and they also had the support of
Callibius and his Peloponnesians, together with several of
the Knights; for some of the members of this class were
the most zealous among the citizens to prevent the return
3 of the exiles from Phyle. When, however, the party in
Piraeus and Munichia began to gain the upper hand in the
war, through the defection of the whole populace to them,
the party in the city deposed the original Ten, and elected
another Ten,[2] consisting of men of the highest repute. Under

[1] This is quite different from Xenophon's dramatic account
(ii. 3. 23–56) of the totally illegal arrest and execution of Theramenes.
[2] No other authority seems to distinguish between these two boards
of Ten. Practically, the rule of the first is ignored, and only that of
the second, which brought the war to a conclusion, is recognized; but
the appointment of this board is assigned to the days immediately
following the defeat of the Thirty, and it is not recognized that a con-

CHAPTER 38

their administration, and with their active and zealous
co-operation, the treaty of reconciliation was made and the
populace returned to the city. The most prominent
members of this board were Rhinon of Paeania and Phayllus
of Acherdus, who, even before the arrival of Pausanias,
opened negotiations with the party in Piraeus, and after
his arrival seconded his efforts to bring about the return of
the exiles. For it was Pausanias, the king of the Lacedae- 4
monians, who brought the peace and reconciliation to a
fulfilment, in conjunction with the ten [1] commissioners of
arbitration who arrived later from Lacedaemon, at his own
earnest request. Rhinon and his colleagues received a vote
of thanks for the goodwill shown by them to the people,
and though they received their charge under an oligarchy
and handed in their accounts under a democracy, no one,
either of the party that had stayed in the city or of the exiles
that had returned from the Piraeus, brought any complaint
against them. On the contrary, Rhinon was immediately
elected general on account of his conduct in this office.

This reconciliation was effected in the archonship of 39
Eucleides,[2] on the following terms. All persons who, having
remained in the city during the troubles, were now anxious
to leave it, were to be free to settle at Eleusis, retaining
their civil rights and possessing full and independent powers
of self-government, and with the free enjoyment of their own
personal property. The temple at Eleusis should be com- 2
mon ground for both parties, and should be under the
superintendence of the Ceryces and the Eumolpidae,[3] according to primitive custom. The settlers at Eleusis should
not be allowed to enter Athens, nor the people of Athens to
enter Eleusis, except at the season of the mysteries, when
both parties should be free from these restrictions. The
secessionists should pay their share to the fund for the

siderable time, apparently about six months, elapsed between this event
and the restoration of the democracy.

[1] Xenophon says fifteen, and some editors alter the present text
accordingly.

[2] i.e. late in the summer of 403 B.C.

[3] Two ancient Athenian families, who from the earliest times had
retained the duty of superintending the Eleusinian mysteries. See
ch. 57, 1.

common defence out of their revenues, just like all the
3 other Athenians. If any of the seceding party wished to
take a house in Eleusis, the people would help them
to obtain the consent of the owner; but if they could not
come to terms, they should appoint three valuers on either
side, and the owner should receive whatever price they
should appoint. Of the inhabitants of Eleusis, those whom
the secessionists wished to remain should be allowed to do
4 so. The list of those who desired to secede should be made
up within ten days after the taking of the oaths in the case
of persons already in the country, and their actual departure
should take place within twenty days; persons at present
out of the country should have the same terms allowed to
5 them after their return. No one who settled at Eleusis
should be capable of holding any office in Athens until he
should again register himself on the roll as a resident in the
city. Trials for homicide, including all cases in which one
party had either killed or wounded another, should be
6 conducted according to ancestral practice.[1] There should be
a general amnesty concerning past events towards all persons
except the Thirty, the Ten, the Eleven, and the magistrates
in Piraeus; and these too should be included if they should
submit their accounts in the usual way. Such accounts
should be given by the magistrates in Piraeus before a
court of citizens rated in Piraeus, and by the magistrates in
the city before a court of those rated in the city.[2] On these
terms those who wished to do so might secede. Each
party was to repay separately the money which it had
borrowed for the war.

40 When the reconciliation had taken place on these terms,
those who had fought on the side of the Thirty felt considerable apprehensions, and a large number intended to
secede. But as they put off entering their names till the last
moment, as people will do, Archinus, observing their numbers,
and being anxious to retain them as citizens, cut off the
remaining days during which the list should have remained

---

[1] The reading of this passage is rather doubtful.
[2] The exact reading of this passage also is doubtful, but the general
sense appears to be that here given (inserting ἐν τῷ ἄστει after ἐν τοῖς).

open; and in this way many persons were compelled
to remain, though they did so very unwillingly until they
recovered confidence. This is one point in which Archinus 2
appears to have acted in a most statesmanlike manner, and
another was his subsequent prosecution of Thrasybulus on
the charge of illegality, for a motion by which he proposed
to confer the franchise on all who had taken part in the
return from Piraeus, although some of them were notoriously
slaves. And yet a third such action was when one of the
returned exiles began to violate the amnesty, whereupon
Archinus haled him to the Council and persuaded them
to execute him without trial, telling them that now they
would have to show whether they wished to preserve the
democracy and abide by the oaths they had taken; for
if they let this man escape they would encourage others
to imitate him, while if they executed him they would make
an example for all to learn by. And this was exactly what
happened; for after this man had been put to death no
one ever again broke the amnesty. On the contrary, the 3
Athenians seem, both in public and in private, to have
behaved in the most unprecedentedly admirable and public-
spirited way with reference to the preceding troubles.
Not only did they blot out all memory of former offences,
but they even repaid to the Lacedaemonians out of the
public purse the money which the Thirty had borrowed for
the war, although the treaty required each party, the party
of the city and the party of Piraeus, to pay its own debts
separately. This they did because they thought it was
a necessary first step in the direction of restoring harmony;
but in other states, so far from the democratic parties [1]
making advances from their own possessions, they are rather
in the habit of making a general redistribution of the land.
A final reconciliation was made with the secessionists at 4
Eleusis two years after the secession, in the archonship of
Xenaenĕtus.[2]

This, however, took place at a later date; at the time of 41
which we are speaking the people, having secured the control

---

[1] Or 'victorious democracies' (reading οἱ δῆμοι κρατήσαντες).

[2] 401 B. C. The date is not elsewhere definitely recorded.

of the state, established the constitution which exists at the present day. Pythodōrus was Archon at the time, but the democracy seems to have assumed the supreme power with perfect justice, since it had effected its own return by its
2 own exertions.[1] This was the eleventh change which had taken place in the constitution of Athens. The first modification of the primaeval condition of things was when Ion and his companions brought the people together into a community, for then the people was first divided into the four tribes, and the tribe-kings were created. Next, and first after this, having now some semblance of a constitution,[2] was that which took place in the reign of Theseus, consisting in a slight deviation from absolute monarchy. After this came the constitution formed under Draco, when the first code of laws was drawn up. The third was that which followed the civil war, in the time of Solon ; from this the democracy took its rise. The fourth was the tyranny of Pisistratus; the fifth the constitution of Cleisthenes, after the overthrow of the tyrants, of a more democratic character than that of Solon. The sixth was that which followed on the Persian wars, when the Council of Areopagus had the direction of the state. The seventh, succeeding this, was the constitution which Aristides sketched out, and which Ephialtes brought to completion by overthrowing the Areopagite Council ; under this the nation, misled by the demagogues, made the most serious mistakes in the interest of its maritime empire. The eighth was the establishment of the Four Hundred, followed by the ninth, the restored democracy. The tenth was the tyranny of the Thirty and the Ten. The eleventh was that which followed the return from Phyle and Piraeus ; and this has continued from that day to this, with continual accretions of power to the masses. The democracy has made itself master of

[1] The text here is corrupt. There is no natural contrast between the fact that Pythodorus was Archon and the assumption of the control of the state by the democracy, since the Archon had for a long time been nothing more than a figure-head. Probably some words have dropped out.
[2] This is the first of the eleven changes to which Aristotle has just referred. The constitution of Ion is not reckoned in the enumeration, since it was the original establishment and not a change.

everything and administers everything by its votes in the Assembly and by the law-courts, in which it holds the supreme power. Even the jurisdiction of the Council has passed into the hands of the people at large; and this appears to be a judicious change, since small bodies are more open to corruption, whether by actual money or influence, than large ones. At first they refused to allow 3 payment for attendance at the Assembly; but the result was that people did not attend. Consequently, after the Prytanes had tried many devices in vain in order to induce the populace to come and ratify the votes, Agyrrhius,[1] in the first instance, made a provision of one obol a day, which Heracleides of Clazomenae,[2] nicknamed 'the king', increased to two obols, and Agyrrhius again to three.

The present state of the constitution is as follows. The 42 franchise is open to all who are of citizen birth by both parents. They are enrolled among the demesmen at the age of eighteen. On the occasion of their enrolment the demesmen give their votes on oath, first whether the candidates appear to be of the age prescribed by the law (if not, they are dismissed back into the ranks of the boys), and secondly whether the candidate is free born and of such parentage as the laws require.[3] Then if they decide that he is not a free man, he appeals to the law-courts, and the demesmen appoint five of their own number to act as accusers; if the court decides that he has no right to be enrolled, he is sold by the state as a slave, but if he wins his case he has a right to be enrolled among the demesmen without further question. After this the Council examines those who have been 2

---

[1] A politician of no very great repute, who flourished at the end of the fifth century and in the early part of the fourth. It is clear from many allusions in the *Ecclesiazusae* of Aristophanes that the rate of pay had been raised to three obols shortly before the performance of that play in 392 B.C.; and the first establishment of payment for attendance at the Assembly cannot be placed many years before that date.

[2] Heracleides is only known otherwise by a mention in the *Ion* attributed to Plato, in which he is referred to as a foreigner who had held office at Athens.

[3] i. e. whether he is born of two citizen parents.

enrolled, and if it comes to the conclusion that any of them is less than eighteen years of age, it fines the demesmen who enrolled him. When the youths [Ephēbi] have passed this examination, their fathers meet by their tribes, and appoint on oath three of their fellow tribesmen, over forty years of age, who, in their opinion, are the best and most suitable persons to have charge of the youths ; and of these the Assembly elects one from each tribe as guardian, together with a director, chosen from the general body 3 of Athenians, to control the while. Under the charge of these persons the youths first of all make the circuit of the temples ; then they proceed to Piraeus, and some of them garrison Munichia and some the south shore.[1] The Assembly also elects two trainers, with subordinate instructors, who teach them to fight in heavy armour, to use the bow and javelin, and to discharge a catapult. The guardians receive from the state a drachma apiece for their keep, and the youths four obols apiece. Each guardian receives the allowance for all the members of his tribe and buys the necessary provisions for the common stock (they mess together by tribes), and generally superintends everything. 4 In this way they spend the first year. The next year, after giving a public display of their military evolutions, on the occasion when the Assembly meets in the theatre,[2] they receive a shield and spear from the state ; after which they 5 patrol the country and spend their time in the forts. For these two years they are on garrison duty, and wear the military cloak, and during this time they are exempt from all taxes. They also can neither bring an action at law, nor have one brought against them, in order that they may have no excuse for requiring leave of absence ; though exception is made in cases of actions concerning inheritances and wards of state,[3] or of any sacrificial ceremony connected

[1] 'Ακτή = the southern side of Piraeus.
[2] This was on the occasion of the great Dionysiac festival in each year, when the whole people was gathered together in the theatre, together with numbers of visitors from foreign countries.
[3] When a man died leaving a daughter, but no son, his estate, though not becoming her property, was attached to her, and the nearest of kin could claim her in marriage ; and the property went to the sons born of such marriage. If she was poor, the nearest of kin

with the family.[1] When the two years have elapsed they thereupon take their position among the other citizens. Such is the manner of the enrolment of the citizens and the **43** training of the youths.

All the magistrates that are concerned with the ordinary routine of administration are elected by lot, except the Military Treasurer, the Commissioners of the Theoric fund,[2] and the Superintendent of Springs.[3] These are elected by vote, and hold office from one Panathenaic festival to the next.[4] All military officers are also elected by vote.

The Council of Five Hundred is elected by lot, fifty from **2** each tribe. Each tribe holds the office of Prytanes in turn, the order being determined by lot; the first four serve for thirty-six days each, the last six for thirty-five, since the reckoning is by lunar years.[5] The Prytanes for the time **3** being, in the first place, mess together in the Tholus,[6] and receive a sum of money from the state for their maintenance; and, secondly, they convene the meetings of the Council

was obliged either to marry her or to provide her with a dowry. If there were more daughters than one, the estate seems to have been divided among them under similar conditions. These heiresses were under the special protection of the Archon (see ch. 56, 6, 7), and may therefore be described as wards of state.

[1] Only members of the older houses belonged to 'families' in the technical sense, these being one of the earliest subdivisions of the population of Attica, and having sacrificial observances connected with them. See ch. 21, 6, where it is said that Cleisthenes, though breaking up the old tribal organization and introducing new citizens, allowed the families and the sacrificial observances to remain according to the ancient system.

[2] This was the fund which provided the populace with the price of admission to the theatre (and, eventually, with something in addition) at the festivals.

[3] Athens was scantily supplied with fresh water, and consequently this officer was of some importance.

[4] The Panathenaic festival was at the end of the first month of the Attic year (July). The other magistrates probably came into office at the beginning of that month; the Archons certainly did so.

[5] The ordinary Attic year was of 354 days, divided into twelve lunar months of thirty and twenty-nine days alternately. The deficiency was made up by inserting intercalary months, at first every alternate year, then three in eight years, and subsequently seven in nineteen. In an intercalary year the duration of the prytanies was thirty-nine and thirty-eight days, in place of thirty-six and thirty-five.

[6] The official residence of the Prytanes, supposed to represent the centre of the public life of Athens.

and the Assembly. The Council they convene every day, unless it is a holiday, the Assembly four times in each prytany. It is also their duty to draw up the programme of the business of the Council and to decide what subjects are to be dealt with on each particular day, and where the 4 sitting is to be held. They also draw up the programme for the meetings of the Assembly. One of these in each prytany is called the 'sovereign' Assembly; in this the people have to ratify the continuance of the magistrates in office, if they are performing their duties properly, and to consider the supply of corn and the defence of the country. On this day, too, impeachments are introduced by those who wish to do so, the lists of property confiscated by the state are read, and also applications for inheritances and wards of state,[1] so that nothing may pass unclaimed 5 without the cognizance of any person concerned. In the sixth prytany, in addition to the business already stated, the question is put to the vote whether it is desirable to hold a vote of ostracism or not; and complaints against professional accusers, whether Athenian or aliens domiciled in Athens, are received, to the number of not more than three of either class, together with cases in which an individual has made some promise to the people and has not performed 6 it. Another Assembly in each prytany is assigned to the hearing of petitions, and at this meeting any one is free, on depositing the petitioner's olive-branch, to speak to the people concerning any matter, public or private. The two remaining meetings are devoted to all other subjects, and the laws require them to deal with three questions connected with religion, three connected with heralds and embassies, and three on secular subjects. Sometimes questions are brought forward without a preliminary vote of the Assembly to take them into consideration.

Heralds and envoys appear first before the Prytanes, and the bearers of dispatches also deliver them to the same officials.

---

[1] If there was no direct heir, the next of kin had to apply to the state, in the person of the Archon, to have his claim recognized. The claims on wards of state have been mentioned in note 3 to ch. 42, 5.

There is a single President of the Prytanes, elected by lot, **44** who presides for a night and a day; he may not hold the office for more than that time, nor may the same individual hold it twice. He keeps the keys of the sanctuaries in which the treasures and public records of the state are preserved, and also the public seal; and he is bound to remain in the Tholus, together with one-third of the Prytanes, named by himself. Whenever the Prytanes **2** convene a meeting of the Council or Assembly, he appoints by lot nine Proedri, one from each tribe except that which holds the office of Prytanes for the time being; and out of these nine he similarly appoints one as President, and hands over the programme for the meeting to them. They take **3** it and see to the preservation of order, put forward the various subjects which are to be considered, decide the results of the votings, and direct the proceedings generally.[1] They also have power to dismiss the meeting. No one may act as President more than once in the year, but he may be a Proedrus once in each prytany.

Elections to the offices of General and Hipparch and all **4** other military commands are held in the Assembly, in such manner as the people decide; they are held after the sixth prytany by the first board of Prytanes in whose term of office the omens are favourable. There has, however, to be a preliminary consideration by the Council in this case also.[2]

In former times the Council had full powers to inflict **45** fines and imprisonment and death; but[3] when it had consigned Lysimachus[4] to the executioner, and he was sitting in the immediate expectation of death, Eumelides of Alopĕcē rescued him from its hands,[5] maintaining that no citizen ought to be put to death except on the decision of a court

---

[1] In the fifth century the Prytanes themselves acted as presidents at meetings of the Council and Assembly; but in the fourth century the Proedri appear to have been instituted, as here described.

[2] As with all business submitted to the Assembly: see ch. 45, 4.

[3] The MS. has 'and', but is perhaps imperfect.

[4] Neither the story nor the person is otherwise known. He may have been one of the partisans of the Thirty (Xen. *Hell.* ii. 4, 8).

[5] Or 'deprived it of its powers'.

of law.[1] Accordingly a trial was held in a law-court, and Lysimachus was acquitted, receiving henceforth the nickname of 'the man from the drum-head';[2] and the people deprived the Council thenceforward of the power to inflict death or imprisonment or fine, passing a law that if the Council condemn any person for an offence or inflict a fine, the Thesmothetae shall bring the sentence or fine before the law-court, and the decision of the jurors shall be the final judgement in the matter.

2 The Council passes judgement on nearly all magistrates, especially those who have the control of money; its judgement, however, is not final, but is subject to an appeal to the law-courts. Private individuals, also, may lay an information against any magistrate they please for not obeying the laws, but here too there is an appeal to the 3 law-courts if the Council declare the charge proved. The Council also examines those who are to be its members for the ensuing year, and likewise the nine Archons.[3] Formerly the Council had full power to reject candidates for office as unsuitable, but now they have an appeal to the law-courts. 4 In all these matters, therefore, the Council has no final jurisdiction. It takes, however, preliminary cognizance of all matters brought before the Assembly, and the Assembly cannot vote on any question unless it has first been considered by the Council and placed on the programme by the Prytanes; since a person who carries a motion in the Assembly is liable to an action for illegal proposal on these grounds.[4]

46 The Council also superintends the triremes that are already in existence, with their tackle and sheds,[5] and builds new triremes or quadriremes,[6] whichever the Assembly

---

[1] It should be observed that throughout the treatise a 'law-court' (δικαστήριον) always means one of the large popular jury-courts, the constitutional importance of which is described in ch. 9.

[2] This, though verbally close to the original, is rather a paraphrase than a translation. The original apparently denotes that Lysimachus was about to be executed by the method of beating or bastinadoing to death.

[3] See ch. 55, 2.

[4] i. e. if this procedure has been omitted.

[5] i. e. the sheds in which the ships were laid up when in dock.

[6] Quadriremes were first built at Athens a few years before 330 B. C.,

votes, with tackle and sheds to match. The Assembly appoints master-builders for the ships by vote; and if they do not hand them over completed to the next Council, the old Council[1] cannot receive the customary donation—that being normally given to it during its successor's term of office. For the building of the triremes it appoints ten commissioners, chosen from its own members. The Council[2] also inspects all public buildings, and if it is of opinion that the state is being defrauded, it reports the culprit to the Assembly, and on condemnation[2] hands him over to the law-courts.

The Council also co-operates with the other magistrates **47** in most of their duties. First there are the treasurers of Athena,[3] ten in number, elected by lot, one from each tribe. According to the law of Solon—which is still in force—they must be Pentacosiomedimni, but in point of fact the person on whom the lot falls holds the office even though he be quite a poor man. These officers take over charge of the statue of Athena, the figures of Victory, and all the other ornaments of the temple, together with the money, in the presence of the Council. Then there are the Commissioners[2] for Public Contracts [Poletae], ten in number, one chosen by lot from each tribe, who farm out the public contracts. They lease the mines and taxes, in conjunction with the Military Treasurer and the Commissioners of the Theoric fund, in the presence of the Council, and grant, to the persons indicated by the vote of the Council, the mines which are let out by the state, including both the workable

and in 325 B.C. they began to build quinqueremes. As the latter are not mentioned here, we seem to get a lower limit of date for the composition (or revision) of the treatise. The upper limit is fixed by ch. 54, 7 as 329 B.C.

[1] Grammatically the subject of this sentence should be the master-builders, but the facts are stated in the speech of Demosthenes against Androtion in closely parallel language.

[2] According to the text of the MS. (καταγνοῦσα), the condemnation is by the Council; but this has already been expressed before the reference to the Assembly (ἀδικεῖν δόξῃ), and if condemnation by the Council sufficed for the case to be brought before the courts, the reference to the Assembly would be otiose. Hence the emendation καταγνόντος.

[3] Each of the temples seems to have possessed a treasury, but that of the temple of Athena was far the most important.

ones, which are let for three years, and those which are
let under special agreements for [ten?] years.[1]   They
also sell, in the presence of the Council, the property
of those who have gone into exile from the court of the
Areopagus, and of others whose goods have been confiscated,
and the nine Archons ratify the contracts.   They also
hand over to the Council lists of the taxes which are farmed
3 out for the year, entering on whitened tablets the name of
the lessee and the amount paid.   They make separate
lists, first of those who have to pay their instalments in each
prytany, on ten several tablets, next of those who pay thrice
in the year, with a separate tablet for each instalment, and
finally of those who pay in the ninth prytany.   They also
draw up a list of farms and dwellings which have been
confiscated and sold by order of the courts; for these
too come within their province.   In the case of dwellings
the value must be paid up in five years, and in that of farms,
4 in ten.   The instalments are paid in the ninth prytany.
Further, the King-archon brings before the Council the
leases of the sacred enclosures, written on whitened tablets.
These too are leased for ten years, and the instalments are
paid in the [ninth] prytany; consequently it is in this
5 prytany that the greatest amount of money is collected.
The tablets containing the lists of the instalments are
carried into the Council, and the public clerk takes charge
of them.   Whenever a payment of instalments is to be
made he takes from the pigeon-holes[2] the precise list of the
sums which are to be paid and struck off on that day, and
delivers it to the Receivers-General.   The rest are kept
apart, in order that no sum may be struck off before it is paid.

48   There are ten Receivers-General [Apodectae], elected by
lot, one from each tribe.   These officers receive the tablets,
and strike off the instalments as they are paid, in the
presence of the Council in the Council-chamber, and give
the tablets back to the public clerk.   If any one fails to pay

---

[1] This is the apparent reading of the passage, but the MS. is considerably damaged in this part.
[2] The exact meaning of the word here (following Sir. J. Sandys) translated 'pigeon-holes' is doubtful.

his instalment, a note is made of it on the tablet; and he is bound to pay double the amount of the deficiency, or, in default, to be imprisoned. The Council has full power by the laws to exact these payments and to inflict this imprisonment. They receive all the instalments, therefore, on 2 one day, and portion the money out among the magistrates; and on the next day they bring up the report of the apportionment, written on a wooden notice-board, and read it out in the Council-chamber, after which they ask publicly in the Council whether any one knows of any malpractice in reference to the apportionment, on the part of either a magistrate or a private individual, and if any one is charged with malpractice they take a vote on it.

The Council also elects ten Auditors [Logistae] by lot 3 from its own members, to audit the accounts of the magistrates for each prytany. They also elect one Examiner of 4 Accounts [Euthūnus] by lot from each tribe, with two assessors [Paredri] for each examiner, whose duty it is to sit at the ordinary market hours,[1] each opposite the statue of the eponymous hero of his tribe; and if any one wishes to prefer a charge, on either public or private grounds, against any magistrate who has passed his audit before the law-courts, within three days of his having so passed, he enters on a whitened tablet his own name and that of the magistrate prosecuted, together with the malpractice that is alleged against him. He also appends his claim for a penalty of such amount as seems to him fitting, and gives in the record to the Examiner. The latter takes it, and if 5 after reading it he considers it proved he hands it over, if a private case, to the local justices who introduce cases[2] for the tribe concerned, while if it is a public case he enters it on the register of the Thesmothetae. Then, if the Thesmothetae accept it, they bring the accounts of this magistrate once

---

[1] Reading ταῖς ἀγοραῖς, and accepting Wilamowitz's interpretation. The alternative translation, 'on the days of the tribal meetings', is not satisfactory, since the complaints had to be lodged within three days.

[2] All cases had to be brought before the courts by some magistrate. Several instances in which one of the Archons, or the Thesmothetae collectively, or the Arbitrators, or some other magistrate, performed this function for specific classes of cases are mentioned in the following chapters.

E

more before the law-court, and the decision of the jury stands as the final judgement.

49 The Council also inspects the horses belonging to the state. If a man who has a good horse is found to keep it in bad condition, he is mulcted in his allowance of corn ; while those which cannot keep up or which shy and will not stand steady, it brands with a wheel on the jaw, and the horse so marked is disqualified for service. It also inspects those who appear to be fit for service as scouts, and any one whom it rejects is deprived of his horse. It also examines the infantry who serve among the cavalry,[1] 2 and any one whom it rejects ceases to receive his pay. The roll of the cavalry is drawn up by the Commissioners of Enrolment [Catalŏgeis], ten in number, elected by the Assembly by open vote. They hand over to the Hipparchs and Phylarchs the list of those whom they have enrolled, and these officers take it and bring it up before the Council, and there open the sealed tablet containing the names of the cavalry.[2] If any of those who have been on the roll previously make affidavit that they are physically incapable of cavalry service, they strike them out; then they call up the persons newly enrolled, and if any one makes affidavit that he is either physically or pecuniarily incapable of cavalry service they dismiss him, but if no such affidavit is made the Council vote whether the individual in question is suitable for the purpose or not. If they vote in the affirmative his name is entered on the tablet; if not, he is dismissed with the others.

3 Formerly the Council used to decide on the plans for public buildings and the contract for making the robe of Athena ;[3] but now this work is done by a jury in the law-

---

[1] This means infantry who fought among the ranks of the cavalry. The πρόδρομοι above are also a military body, meaning light cavalry who acted as advance guard or skirmishers. There was a special corps so named in the army of Alexander.

[2] i. e. the names of those already in the cavalry, before the new enrolment.

[3] This was the robe which was carried in procession at the great Panathenaic festival. It was embroidered with mythological subjects, and was woven on each occasion by a number of girls, under the superintendence of two of superior family.

courts appointed by lot, since the Council was considered to have shown favouritism in its decisions. The Council also shares with the Military Treasurer the superintendence of the manufacture of the images of Victory and the prizes at the Panathenaic festival.

The Council also examines infirm paupers; for there is a 4 law which provides that persons possessing less than three minas, who are so crippled as to be unable to do any work, are, after examination by the Council, to receive two obols a day from the state for their support. A treasurer is appointed by lot to attend to them.

The Council also, speaking broadly, co-operates in most 5 of the duties of all the other magistrates; and this ends the list of the functions of that body.

There are ten Commissioners for Repairs of Temples, 50 elected by lot, who receive a sum of thirty minas from the Receivers-General, and therewith carry out the most necessary repairs in the temples.

There are also ten City Commissioners [Astynŏmi], of 2 whom five hold office in Piraeus and five in the city. Their duty is to see that female flute- and harp- and lute-players are not hired at more than two drachmas, and if more than one person is anxious to hire the same girl, they cast lots and hire her out to the person to whom the lot falls. They also provide that no collector of sewage shall shoot any of his sewage within ten stadia of the walls; they prevent people from blocking up the streets by building, or stretching barriers across them, or making drain-pipes in mid-air with a discharge into the street, or having doors[1] which open outwards; they also remove the corpses of those who die in the streets, for which purpose they have a body of state slaves assigned to them.

Market Commissioners [Agoranŏmi] are elected by lot. 51 five for Piraeus, five for the city. Their statutory duty is to see that all articles offered for sale in the market are pure and unadulterated.

Commissioners of Weights and Measures [Metronŏmi] 2

---

[1] Or possibly 'windows'.

are elected by lot, five for the city, and five for Piraeus. They see that sellers use fair weights and measures.

3   Formerly there were ten Corn Commissioners [Sitophy-lăces], elected by lot, five for Piraeus, and five for the city ; but now there are twenty for the city and fifteen for Piraeus. Their duties are, first, to see that the unprepared corn in the market is offered for sale at reasonable prices, and secondly, to see that the millers sell barley meal at a price proportionate to that of barley, and that the bakers sell their loaves at a price proportionate to that of wheat, and of such weight as the Commissioners may appoint ; for the law requires them to fix the standard weight.

4   There are ten Superintendents of the Mart, elected by lot, whose duty is to superintend the Mart, and to compel merchants to bring up into the city two-thirds of the corn which is brought by sea to the Corn Mart.

52   The Eleven also are appointed by lot to take care of the prisoners in the state gaol. Thieves, kidnappers, and pick-pockets are brought to them, and if they plead guilty they are executed, but if they deny the charge the Eleven bring the case before the law-courts ; if the prisoners are acquitted, they release them, but if not, they then execute them. They also bring up before the law-courts the list of farms and houses claimed as state-property ; and if it is decided that they are so, they deliver them to the Commissioners for Public Contracts. The Eleven also bring up informations laid against magistrates alleged to be disqualified ; this function comes within their province, but some such cases are brought up by the Thesmothetae.

2   There are also five Introducers of Cases [Eisagōgeis], elected by lot, one for each pair of tribes, who bring up the ' monthly ' cases [1] to the law-courts. ' Monthly ' cases are these : refusal to pay up a dowry where a party is bound to do so, refusal to pay interest on money borrowed at 12 per cent.[2],

---

[1] i. e. cases which have to be decided within a month, as being considered to be of a pressing nature.
[2] If the rate of interest was higher, the creditor could not make use of this procedure.

or where a man desirous of setting up business in the market has borrowed from another man capital to start with; also cases of slander, cases arising out of friendly loans or partnerships, and cases concerned with slaves, cattle, and the office of trierarch, or with banks. These are brought 3 up as 'monthly' cases and are introduced by these officers; but the Receivers-General perform the same function in cases for or against the farmers of taxes. Those in which the sum concerned is not more than ten drachmas they can decide summarily, but all above that amount they bring into the law-courts as 'monthly' cases.

The Forty [1] are also elected by lot, four from each 53 tribe, before whom suitors bring all other cases. Formerly they were thirty in number, and they went on circuit through the demes to hear causes; but after the oligarchy of the Thirty they were increased to forty. They have full 2 powers to decide cases in which the amount at issue does not exceed ten drachmas, but anything beyond that value they hand over to the Arbitrators. The Arbitrators take up the case, and, if they cannot bring the parties to an agreement, they give a decision. If their decision satisfies both parties, and they abide by it, the case is at an end; but if either of the parties appeals to the law-courts, the Arbitrators enclose the evidence, the pleadings, and the laws quoted in the case in two urns, those of the plaintiff in the one, and those of the defendant in the other. These they 3 seal up and, having attached to them the decision of the arbitrator, written out on a tablet, place them in the custody of the four justices whose function it is to introduce cases on behalf of the tribe of the defendant. These officers take them and bring up the case before the law-court, to a jury of two hundred and one members in cases up to the value of a thousand drachmas, or to one of four hundred and one in cases above that value. No laws or pleadings or evidence may be used except those which were adduced

---

[1] These are the officials elsewhere described as the local justices, who were instituted by Pisistratus (ch. 16, 5) and revived in 453 B.C. (ch. 26, 3).

before the Arbitrator, and have been enclosed in the urns.

4 The Arbitrators are persons in the sixtieth year of their age ; this appears from the schedule of the Archons and the Eponymi. There are two classes of Eponymi, the ten who give their names to the tribes, and the forty-two of the years of service.[1] The youths, on being enrolled among the citizens, were formerly registered upon whitened tablets, and the names were appended of the Archon in whose year they were enrolled, and of the Eponymus who had been in course in the preceding year ; at the present day they are written on a bronze pillar, which stands in front of the Council-chamber, near the Eponymi of the tribes. Then the Forty take the

5 last of the Eponymi of the years of service, and assign the arbitrations to the persons belonging to that year, casting lots to determine which arbitrations each shall undertake ; and every one is compelled to carry through the arbitrations which the lot assigns to him. The law enacts that any one who does not serve as Arbitrator when he has arrived at the necessary age shall lose his civil rights, unless he happens to be holding some other office during that year, or to be out of the country. These are the only persons who escape

6 the duty. Any one who suffers injustice at the hands of the Arbitrator may appeal to the whole board of Arbitrators, and if they find the magistrate guilty, the law enacts that he shall lose his civil rights. The persons thus condemned

7 have, however, in their turn an appeal. The Eponymi are also used in reference to military expeditions ; when the men of military age are despatched on service, a notice is put up stating that the men from such-and-such an Archon and

---

[1] These Eponymi are unknown except from this passage and quotations from it in the grammarians. It would appear that, just as the Eponymi of the tribes were the ten heroes who gave their names to the ten tribes, so a cycle of forty-two years was arranged, to each of which the name of a hero was assigned as its Eponymus. Then, as every Athenian was liable to military service for forty-two years (18 to 59 inclusive), each man had to go through the complete cycle before he was free from liability to serve. During the last year of his cycle, however, he was required to serve not as a soldier but as an Arbitrator ; and accordingly each year the Forty took the list of those who were commencing their last year of service, and assigned to them the duties which they were to undertake as arbitrators during the year.

Eponymus to such-and-such another Archon and Eponymus are to go on the expedition.

The following magistrates also are elected by lot: Five 54 Commissioners of Roads [Hodopoei], who, with an assigned body of public slaves, are required to keep the roads in order: and ten Auditors, with ten assistants, to whom all 2 persons who have held any office must give in their accounts. These are the only officers who audit the accounts of those who are subject to examination,[1] and who bring them up for examination before the law-courts. If they detect any magistrate in embezzlement, the jury condemn him for theft, and he is obliged to repay tenfold the sum he is declared to have misappropriated. If they charge a magistrate with accepting bribes and the jury convict him, they fine him for corruption, and this sum too is repaid tenfold. Or if they convict him of unfair dealing, he is fined on that charge, and the sum assessed is paid without increase, if payment is made before the ninth prytany, but otherwise it is doubled. A tenfold fine is not doubled.

The Clerk of the Prytany, as he is called, is also elected by 3 lot. He has the charge of all public documents, and keeps the resolutions which are passed by the Assembly, and checks the transcripts of all other official papers and attends at the sessions of the Council. Formerly he was elected by open vote, and the most distinguished and trustworthy persons were elected to the post, as is known from the fact that the name of this officer is appended on the pillars recording treaties of alliance and grants of consulship[2] and citizenship. Now, however, he is elected by lot. There is, in addition, 4 a Clerk of the Laws, elected by lot, who attends at the sessions of the Council; and he too checks the transcript of all the laws. The Assembly also elects by open vote 5 a clerk to read documents to it and to the Council; but he has no other duty except that of reading aloud.

---

[1] Every person who had held any public office had to submit himself and his accounts to examination before a jury at the end of his term of office; on which occasion any citizen might impeach his conduct during his office.

[2] i. e. of representation of a foreign state.

6   The Assembly also elects by lot the Commissioners of Public Worship [Hieropoei], known as the Commissioners for Sacrifices, who offer the sacrifices appointed by oracle, and, in conjunction with the seers, take the auspices whenever 7 there is occasion.   It also elects by lot ten others, known as Annual Commissioners, who offer certain sacrifices and administer all the quadrennial festivals except the Panathenaea.   There are the following quadrennial festivals: first that of Delos (where there is also a sexennial festival), secondly the Brauronia, thirdly the Heracleia, fourthly the Eleusinia, and fifthly the Panathenaea; and no two of these are celebrated in the same place.[1] To these the Hephaestia has now been added, in the archonship of Cephisophon.[2]

8   An Archon is also elected by lot for Salamis, and a Demarch for Piraeus.   These officers celebrate the Dionysia in these two places, and appoint Chorēgi.   In Salamis, moreover, the name of the Archon is publicly recorded.

55   All the foregoing magistrates are elected by lot, and their powers are those which have been stated.   To pass on to the nine Archons, as they are called, the manner of their appointment from the earliest times has been described already.   At the present day six Thesmothetae are elected by lot, together with their clerk, and in addition to these an Archon, a King, and a Polemarch.   One is elected from 2 each tribe.   They are examined first of all by the Council of Five Hundred, with the exception of the clerk.   The latter is examined only in the law-court, like other magistrates (for all magistrates, whether elected by lot or by open vote, are examined before entering on their offices); but the nine Archons are examined both in the Council and again in the law-court.   Formerly no one could hold the office if the Council rejected him, but now there is an appeal to the law-court, which is the final authority in the 3 matter of the examination.   When they are examined, they

---

[1] The reading is rather doubtful, and the meaning might be 'no two of them take place in the same year'; but with five festivals in four years, two of them must have fallen in the same year.

[2] This date (329 B. C.) gives us a limit of time after which this work must have been written, or (since the words have the air of a parenthetical or later addition) at least revised. See note 5 on ch. 46, 1.

are asked, first, 'Who is your father, and of what deme? who is your father's father? who is your mother? who is your mother's father, and of what deme?' Then the candidate is asked whether he possesses an ancestral Apollo and a household Zeus, and where their sanctuaries are; next if he possesses a family tomb, and where; then if he treats his parents well, and pays his taxes, and has served on the required military expeditions. When the examiner has put these questions, he proceeds, 'Call the witnesses to these facts'; and when the candidate has produced his witnesses, 4 he next asks, 'Does any one wish to make any accusation against this man?' If an accuser appears, he gives the parties an opportunity of making their accusation and defence, and then puts it to the Council to pass the candidate or not, and to the law-court to give the final vote. If no one wishes to make an accusation, he proceeds at once to the vote. Formerly a single individual gave the vote, but now all the members are obliged to vote on the candidates, so that if any unprincipled candidate has managed to get rid of his accusers,[1] it may still be possible for him to be disqualified before the law-court. When the examination 5 has been thus completed, they proceed to the stone on which are the pieces of the victims, and on which the Arbitrators take oath before declaring their decisions, and witnesses swear to their testimony. On this stone the Archons stand, and swear to execute their office uprightly and according to the laws, and not to receive presents in respect of the performance of their duties, or, if they do, to dedicate a golden statue. When they have taken this oath they proceed to the Acropolis, and there they repeat it; after this they enter upon their office.

The Archon, the King, and the Polemarch have each two **56** assessors, nominated by themselves. These officers are

---

[1] i.e. by inducing them not to press their charges. It appears that originally, if no accusation was brought before the Council, the examination by the law-court was a mere formality, a single member voting for the whole jury. But it was found that candidates sometimes escaped an accusation before the Council by 'squaring' their accusers; and to meet this the law-court was made to examine and vote independently.

examined in the law-court before they begin to act, and give in accounts on each occasion of their acting.

2 As soon as the Archon enters office, he begins by issuing a proclamation that whatever any one possessed before he entered into office, that he shall possess and hold until the 3 end of his term. Next he assigns Chorēgi to the tragic poets, choosing three[1] of the richest persons out of the whole body of Athenians. Formerly he used also to assign five Choregi to the comic poets, but now the tribes provide the Choregi for them. Then he receives the Choregi who have been appointed by the tribes for the men's and boys' choruses[2] and the comic poets at the Dionysia, and for the men's and boys' choruses at the Thargelia (at the Dionysia there is a chorus for each tribe, but at the Thargelia one between two tribes, each tribe bearing its share in providing it); he transacts the exchanges of properties for them,[3] and reports any excuses that are tendered, if any one says that he has already borne this burden, or that he is exempt because he has borne a similar burden and the period of his exemption has not yet expired, or that he is not of the required age; since the Choregus of a boys 4 chorus must be over forty years of age. He also appoints Choregi for the festival at Delos, and a chief of the mission[4] for the thirty-oar boat which conveys the youths thither. He also superintends sacred processions, both that in honour of Asclepius, when the initiated keep house, and that of the

---

[1] Only three tragic poets might contend at the festivals, and it was the duty of the Archon to decide what poets should be admitted to the honour. In Comedy, as stated below, five competitors were allowed, but this number applies only to the fourth century, before which time the number was limited to three. The duty of the Choregus was to defray the expense of training, maintaining, and equipping the chorus required for a play or a dithyrambic contest.

[2] These are dithyrambic choruses, which were quite unconnected with the dramatic representations, and in which the several tribes competed against one another.

[3] If any person considered that he had been unduly saddled with one of the burdens which rich men were called upon to bear for the state (such as the equipment of a chorus or a trireme), he might require any one on whom he thought the burden should rather have been laid either to undertake it, or else to submit to an exchange of properties.

[4] i.e. chiefs of the sacred deputation sent from Athens to the Delian festival. It is uncertain whether there was more than one such chief, and some editors read ἀρχιθεώ[ρους].

great Dionysia—-the latter in conjunction with the Superintendents of that festival. These officers, ten in number, were formerly elected by open vote in the Assembly, and used to provide for the expenses of the procession out of their private means; but now one is elected by lot from each tribe, and the state contributes a hundred minas for the expenses. The Archon also superintends the procession 5 at the Thargelia, and that in honour of Zeus the Saviour. He also manages the contests at the Dionysia and the Thargelia.

These, then, are the festivals which he superintends. The suits and indictments which come before him, and 6 which he, after a preliminary inquiry, brings up before the law-courts, are as follows. Injury to parents (for bringing these actions the prosecutor cannot suffer any penalty);[1] injury to orphans (these actions lie against their guardians); injury to a ward of state (these lie against their guardians or their husbands);[2] injury to an orphan's estate (these too lie against the guardians); mental derangement, where a party charges another with destroying his own property through unsoundness of mind; for appointment of liquidators, where a party refuses to divide property in which others have a share; for constituting a wardship; for determining between rival claims to a wardship; for granting inspection of property to which another party lays claim; for appointing oneself as guardian; and for determining disputes as to inheritances and wards of state. The 7 Archon also has the care of orphans and wards of state, and of women who, on the death of their husbands, declare themselves to be with child; and he has power to inflict a fine on those who offend against the persons under his charge, or to bring the case before the law-courts. He also leases the houses of orphans and wards of state until they reach the age of fourteen, and takes mortgages on them; and if the guardians fail to provide the necessary food for

[1] In most cases the prosecutor was subject to penalties if he failed to receive a fifth part of the votes of the jury.
[2] The state still continued its protection of heiresses even after they were married. It scare only ceased when they had children capable of inheriting the property.

the children under their charge, he exacts it from them. Such are the duties of the Archon.

57   The King in the first place superintends the mysteries, in conjunction with the Superintendents of Mysteries. The latter are elected in the Assembly by open vote, two from the general body of Athenians, one from the Eumolpidae, and one from the Cerӯces. Next, he superintends the Lenaean Dionysia,[1] which consists of a procession and a contest. The procession is ordered by the King and the Superintendents in conjunction ; but the contest is managed by the King alone. He also manages all the contests of the torch-race ; and to speak broadly, he administers all the
2 ancestral sacrifices. Indictments for impiety come before him, or any disputes between parties concerning priestly rites ; and he also determines all controversies concerning sacred rites for the ancient families [2] and the priests. All actions for homicide come before him, and it is he that makes the proclamation requiring polluted persons to keep away from
3 sacred ceremonies. Actions for homicide and wounding are heard, if the homicide or wounding be wilful, in the Areopagus ; so also in cases of killing by poison, and of arson. These are the only cases heard by that Council. Cases of unintentional homicide, or of intent to kill, or of killing a slave or a resident alien or a foreigner, are heard by the court of Palladium. When the homicide is acknowledged, but legal justification is pleaded, as when a man takes an adulterer in the act, or kills another by mistake in battle, or in an athletic contest, the prisoner is tried in the court of Delphinium. If a man who is in banishment for a homicide which admits of reconciliation [3] incurs a further charge of killing or wounding, he is tried in Phreatto, and he makes

[1] The lesser of the two chief festivals of Dionysus, held in January. Many of the plays which have come down to us were first performed at this festival, but it was not such a magnificent occasion as the great Dionysia, at which strangers from the rest of Greece were usually present in great numbers.

[2] See note 2 on ch. 20, 2.

[3] A person who committed an involuntary homicide had to give pecuniary satisfaction to the relatives of the deceased, and he was compelled to go into exile for a year unless they gave him leave to return earlier.

his defence from a boat moored near the shore. All these 4 cases, except those which are heard in the Areopagus, are tried by the Ephetae on whom the lot falls.[1] The King introduces them, and the hearing is held within sacred precincts and in the open air. Whenever the King hears a case he takes off his crown. The person who is charged with homicide is at all other times excluded from the temples, nor is it even lawful for him to enter the market-place; but on the occasion of his trial he enters the temple and makes his defence. If the actual offender is unknown, the writ runs against 'the doer of the deed'. The King and the tribe-kings also hear the cases in which the guilt rests on inanimate objects and the lower animals.[2]

The Polemarch performs the sacrifices to Artemis the 58 huntress and to Enyalius, and arranges the contest at the funeral of those who have fallen in war, and makes offerings to the memory of Harmodius and Aristogeiton. Only private actions come before him, namely those in which 2 resident aliens, both ordinary and privileged, and agents of foreign states are concerned. It is his duty to receive these cases and divide them into ten groups, and assign to each tribe the group which comes to it by lot; after which the magistrates who introduce cases for the tribe hand them over to the Arbitrators. The Polemarch, however, brings 3 up in person cases in which an alien is charged with deserting his patron or neglecting to provide himself with one,[3] and also of inheritances and wards of state where aliens are concerned; and in fact, generally, whatever the Archon does for citizens, the Polemarch does for aliens.

The Thesmothetae in the first place have the power of 59

[1] The Ephetae were a very ancient board of magistrates who used to hear these kinds of cases, but whether they are spoken of here is doubtful, as the word in the MS. is lost in a lacuna. It is, however, supplied from passages in Harpocration and other grammarians.
[2] This is a relic of a very primitive custom, by which any object that had caused a man's death was put upon its trial. In later times it may have served the purpose of a coroner's inquest. Cases of this kind, and those in which the culprit was unknown, were tried in the court of the Prytaneum, and it is probable that the name occurred in the treatise, but has dropped out of the MS.
[3] Every alien resident in Athens was required to provide himself with a patron from among the citizens.

prescribing on what days the law-courts are to sit, and next of assigning them to the several magistrates; for the latter must follow the arrangement which the Thesmothetae assign.
2 Moreover they introduce impeachments before the Assembly, and bring up all votes for removal from office, challenges of a magistrate's conduct before the Assembly, indictments for illegal proposals, or for proposing a law which is contrary to the interests of the state, complaints against Proedri or their president for their conduct in office, and the accounts
3 presented by the generals. All indictments also come before them in which a deposit has to be made by the prosecutor, namely, indictments for concealment of foreign origin, for corrupt evasion of foreign origin (when a man escapes the disqualification by bribery), for blackmailing accusations, bribery, false entry of another as a state debtor, false testimony to the service of a summons, conspiracy to enter a man as a state debtor, corrupt removal from the list
4 of debtors, and adultery. They also bring up the examinations of all magistrates,[1] and the rejections by the demes
5 and the condemnations by the Council. Moreover they bring up certain private suits in cases of merchandise and mines, or where a slave has slandered a free man. It is they also who cast lots to assign the courts to the various magis-
6 trates, whether for private or public cases. They ratify commercial treaties, and bring up the cases which arise out of such treaties; and they also bring up cases of perjury
7 from the Areopagus. The casting of lots for the jurors is conducted by all the nine Archons, with the clerk to the Thesmothetae as the tenth, each performing the duty for his own tribe. Such are the duties of the nine Archons.

60   There are also ten Commissioners of Games[Athlothĕtae], elected by lot, one from each tribe. These officers, after passing an examination, serve for four years; and they manage the Panathenaic procession, the contest in music and that in gymnastic, and the horse-race; they also provide the robe of Athena[2] and, in conjunction with the Council,

---

[1] i. e. the examination to which all magistrates were subjected before entering office. See ch. 55, 2.
[2] See note 3 on ch. 49, 3.

the vases,[1] and they present the oil to the athletes. This oil is collected from the sacred olives. The Archon 2 requisitions it from the owners of the farms on which the sacred olives grow, at the rate of three-quarters of a pint from each plant. Formerly the state used to sell the fruit itself, and if any one dug up or broke down one of the sacred olives, he was tried by the Council of Areopagus, and if he was condemned, the penalty was death. Since, however, the oil has been paid by the owner of the farm, the procedure has lapsed, though the law remains; and the oil is a state charge upon the property instead of being taken from the individual plants.[2] When, then, the Archon has 3 collected the oil for his year of office, he hands it over to the Treasurers to preserve in the Acropolis, and he may not take his seat in the Areopagus until he has paid over to the Treasurers the full amount. The Treasurers keep it in the Acropolis until the Panathenaea, when they measure it out to the Commissioners of Games, and they again to the victorious competitors. The prizes for the victors in the musical contest consist of silver and gold, for the victors in manly vigour, of shields, and for the victors in the gymnastic contest and the horse-race, of oil.

All officers connected with military service are elected by 61 open vote. In the first place, ten Generals [Strategi], who were formerly elected one from each tribe, but now are chosen from the whole mass of citizens. Their duties are assigned to them by open vote; one is appointed to command the heavy infantry, and leads them if they go out to war; one to the defence of the country, who remains on the defensive, and fights if there is war within the borders of the country; two to Piraeus, one of whom is assigned to Munichia, and one to the south shore, and these have charge of the defence of the Piraeus; and one to superintend the

---

[1] The vases given as prizes at the Panathenaea, of which a considerable number still exist.

[2] The meaning is that the oil is now a fixed charge on the estate, so that the owner would be liable for the amount, whatever happened to the plants.

symmories,[1] who nominates the trierarchs[2] and arranges exchanges of properties[3] for them, and brings up actions to decide on rival claims in connexion with them. The rest are dispatched to whatever business may be on hand at the moment. The appointment of these officers is submitted for confirmation in each prytany, when the question is put whether they are considered to be doing their duty. If any officer is rejected on this vote, he is tried in the law-court, and if he is found guilty the people decide what punishment or fine shall be inflicted on him ; but if he is acquitted he resumes his office. The Generals have full power, when on active service, to arrest any one for insubordination, or to cashier him publicly, or to inflict a fine ; the latter is, however, unusual.

There are also ten Taxiarchs, one from each tribe, elected by open vote; and each commands his own tribesmen and appoints captains of companies [Lochāgi]. There are also two Hipparchs, elected by open vote from the whole mass of the citizens, who command the cavalry, each taking five tribes. They have the same powers as the Generals have in respect of the infantry, and their appointments are also subject to confirmation. There are also ten Phylarchs, elected by open vote, one from each tribe, to command the cavalry, as the Taxiarchs do the infantry. There is also a Hipparch for Lemnos, elected by open vote, who has charge of the cavalry in Lemnos. There is also a treasurer of the Paralus, and another of the Ammonias, similarly elected.[4]

62 Of the magistrates elected by lot, in former times some

---

[1] The companies into which the richer members of the community were formed (first in 377 B.C.) for the payment of the extraordinary charges in war-time.
[2] The trierarchs were the persons (chosen from the richest men in the community) who were required to undertake the equipment of a trireme at their own expense. Like the office of Choregus (ch. 56, 3, 4) it was a public duty performed by private individuals.
[3] See note 3 on ch. 56, 3.
[4] These are the two triremes, usually known as 'sacred', which were used for special state services. According to the grammarians the two originally so employed were the Paralus and Salaminia ; e. g. it was the latter that was sent to fetch Alcibiades back from Sicily to stand his trial. The Ammonias appears to have taken the place of the Salaminia in the time of Alexander, when the Athenians sent sacrifices to the god Ammon in it.

including the nine Archons, were elected out of the tribe as a whole, while others, namely those who are now elected in the Theseum, were apportioned among the demes; but since the demes used to sell the elections, these magistrates too are now elected from the whole tribe, except the members of the Council and the guards of the dockyards, who are still left to the demes.

Pay is received for the following services. First the 2 members of the Assembly receive a drachma for the ordinary meetings, and nine obols for the 'sovereign' meeting. Then the jurors at the law-courts receive three obols; and the members of the Council five obols. The Prytanes receive an allowance of an obol for their maintenance. The nine Archons receive four obols apiece for maintenance, and also keep a herald and a flute-player; and the Archon for Salamis receives a drachma a day. The Commissioners for Games dine in the Prytaneum during the month of Hecatombaeon in which the Panathenaic festival takes place, from the fourteenth day onwards. The Amphictyonic deputies to Delos receive a drachma a day from the exchequer of Delos. Also all magistrates sent to Samos, Scyros, Lemnos, or Imbros receive an allowance for their maintenance. The military offices may be held any number of times, but 3 none of the others more than once, except the membership of the Council, which may be held twice.

The juries for the law-courts are chosen by lot by the nine 63 Archons, each for their own tribe, and by the clerk to the Thesmothetae for the tenth. There are ten entrances into 2 the courts, one for each tribe; twenty rooms in which the lots are drawn, two for each tribe; a hundred chests, ten for each tribe; other chests, in which are placed the tickets of the jurors on whom the lot falls; and two vases. Further, staves, equal in number to the jurors required, are placed by the side of each entrance; and counters are put into one vase, equal in number to the staves. These are inscribed with letters of the alphabet beginning with the eleventh (*lambda*), equal in number to the courts which require to be filled. All persons above thirty years of age are qualified to 3

F

serve as jurors, provided they are not debtors to the state and have not lost their civil rights. If any unqualified person serves as juror, an information is laid against him, and he is brought before the court; and, if he is convicted, the jurors assess the punishment or fine which they consider him to deserve. If he is condemned to a money fine, he must be imprisoned until he has paid up both the original debt, on account of which the information was laid against him, and also the fine which the court has imposed upon him. 4 Each juror has his ticket of box-wood, on which is inscribed his name, with the name of his father and his deme, and one of the letters of the alphabet up to *kappa*;[1] for the jurors in their several tribes are divided into ten sections, with approximately an equal number in each letter. When the Thesmothetes has decided by lot which letters are required to attend at the courts, the servant puts up above each court the letter which has been assigned to it by the lot.

64 The ten chests above mentioned are placed in front of the entrance used by each tribe, and are inscribed with the letters of the alphabet from *alpha* to *kappa*. The jurors cast in their tickets, each into the chest on which is inscribed the letter which is on his ticket; then the servant shakes them all up, and the Archon draws one 2 ticket from each chest. The individual so selected is called the Ticket-hanger [Empēctes], and his function is to hang up the tickets out of his chest on the bar which bears the same letter as that on the chest. He is chosen by lot, lest, if the Ticket-hanger were always the same person, he might tamper with the results. There are five of these bars in each of the 3 rooms assigned for the lot-drawing. Then the Archon casts in the dice and thereby chooses the jurors from each tribe, room by room. The dice are made of brass, coloured black or white; and according to the number of jurors required, so many white dice are put in, one for each five tickets, while

---

[1] The tenth letter of the alphabet. Thus the whole body of jurors was divided into ten sections, indicated by the letters from *alpha* to *kappa*; and the courts for which jurors were required were indicated by the requisite number of letters from *lambda* onwards.

the remainder are black, in the same proportion.[1] As the
Archon draws out the dice, the crier calls out the names
of the individuals chosen. The Ticket-hanger is included
among those selected. Each juror, as he is chosen and [4]
answers to his name, draws a counter from the vase, and
holding it out with the letter uppermost shows it first to the
presiding Archon ; and he, when he has seen it, throws the
ticket of the juror into the chest on which is inscribed the
letter which is on the counter, so that the juror must go into
the court assigned to him by lot, and not into one chosen by
himself, and that it may be impossible for any one to collect
the jurors of his choice into any particular court. For this [5]
purpose chests are placed near the Archon, as many in
number as there are courts to be filled that day, bearing the
letters of the courts on which the lot has fallen.

The juror thereupon, after showing his counter again to [65]
the attendant, passes through the barrier into the court.
The attendant gives him a staff of the same colour as the
court bearing the letter which is on his counter, so as to
ensure his going into the court assigned to him by lot ;
since, if he were to go into any other, he would be betrayed
by the colour of his staff. Each court has a certain colour [2]
painted on the lintel of the entrance. Accordingly the
juror, bearing his staff, enters the court which has the same
colour as his staff, and the same letter as his counter. As
he enters, he receives a voucher from the official to whom
this duty has been assigned by lot. So with their counters [3]
and their staves the selected jurors take their seats in the
court, having thus completed the process of admission. The
unsuccessful candidates receive back their tickets from the
Ticket-hangers. The public servants carry the chests from [4]
each tribe, one to each court, containing the names of the
members of the tribe who are in that court, and hand them

---

[1] Thus the process of selection is as follows. The Ticket-hanger
arranges all the tickets on a bar, which establishes their order. Then
the Archon draws a die ; if it is white, the owners of the first five
tickets on the bar serve on the jury, while if it is black they are
rejected ; and so on through the whole number. The selected jurors
are then assigned to the several courts in accordance with the lots
drawn from the vases.

over to the officials[1] assigned to the duty of giving back their tickets to the jurors in each court, so that these officials may call them up by name and pay them their fee.

66 When all the courts are full, two ballot boxes are placed in the first court, and a number of brazen dice, bearing the colours of the several courts, and other dice inscribed with the names of the presiding magistrates. Then two of the Thesmothetae, selected by lot, severally throw the dice with the colours into one box, and those with the magistrates' names into the other. The magistrate whose name is first drawn is thereupon proclaimed by the crier as assigned for duty in the court which is first drawn, and the second in the second, and similarly with the rest. The object of this procedure is that no one may know which court he will have, but that each may take the court assigned to him by lot.

2 When the jurors have come in, and have been assigned to their respective courts, the presiding magistrate in each court draws one ticket out of each chest (making ten in all, one out of each tribe), and throws them into another empty chest. He then draws out five of them, and assigns one to the superintendence of the water-clock, and the other four to the telling of the votes. This is to prevent any tampering beforehand with either the superintendent of the clock or the tellers of the votes, and to secure that there is 3 no malpractice in these respects. The five who have not been selected for these duties receive from them a statement of the order in which the jurors shall receive their fees, and of the places where the several tribes shall respectively gather in the court for this purpose when their duties are completed ; the object being that the jurors may be broken up into small groups for the reception of their pay, and not all crowd together and impede one another.

67 These preliminaries being concluded, the cases are called on. If it is a day for private cases, the private litigants are called. Four cases are taken in each of the categories

[1] The correct reading is perhaps 'the five officials'.

defined in the law, and the litigants swear to confine their speeches to the point at issue. If it is a day for public causes, the public litigants are called, and only one case is tried. Water-clocks are provided, having small supply-tubes,[1] into which the water is poured by which the length of the pleadings is regulated. Ten gallons[2] are allowed for a case in which an amount of more than five thousand drachmas is involved, and three for the second speech on each side. When the amount is between one and five thousand drachmas, seven gallons are allowed for the first speech and two for the second ; when it is less than one thousand, five and two. Six gallons are allowed for arbitrations between rival claimants, in which there is no second speech. The official chosen by lot to superintend the water-clock places his hand on the supply-tube whenever the clerk is about to read a resolution or law or affidavit or treaty. When, however, a case is conducted according to a set measurement of the day, he does not stop the supply, but each party receives an equal allowance of water.[3] The standard of measurement is the length of the days in the month Poseideon[4] . . . . The measured day is employed in cases when imprisonment, death, exile, loss of civil rights, or confiscation of goods is assigned as the penalty.

Most of the courts consist of 500 members . . . ; and **68** when it is necessary to bring public cases before a jury of 1,000 members, two courts combine for the purpose, [while the most important cases of all are brought before] 1,500 jurors, or three courts. The ballot balls are made of brass

---

[1] Or, reading αὐλοὺς τε ἔχουσαι καὶ ἔκρους, with Sandys, 'having supply-tubes and outlets'; but it is difficult to say that water is poured into an outlet. The water is poured in through the supply-tube, and trickles out through an opening at the bottom. When the aperture at the top is closed, the water ceases to run out.

[2] The χοῦς is really equivalent to about three-quarters of a gallon.

[3] In ordinary suits, fixed allowances of water (i. e. of time as measured by the water-clock) were given for each speech, and the time occupied in the reading of affidavits, &c., was not included in the allowances, so that the water-clock was stopped while they were read. In more important cases a certain portion of the day was allotted to either side, without allowance for the time occupied by reading documents.

[4] i. e. December to January, when the days are shortest. A mutilated passage follows.

with stems running through the centre, half of them having the stem pierced and the other half solid. When the speeches are concluded, the officials assigned to the taking of the votes give each juror two ballot balls, one pierced and one solid. This is done in full view of the rival litigants, to secure that no one shall receive two pierced or two solid balls. Then the official designated for the purpose takes away the jurors' staves, in return for which each one as he records his vote receives a brass voucher marked with the numeral 3 (because he gets three obols when he gives it up). This is to ensure that all shall vote; since no one can get a voucher

3 unless he votes. Two urns, one of brass and the other of wood, stand in the court, in distinct spots so that no one may surreptitiously insert ballot balls; in these the jurors record their votes. The brazen urn is for effective votes,[1] the wooden for unused votes; and the brazen urn has a lid pierced so as to take only one ballot ball, in order that no one may put in two at a time.

4 When the jurors are about to vote, the crier demands first whether the litigants enter a protest against any of the evidence; for no protest can be received after the voting has begun. Then he proclaims again, 'The pierced ballot for the plaintiff, the solid for the defendant'; and the juror, taking his two ballot balls from the stand, with his hand closed over the stem so as not to show either the pierced or the solid ballot to the litigants, casts the one which is to count into the brazen urn, and the other into the wooden urn.

69 When all the jurors have voted, the attendants take the urn containing the effective votes and discharge them on to a reckoning board having as many cavities as there are ballot balls, so that the effective votes, whether pierced or solid, may be plainly displayed and easily counted. Then the officials assigned to the taking of the votes tell them off on the board, the solid in one place and the pierced in another, and the crier announces the numbers of the

---

[1] i. e. those which record the juror's actual vote. Each juror receives two ballots, and uses one (pierced or solid according as he votes for the plaintiff or the defendant) to record his vote, and throws the other away.

votes, the pierced ballots being for the prosecutor and the solid for the defendant. Whichever has the majority is victorious; but if the votes are equal the verdict is for the defendant. Then, if damages have to be awarded, they vote again in the same way, first returning their pay-vouchers and receiving back their staves. Half a gallon of water is allowed to each party for the discussion of the damages. Finally, when all has been completed in accordance with the law, the jurors receive their pay in the order assigned by the lot.

INDEX

References are to chapters and sections.

Acastus, 3, 3.
Acherdus, deme of, 38, 3.
Acropolis, 7, 4; 8, 4; 14, 1; 15, 4; 18, 3; 19, 6; 20, 3; 37, 2; 55, 5; 60, 3.
Acté (south shore of Piraeus), 42, 3; 61, 1.
Aegospotami, battle of, 34, 2.
Agoranomi (Market Commissioners), 51, 1.
Agroeci, 13, 2.
Agyrrhius, 41, 3.
Alcmeonidae, 1; 19, 3; 20, 2, 4, 5; 28, 2.
Alexias, archon, 34, 2.
Aliens, jurisdiction of Polemarch over, 58, 3.
Alopece, deme of, 22, 5; 45, 1.
Ammonias, sacred trireme, 61, 7.
Amphictyonic deputies, 62, 2.
Anacreon, 18, 1.
Anaphlystus, deme of, 29, 1.
Anchimolus, 19, 5.
Angele, deme of, 34, 1.
Anthemion, 7, 4.
Antidotus, archon, 26, 4.
Antiphon, 32, 2.
Anytus, 27, 5; 34, 3.
Aphidna, deme of, 34, 3.
Apodectae (Receivers), 47, 5; 48, 1, 2; 50; 52, 3.
Arbitrators, 53, 2–6; 58, 2; oath of, 55, 5.
Archestratus, 35, 2.
Archinus of Ambracia, 17, 4.
Archinus, political leader, 34, 3; 40, 1, 2.
Archon, the, 3, 2–3, 5; 60, 2, 3; constitutional importance of, 13, 2; functions of, 56.
Archon, for Salamis, 54, 8; 62, 2.
Archons, the nine, 3; 4, 2; 7, 1, 3; 8, 1, 2; 29, 5; 30, 2; 47, 2; 63, 1; 64; 66, 1; election of, 22, 5; 26, 2; 55; examination of, 45, 3; oath of, 55, 5; pay of, 62, 2. See also King-Archon, Polemarch, Thesmothetae.

Archons, in Piraeus, 35, 1.
Archons, chronological sequence of, B.C.
621 Aristaichmus, 4, 1.
594 Solon, 5, 2.
582 (?) Damasias, 13, 2.
560 Comeas, 14, 1.
555 Hegesias, 14, 3.
528 Philoneos, 17, 1.
511 Harpactides, 19, 6.
508 Isagoras, 21, 1.
501 Hermocreon, 22, 2.
490 Phaenippus, 22, 3.
487 Telesinus, 22, 5.
483 Nicodemus, 22, 7.
481 Hypsichides, 22, 8.
478 Timosthenes, 23, 5.
462 Conon, 25, 2.
457 Mnesitheides, 26, 2.
453 Lysicrates 26, 3.
451 Antidotus, 26, 4.
432 Pythodorus 27, 2.
412 Callias 32, 1, 2.
[411 Mnasilochus, 33, 1.]
411 Theopompus, 33, 1.
406 Callias, 34, 1.
405 Alexias, 34, 2.
404 Pythodorus, 35, 1; 41, 1.
403 Eucleides, 39, 1.
401 Xenaenetus, 40, 4.
329 Cephisophon, 54, 7.
Archons, ten, 13, 2.
Areopagus, Council of, 3, 6; 4, 4; 8, 2, 4; 16, 8; 23, 1; 25, 1–4; 27, 1; 35, 2; 47, 2; 57, 3; 60, 2, 3.
Arginusae, battle of, 34, 1.
Argos, 17, 4; 19, 4.
Aristaichmus, archon, 4, 1.
Aristides, 22, 7; 23, 3–5; 24, 3; 28, 2; 41, 2.
Aristion, 14, 1.
Aristocrates, 33, 2.
Aristodicus, of Tanagra, 25, 4.
Aristogeiton, 18, 2–6; 58, 1.
Aristomachus, 32, 1.

INDEX

Draco, legislation of, 4 ; 7, 1 ; 41, 2.
Dracontides, 34, 3.

Eetioneia, fort of, 37, 1.
Eisagogeis (Introducers of Cases), 52, 2 ; 58, 2.
Elections by lot, 43, 1, 2 ; 44, 1 ; 47, 1, 2 ; 48, 1, 3, 4 ; 50 ; 51, 1-4 ; 52, 1, 2 ; 53, 1 ; 54, 1-4, 6-8 ; 55, 1 ; 56, 4 ; 60, 1 ; 62, 1.
— by vote, 43, 1 ; 44, 4 ; 46, 1 ; 49, 2 ; 54, 3, 5 ; 56, 4 ; 57, 1 ; 61, 1, 3-7.
Eleusinia, festival of, 54, 7.
Eleusis, 39, 1-4 ; 40, 4.
Eleven, the (Police Commissioners), 7, 3 ; 29, 4 ; 35, 1 ; 39, 5 ; 52, 1.
Empectes (Ticket-hanger), 64, 2, 3 ; 65, 3.
Enrolment, Commissioners of, 49, 2.
Enyalius, sacrifices to, 58, 1.
Ephebi, examination of, 42, 1, 2 ; 53, 4 ; training, 42, 2-5.
Ephetae, 57, 4.
Ephialtes, 25 ; 28, 2 ; laws of, 35, 2 ; 41, 2.
Epilyceum, 3, 5.
Epimenides, 1.
Eponymi (eponymous heroes), of tribes, 21, 5 ; 48, 4 ; 53, 4.
— of years of service, 53, 4-7.
Eretria, 15, 2 ; battle of, 33, 1.
Euboea, 33, 1.
Eucleides, archon, 39, 1.
Eumelides, 45, 1.
Eumolpidae, 39, 2 ; 57, 1.
Eupatridae, 13, 2.
Euthuni (Examiners of Accounts), 48, 4.
Examination of Magistrates, 45, 2, 3 ; 48, 4, 5 ; 55.
Examiner of Accounts, 48, 4.

Family deities, 55, 3.
Festivals, Commissioners for, 54, 7.
Festivals, quadriennial, 54, 7.
Five Thousand, Assembly of, 29, 5 ; 30, 1 ; 31, 2, 3 ; 32, 1, 3 ; 33, 1 ; 34, 1.
Forty, the. *See* Justices, Local.
Four Hundred, constitution of, 29-33.
Four Hundred, Council of, 8, 4 ; 21, 3 ; 31, 1 ; 32, 1, 3.
Franchise, citizen, 4, 1 ; 7, 3, 4 ; 21, 2 ; 26, 4 ; 42.

Games, Commissioners of, 60, 1, 3 ; 62, 2.
— prizes in, 60, 3.
Geraestus, 22, 8.
Gorgilus, 17, 4.

Harmodius, 18, 2-4.
-- and Aristogeiton, memorial offerings to, 58, 1.
Harpactides, archon, 19, 6.
Hectemori, 2, 2.
Hegesias, archon, 14, 3.
Hegesistratus (Thessalus), 17, 3.
Hellenotamiae, 30, 2.
Hephaestia, festival of, 54, 7.
Heracleia, festival of, 54, 7.
Heracleides, of Clazomenae, 41, 3.
Hermocreon, archon, 22, 2.
Hieromnemon, 30, 2.
Hieropoei (Commissioners of Public Worship), 30, 2 ; 54, 6.
Hipparchs, 4, 2 ; 30, 2 ; 31, 3 ; 49, 2 ; 61, 4 ; election of, 44, 4.
— for Lemnos, 61, 6.
Hipparchus, son of Charmus, 22, 4.
Hipparchus, son of Pisistratus, 17, 3-18.
Hippias, son of Pisistratus, 17, 3-19, 5.
Hodopoei (Commissioners of Roads), 54, 1.
Homicide, cases of, 57, 3, 4.
Horses, state examination of, 49, 1, 2.
Hypsichides, archon, 22, 8.

Imbros, magistrates for, 62, 2.
Introducers of Cases, 52, 2 ; 58, 2.
Ion, 3, 2 ; 41, 2.
Iophon, 17, 3.
Isagoras, son of Tisander, 20, 1-3 ; 21, 1 ; 28, 2.

Jurors, qualifications of, 63, 3.
Justices, local, 16, 5 ; 26, 3 ; 48, 5 ; 53.

King-Archon, 3, 2, 3, 5 ; 47, 4 ; 55, 1 ; 56, 1 ; functions of, 57.
Knights, 4, 3 ; 7, 3, 4 ; 24, 3 ; 26, 2 ; 38, 2.

Laciadae, deme of, 27, 3.
Law-courts, appeal to, 42, 1 ; 45, 1-3 ; 48, 4, 5 ; 49, 3 ; 55, 2.
— jurisdiction of, 52, 2 ; 53, 2, 3 ; 54, 2 ; 55, 2, 4 ; 56, 6, 7 ; 61, 2.
— pay for service in, 27, 3.

INDEX

INDEX

Pythia, of Delphi, 19, 4 ; 21, 6.
Pythodorus, archon (432–431 B.C.), 27, 2.
Pythodorus, archon (404–403 B.C.), 35, 1 ; 41, 1.
Pythodorus, of Anaphlystus, 29, 1.

Quadriremes, 46, 1.

Receivers-General, 47, 5 ; 48, 1, 2 ; 50 ; 52, 3.
Rhaicelus, 15, 2.
Rhinon, 38, 3, 4.
Roads, Commissioners of, 54, 1.

Salamis, archon for, 54, 8 ; 62, 2.
— battle of, 22, 7 ; 23, 1.
Samos, magistrates for, 62, 2.
Sanitation, control of, 50.
Scouts, 49, 1.
Scyllaeum, 22, 8.
Scyros, magistrates for, 62, 2.
Seal, public, 44, 1.
Seisachtheia, 6 ; 12, 4.
Shipbuilding, 46.
Sicily, Athenian defeat in, 29, 1.
Simonides, 18, 1.
Sitophylaces (Corn Commissioners), 51, 3.
Solon, 5–14 ; 17, 2 ; 22, 1 ; 28, 2 ; laws of, 7–10 ; 35, 2 ; poetry of, 5, 2, 3 ; 12.
Sophronistae (guardians), 42, 2, 3.
Sparta, 19, 2, 4–6 ; 23, 2, 4 ; 37, 2 ; 38, 41.
Springs, Superintendent of, 43, 1.
Strategi, 4, 2 ; 22, 2 ; 26, 1 ; 30, 2 ; 31, 2 ; 61, 1, 2 ; election of, 44, 4.
Symmories, 61, 1.

'Tax-Free Farm', 16, 6.
Taxiarchs, 30, 2 ; 61, 3.
Telesimus, archon, 22, 5.
Temples, Commissioners for repair of, 50.
Ten, the (first board of), 38, 1 ; 39, 5.
Ten, the (second board of), 38, 3.
Thargelia, festival of, 56, 3, 5.
Theatre, pay for attendance at, 28, 3.
Thebes, 15, 2.

Themistocles, 22, 7 ; 23, 3 ; 25, 3, 4 ; 28, 2.
Theopompus, archon, 33, 1.
Theoric Fund, Commissioners of, 43, 1 ; 47, 2.
Theramenes, 28, 3, 5 ; 32, 2 ; 33, 2 ; 34, 3 ; 36, 1, 2 ; 37, 1, 2.
Theseum, 15, 4 ; 62, 1.
Thesmothetae, 3, 4 ; 45, 1 ; 48, 5 ; 52, 1 ; functions of, 59 ; 63, 4. *See also* Archons.
Thesmotheteum, 3, 5.
Thessalus, 17, 3 ; 18, 1.
Thetes, 7, 3, 4.
Thirty, the, 34, 2 ; 35–40.
Tholus, 43, 3 ; 44, 1.
Thrasybulus, 37, 1 ; 40, 2.
Three Thousand, Assembly of (under the Thirty), 36, 1, 2 ; 37, 1.
Thucydides, 28, 2, 5.
Ticket-hangers, 64, 2, 3.
Timonassa, 17, 4.
Timosthenes, archon, 23, 5.
Treasurers, 4, 2 ; 7, 3 ; 8, 1 ; 30, 2 ; 60, 3.
— Military, 43, 1 ; 47, 2 ; 49, 3.
— of Ammonias and Paralus, 61, 7.
— of Athena, 47, 1.
Tribe-kings, 8, 3 ; 41, 2 ; 57, 4.
Tribes, four, 8, 3 ; 41, 2.
— ten, 21, 2 ; election by, 8, 1 ; 43, 2 ; 44, 2 ; 47, 1, 2 ; 48, 1, 3, 4 ; 52, 2 ; 53, 1 ; 56, 3 ; 60, 1 ; 61, 1, 3 ; 62, 1 ; tribal division of jurors, 63–69, *passim*.
Trierarchs, 61, 1.
Triremes, 22, 7 ; 46.
Trittyes, 8, 3 ; 21, 3, 4.

Victory, figures of, 47, 1 ; 49, 3.

Wards of state, 42, 5 ; 43, 4 ; 56, 7.
Weights and Measures, Commissioners of, 51, 2.
— Solon's reform of, 10.
Worship, Commissioners of, 54, 6.

Xanthippus, son of Ariphron, 22, 6 ; 28, 2.
Xenaenetus, archon, 40, 4.

Zeugites, 4, 3 ; 7, 3, 4 ; 26, 2.